Future of Business and Finance

The Future of Business and Finance book series features professional works aimed at defining, analyzing, and charting the future trends in these fields. The focus is mainly on strategic directions, technological advances, challenges and solutions which may affect the way we do business tomorrow, including the future of sustainability and governance practices. Mainly written by practitioners, consultants and academic thinkers, the books are intended to spark and inform further discussions and developments.

Nils Urbach • Daniel Feulner
Editors

Managing Artificial Intelligence

How Organizations Succeed with AI

Springer

Editors
Nils Urbach
Frankfurt University of Applied Sciences
Frankfurt am Main, Germany

Daniel Feulner
University of Bayreuth
Bayreuth, Germany

ISSN 2662-2467 ISSN 2662-2475 (electronic)
Future of Business and Finance
ISBN 978-3-032-13307-6 ISBN 978-3-032-13308-3 (eBook)
https://doi.org/10.1007/978-3-032-13308-3

This Springer imprint is published by the registered company Springer Nature Switzerland AG
The registered company address is: Gewerbestrasse 11, 6330 Cham, Switzerland

Preface

Artificial intelligence (AI) represents one of the most profound and transformative phenomena of our time. The rapid advancements in AI technology have permeated various facets of modern life, revolutionized industries, and reshaped the future of work. While initial enthusiasm surrounding AI saw a wave of innovations and high expectations, the emergence of Generative AI reinvigorated interest and profoundly accelerated AI adoption within corporate environments, underscoring its immense potential for enhancing personal productivity through Generative AI.

The advent of ChatGPT and other Generative AI tools serves as a pivotal moment in the evolution of AI, demonstrating the technology's capacity to perform complex tasks, generate human-like text, and assist in various domains, ranging from customer service to content creation. This breakthrough is an example of how AI can be transformed from a theoretical construct into a practical tool that can be integrated into everyday business. Consequently, the pressing question of how to effectively integrate AI into business processes has surfaced. Such integration necessitates not just the adoption of novel technologies but also the rethinking and redesigning of workflows to ensure AI complements and enhances human efforts.

Despite the promising potential, the path toward effective AI integration is beset with uncertainties and challenges. Organizations frequently face decision-making uncertainty and lack clear guidance for how best to incorporate AI into their operations. They grapple with identifying viable AI use cases, developing tailored AI solutions, and understanding the broader implications of AI on their business models. The fear of the unknown, coupled with the rapid pace of technological advancements, adds to the complexity of the task. In this context, comprehensive guidance and strategic planning become indispensable.

One of the primary challenges businesses are facing is identifying AI use cases that align with their strategic objectives and provide a clear value proposition. This requires a deep understanding of both the technological capabilities and the specific needs of the organization. Once potential use cases are identified, the process of developing and implementing AI solutions begins. This stage involves overcoming technical hurdles, ensuring data quality, and building robust models that can be scaled and maintained over time. Moreover, integrating AI solutions into existing systems necessitates meticulous planning and coordination across various departments.

In addition to the technological challenges, there is also the question of comprehensive AI management. Effective AI management encompasses strategic oversight, ethical considerations, and ongoing monitoring. It involves setting clear objectives, establishing governance frameworks, and ensuring transparency and accountability. Ethical considerations, such as bias mitigation, privacy concerns, and the societal impact of AI, must be addressed proactively. Additionally, AI systems require continuous monitoring and improvement to ensure they remain effective and aligned with the evolving needs of the business.

This book aims to address these pressing concerns by covering all essential aspects of managing artificial intelligence. It is designed to cater to both academics seeking theoretical insights and practitioners in search of practical guidance. The chapters are structured to provide a comprehensive overview, starting with the fundamentals of AI and progressing to advanced topics such as AI innovation, transformation, management, and ethics.

Through its comprehensive approach, this book endeavors to equip readers with the knowledge and tools necessary for successful AI management. It deals with the intricacies of AI technology, offering a balanced perspective that bridges the gap between theory and practice. By addressing key challenges and providing actionable insights, the book seeks to empower organizations to navigate the complexities of AI integration and harness its full potential.

We invite you to embark on this journey with us and hope you find the insights both enlightening and stimulating. The realm of AI is dynamic and ever evolving, and this book aspires to be your trusted companion in understanding and managing this transformative technology. Whether you are an academic, a student, a practitioner, or an enthusiast, we believe this volume will provide valuable insights and inspire you to explore the boundless possibilities of artificial intelligence.

We would like to deeply thank all authors and all involved people who supported the project from the publisher's side. Our special thanks go to Peter Hofmann and Luis Lämmermann, who were instrumental in setting up our AI research activities, and to the ABBA project team for their support of this book project. Furthermore, we gratefully acknowledge funding by the Federal Ministry of Education and Research (BMBF), the Bavarian State Ministry of Science and Art (STMWK), and the Hessian Ministry of Higher Education, Research, Science and the Arts (HMWK) for the ABBA project (Grant Numbers 16DHBKI004, 16DHBKI005).

We hope you enjoy this book and invite all readers to enter into a dialogue with us. Please feel free to contact us for questions, discussions, and suggestions.

Frankfurt, Germany
Bayreuth, Germany
April 2025

Nils Urbach
Daniel Feulner

Contents

Introduction to Managing Artificial Intelligence

1

Nils Urbach, Daniel Feulner, and Philipp Dilger

Artificial intelligence (AI) has become one of the most transformative forces of our time, driving innovation, efficiency, and entirely new ways of doing business. As AI systems grow in sophistication, their impact extends across industries, reshaping operational processes, decision-making, and competitive dynamics. For organizations, effectively managing AI is no longer a choice but a necessity – one that determines their ability to innovate, scale, and remain competitive in a rapidly evolving digital landscape. This requires not only a technical understanding of AI but also a structured approach to its strategic integration, governance, and operational deployment. Organizations must navigate challenges such as identifying high-impact use cases, aligning AI with business objectives, and ensuring seamless adoption at scale.

This chapter sets the stage for understanding AI and its management. It explores the rise of AI, defines its core concepts, and traces its historical milestones. These foundational insights are followed by a discussion of the essential themes in AI management, structured around the key areas covered in this book: establishing a technical foundation, identifying and designing AI use cases, developing AI strategies and governance frameworks, translating AI strategies into functional solutions, and scaling them effectively. Together, these elements provide a comprehensive framework to navigate the complexities and opportunities of AI in a business context.

N. Urbach (✉)
Frankfurt University of Applied Sciences, Frankfurt am Main, Germany
e-mail: nils.urbach@fim-rc.de

D. Feulner
University of Bayreuth, Bayreuth, Germany
e-mail: daniel.feulner@fim-rc.de

P. Dilger
University of Hohenheim, Stuttgart, Germany
e-mail: philipp.dilger@fim-rc.de

N. Urbach, D. Feulner (eds.), *Managing Artificial Intelligence*, Future of Business and Finance, https://doi.org/10.1007/978-3-032-13308-3_1

1.1 The Rise of AI

The rapid advancements in AI have increasingly blurred the boundaries between human creativity and machine-generated output, sparking a profound discussion on the capabilities of AI in comparison to human intelligence. This debate can be illustrated through a compelling and thought-provoking exercise: distinguishing between images created by humans and those generated by AI.

The images presented in Fig. 1.1 challenge conventional perceptions of intelligence, creativity, and authenticity. Some of these images are the result of human artistic expression, while others have been produced by sophisticated AI systems. This exercise highlights how AI, through advanced learning algorithms, has begun to emulate human-like abilities in fields traditionally associated with human creativity, such as painting and photographic composition.

This exercise serves as an entry point into the growing influence of AI on fields traditionally reserved for human intelligence. The ability of AI to produce works that rival human creations in artistry, realism, and complexity highlights its capacity to replicate even nuanced and sophisticated tasks. These advancements are not limited to the arts but extend across various domains, raising critical questions about how AI reshapes the nature of work and the roles humans play in it.

In the business context, AI's transformative potential is equally profound. Its applications go far beyond creativity, enabling organizations to optimize processes, enhance decision-making, and unlock new opportunities for value creation. A compelling example is Morgan Stanley's integration of generative AI (GenAI) (OpenAI, 2023), specifically GPT-4, into its knowledge management systems. By leveraging AI to streamline information retrieval and synthesis, the company has significantly improved the efficiency of its financial advisory services, demonstrating how AI can enhance productivity and strategic insights in complex, high-stakes environments.

Morgan Stanley utilizes a GPT-4-powered chatbot to support its financial advisors, addressing the critical need for quick and accurate access to information in the fast-paced world of wealth management. Previously, advisors faced inefficiencies navigating scattered resources to find answers or data for decision-making. The chatbot has streamlined this process, enabling natural language queries and delivering concise, actionable insights drawn from extensive internal databases. Beyond information retrieval, the AI tool converts raw data into actionable insights, accelerating decision-making and enhancing the client experience. This system has significantly improved Morgan Stanley's operations by reducing the time spent on information searches and automating complex data processing. Advisors can now focus on strategic tasks requiring human judgment, while the AI augments productivity and decision-making. This example highlights how AI is transforming business processes, driving both innovation and operational efficiency across industries.

AI as a Catalyst for Digital Transformation

The rise of AI and the availability of data have become powerful catalysts for digital transformation, fundamentally reshaping industries and business models on a global scale. Building on the advancements of Industry 4.0 – which revolutionized

Fig. 1.1 A selection of human and AI-created images

- **Image 1**: On the left is a classical portrait in the style of Rembrandt. Was this painting created by a human artist, or is it the result of AI learning to emulate one of history's most renowned painters? *Answer:* This image was created by a human. The detailed brushstrokes and subtle play of light and shadow indicate traditional human artistry.
- **Image 2:** The next image presents a portrait that bears striking similarities to classical works. Is this a product of human creativity, or has AI learned to replicate centuries of artistic tradition with surprising accuracy? *Answer:* This image was created by an AI. It demonstrates the power of machine learning (ML) algorithms to analyze vast amounts of historical artwork and produce realistic recreations that mimic human-made portraits.
- **Image 3:** This image appears to be a realistic, modern-day photograph of a woman. However, is this a real person captured by a camera, or is it an AI-generated image designed to look indistinguishably human? *Answer:* This image was created by AI. While highly realistic, subtle artifacts like irregular skin textures and unnatural blending of features hint at its synthetic nature, revealing its digital origin.
- **Image 4:** Finally, a modern portrait is presented. The realism in this photograph suggests that it could be an actual person. Is this human, or could it be another AI-generated creation? *Answer:* This image was captured by a camera but likely underwent significant editing. Despite retouching and enhancements, it remains a genuine portrait of a real person, highlighting modern photography techniques

manufacturing through digitalization, automation, and interconnected systems – the emerging concept of Industry 5.0 introduces a transformative paradigm. This new approach goes beyond efficiency and automation, emphasizing the harmonious collaboration between humans and intelligent systems while placing sustainability and societal value at its core (European Commission, 2021; Özdemir & Hekim, 2018)

At the heart of this evolution is the availability of data, now more abundant and accessible than ever before. During earlier industrial revolutions – from the steam power of Industry 1.0 to the automation breakthroughs of Industry 3.0 – data was a limited resource, often collected manually and processed at a slow pace. In contrast, Industry 4.0 ushered in the era of Big Data, enabling businesses to gather and analyze vast amounts of information in real time. Now, with the integration of AI in Industry 5.0, this data becomes the foundation for systems that not only optimize production lines and customer interactions but also foster collaboration between humans and intelligent machines.

The growth of data has been accompanied by a profound shift in business models, especially evident among the world's largest companies (see Fig. 1.2). In 2009, the industry leaders were primarily concentrated in traditional sectors such as energy and financial services, with companies such as ExxonMobil, PetroChina, and ICBC dominating the global stage. However, by 2024, the corporate landscape has undergone a dramatic transformation. Companies such as Apple, Microsoft, and Nvidia have surged ahead, dominating the global market by capitalizing on digital platforms and data-driven business strategies (PwC, 2024). These firms have recognized that data, combined with AI, is a key driver of value in the modern economy. Their market dominance underscores the fact that companies able to harness the power of data and AI are not just disrupting industries – they are fundamentally reshaping them.

Data has thus been likened to a new form of oil, a valuable resource in the digital age. However, unlike oil, data's true value lies in how it is processed and analyzed. As The Economist (2017) famously noted: "The world's most valuable resource is no longer oil, but data." This shift in perspective signals the immense role that data now plays in driving economic value. Just as oil once fueled the engines of

2009 (first quarter)		**2014** (first quarter)		**2024** (first quarter)	
1. Exxon Mobil	337	1. Apple	469	1. Microsoft	3.126
2. PetroChina	287	2. Exxon Mobil	416	2. Apple	2.648
3. Walmart	204	3. Google	409	3. Nvidia	2.224
4. ICBC	188	4. Microsoft	318	4. Saudi Arabian Oil	1.991
5. China Mobile	175	5. Berkshire Hathaway	286	5. Alphabet	1.884
6. Microsoft	163	6. Roche Holding	266	6. Amazon	1.874
7. AT&T	149	7. Johnson & Johnson	261	7. Meta	1.238

All market capitalization figures are in billions of USD.

Fig. 1.2 Largest companies in the world by market value (PwC, 2014, 2024)

industrial progress, data now powers digital transformation, enabling businesses to innovate faster, respond to market demands more efficiently, and create highly personalized experiences for their customers.

Yet, data alone is not enough. AI is the "engine" that turns this raw material into something useful. Agrawal et al. (2018) provide a fitting analogy, stating that if data is the new oil, then AI is the engine refining this resource into actionable insights. AI's ability to process vast quantities of data, recognize patterns, and generate predictive models has redefined how businesses operate. Through AI, companies can automate decision-making processes, optimize supply chains, and enhance customer engagement – all in real time. This automation not only reduces costs but also enables companies to innovate at speeds previously unimaginable.

Summary
AI is handling increasingly complex tasks that were once considered uniquely human, from creating art to supporting strategic decisions. Across industries, organizations leverage AI-powered solutions such as GPT-4 to streamline knowledge retrieval, optimize processes, and enhance decision-making. Meanwhile, AI-driven companies such as Apple, Microsoft, and Nvidia have overtaken traditional industry leaders, illustrating AI's role as a catalyst for innovation, automation, and competitive advantage. AI is not just a tool for processing data – but it is reshaping industries, changing the way companies work, and driving new opportunities for growth.

1.2 What Is AI?

When people think of AI, they often envision a range of capabilities – from cold, logical reasoning to human-like behavior or even emotions. This mix of perceptions reflects both the transformative potential of AI and widespread misunderstandings about its current capabilities. Figure 1.3 provides a snapshot of how 1000 people perceive AI, revealing insights into what the general public believes AI can achieve today.

The survey results show that the most common association with AI is its ability to think logically, with 58% of respondents identifying this as a key capability. Learning is the second most recognized ability, with 57%, followed by problem-solving at 52%. These results highlight AI's core strengths in logical reasoning, ML, and decision-making processes. Understanding languages (42%) and behaving like a human (39%) are also frequently mentioned, demonstrating that a significant portion of people believe AI can emulate human interaction. Additionally, 35% think that AI can take over human jobs, reflecting concerns about automation in the workforce.

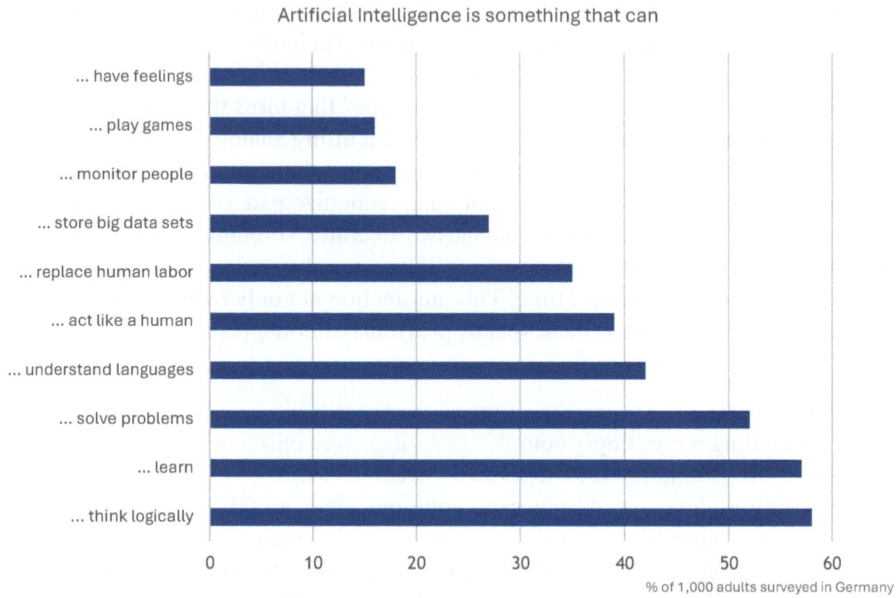

Fig. 1.3 What 1000 people think of when they think of AI. (Adapted from Statista, 2017)

Regarding data management, 27% of respondents associate AI with storing large datasets, while 18% believe that it is capable of monitoring people, reflecting awareness of AI's role in surveillance and privacy issues. Notably, only 16% of respondents think AI can play games, despite its demonstrated proficiency in complex games such as chess and Go. At the lower end, 15% of respondents mistakenly believe that AI can experience emotions, a misconception given that AI can simulate emotional responses but lacks actual consciousness.

Overall, this figure illustrates the public's blend of accurate views and misconceptions about AI. While AI's strengths lie in learning, reasoning, and data analysis, more complex human-like traits, such as feelings or full human behavior, remain beyond its current capabilities. Understanding this distinction is critical as society navigates the growing role of AI in our lives.

1.2.1 Definition of AI

The term AI has evolved significantly since its introduction in the 1950s. First coined at the Dartmouth Conference, AI was initially defined as the development of machines that behave as if they possess intelligence. This notion of imitating human intelligence has been central to many definitions of AI, though the understanding of what AI entails has changed over time.

As shown by various definitions, AI can be understood in both classical and modern terms. Early definitions, such as McCarthy et al. (1955), emphasized the goal of building machines that act intelligently. Similarly, Rich and Knight (1991) described AI as the study of how to make computers perform tasks at which humans currently excel. These early definitions focused on mimicking human abilities and automating tasks previously done by people.

More contemporary definitions focus on AI's ability to function autonomously and adaptively. For example, the European Commission's high-level expert group on AI (2018) defines AI as "systems that display intelligent behavior by analyzing their environment and taking actions – with some degree of autonomy – to achieve specific goals." Copeland (2023) expands on this by describing AI as "the ability of a digital computer or computer-controlled robot to perform tasks commonly associated with intelligent beings."

These varying definitions show that AI is a broad concept with no single, all-encompassing definition. At its core, AI refers to systems that imitate human intelligence to solve problems and perform tasks, often at a level that surpasses human capabilities in certain domains. However, AI is not limited to a singular concept or technology. Instead, AI encompasses a wide range of perspectives, disciplines, and research fields, each contributing uniquely to the development of AI technologies. As Russell and Norvig (2010) illustrate, several key disciplines have significantly shaped the ideas and techniques underlying modern AI.

- **Philosophy** has influenced AI by raising foundational questions: Can valid conclusions be drawn using formal rules? How does the mind emerge from a physical brain, and how does knowledge lead to action? Philosophy also questions the origins of knowledge itself.
- **Mathematics** contributes through formalization and logic, addressing how valid reasoning can be computed, what can be programmed, and how uncertain information can be processed or inferred. This field provides the tools for managing uncertainty and developing algorithms.
- **Economics** has provided models for decision-making, particularly in the context of maximizing utility. It also explores how to make decisions with delayed rewards, which is critical for long-term planning and AI strategies like reinforcement learning.
- **Neuroscience** offers insights into how the brain processes information, helping to inspire models that emulate human cognition. Questions such as how sensory inputs lead to thoughts, actions, or even consciousness guide AI researchers in creating intelligent systems.
- **Psychology,** especially cognitive psychology, examines how humans and animals think, learn, and act. Understanding the brain as an information-processing tool helps develop AI models that mimic human problem-solving and learning behaviors.
- **Computer engineering** focuses on building efficient systems capable of running AI algorithms. This discipline addresses how to construct effective hardware, solve computational problems, and convert inputs into meaningful outputs through programming languages and operating systems.

Together, these disciplines illustrate that AI is a multidisciplinary field, drawing on various ideas and techniques to develop intelligent systems. The convergence of these perspectives allows AI to progress and tackle increasingly complex problems across different domains.

The Hierarchical Structure of AI

When discussing AI, it is important to understand the distinction between AI, ML, deep learning (DL), and GenAI as they represent different layers of complexity (see Fig. 1.4) (Stryker & Kavlakoglu, 2024).

AI is the broadest concept, referring to systems that mimic human intelligence to solve problems and perform tasks. AI can be based on pre-programmed rules or utilize learning algorithms to make decisions.

ML is a subset of AI that enables systems to learn from data without being explicitly programmed for each specific task. It focuses on identifying patterns or relationships in data and making predictions based on them.

DL is a more specialized branch of ML that leverages artificial neural networks with multiple layers. These networks allow the system to process and learn from vast amounts of data, enabling highly sophisticated models like those used in image and speech recognition.

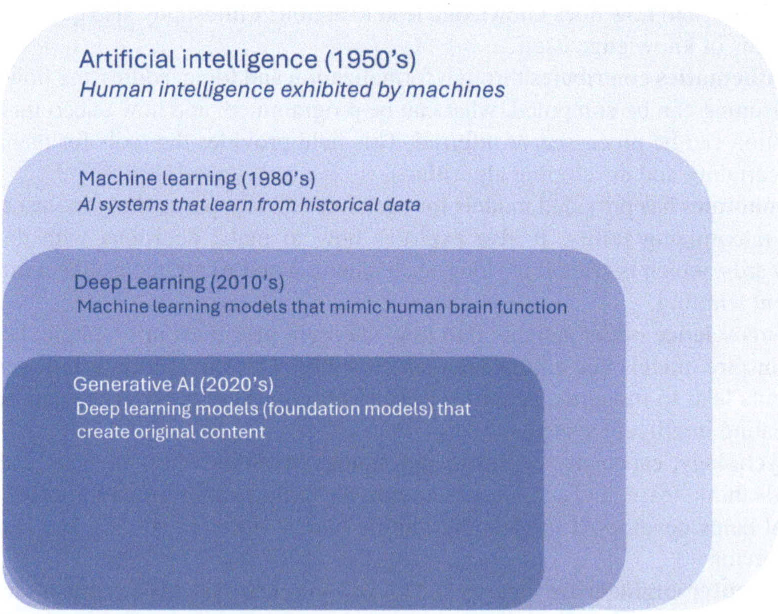

Fig. 1.4 The hierarchical structure of AI. (Adapted from Stryker & Kavlakoglu, 2024)

GenAI is a specific category within AI, particularly DL, that involves algorithms capable of creating new and original content, such as text, images, audio, or videos.

Summary
AI encompasses a wide range of capabilities, from logical reasoning to learning and problem-solving. Public perceptions of AI often reflect both its potential and common misconceptions, such as believing that AI can experience emotions or fully replace human behavior. AI is broadly defined as systems that imitate human intelligence to perform tasks, with modern definitions focusing on autonomy and adaptability. AI draws from multiple disciplines, including philosophy, mathematics, economics, and neuroscience. Within AI, ML allows systems to learn from data, while DL leverages neural networks for more advanced applications, such as image and speech recognition. GenAI enables systems not only to analyze data but also to produce original content, such as text, images, audio, or video, thereby expanding AI's creative potential and practical applications.

1.3 AI: Past and Present

The history of AI is marked by ambitious predictions and visionary pioneers. A notable example is Marvin Minsky, co-founder of the first AI conference in 1956, who optimistically predicted in 1970 that within 3–8 years, machines would achieve the general intelligence of an average human (Darrach, 1970). These forecasts reflected the early excitement and high expectations that characterized the field of AI. Similarly, Simon and Newell in 1958 predicted that, within 10 years, a computer would become a chess world champion and discover as well as prove a major mathematical theorem (Simon & Newell, 1958).

These overly optimistic assessments stemmed from the initial successes in AI, where researchers anticipated rapid advancements. However, in the following decades, technological challenges and the complexity of human intelligence slowed progress. These early forecasts underestimated the difficulty of developing machines that could replicate not only computational power but also the nuanced capabilities of human intelligence. The early decades of AI research reveal how challenging it was to accurately predict the boundaries and potential of AI.

1.3.1 Major Milestones in the History of AI

The history of AI is punctuated by numerous significant milestones, each contributing to the development and popularization of the technology. Understanding these key moments helps illustrate both the progress AI has made and the challenges it has faced along the way. Here, we take a closer look at several important milestones in AI's long journey (Manhart, 2024):

Turing Test (1950)

The Turing Test, proposed by British mathematician and computer scientist Alan Turing, was a foundational moment in AI's conceptualization. Turing's test was designed to measure a machine's ability to exhibit behavior indistinguishable from that of a human. If a machine could convince a human interlocutor that it was also human during a conversation, Turing argued, then that machine could be said to have intelligence. While the Turing Test remains a philosophical touchstone in discussions about AI, it also sparked the imagination of researchers, motivating them to explore the boundaries of machine cognition. However, it remains an open debate as to whether passing the Turing Test is a sufficient measure of true machine intelligence (Gillis, 2023).

ELIZA (1966)

In 1966, Joseph Weizenbaum developed ELIZA, one of the first chatbots designed to simulate human conversation. ELIZA mimicked a psychotherapist, mainly by reflecting back users' statements with simple questions. Although limited by today's standards, ELIZA was groundbreaking in its ability to use natural language processing (NLP) to create the illusion of understanding. ELIZA highlighted both the potential and limitations of early AI systems – while users often felt that they were conversing with an intelligent entity, the chatbot relied on pattern matching rather than genuine comprehension. ELIZA sparked discussions around human–computer interaction, laying the groundwork for future developments in conversational AI (Gobiet, 2024).

MYCIN (1972)

Developed at Stanford University, MYCIN was an expert system designed to diagnose bacterial infections and recommend appropriate antibiotics. MYCIN could perform at a level comparable to or better than medical experts in specific diagnostic scenarios. This system used a rule-based approach, drawing on an extensive database of expert knowledge to make decisions. MYCIN is one of the earliest examples of AI being used in specialized domains, demonstrating the power of expert systems to enhance decision-making in highly technical fields like medicine. However, due to concerns about accountability and liability, MYCIN was never implemented in clinical settings, showcasing some of the challenges that continue to accompany AI deployment in critical areas like healthcare (Copeland, 2024).

R1 (1978)

R1, also known as the Digital Equipment Corporation's XCON system, was one of the first expert systems to achieve commercial success. R1 was used to configure orders for new computer systems, automating tasks that previously required significant human expertise. This expert system helped to improve both the efficiency and accuracy of the configuration process, saving time and reducing errors. R1's success demonstrated that AI could offer practical, real-world business applications beyond research laboratories. It also marked the beginning of AI's integration into industry, highlighting the value of expert systems in automating complex tasks and improving productivity (McDermott, 1982).

Deep Blue (1997)

In 1997, IBM's Deep Blue made headlines by defeating world chess champion Garry Kasparov in a six-game match. Deep Blue's victory was a monumental achievement, showcasing the immense computing power that could be harnessed to solve complex problems. The system used brute-force search algorithms, evaluating millions of possible chess positions per second. While Deep Blue's method was not "intelligent" in the human sense, it underscored the capability of machines to surpass human experts in highly specialized tasks. The event not only propelled AI into the public consciousness but also raised questions about the nature of intelligence and the boundaries between human and machine capabilities (Bellinghausen, 2022).

IBM Watson (2011)

IBM Watson's victory in the quiz show Jeopardy! in 2011 marked another leap forward in AI's abilities. Unlike Deep Blue, Watson combined NLP, information retrieval, and ML to compete in a game that required understanding ambiguous, context-dependent questions. Watson's win against human champions demonstrated AI's growing capacity to handle unstructured data – text, in this case – and make sense of it in real time. Watson's success laid the foundation for AI applications in fields like healthcare, law, and finance, where handling vast amounts of information and providing timely insights is critical (Walsh, 2021).

AlphaGo (2016)

In 2016, Google's DeepMind shocked the world when its AI, AlphaGo, defeated Lee Sedol, the reigning world champion of Go, a complex board game with far more possible moves than chess. AlphaGo's victory was particularly impressive because it used DL techniques, specifically neural networks, to analyze the board and predict optimal moves. Unlike traditional expert systems that relied on preprogrammed rules, AlphaGo learned from millions of examples and refined its strategy through self-play. This milestone demonstrated the power of DL, not just in mastering complex games but also in showing the potential for AI to tackle other tasks that involve high-dimensional decision-making, like drug discovery or autonomous driving (DeepMind, 2023).

ChatGPT (2022)

The release of ChatGPT by OpenAI in 2022 marked a significant milestone in the history of AI. As one of the first widely accessible chatbots based on large language models, ChatGPT showcased the transformative potential of GenAI to produce coherent and context-sensitive human language. Within days, the system attracted millions of users and quickly found its way into everyday life, education, and the workplace. Unlike earlier systems such as ELIZA or IBM Watson, which were confined to narrow domains or scripted responses, ChatGPT could flexibly handle a broad range of prompts – from creative writing and coding assistance to problem-solving and tutoring. It came to symbolize a new era in which AI is increasingly seen not only as a specialized tool but as a general-purpose assistant capable of supporting human thinking and communication across diverse contexts (Marr, 2023).

These milestones collectively highlight the evolution of AI from theoretical concepts to practical applications across various fields. While early systems such as ELIZA and MYCIN showed the promise of AI, more recent advancements such as Watson and AlphaGo underscore the incredible strides made through ML and DL. Despite the setbacks of AI winters – periods of reduced interest and funding – these milestones demonstrate that AI's progress is cumulative, with each breakthrough building on the foundations laid by earlier innovations. Today, AI is poised to influence nearly every sector of society, from healthcare and finance to education and transportation, making an understanding of its history essential for grasping its future potential.

1.3.2 Why Now?

The question of "why now?" in the context of AI reflects a shift from academic experimentation to real-world business applications. In the past, AI was largely confined to research labs, with early projects like the Stanford Cart (one of the first autonomous cars) in the 1970s representing significant technological achievements but having little immediate commercial value. Today, however, AI is being integrated into business models, products, and services, generating tangible revenue. For example, Tesla's Autopilot, launched in 2014 (Groom, 2014), illustrates how AI has moved from theoretical constructs to practical, market-driven solutions. This transformation marks AI's journey from ivory tower research to everyday business applications, driven by a surge in patent filings and scientific publications, as depicted in Fig. 1.5.

The application of AI has made significant strides in recent years, driven by advancements in technology and infrastructure. Four main factors have transformed

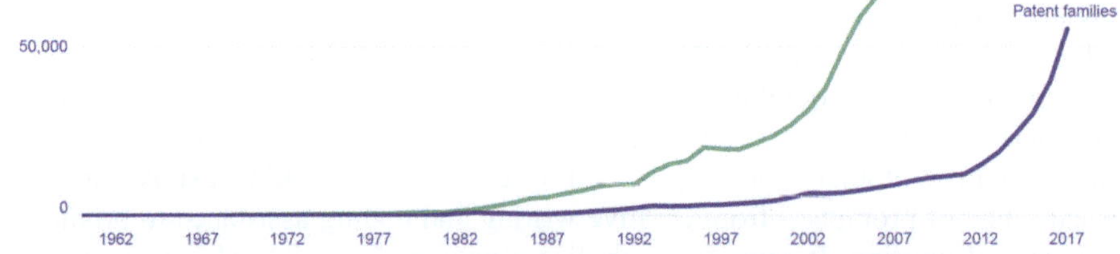

Fig. 1.5 AI patent families and scientific publications by publication year. (Adapted from WIPO, 2019)

AI from a largely theoretical concept into a practical tool that is being widely integrated into business processes, products, and services:

Necessary Data Is Available and Usable

One of the fundamental drivers behind AI's rise is the exponential growth of data. With the proliferation of digital technologies, such as Big Data and the Internet of Things, vast amounts of data are continuously generated and stored. These datasets are essential for training AI algorithms, which rely on large quantities of structured and unstructured data to identify patterns, make predictions, and optimize decision-making processes. Advances in data processing technologies have also improved the ability to clean, store, and analyze data efficiently, making it usable for AI applications (Marr, 2018).

The ML Algorithms Have Been Improved

ML and, more specifically, DL algorithms have seen remarkable improvements in recent years. These enhancements are particularly evident in fields such as image recognition, NLP, and autonomous systems. DL, which leverages neural networks with multiple layers, allows AI systems to learn from vast amounts of data and improve their performance over time. This capability enables AI to tackle complex problems, such as interpreting images or human language, which were previously beyond the reach of traditional algorithms (Vaswani et al., 2017).

Cloud Services Provide the Required Computing Power

A key challenge for AI in its early stages was the lack of affordable and scalable computing power. However, with the rise of cloud computing, businesses now have on-demand access to the computational resources required for AI tasks. High-performance computing power, which was once prohibitively expensive, is now available through cloud platforms such as Microsoft Azure, Amazon Web Services (AWS), and Google Cloud. This flexibility allows organizations to run AI models without significant upfront investments in infrastructure. In 1961, the cost of performing 1 GFLOP (1 billion floating-point operations per second) was $145 billion, whereas in 2017, the same computational power cost just 3 cents. This dramatic reduction in computing costs has been a game-changer, enabling AI to scale rapidly across industries (Rittershaus, 2023).

The Application of AI Is Becoming Increasingly Accessible

The final driver is the simplification of AI applications through high-performance toolkits and libraries. In the past, implementing AI required highly specialized knowledge and extensive resources. Today, however, many open-source tools and libraries are available, enabling developers and data scientists to build and deploy AI systems with relative ease. Platforms such as Microsoft's ML.NET, TensorFlow, and Azure AI Services provide pre-built models, APIs, and resources, lowering the barrier to entry for businesses looking to leverage AI. These tools allow organizations to experiment, iterate, and scale AI solutions without needing deep technical expertise in every aspect of AI development.

These four drivers – available data, improved ML algorithms, cloud computing, and accessible toolkits – collectively accelerated the adoption of AI across industries. While the technical challenges of AI are being addressed, businesses must also tackle organizational hurdles to successfully implement AI at scale. Beyond technological readiness, companies need to establish clear strategies, governance structures, and operational frameworks to integrate AI effectively.

Summary
AI has evolved from early optimism and limited expert systems to powerful, widely accessible tools like ChatGPT. Key historical milestones, such as the Turing Test, ELIZA, Deep Blue, and AlphaGo, illustrate both breakthroughs and challenges in AI's development. Today's AI success is driven by four main factors: the availability of vast datasets, advances in ML algorithms, scalable cloud computing, and accessible development tools. Together, these enablers have lowered technical barriers, accelerated adoption, and allowed AI to be embedded in products, services, and decision-making processes across industries, fundamentally reshaping how organizations innovate, compete, and create value.

1.4 Managing AI

As businesses increasingly integrate AI into their operations, they face a range of challenges that emphasize the necessity of effective AI management. While AI offers transformative benefits such as efficiency, automation, and data-driven decision-making, it also introduces complexities that companies must address to fully realize its potential. This chapter introduces the critical dimensions of AI management, structured around five key areas that align with the broader framework of this book (see Fig. 1.6): AI Foundations, AI Ideation, AI Strategizing, AI Design and Development, and AI Operations at Scale.

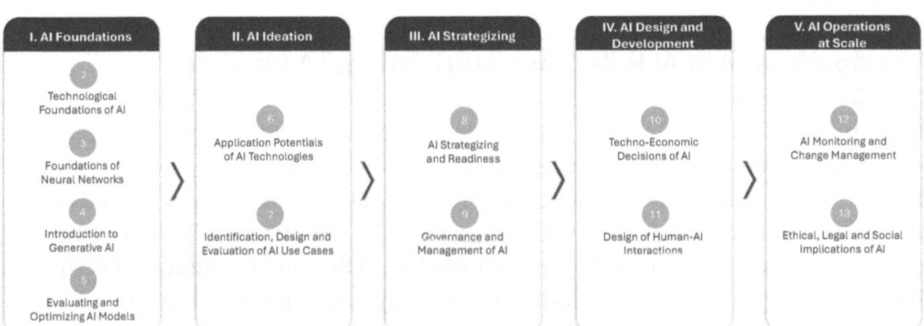

Fig. 1.6 Key areas of managing AI

I. AI Foundations: Establishing Core Concepts

AI management begins with a deep understanding of its technical and conceptual foundations. Companies must grasp the capabilities and limitations of AI technologies, from learning methods and algorithms to neural networks. This foundational knowledge is critical for designing systems that are both technically robust and aligned with business goals. Without this grounding, organizations risk deploying systems that fail to deliver value or are overly complex for their intended use. These fundamentals are detailed in *Part I: AI Foundations*, equipping readers with the knowledge required to navigate the complexities of AI technology.

II. AI Ideation: Identifying and Designing AI Use Cases

The successful integration of AI starts with identifying use cases that address specific business challenges or create opportunities for innovation. A structured approach to ideation ensures that AI investments are both targeted and impactful. Businesses must evaluate the operational and innovative potential of AI, considering how it can optimize processes, enable cross-technology innovation, or unlock entirely new business models. The design and evaluation of these use cases, explored in *Part II: AI Ideation*, are critical for ensuring AI initiatives deliver measurable outcomes and align with organizational priorities.

III. AI Strategizing: Preparing for AI Integration

Once promising use cases are identified, businesses must strategically prepare to integrate AI into their operations. This involves evaluating AI readiness, including aligning initiatives with business objectives, securing resources such as personnel and infrastructure, and fostering an environment that supports innovation and process transformation. Readiness assessments ensure that organizations can effectively position AI as a driver of value and competitiveness. In parallel, management and governance frameworks are essential to guide AI initiatives. Clear accountability structures, well-organized teams, and robust governance practices help ensure that AI systems remain compliant, reliable, and aligned with organizational priorities. These considerations are explored in *Part III: AI Strategizing*, offering tools for both assessing readiness and managing AI effectively to enable sustainable integration.

IV. AI Design and Development: From Strategy to Execution

With a clear strategy in place, the next step involves translating AI plans into functional solutions. This requires making techno-economic decisions about infrastructure, deployment, and platform integration while ensuring that systems are designed to optimize human–AI collaboration. Key considerations include the implementation of MLOps frameworks to streamline the lifecycle of AI models and the design of systems that enhance workforce transformation through human–AI interaction. These aspects, covered in *Part IV: AI Design and Development*, are critical for bridging the gap between strategic planning and operational execution.

V. AI Operations at Scale: Operationalizing and Sustaining Success

The final step in managing AI involves scaling and sustaining AI solutions across the organization. Businesses must establish robust monitoring frameworks to measure performance, address potential issues, and adapt systems to evolving business needs. Change management builds trust, addresses concerns, and enables the long-term integration of AI into everyday work. Furthermore, as AI systems become integral to operations, companies must address the ethical, legal, and societal implications of their use, ensuring compliance with regulations and fostering public trust. These challenges and opportunities are the focus of *Part V: AI Operations at Scale*, which prepares organizations for the long-term impact of AI.

Managing AI requires a holistic approach that spans the entire lifecycle of AI solutions, from foundational understanding to large-scale operationalization. Each phase presents unique challenges and opportunities that must be addressed through strategic planning, robust governance, and effective implementation. By following the structured approach outlined in this book, businesses can harness the transformative power of AI to drive innovation, improve efficiency, and achieve long-term success.

References

Agrawal, A., Gans, J., & Goldfarb, A. (2018). Is your company's data actually valuable in the AI era? *Harvard Business Review*. Retrieved November 18, 2018, from https://hbr.org/2018/01/is-your-companys-data-actually-valuable-in-the-ai-era

Bellinghausen, Y. (2022). Schachcomputer Deep Blue: Der Tag, an dem die Maschine gewann. *Zeit.de*. Retrieved September 28, 2024, from https://www.zeit.de/digital/2022-05/deep-blue-ibm-schachcomputer-garri-kasparov-kuenstliche-intelligenz

Copeland, B. J. (2023). Artificial intelligence. *Encyclopedia Britannica*. Retrieved September 20, 2023, from https://www.britannica.com/technology/artificial-intelligence

Copeland, B. J. (2024). *MYCIN*. Retrieved September 28, 2024, from https://www.britannica.com/technology/MYCIN

Darrach, B. (1970). Meet Shaky, the first electronic person. *Life Magazine*, 58–68.

DeepMind. (2023). *AlphaGo: Mastering the Game of Go with AI*. Retrieved September 26, 2024, from https://deepmind.com/research/case-studies/alphago-the-story-so-far

European Commission. (2021*). Industry 5.0, a transformative vision for Europe – Governing systemic transformations towards a sustainable industry*. Publications Office of the European Union. Retrieved September 28, 2024, from https://data.europa.eu/doi/10.2777/17322

European Commission High-Level Expert Group on Artificial Intelligence. (2018). *Ethics guidelines for trustworthy AI*. [pdf]. Retrieved September 28, 2024, from https://ec.europa.eu/futurium/en/system/files/ged/ai_hleg_definition_of_ai_18_december_1.pdf

Gillis, A. (2023). *Turing-Test*. Retrieved September 28, 2024, from https://www.computerweekly.com/de/definition/Turing-Test

Gobiet, M. (2024). *Die Geschichte und Entwicklung von Chatbots*. Retrieved September 28, 2024, from https://onlim.com/die-geschichte-und-entwicklung-von-chatbots/

Groom, N. (2014). *Tesla unveils all-wheel-drive Model S with Autopilot features*. Retrieved September 26, 2024, from https://www.reuters.com/article/business/tesla-unveils-all-wheel-drive-model-s-autopilot-features-idUSKCN0HZ07N

Manhart, K. (2024). *Eine kleine Geschichte der Künstlichen Intelligenz*. Retrieved September 28, 2024, from https://www.computerwoche.de/article/2756938/eine-kleine-geschichte-der-kuenstlichen-intelligenz.html

Marr, B. (2018). How much data do we create every day? The mind-blowing stats everyone should read. *Forbes*. Retrieved September 26, 2024, from https://www.forbes.com/sites/bernard-marr/2018/05/21/how-much-data-do-we-create-every-day-the-mind-blowing-stats-everyone-should-read/

Marr, B. (2023). A short history of ChatGPT: How we got to where we are today. *Forbes*. Retrieved March 29, 2025, from https://www.forbes.com/sites/bernardmarr/2023/05/19/a-short-history-of-chatgpt-how-we-got-to-where-we-are-today/

McCarthy, J., Minsky, M. L., Rochester, N., & Shannon, C. E. (1955). *A proposal for the Dartmouth summer research project on artificial intelligence*. Retrieved from http://jmc.stanford.edu/articles/dartmouth/dartmouth.pdf

McDermott, J. (1982). R1: A rule-based configurer of computer systems. *Artificial Intelligence, 19*(1), 39–88.

OpenAI. (2023). *Morgan Stanley and OpenAI partnership*. Retrieved September 28, 2024, from https://openai.com/index/morgan-stanley/

Özdemir, V., & Hekim, N. (2018). Birth of Industry 5.0: Making sense of big data with artificial intelligence, "The Internet of Things" and next-generation technology policy. *Omics: A Journal of Integrative Biology*. https://doi.org/10.1089/omi.2017.0194

PwC. (2014). *Global top 100 companies by market capitalisation: 31 March 2014 update*. IPO Centre. Retrieved February 3, 2025, from https://www.pwc.com/gx/en/audit-services/capital-market/publications/assets/pwc-top-100-2014.pdf

PwC. (2024). *Global top 100 companies – By market capitalisation*. April 2024. Retrieved February 3, 2025, from https://www.pwc.co.uk/audit/assets/pdf/global-100/global-top-100-companies-2024.pdf

Rich, E., & Knight, K. (1991). *Artificial intelligence* (2nd ed.). McGraw-Hill.

Rittershaus, A. (2023). *What you need to know about AI and what it could mean for our future: FAQ*. Retrieved September 26, 2024, from c

Russell, S., & Norvig, P. (2010). *Artificial intelligence: A modern approach* (3rd ed.). Pearson Education.

Simon, H. A., & Newell, A. (1958). Heuristic problem solving: The next advance in operations research. *Operations Research, 6*(1), 1–10.

Statista. (2017). *Was macht künstliche Intelligenz aus*? Retrieved September 28, 2024, from https://de.statista.com/infografik/8943/was-macht-kuenstliche-intelligenz-aus/

Stryker, C. & Kavlakoglu, E. (2024). *What is AI?* Retrieved March 18, 2025, from https://www.ibm.com/think/topics/artificial-intelligence

The Economist. (2017). *The world's most valuable resource is no longer oil, but data*. Retrieved September 28, 2024, from https://www.economist.com/leaders/2017/05/06/the-worlds-most-valuable-resource-is-no-longer-oil-but-data

Vaswani, A., Shazeer, N., Parmar, N., Uszkoreit, J., Jones, L., Gomez, A. N., Kaiser, Ł., & Polosukhin, I. (2017). Attention is all you need. In *Advances in neural information processing systems*.

Walsh, B. (2021). *Looking back at Watson's 2011 "Jeopardy!" win*. Retrieved September 26, 2024, from https://www.axios.com/2021/02/13/ibm-watson-jeopardy-win-language-processing

WIPO. (2019). *WIPO technology trends 2019: Artificial intelligence*. World Intellectual Property Organization.

Nils Urbach is Professor of Information Systems and Digital Business as well as Director of the Research Lab for Digital Innovation & Transformation at the Frankfurt University of Applied Sciences, Germany. Furthermore, he is Director at the FIM Research Center for Information Management, and the Branch Business & Information Systems Engineering of Fraunhofer FIT. Nils Urbach has been working in the fields of digital innovation and transformation for several years. His work has been published in several academic journals such as Information Systems Research (ISR), the Journal of the Association for Information Systems (JAIS), the Journal of Strategic Information Systems (JSIS), the Journal of Information Technology (JIT), MIS Quarterly Executive (MISQE), IEEE Transactions on Engineering Management (IEEE TEM), Information and Management (I&M), Business & Information Systems Engineering (BISE), and Electronic Markets (EM). He advises several companies on digitalization issues and regularly appears as a speaker on this topic.

Daniel Feulner received his M.Sc. in information system from the Otto-Friedrich University of Bamberg, Germany in 2023. He is an affiliated researcher at the Branch Business & Information Systems Engineering of the Fraunhofer FIT and FIM Research Center for Information Management at the University of Bayreuth. In his research, he aims to understand how Business Analytics and Artificial Intelligence can be effectively and responsibly utilized in organizations. His goal is to enable companies to drive innovation and achieve sustainable growth in a rapidly evolving technological landscape.

Philipp Dilger received his M.Sc. in business administration from the University of Augsburg, Germany, in 2022. He is an affiliated researcher at the Branch Business & Information Systems Engineering of the Fraunhofer FIT and FIM Research Center for Information Management at the University of Bayreuth. His research interest centers on on how interactions between individuals with varying levels of digital proficiency and AI systems can be effectively designed. He explores different design approaches for AI systems that are tailored to users' capabilities to ensure accessibility, usability, and meaningful engagement.

Part I

AI Foundations

Technological Foundations of AI 2

Nils Urbach, Daniel Feulner, and Tobias Guggenberger

Artificial intelligence (AI) has become a key driver of innovation, fundamentally changing how businesses operate, make decisions, and create value. The increasing adoption of AI across sectors has been driven by continuous advancements in computational power, algorithmic sophistication, and the proliferation of data. As AI systems become more integrated into business operations, understanding their underlying technical fundamentals is crucial for organizations aiming to harness AI effectively. Mastering these fundamentals enables businesses to make informed decisions about AI adoption, ensuring that their AI initiatives are built on a strong technological foundation.

This chapter explores the core technical components that make AI possible, including data quality, storage architectures, computational power, and tools for AI development and deployment. It examines key learning methods – supervised, unsupervised, and reinforcement learning – alongside foundational algorithms such as regression, classification, and clustering, which drive AI-driven insights and automation. The goal is to provide a structured introduction to AI's technological foundations, enabling readers to understand its core mechanisms and make informed decisions about its application.

N. Urbach (✉)
Frankfurt University of Applied Sciences, Frankfurt am Main, Germany
e-mail: nils.urbach@fim-rc.de

D. Feulner · T. Guggenberger
University of Bayreuth, Bayreuth, Germany
e-mail: daniel.feulner@fim-rc.de; tobias.guggenberger@fim-rc.de

N. Urbach, D. Feulner (eds.), *Managing Artificial Intelligence*, Future of Business and Finance, https://doi.org/10.1007/978-3-032-13308-3_2

2.1 Technical Fundamentals

To fully understand the role of AI in modern business, it is essential to examine the underlying technical fundamentals that make AI possible. These core elements have evolved significantly in recent years, enabling AI to become more powerful, efficient, and widely applicable. The four primary components (see Fig. 2.1) of the technical framework for AI – data, storage, computing power and algorithms, as well as tools and services – are the building blocks of any AI system. Each of these areas has seen important developments, contributing to the rapid advancement of AI technologies (Buxmann & Schmidt, 2019).

2.1.1 Data

In the digital age, data is increasingly recognized as a strategic asset. However, its value is only realized when it is effectively processed, analyzed, and interpreted. The DIKW pyramid (Frické, 2019) in Fig. 2.2 illustrates the transformation of raw data into meaningful insights, moving from data at the base to wisdom at the top. This model emphasizes the increasing value added at each level of data refinement.

At the base level of the DIKW pyramid is **data**, which consists of unprocessed facts, figures, or values. For example, the number 1000 on its own represents raw data – without context, it is unclear whether this refers to 1000 units sold, 1000 Euros in revenue, or something else entirely. Data in this raw form lacks meaning and cannot be used effectively in decision-making.

Once data is processed, organized, or structured, it becomes **information**. For instance, if we know that 1000 refers to 1000 products sold in the last quarter, this data has been transformed into information. The number is now placed within a meaningful context, providing insight into the company's sales performance over a specific period.

Knowledge is created when information is further synthesized and applied. For example, using quarterly sales information (1000 products sold), along with additional insights such as customer behavior trends or seasonal demand fluctuations,

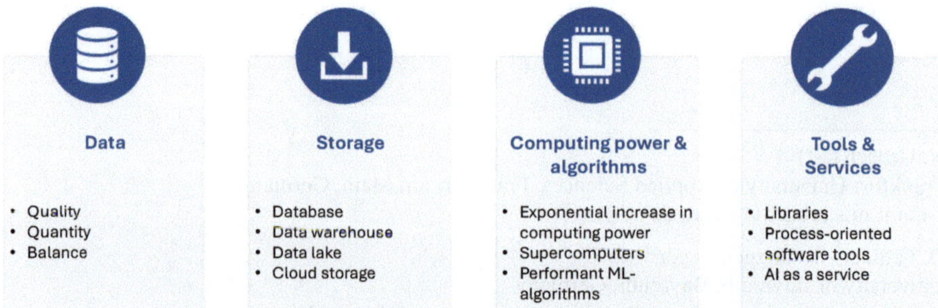

Fig. 2.1 Technical framework for the use of AI

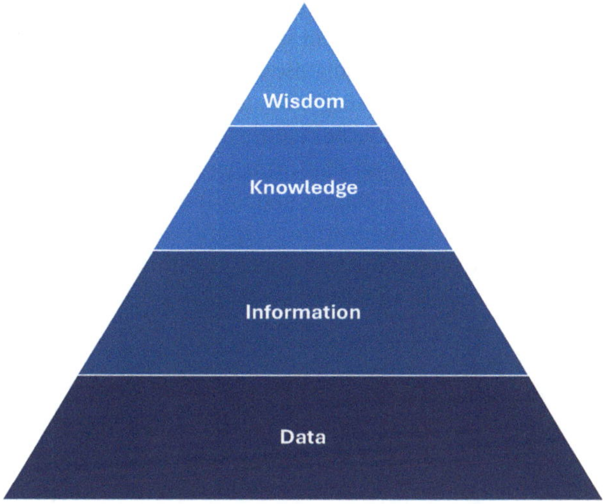

Fig. 2.2 DIKW pyramid. (Adapted from Frické, 2019)

allows the business to forecast future sales or adjust inventory management. This application of information enables more informed decision-making and problem-solving.

At the top of the hierarchy, **wisdom** represents the ability to apply knowledge in a broader context for sound judgment. Using past sales data and knowledge of market trends, the business may decide to diversify its product line or enter new markets to capitalize on future opportunities. Wisdom is the ability to make strategic, long-term decisions that go beyond immediate problem-solving and consider deeper insights and experience.

While the process from data to wisdom highlights the importance of data transformation, it also emphasizes the necessity of data quality at each stage. Data quality is foundational to ensure that the higher levels of this hierarchy are accurate and reliable. As we move forward, we will explore the key criteria for ensuring high-quality data, which is critical for the success of AI models and systems.

Data Quality

The quality of the data is crucial for AI (Monolith AI, 2023). High-quality data ensures effective training of AI models, which, in turn, yields more accurate predictions and insights. Incomplete, erroneous, or anomalous data often yield unsatisfactory or misleading results. To ensure the quality of data, it is essential to implement a series of checks. The **accuracy** of data is ensured through the implementation of rigorous quality control measures. This guarantees that the data is an accurate reflection of reality. In the absence of representative data, any insights derived from it may be flawed. **Completeness** pertains to the presence of all requisite data. The presence of missing values has the potential to impact the performance of the model and introduce inaccuracies, particularly in areas where the data is scarce.

Purity refers to the absence of errors or extraneous information. Inconsistencies, outliers, and irrelevant features in data can significantly degrade model performance by introducing noise that distorts outputs. Beyond purity, the **recency** of data is also critical for ensuring its relevance. Using outdated information can result in insights that no longer reflect present trends or realities, thereby diminishing the model's effectiveness. **Consistency** across all platforms and databases is equally important. Conflicting information between datasets undermines trust in the model, as inconsistencies can mislead or confuse learning algorithms. Without rigorous quality assurance, AI models risk producing erroneous insights, which can lead to costly decisions or the implementation of flawed systems.

Data Quantity

A further essential factor for the success of a machine learning (ML) project is the quantity of data used (Monolith AI, 2023). The efficacy of ML models is contingent upon the availability of a substantial quantity of data, which is necessary for effective learning, pattern recognition, and the generation of accurate predictions. This is especially true for deep learning algorithms, which require large datasets to efficiently train their complex neural networks. Sufficient data is necessary to ensure that the model can be generalized and to prevent overfitting, whereby the model performs well on training data but poorly on new, unseen data. Insufficient data can lead to the creation of unreliable models with a compromised ability to accurately predict outcomes. Furthermore, the greater the diversity of the data, the more effectively the model will be able to cope with varying conditions, thereby enhancing its robustness. However, data collection must be complemented by ensuring the quality of the data set, as an abundance of low-quality data will not lead to useful insights.

Data Balance

In the context of data, balance refers to the distribution of data samples among different categories or classes (Buhl, 2022). The presence of imbalanced data can restrict the efficacy of ML models, particularly in the context of classification tasks. For example, if one class is represented by a significantly larger number of instances than the others, the model may become biased toward that dominant class, resulting in inaccurate predictions for the minority class, which can be problematic in applications such as fraud detection or disease diagnosis.

The use of balanced datasets enables the model to comprehend the diversity among different classes, thereby enhancing its capacity to make impartial and precise predictions across categories. The issue of imbalance can be addressed through the implementation of techniques such as oversampling the minority class, undersampling the majority class, or the utilization of specialized algorithms that are capable of handling datasets that are skewed.

The success of AI projects is contingent upon the suitability of the underlying data. By ensuring that the data meets the requisite criteria of quality, quantity, and balance, organizations can enhance the effectiveness and reliability of AI models. Such efforts lead to improved decision-making, more sophisticated automation, and, ultimately, competitive advantage in the use of AI for strategic objectives.

2.1.2 Data Storage

In data management, selecting the right storage approach is critical for effectively handling and utilizing data. The decision on which method to use depends on the structure of the data, its volume, and the specific business requirements for processing, analysis, and accessibility. Four major storage approaches are commonly used: databases, data warehouses, data lakes, and data lakehouses. Each approach has distinct characteristics that make it suitable for specific tasks in data management and analytics.

A **database** is a structured system designed to store, organize, and manage data efficiently, facilitating access and processing for various applications (Petrov, 2019). Databases are ideal for real-time applications such as e-commerce platforms, customer relationship management systems, and inventory management systems. Optimized for quick read and write operations, databases ensure efficient data retrieval and updates, making them highly suitable for handling structured data where consistency and transactional integrity are critical. Access to databases is managed through database management systems, which provide tools to manipulate and maintain the stored data.

Databases generally handle smaller volumes of data compared to other approaches and are specialized for environments where the consistency and integrity of structured data are essential. They are designed to meet high demands for transactional accuracy, especially in applications where frequent updates are necessary.

A **data warehouse** is a centralized repository designed to store processed and structured data, making it a key component in business intelligence (BI) and analytics processes (Harby & Zulkernine, 2022). Data warehouses facilitate complex queries and reporting, offering organizations the ability to gain insights into their operations. They typically aggregate information from various sources, such as operational databases, external application programming interfaces, or flat files, providing a comprehensive view of an organization's structured data.

Data warehouses are optimized for read-heavy operations, focusing on analytical workloads rather than frequent data updates. They are particularly effective for analyzing historical data, identifying trends, and supporting strategic decision-making. Business analytics tools are used to extract insights from data warehouses, making them crucial for organizations that rely on historical reporting and performance analysis.

A **data lake** is a centralized repository that allows for the storage of vast amounts of raw, unprocessed data in its native form (El Aissi et al., 2022). Unlike data warehouses, data lakes can store structured, semi-structured, and unstructured data, making them highly flexible for organizations managing large datasets, such as logs, sensor data, or social media feeds. Data lakes are particularly useful for advanced analytics tasks, including ML and big data analysis, where various forms of data need to be processed and transformed at scale.

While data lakes offer flexibility and cost-efficiency by allowing data to be stored at a lower cost, the data is often in a raw state and requires significant processing before it can be used for decision-making or reporting. This makes data lakes well-suited for organizations that prioritize flexibility and scalability in managing large volumes of data but are willing to invest in the necessary data preparation and transformation tasks.

A **data lakehouse** is an emerging storage approach that combines the benefits of both data lakes and data warehouses (Harby & Zulkernine, 2022). It provides the flexibility and scalability of a data lake for handling large volumes of unstructured or semi-structured data, while also offering data management, governance, and performance features traditionally associated with data warehouses. By integrating both capabilities, a data lakehouse allows for advanced analytics and real-time decision-making without the need for extensive data movement between different storage systems.

The data lakehouse architecture supports both transactional and analytical workloads, offering organizations the ability to run ML models, perform big data analytics, and execute traditional BI queries from a single platform. This convergence reduces the complexity of managing separate systems for structured and unstructured data, thus enabling a more streamlined and cost-effective data management solution.

The selection of an appropriate data storage approach depends on the nature of the data, its volume, and the specific use cases. Databases are ideal for managing structured data in real-time, transactional environments. Data warehouses, on the other hand, are optimized for processed, structured data, particularly in BI and reporting scenarios. Data lakes offer flexibility and scalability for storing unprocessed, large-scale data that may require future transformation, while data lakehouses provide a unified solution that supports both analytical and operational tasks. Many modern organizations integrate multiple storage solutions to create a comprehensive data architecture, tailored to meet both their operational and analytical needs efficiently.

2.1.3 Computing Power and Algorithms

The exponential increase in **computing power** has been a principal factor driving the rapid advancements in AI and ML over recent decades. As computing hardware has evolved, AI models have become increasingly sophisticated, demonstrating the capacity to handle complex tasks and process vast amounts of data. This progress is closely correlated with Moore's law, which postulates that the number of transistors on a microchip will double approximately every 18–24 months, resulting in an exponential increase in computational capacity. For years, this trend has permitted the continual enhancement of both the performance and cost-effectiveness of AI systems. Nevertheless, there is a growing concern that physical limitations may eventually impede this exponential growth, as further miniaturization of components reaches its limits. However, the advances made thus far in computing power have established a robust foundation for both current and future developments in AI (Peper, 2017).

In response to these potential limitations, the development of specialized hardware, such as graphics processing units (GPUs) and tensor processing units (TPUs), has emerged as a solution to further accelerate and optimize AI processing (Bigelow, 2024). Originally designed for rendering graphics, GPUs have become indispensable for parallel processing in AI, particularly in deep learning, due to their ability to perform multiple calculations simultaneously. Complementing this, Google's TPUs, engineered specifically to accelerate AI tasks, have further enhanced the scale and efficiency of data processing. Together, these hardware innovations have been key in meeting the growing computational demands of modern ML algorithms, significantly improving both performance and reducing training times.

A crucial component of these advancements is the function of **supercomputers**, which are designed to address the most challenging computational tasks. Supercomputers are equipped with hundreds or even thousands of processors that operate in parallel, allowing them to process large datasets with remarkable speed. These machines are employed in high-performance computing for simulations in domains such as astrophysics, climate modeling, quantum mechanics, and cryptanalysis, where their computational capabilities can be fully exploited.

In recent decades, the performance of supercomputers has improved dramatically, as measured in teraflops (trillions of floating-point operations per second). For instance, in 2001, the top-performing supercomputers operated at approximately 7 teraflops, but by 2021, this performance had surged to over 442,000 teraflops (Janson, 2022). This exponential growth in computational power has significantly impacted the development of ML algorithms, many of which require immense processing capabilities. Consequently, supercomputers have played a crucial role in advancing AI and other fields reliant on high-performance computing.

As computing power has increased, there have been substantial improvements in the **effectiveness and efficiency of AI algorithms**. This improvement has been driven by a combination of factors, one of which is the increasing availability of high-quality data. The advent of big data has enabled AI models to be trained on extensive and heterogeneous datasets, thereby enhancing their capacity to generalize and perform effectively in real-world applications. Techniques such as data augmentation have also emerged, enabling the creation of supplementary, diverse data from existing datasets, which further optimizes model training and performance. The combination of greater data availability and more powerful computing resources has enabled AI systems to make more accurate predictions, identify patterns with greater precision, and address complex problems that were previously intractable.

Building on these foundational advancements, novel learning methodologies have revolutionized how AI acquires and utilizes knowledge. One of the most significant advancements has been the advent of deep learning, particularly the utilization of neural networks comprising numerous layers, designated as deep neural networks (Goodfellow, 2016). These networks have demonstrated remarkable efficacy in image recognition, natural language processing, and other complex tasks. The processing of data through multiple layers of abstraction enables deep learning models to identify intricate patterns and relationships within data that may be overlooked by simpler models. Another significant advancement has been the emergence of reinforcement learning, a technique whereby AI agents learn through interaction with their environment, adjusting their actions based on received feedback (Li, 2023). This approach has resulted in notable advancements in domains such as autonomous driving and gaming.

Complementing these learning methodologies, the development of innovative algorithms has further propelled the capabilities of AI systems. Over time, researchers have developed new algorithms that enable AI to perform tasks in a more efficient and effective manner. For example, the advent of generative adversarial networks (GANs) has marked a significant turning point in AI's capacity to generate realistic images, videos, and data (Creswell et al., 2018). Such algorithms have been deployed in creative domains, including art and content creation, as well as in sectors that necessitate the generation of synthetic data. Similarly, attention mechanisms have facilitated significant advancements in the field of natural language processing, enabling AI models to process sequential data more effectively and enhance capabilities in areas such as translation, summarization, and other tasks involving human language (Soydaner, 2022). These innovations in algorithms represent a significant advancement in AI systems, exceeding the capabilities of earlier iterations.

2.1.4 Tools and Services

The success of AI and ML projects relies not only on data, storage, computing power, and algorithms but also on a comprehensive set of tools and services that facilitate the development, deployment, and maintenance of AI systems. These tools are essential for streamlining processes, managing complex workflows, and enabling collaboration among data scientists, developers, and business stakeholders.

AI libraries are pre-built modules that provide functionalities for building ML models, processing data, and executing algorithms. These libraries enable developers to quickly implement complex AI systems without having to write low-level code from scratch. Popular libraries such as TensorFlow, PyTorch, and Keras offer pre-built functions for tasks such as deep learning, natural language processing, and computer vision (Vasilev, 2019). They allow for seamless experimentation, prototyping, and scaling of models to production environments. Other libraries, such as scikit-learn, specialize in traditional ML techniques, making them versatile tools for a variety of applications.

To manage the complexity of developing, testing, and deploying AI systems, **lifecycle management tools** have become indispensable. These tools help manage the end-to-end ML lifecycle, from data preparation to model deployment and monitoring. Model management platforms such as MLflow and Weights & Biases assist in tracking experiments, managing versions of models, and ensuring reproducibility (Alla & Adari, 2021). Additionally, ML operations tools, such as Azure Machine Learning, Google AI Platform, and DataRobot, help organizations automate and standardize their AI workflows, ensuring efficiency, consistency, and compliance throughout the process.

AI as a Service (AIaaS) is a cloud-based solution that allows organizations to leverage AI technologies without investing heavily in infrastructure or specialized skills (Lins et al., 2021). AIaaS platforms provide pre-trained models and tools for building, training, and deploying AI systems in a scalable manner. Cloud providers such as Amazon Web Services, Google Cloud Platform, and Microsoft Azure offer AI services such as natural language processing, image recognition, recommendation systems, and custom ML models. These platforms also offer AI model hosting services, enabling organizations to easily deploy their AI models in production with minimal setup and maintenance.

Together, these tools and services are essential in creating efficient, scalable, and robust AI systems. AI libraries provide the foundational building blocks for ML, while process-oriented tools and platforms like AIaaS help manage the complexity of AI development and deployment. The availability of these tools enables organizations to integrate AI into their operations more effectively, helping to drive innovation and maintain a competitive edge in a rapidly evolving technological landscape.

Summary

The technical fundamentals of artificial intelligence in modern business are built on four key components: data, storage, computing power and algorithms, as well as tools and services. High-quality, diverse, and balanced data is essential for successful AI model training and decision-making. Different data storage approaches, such as databases, data warehouses, data lakes, and data lakehouses, support various business requirements for processing and analysis. The exponential growth in computing power, alongside innovations in algorithms such as deep learning and GANs, has enabled AI's rapid advancement. Furthermore, AI tools and services streamline the development, deployment, and maintenance of AI systems.

2.2 AI Learning Methods

ML methods can be classified into three principal categories: supervised learning, unsupervised learning, and reinforcement learning (Li, 2023). Each method possesses distinctive strengths and is best suited to a particular class of tasks. Supervised learning is particularly well-suited to scenarios where labeled data is available and the objective is to make future predictions based on past data. Unsupervised learning is an effective method for identifying patterns and structures within unlabeled data. Finally, reinforcement learning is optimal for dynamic environments where learning is based on interaction and feedback. An understanding of these different approaches allows for the selection of the most appropriate method, depending on the nature of the problem and the available data.

2.2.1 Supervised Learning

Supervised learning is one of the foundational methods in ML, widely applied across industries for applications such as image classification and predictive analytics (Li, 2023; Buxmann & Schmidt, 2019). In this approach, an algorithm is trained on a labeled dataset, where each input is paired with its corresponding correct output. The primary goal of the algorithm is to learn from these examples to accurately predict outputs for new, unseen inputs. Traditionally, human experts provide the labeled data that guides the training phase, although automated systems can also be used to generate labels in certain cases. Regardless of the source, these input–output pairs enable the model to identify patterns and relationships within the data. The supervised learning process is typically divided into two main stages: the training phase and the prediction phase.

In the example illustrated in Fig. 2.3, the process of supervised learning is demonstrated through a simple scenario involving vehicle classification. During the training phase, the algorithm is provided with labeled data – images of buses and cars, each paired with their corresponding labels ("Bus" or "Car"). This allows the algorithm to learn the distinguishing features between these two vehicles. Once the training is complete, the algorithm produces a trained model, which can then be used in the prediction phase. In this phase, when a new, unlabeled input is presented (in this case, an image of a car), the model applies the patterns it has learned to predict the correct label ("Car"). This cycle of training on labeled examples and then making predictions on unseen inputs is the essence of supervised learning (Vaseekaran, 2018).

The fundamental concept underlying supervised learning can be expressed mathematically as the identification of a mapping function, $f(x)$, that predicts the output y for a given input x. In the context of the vehicle classification example, the input x represents an image of a vehicle, such as a bus or a car, and the output y is the correct label, either "Bus" or "Car." The goal of the algorithm is to learn this function $f(x)$ by analyzing labeled training data, which pairs inputs (vehicle images) with known outputs (labels).

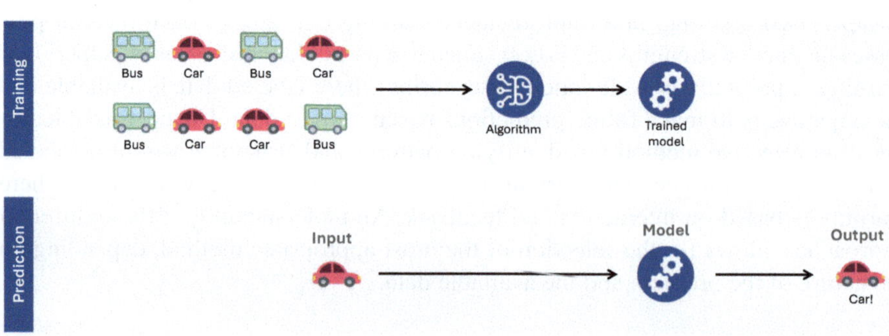

Fig. 2.3 Learning process in supervised learning

During the training process, the algorithm makes initial predictions based on its current parameters. It then compares these predictions to the actual labels in the dataset and calculates the difference using a loss function (see Chap. 3). By iteratively adjusting its internal parameters – often through optimization techniques like gradient descent – the algorithm aims to minimize the discrepancy between its predictions and the true labels. As the model processes more data, it gradually improves its ability to generalize from the training examples, allowing it to correctly predict the label for new, unseen vehicle images in the prediction phase. This ability to generalize effectively is the core objective of supervised learning.

The principal strength of supervised learning lies in its capacity to model relationships between input and output data with high accuracy, if there is sufficient high-quality labeled data available. The training process allows the algorithm to learn from past experience and apply this knowledge to make accurate future predictions. For instance, in the field of financial services, supervised learning is frequently employed to anticipate loan defaults by examining historical data on borrower behavior. In the field of healthcare, the application of supervised learning enables the prediction of patient outcomes based on an analysis of their medical history and other factors, helping doctors make informed decisions about treatment plans.

Nevertheless, supervised learning is not without its inherent difficulties. One of the principal constraints is the dependence on labeled data, which can be costly and time-consuming to procure. In many cases, the acquisition of a sufficient number of labeled examples to adequately train a model can present a significant challenge. Furthermore, the efficacy of the model is contingent upon the quality of the data. If the input–output pairs are noisy, incomplete, or biased, the model's predictions will be reflective of these shortcomings. Another challenge is that of overfitting, whereby the model becomes excessively calibrated to the training data and exhibits suboptimal performance on new, unseen data. It is therefore crucial to achieve an appropriate balance between model complexity and generalization ability.

Notwithstanding these challenges, supervised learning remains one of the most effective and widely utilized methods in ML. Its versatility, coupled with the wealth of algorithms available, makes it applicable to a wide range of tasks, from simple linear regression to complex image and speech recognition. As a result of ongoing developments in data collection and labeling techniques, supervised learning is undergoing a period of significant evolution, with the emergence of increasingly sophisticated tools for prediction and decision-making across a range of disciplines.

2.2.2 Unsupervised Learning

Unsupervised learning represents a powerful approach in ML, whereby the algorithm is tasked with the analysis and interpretation of data without any prior labels or human-provided categories (Li, 2023; Buxmann & Schmidt, 2019). In contrast to supervised learning, where human involvement is pivotal in the process of labeling data and providing guidance through the presentation of example outputs, unsupervised learning functions in an autonomous manner. The objective of unsupervised learning is to identify patterns, relationships, or groupings within the data, thereby serving as an exploratory tool that discovers the hidden structure within datasets. This makes unsupervised learning an optimal choice in scenarios where the underlying patterns in the data are not yet fully understood.

In the context of unsupervised learning, the role of humans is largely limited. In contrast to supervised learning, where humans provide labeled data and act as teachers, there is no human intervention in terms of labeling or guiding the model in unsupervised learning. The algorithm is provided with raw data, which may be in any format, including images, text, or numerical values. Its objective is to autonomously process and comprehend this data. The model itself must be capable of detecting patterns, grouping similar data points, or uncovering relationships between data points. This characteristic renders unsupervised learning an invaluable tool for exploratory data analysis, where human experts may lack prior knowledge of the patterns or groupings that exist within the dataset. To illustrate, consider an algorithm presented with a set of images depicting various vehicles, such as buses, cars, and scooters, without any accompanying labeling indicating the specific types of vehicles depicted (see Fig. 2.4). The algorithm must then autonomously discern the similarities and differences between these images and organize them into meaningful groups.

This process is divided into several stages, beginning with data analysis. Here, the algorithm receives raw, unlabeled data and starts by interpreting it to uncover underlying patterns, trends, or anomalies. Based on this interpretation, the algorithm enters the processing phase, where it organizes the data into clusters or extracts meaningful information from it. In this example, the algorithm might group all buses, cars, and scooters into separate clusters based on their shared visual characteristics. This unsupervised approach, which involves the model learning to distinguish and categorize items without guidance, is similar to how a human infant

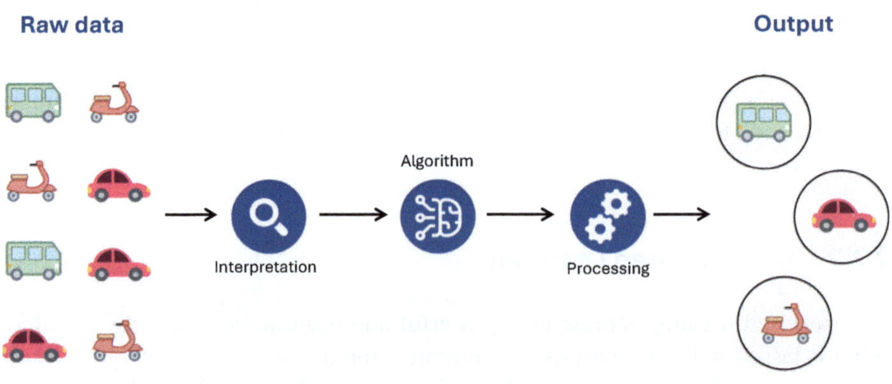

Fig. 2.4 Learning process in unsupervised learning

can visually discriminate between different types of vehicles without explicit instruction.

The Netflix recommendation system provides an illustrative example of unsupervised learning in a real-world context (Lutins, 2017). It employs unsupervised learning to categorize users based on their viewing patterns. For instance, users who watch the television series "Shameless" may also enjoy the television series "Orange is the New Black" or "American Horror Story." By identifying the characteristics that differentiate these users, Netflix can make precise recommendations without requiring explicit labels indicating each user's content preferences. The application of this method of clustering users based on shared behaviors enables Netflix to create a highly personalized viewing experience for each customer.

Unsupervised learning offers several key advantages, making it an invaluable tool in modern data analysis. One of its primary strengths is the ability to detect patterns and relationships within data without requiring prior knowledge or manually labeled data. This feature enables businesses and researchers to uncover entirely new insights from unstructured data, which may not be possible using traditional methods. In fields such as image and text analysis, as well as customer behavior analysis, unsupervised learning provides entirely new opportunities, as exemplified by the Netflix recommendation system. Additionally, this method is highly flexible, as it is not dependent on large, expensive, and time-consuming labeled datasets, allowing it to be applied in situations where labeled data is scarce or nonexistent.

Despite its strengths, unsupervised learning comes with several challenges. One of the main difficulties is the lack of clear evaluation metrics for the model's performance. Unlike supervised learning, where labeled data provides a benchmark for accuracy, the outcomes of unsupervised learning can be more ambiguous and subjective. Moreover, since the algorithm operates without human guidance, it may sometimes identify patterns that are not meaningful or relevant, leading to misinterpretations. Another significant challenge is the complexity of the algorithms involved, which can require substantial computational power and time, particularly when working with large datasets. Furthermore, unsupervised models often struggle with overfitting or producing results that lack generalization when applied to new data.

In summary, unsupervised learning is a powerful and versatile approach in ML, capable of revealing hidden patterns in unstructured data and offering new insights, particularly in exploratory data analysis. However, its utility is tempered by the challenges of assessing model performance and ensuring meaningful results. Despite these obstacles, unsupervised learning remains an essential tool in scenarios where prior knowledge of data patterns is limited, and its strengths far outweigh the inherent difficulties when applied judiciously.

2.2.3 Reinforcement Learning

Reinforcement learning represents a distinctive approach within the field of ML, whereby an agent learns through interactions with its surrounding environment and receives feedback based on its actions (Buxmann & Schmidt, 2019, Fumo, 2017, Li, 2023). In contrast to supervised learning, where an algorithm is provided with labeled data, reinforcement learning operates without predefined labels or direct human guidance. In contrast, the agent explores its environment, performs actions, and receives rewards or penalties as feedback. With the passage of time, this feedback enables the agent to modify its strategy in a manner that optimizes long-term rewards. The objective of the agent is to develop an optimal policy that determines the most appropriate action to take in each situation to achieve the highest cumulative reward.

The process of learning in reinforcement learning (see Fig. 2.5) commences with the agent's evaluation of the prevailing state of the environment. A state represents the conditions of the environment at a specific point in time, thereby providing the agent with the requisite context to make an informed decision. Based on the aforementioned state, the agent employs a decision-making function to select an action from a set of potential actions. Subsequently, the environment responds to the action performed by the agent, undergoing a transition to a new state and providing the agent with a reward. The reward is a numerical value that indicates the degree of success or failure of the action taken. For example, a positive reward indicates a favorable outcome, whereas a negative reward signifies that the action resulted in an unfavorable outcome. The agent utilizes this feedback to modify its behavior, learning from the rewards it receives and gradually refining its decision-making process to maximize its overall reward.

In reinforcement learning, humans play an indirect role. Although humans do not actively label data or train the algorithm, they are nevertheless responsible for defining the environment and designing the reward structure that drives the agent's

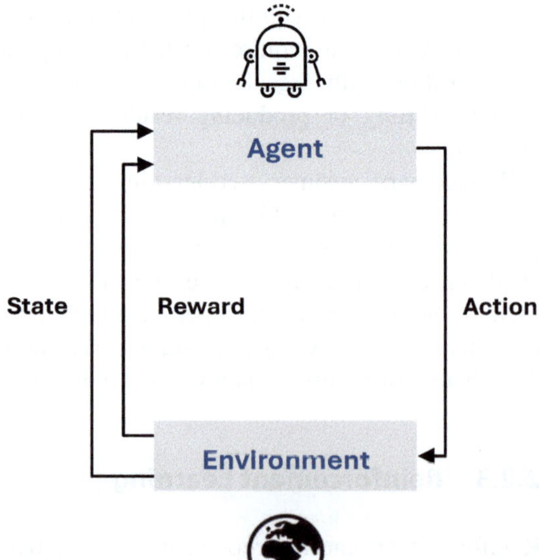

Fig. 2.5 Learning process in reinforcement learning. (Adapted from Li, 2023)

learning. By shaping the environment and rewards, humans exert influence over the outcomes that the agent is driven to pursue. However, the learning process itself is performed autonomously by the agent, which interacts with the environment, collects rewards, and uses that information to improve its performance over time.

Reinforcement learning has a wide range of real-world applications, particularly in domains that require autonomous decision-making. One of the most well-known applications of reinforcement learning is in the domain of gaming. In this context, AI agents have been trained to play games such as Go, Chess, and video games at levels that are perceived to be superhuman. In such instances, the agent acquires knowledge through repeated engagement with the game, modifying its strategy in accordance with the rewards (either winning or losing) it receives. By means of a process of trial and error, the agent identifies the optimal strategies for achieving victory, thereby attaining mastery of complex games.

Furthermore, reinforcement learning is a prominent field in robotics, where robots are trained to perform tasks, such as walking, navigating environments, or manipulating objects. In these scenarios, the agent (the robot) interacts with the physical world, learns from the outcomes of its actions, and gradually improves its performance. Similarly, reinforcement learning is employed in the context of autonomous vehicles, wherein the vehicle (agent) is tasked with making real-time decisions based on its interactions with the road, other vehicles, and obstacles. The vehicle receives feedback based on its adherence to traffic rules, ability to avoid collisions, and safety in navigation. This feedback is then used to refine the vehicle's driving strategy.

Reinforcement learning is highly effective in dynamic environments where agents must continuously adapt based on their interactions with the surrounding system. One of its key strengths lies in its ability to handle complex, sequential decision-making problems. Unlike other learning paradigms, reinforcement learning allows agents to improve through trial and error, making it particularly well-suited for applications such as robotics, game playing (e.g., AlphaGo), and real-time decision-making systems. Reinforcement learning's capacity to optimize actions based on long-term rewards rather than short-term gains ensures that agents learn more effective and efficient strategies over time. This adaptability allows reinforcement learning to excel in environments where optimal solutions are not immediately apparent and must be learned incrementally.

However, reinforcement learning is not without its limitations. One common problem is state overload, where the sheer number of possible states becomes overwhelming for the agent to process. This issue is particularly pronounced in large or complex environments, where managing and optimizing the learning process requires significant computational resources. Additionally, reinforcement learning is generally not suitable for simpler problems, where other learning paradigms, such as supervised learning, may provide more straightforward and efficient solutions. Insufficient data quantity can also impede the learning process, as reinforcement learning requires a vast amount of interaction data to effectively learn policies. Moreover, reinforcement learning is highly computationally intensive, with significant demands on computing power, further limiting its scalability. Finally, reinforcement learning struggles with limited dimensionality when tasked with handling highly detailed environments, which can restrict its capacity to generalize across various applications.

In summary, reinforcement learning is a powerful tool for solving complex, dynamic problems, offering substantial potential for long-term optimization in areas such as robotics and autonomous systems. However, its demanding computational requirements, inefficiency for simpler tasks, and susceptibility to state overload necessitate careful consideration. When appropriately applied in environments with sufficient computational resources and interaction data, reinforcement learning can produce highly effective solutions, but it is not always the most suitable choice for less complex or resource-constrained problems. Selecting the right learning paradigm requires balancing problem complexity, data availability, and computational resources, ensuring that the strengths of reinforcement learning are harnessed in the correct context.

Summary
AI learning methods are divided into three main categories: supervised, unsupervised, and reinforcement learning. Each approach excels in different scenarios, depending on the availability of data and the complexity of the task. Supervised learning works well for tasks with labeled data, enabling accurate predictions based on past examples. Unsupervised learning, in contrast, identifies patterns in unlabeled data, making it ideal for exploratory analysis. Reinforcement learning is best suited for dynamic environments, where agents learn by interacting with the system and receiving feedback. Each method's strengths and weaknesses must be carefully considered to select the most appropriate approach for the task.

2.3 Functional Groups of AI Algorithms and Architectures

The field of AI relies on a wide range of algorithms and architectures, which can be grouped into five primary categories: regression, classification, clustering, generation, and action (see Fig. 2.6). These categories represent the core functions AI can perform and are essential for understanding its applications in both business and research contexts. With the increasing prevalence of neural networks (see Chap. 3), the distinction between algorithms and architectures has become increasingly important:

- **Algorithms** are step-by-step computational procedures designed to solve a specific task (e.g., linear regression for regression tasks and K-means for clustering).
- **Architectures** define the overall structure of a model, specifying how information is processed but typically requiring separate algorithms for optimization and inference (e.g., Transformer Models for generation tasks or deep Q-networks (DQNs) for action tasks).

Functional Group	Definition	Example
Regression	Predicting continuous values based on relationships between variables	Predicting continuous values based on relationships between variables
Classification	Assigning data points to predefined categories	Classify customers into predefined groups in terms of purchasing power
Clustering	Grouping similar data points without predefined categories	Identify homogeneous groups among customers in terms of purchasing power
Generation	Creating new data instances based on learned patterns	Writing news articles based on structured data (e.g., weather or financial reports)
Action	Making decisions and performing tasks in dynamic environments	Self-driving cars learning optimal navigation strategies

Fig. 2.6 Functional groups of AI algorithms and architectures

Understanding this distinction helps clarify why some methods are classified as algorithms – which execute computations based on predefined rules – whereas others are considered architectures, which provide flexible frameworks for organizing learning processes and structuring models within AI. Notably, many algorithms and architectures are not confined to a single category. For example, decision trees can be used for both regression and classification, while neural network architectures are found across all five categories – regression, classification, clustering, generation, and action – depending on how they are structured and trained.

Regression is a fundamental method in supervised learning, used to predict continuous values by modeling the relationship between dependent and independent variables (Russell & Norvig, 2016; James et al., 2013). A common application in business is demand forecasting, where historical sales data and market factors help predict future product demand. In this context, different approaches are utilized, which can be categorized as either algorithms or architectures. Examples of algorithms used in regression include linear regression, support vector regression, and lasso regression, which follow predefined computational steps to estimate relationships between variables. In contrast, architectures such as feedforward neural networks are commonly used for general regression tasks with structured data, while temporal convolutional networks are designed to process sequential data, making them well-suited for time-series regression.

Classification is a key method within the supervised learning paradigm, used to assign data points to predefined categories (James et al., 2013). This approach is particularly valuable in customer segmentation, where businesses classify customers based on factors such as purchasing power, demographics, or behavioral patterns. By distinguishing different customer groups, companies can tailor their strategies to better meet the needs of each segment. Various approaches are employed in classification tasks. Examples of classification algorithms include random forest, kernelized support vector machines, and decision trees (ID3), which determine decision boundaries based on training data. Meanwhile, architectures such as convolutional neural networks and recurrent neural networks enable more advanced classification tasks, particularly in domains such as image recognition and sequential data analysis.

Clustering is an unsupervised learning method designed to identify patterns in data by grouping similar items into clusters (James et al., 2013). In marketing, clustering techniques help businesses uncover groups of customers who exhibit similar behaviors or preferences. This approach provides valuable insights for product development and the design of targeted promotional strategies. Different methods are employed to perform clustering. Examples of clustering algorithms include K-means, hierarchical clustering, and fuzzy C-means, which categorize data points based on similarity measures. On a more advanced level, architectures such as autoencoders and self-organizing maps allow for high-dimensional data representation and deep clustering tasks, enabling businesses to extract meaningful patterns from complex datasets.

Generation refers to methods in ML that create new data instances resembling input data. These techniques are particularly valuable in unsupervised and semi-supervised learning, enabling applications such as text generation, image synthesis, and data augmentation. Recent advances in generative AI have been driven by transformer-based architectures (e.g., GPT), which enable high-quality text generation, code synthesis, and multimodal applications. Additionally, diffusion models, as used in tools such as DALL·E and Stable Diffusion, have significantly improved AI-generated content in fields such as image and video generation. Beyond these, other generative approaches include GANs and variational autoencoders, which learn underlying data distributions to generate realistic samples (Feuerriegel et al., 2024).

Action refers to AI systems that learn to make decisions and take actions in dynamic environments. These methods are particularly prominent in reinforcement learning, where agents iteratively refine their strategies by interacting with their surroundings and receiving feedback through rewards and penalties. This approach is widely applied in autonomous vehicles and adaptive recommendation systems, where AI must learn and adjust to ever-changing inputs (Plaat, 2022). Examples of action algorithms include Q-learning and asynchronous actor-critic agents, which optimize actions based on reward structures. Architectures such as DQNs improve AI's ability to learn optimal policies from experience, while graph neural networks can enhance decision-making in structured environments, such as traffic networks or robotic motion planning.

The five functional groups of AI algorithms and architectures – regression, classification, clustering, generating, and acting – form the foundation for a multitude of diverse AI applications. Each group addresses distinct needs and offers unique value in optimizing decision-making, enhancing customer experiences, and automating complex processes across industries. An understanding of these categories and their algorithms and architectures enables practitioners and researchers to select the most appropriate techniques for specific business problems, thereby driving innovation and operational efficiency. In the following, we will take a closer look at some of the most popular algorithms within these groups to illustrate their practical relevance and application. Neural networks, which form the foundation for the architectures discussed here, will be examined in detail in Chap. 3.

2.3.1 Linear Regression

Linear regression is a fundamental statistical method used to model the relationship between a dependent variable and one or more independent variables (see Fig. 2.7). It finds applications in areas such as economics, finance, and ML, where predicting trends and understanding relationships between variables are crucial. This technique is particularly useful for elucidating the behavior of the dependent variable, which is often referred to as the target or outcome, based on the values of the independent variables, which are also known as predictors or input features. The principal objective of linear regression is to ascertain a linear relationship between the variables in question, thereby enabling the value of the dependent variable to be predicted for new observations (Russell & Norvig, 2016; James et al., 2013).

The underlying equation of linear regression is typically expressed as follows:

$$y_i = a + x_i b$$

In this equation, y_i represents the predicted value of the dependent variable for the ith observation, x_i denotes the value of the independent variable, a is the intercept of the regression line with the y-axis, and b is the slope of the regression line. The slope, b, indicates the degree to which y changes when x increases by one unit. The intercept, a, represents the value of y when x equals zero. This relationship allows for the prediction of how the dependent variable behaves when the independent variable changes. The method employed to fit the regression line is referred to as the

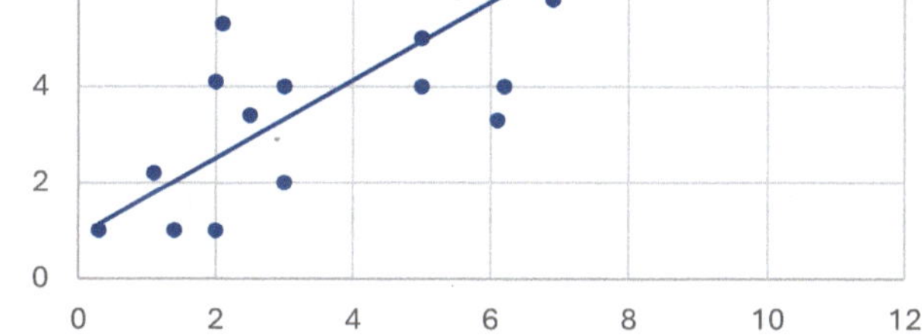

Fig. 2.7 Linear regression example

"least squares estimation," which is designed to minimize the sum of the squared differences between the observed and predicted values, also known as residuals.

In scenarios where multiple independent variables influence the dependent variable, the linear regression model is expanded to a multiple regression model, which is represented as follows:

$$y_i = a + b_1x_1 + b_2x_2 + \ldots + b_ix_i$$

where x_1, x_2, …, x_i are the independent variables and b_1, b_2,..., b_i are the coefficients. The respective coefficients, denoted by b_1, b_2, and so forth, quantify the impact of each independent variable on the dependent variable. The multiple regression model allows for the simultaneous analysis of multiple factors and their combined effect on the target variable.

The calculation of the regression line is based on fundamental statistical concepts, including covariance and correlation. Covariance is a statistical measure that quantifies the joint variability of two variables, indicating the extent to which they exhibit correlated changes. A positive covariance indicates a tendency for the variables to increase or decrease in conjunction with one another, whereas a negative covariance implies that one variable increases, while the other decreases. Correlation serves to normalize covariance, thereby providing a measure of the strength and direction of the linear relationship between variables. The correlation coefficient ranges from –1 (indicating a perfect negative correlation) to +1 (indicating a perfect positive correlation), with 0 indicating the absence of a linear relationship between the variables.

The slope, denoted by b, of the regression line is calculated using the following formula:

$$b = r_{xy} * \frac{s_y}{s_x}$$

The intercept, a, is calculated using the following formula:

$$a = -\frac{s_y}{s_x} * r_{xy} * x_{avg} + y_{avg}$$

where s_x and s_y represent the standard deviation of the independent variable, r_{xy} is the correlation coefficient between the two variables, x_{avg} is the mean of the independent variable, and y_{avg} is the mean of the dependent variable. The correlation coefficient is calculated using the following formula:

$$r_{xy} = \frac{cov(x,y)}{s_x * s_y}$$

The covariance is calculated using the following formula:

$$cov(x,y) = \frac{1}{n-1} * \Sigma\left(x_i - x_{\text{avg}}\right)\left(y_i - y_{\text{avg}}\right)$$

where x_{avg} and y_{avg} are the means of the independent and dependent variables, respectively. These calculations guarantee that the regression line is optimally fitted to the dataset, passing through the mean of the data points.

One of the most significant advantages of linear regression is its simplicity and ease of interpretation, which facilitate the understanding of the underlying relationships between variables. The results of a linear regression model are readily comprehensible, as the coefficients offer direct insights into the manner in which the independent variables exert an influence on the dependent variable. To illustrate, in a business context, the slope of the regression line can demonstrate the extent to which sales increase when the marketing budget is augmented. This transparency renders linear regression a valuable tool in business, particularly in domains such as financial analysis and sales forecasting. Another advantage of linear regression is its efficiency. It requires relatively few computational resources and is capable of handling large datasets with great efficiency, which makes it an ideal choice for exploratory data analysis and rapid prototyping.

Notwithstanding the advantages, linear regression is not without limitations. The most significant limitation of linear regression is its inability to capture non-linear relationships between variables. In practice, many relationships are not linear, which means that linear regression may be inadequate for modeling more complex interactions between variables. To illustrate, the relationship between marketing expenditure and customer acquisition may be more accurately represented by a curve than by a straight line. In such instances, the application of linear regression may result in the generation of inaccurate or misleading outcomes.

Furthermore, linear regression is contingent upon a number of underlying assumptions. A fundamental assumption underlying linear regression is that the relationship between the dependent and independent variables is linear. Other assumptions include the independence of residuals (the differences between observed and predicted values), homoscedasticity (the variance of residuals remains constant across the range of the independent variables), and normally distributed residuals. In the event of a breach of these assumptions, the model's predictive accuracy may be significantly compromised.

Another significant drawback of linear regression is its susceptibility to the influence of outliers. As linear regression strives to identify a line that aligns as closely as possible with all data points, outliers – that is, data points that deviate significantly from the overall pattern – can exert a considerable influence on the regression line and distort the results. This is a particularly problematic issue in business applications, where data is often of poor quality or contains outliers due to operational anomalies. In such cases, it may be necessary to employ alternative models that are more robust to outliers.

Linear regression is a commonly utilized technique for applications such as sales forecasting, cost–benefit analysis, and market evaluations. It provides decision-makers with invaluable insights into the interrelationships between different business variables, thereby enabling them to make well-informed predictions based on historical data. To illustrate, a company may utilize linear regression to ascertain the influence of diverse factors, including advertising budget, pricing strategies, and seasonal trends, on sales. In the field of finance, linear regression is frequently utilized for the purpose of forecasting stock prices or assessing the sensitivity of a portfolio to market fluctuations. Nevertheless, while linear regression is an invaluable tool for rapidly acquiring insights, it is crucial to ascertain that its underlying assumptions are satisfied and to explore alternative models when the relationships between variables are intricate or the data does not align with the linear regression paradigm.

In conclusion, linear regression is a robust and pervasive technique for modeling the relationship between variables. The simplicity and interpretability of linear regression make it a valuable tool for both exploratory and predictive analyses, particularly in business contexts where clear insights into the factors driving outcomes are essential. However, its limitations – especially its inability to handle non-linear relationships, sensitivity to outliers, and reliance on strict assumptions – imply that it should be applied with caution, and more advanced methods may be required for more complex or nuanced analyses.

2.3.2 Decision Tree

A decision tree is a supervised learning algorithm that is frequently utilized in AI and ML, particularly for classification and regression tasks. The structure of a decision tree is analogous to a series of questions or tests that direct the decision-making process (Li, 2023; Blockeel et al., 2023). Each question, represented as a node, partitions the data into smaller subsets based on certain conditions, and the process continues recursively until a final decision is reached. Decision trees can be classified into two main categories:

1. **Classification trees** are employed in situations where the objective is to categorize data into predefined categories or classes. In a classification tree, the target variable is categorical, with each leaf node representing a specific class. For example, in the context of email filtering, a classification tree may be employed to categorize emails as either "spam" or "not spam." At each decision node, the tree evaluates a condition based on a feature of the input data (e.g., whether a specific word appears in the email), and the branches lead to further classifications until a final category is assigned at the leaf node. The process of decision-making continues until the model has sufficiently partitioned the data set to enable an accurate prediction of the class.
2. **Regression trees** are a specific type of tree-based model that is used to predict continuous numerical values. In a regression tree, the target variable is continuous, and each leaf node contains a predicted numerical value based on the input features. To illustrate, a regression tree may be employed to estimate the price of a house based on characteristics such as its size, location, and number of bedrooms. At each decision node, the tree evaluates whether a specific feature exceeds a predefined threshold value (e.g., whether the house size is larger than a given value). Based on this evaluation, the data is split until a final prediction

is made. The model's performance is typically evaluated by minimizing the mean squared error (MSE) at the leaf nodes.

In a decision tree, the process begins at the root node, which represents the initial question or test that will divide the dataset. This node sets the stage for the entire tree by posing a condition based on one of the features in the dataset. The goal of the initial split is to group the data points that share similar characteristics or belong to the same class. From this root node, the tree branches out, with each branch representing one possible answer to the question posed at the node.

Step 1: The Question/Test

At the root node and each subsequent decision node, the algorithm must identify a question or test that will split the data in the most meaningful way. This question is based on the features of the data. For example, in a weather data set, the question might concern the outlook (e.g., "Is the weather sunny, overcast, or rainy?"). The goal is to find a feature that best divides the data into subsets that are homogeneous or as close to homogeneous as possible, meaning that the data points in each subset should belong to the same class (for classification problems) or be as similar as possible (for regression problems).

The selection of the best question or feature for the split is typically driven by optimizing specific criteria. For classification tasks, this often involves minimizing Gini impurity or entropy to ensure that each split results in subsets that contain mostly one class. For regression tasks, the decision-making process aims to minimize MSE, ensuring that each split produces more accurate predictions.

Step 2: Split Decision

Once the test or question is selected, the data is split into subsets based on the possible answers to the question. Each subset represents a group of data points that share the same answer to the question. For example, if the question at the root node is *"What is the outlook?"* with possible values sunny, overcast, and rainy, the dataset is divided into three subsets accordingly.

This process is illustrated in Fig. 2.8, where the decision tree begins by asking about the outlook to determine if it is sunny, overcast, or rainy. Depending on the answer, the tree further splits the data based on additional features, such as humidity or wind. In the case of a sunny outlook, the decision node then checks whether the humidity is high or normal, further dividing the dataset.

Step 3: For Each Subset

After each split, the algorithm evaluates whether additional splits are necessary. This is determined by the homogeneity of the data within each subset:

- If all data points in a subset belong to the same class (classification) or if the variance in the target values is below a predefined threshold (regression), no further splits are needed, and the subset is assigned a leaf node. A leaf node represents

Fig. 2.8 Decision tree example

the final decision, either as a classification label (e.g., "Yes, we should play tennis") or a predicted numerical value (in regression).

- If a subset contains data points from multiple classes (classification) or shows high variance (regression), the algorithm searches for another feature to split the subset further. This process continues until homogeneity is achieved or no further meaningful splits can be made.
- If no further features are available to split on, and some data points still belong to different classes (classification) or have a high variance (regression), the algorithm assigns the most common class (classification) or the average target value (regression) from the parent node to minimize prediction errors on unseen data.

The tree-building process continues recursively, splitting the data into increasingly smaller subsets until one of the following stop conditions is met: all data points in a subset are homogeneous – meaning that they belong to the same class in classification tasks or exhibit sufficiently low variance in regression tasks – no further features remain for splitting, or a predefined stopping criterion is reached. These stopping criteria typically include a maximum tree depth to control model complexity or a minimum number of data points per node to prevent overfitting.

The principal advantages of decision trees are their simplicity and interpretability. The structure of decision trees is designed to mirror the processes by which humans make decisions, which makes them intuitive and easy to understand. The correspondence between each node in the tree and a specific question or condition provides transparency regarding the logic behind the model's predictions. The interpretability of decision trees renders them particularly valuable in fields where an understanding of the rationale behind decisions is of paramount importance, such as healthcare or finance.

Decision trees are typically efficient to train. The training process is scalable with respect to the size of the dataset. In comparison to more complex ML algorithms, such as neural networks, decision trees require relatively little computational power. The time required for training typically increases in a linear manner with the number of samples and features, thereby rendering decision trees a practical option for large datasets.

Furthermore, decision trees are robust to outliers and noise in the data. As each decision node is based on a condition that affects only a subset of the data, the influence of outliers or noisy data points on the overall model is reduced. This renders decision trees more resilient to errors resulting from irregular data, in comparison to alternative models that are more susceptible to such anomalies.

Despite their advantages, decision trees have a number of significant disadvantages. One of the principal difficulties is that of overfitting. The propensity for decision trees to overfit is heightened when they become overly complex, particularly when they become too deep and attempt to model every nuance in the training data. Overfitting results in poor generalization to new data, as the tree becomes tailored to the noise and specificities of the training set, rather than capturing the underlying patterns.

A further disadvantage is instability. Due to the sensitivity of decision trees to variations in the training data, even minor alterations can lead to entirely different tree structures and splits, potentially affecting model predictions and reducing reliability in certain scenarios. This instability can be mitigated by employing ensemble methods such as Random Forests, wherein multiple decision trees are trained on distinct subsets of the data and their predictions are aggregated. Additionally, pruning techniques – which remove branches that contribute little to predictive performance – can help reduce variance and improve the tree's generalization ability.

Additionally, decision trees may be susceptible to bias when dealing with imbalanced classes. In classification tasks where one class is markedly more prevalent than others, decision trees may yield models that are biased toward predicting the dominant class. This can result in suboptimal performance, particularly in instances where correctly identifying the minority class is critical, such as in fraud detection or medical diagnoses. Techniques such as class weighting or the utilization of more sophisticated algorithms, including gradient boosting machines, can assist in addressing this issue.

In summary, decision trees represent a powerful and versatile tool in the domain of AI, exhibiting the capacity to handle both classification and regression tasks. The ease of interpretation and robustness to outliers make them a popular choice for many applications. However, their susceptibility to overfitting and sensitivity to data variations necessitate caution when employing them, particularly in complex or imbalanced datasets. In practice, decision trees often perform optimally when used in conjunction with ensemble methods, which help to offset their limitations while leveraging their strengths.

2.3.3 K-Means

The k-means algorithm is a common approach to cluster analysis in unsupervised learning. It partitions a dataset into a predefined number of k clusters, each

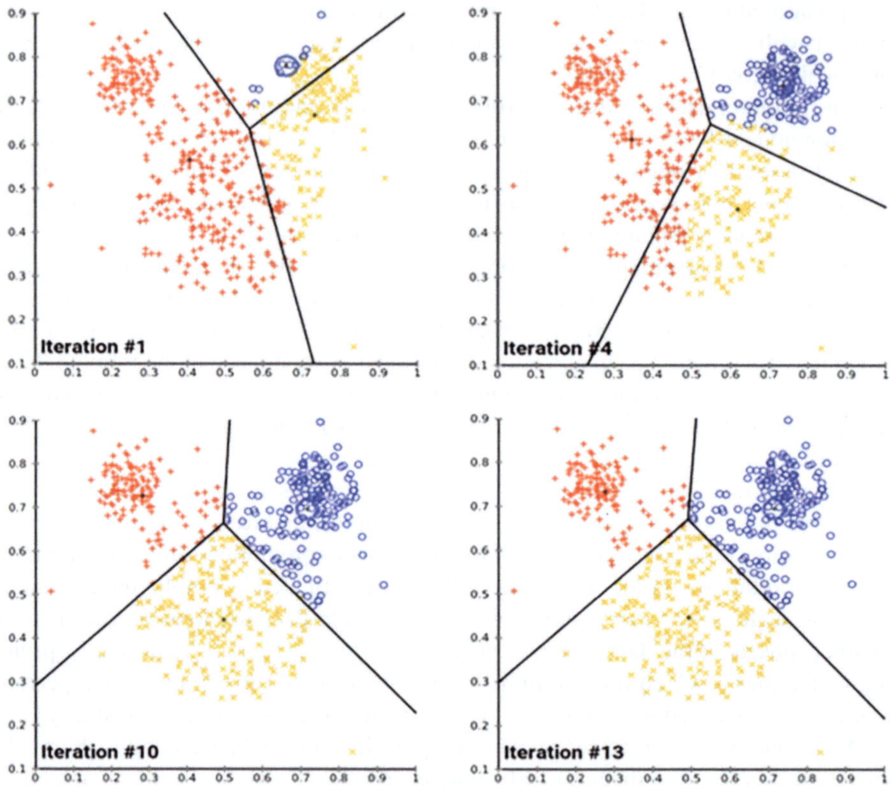

Fig. 2.9 K-means example. (Adapted from Chire, 2017)

represented by a centroid (see Fig. 2.9). The primary objective of the k-means algorithm is to group data points so that those within the same cluster are more similar to each other than to points in different clusters. It is particularly useful for identifying intrinsic structures within unlabeled numerical data. Standard k-means relies on Euclidean distance to measure similarity, but variations such as k-modes allow for clustering categorical data (Li, 2023).

The k-means algorithm employs a two-step iterative process, starting with the selection of initial centroids, which represent the central points of each cluster. In the initial stage of the algorithm, a random selection of k data points from the dataset is made to serve as the starting centroids. The choice of initial centroids is of great consequence, as they determine the eventual shape and composition of the clusters. Subsequently, the algorithm assigns each data point to the nearest centroid, based on a selected distance metric. Once all data points have been assigned to the nearest centroid, the latter is updated by recalculating its position as the mean of all data points within the cluster. This process of assigning points and updating centroids is repeated until the algorithm reaches convergence, which is defined as the point at which the centroids no longer exhibit significant movement or a specified number of iterations has been reached.

One of the biggest advantages of the k-means algorithm is its efficiency and scalability, making it well-suited for large datasets. Due to its simple iterative process – assigning data points to the nearest centroid and updating cluster centers – k-means runs quickly and efficiently, even when handling substantial amounts of data. For Big Data applications, optimized variants such as Mini-Batch K-means can further enhance performance. Another key strength of k-means is its broad applicability across various domains. In marketing, it helps businesses segment customers based on purchasing behavior. In image processing, it simplifies images by grouping similar colors, making it useful for compression and color quantization. In bioinformatics, k-means is used to analyze gene expression patterns and identify similarities in genetic data. While standard k-means is designed for numerical data, alternative versions such as k-modes (for categorical data) and k-prototypes (for mixed data) extend its applicability to a wider range of data types and use cases.

Notwithstanding its advantages, the k-means algorithm has limitations that can impact its performance. One of the primary challenges associated with the k-means algorithm is its sensitivity to the initial placement of centroids. The choice of initial centroids significantly influences the final clustering result, and poor initialization may lead to suboptimal clustering, causing the algorithm to become trapped in a local minimum. To address this issue, techniques such as k-means++, which employs a strategic approach to selecting initial centroids, are frequently employed to enhance the probability of identifying superior clusters. Another challenge is that the number of clusters k must be specified in advance, which can be difficult if the optimal value is unknown. Selecting an inappropriate k can lead to suboptimal clustering, either by merging dissimilar data points or unnecessarily splitting cohesive groups. Techniques such as the elbow method and silhouette analysis can assist in determining a suitable value for k, though this remains an inherent challenge.

Additionally, k-means assumes that clusters are spherical and of similar size, which makes it less effective for real-world data, where clusters may have complex, non-spherical shapes or varying densities. When clusters are elongated or exhibit irregular boundaries, k-means may fail to accurately capture the intrinsic structure of the data. In such cases, alternative clustering methods, such as DBSCAN, may be preferable, as they do not rely on predefined cluster shapes.

The k-means algorithm's reliance on distance measures, particularly Euclidean distance, also implies that it is most effective when the data is evenly scaled. The presence of features with disparate units or scales can result in the generation of biased outcomes, as features exhibiting greater ranges may exert a disproportionate influence on the distance calculations. Consequently, data preprocessing steps, such as normalization or standardization, are frequently required to guarantee that all features contribute equally to the clustering process. Furthermore, because k-means relies on distance-based similarity measures, particularly Euclidean distance, it is highly sensitive to differences in scale between features. If the data contains attributes with varying units or magnitudes, features with larger ranges can disproportionately influence clustering results. To prevent this, preprocessing steps such as normalization or standardization are often necessary to ensure that all features contribute equally to the clustering process.

Summary
AI consists of five functional groups of algorithms and architectures: regression, classification, clustering, generation, and action. Regression predicts continuous values, classification assigns data to predefined categories, and clustering identifies patterns by grouping similar data points. Generation creates new data, such as text or images, using models such as GANs and transformers, while action-oriented AI leverages reinforcement learning for decision-making in dynamic environments. These categories form the foundation of AI applications, enabling businesses to develop tailored solutions that enhance automation, optimize processes, and drive innovation.

References

Alla, S., & Adari, S. K. (2021). *Beginning MLOps with MLFlow*. Apress.

Bigelow, S. J. (2024). Tensor processing unit (TPU). *TechTarget*. Retrieved October 21, 2024, from https://www.techtarget.com/whatis/definition/tensor-processing-unit-TPU

Blockeel, H., Devos, L., Frénay, B., Nanfack, G., & Nijssen, S. (2023). Decision trees: From efficient prediction to responsible AI. *Frontiers in Artificial Intelligence, 6*, 1124553.

Buhl, N. (2022). *An introduction to balanced and imbalanced datasets in machine learning*. Retrieved October 21, 2024, from https://encord.com/blog/an-introduction-to-balanced-and-imbalanced-datasets-in-machine-learning/

Buxmann, P., & Schmidt, H. (2019). *Künstliche Intelligenz*. Springer.

Chire. (2017). Konvergenz von k-means. *Wikipedia*. Retrieved October 21, 2024, from https://de.wikipedia.org/wiki/K-Means-Algorithmus#/media/Datei:K-means_convergence.gif

Creswell, A., White, T., Dumoulin, V., Arulkumaran, K., Sengupta, B., & Bharath, A. A. (2018). Generative adversarial networks: An overview. *IEEE Signal Processing Magazine, 35*(1), 53–65.

El Aissi, M. E. M., Benjelloun, S., Loukili, Y., Lakhrissi, Y., Boushaki, A. E., Chougrad, H., & Elhaj Ben Ali, S. (2022). Data lake versus data warehouse architecture: A comparative study. In *WITS 2020: Proceedings of the 6th International Conference on Wireless Technologies, Embedded, and Intelligent Systems* (pp. 201–210). Springer.

Feuerriegel, S., Hartmann, J., Janiesch, C., Maedche, A., Utz, S., & Weinzierl, S. (2024). Generative AI. *Business & Information Systems Engineering, 66*, 111–126.

Frické, M. (2019). The knowledge pyramid: The DIKW hierarchy. *Ko Knowledge Organization, 46*(1), 33–46.

Fumo, J. (2017). Types of machine learning algorithms you should know. *Towards Data Science*. Retrieved October 21, 2024, from https://medium.com/data-science/types-of-machine-learning-algorithms-you-should-know-953a08248861

Goodfellow, I. (2016). *Deep learning* (Vol. 196). MIT Press.

Harby, A. A., & Zulkernine, F. M. (2022). From data warehouse to lakehouse: A comparative review. In *2022 IEEE International Conference on Big Data (Big Data)* (pp. 389–395). IEEE.

James, G., Witten, D., Hastie, T., & Tibshirani, R. (2013). *An introduction to statistical learning* (Vol. 112, p. 18). Springer.

Janson. (2022). *Rechenleistung von Supercomputern wächst rasant*. Retrieved October 21, 2024, from https://de.statista.com/infografik/26868/rechenleistung-des-jeweils-staerksten-supercomputers-der-welt/

Li, H. (2023). *Machine learning methods*. Springer Nature.

Lins, S., Pandl, K. D., Teigeler, H., Thiebes, S., Bayer, C., & Sunyaev, A. (2021). Artificial intelligence as a service: Classification and research directions. *Business & Information Systems Engineering, 63*, 441–456.

Lutins, E. (2017). DBSCAN: What is it? When to use it? How to use it. *Medium*. Retrieved October 21, 2024, from https://elutins.medium.com/dbscan-what-is-it-when-to-use-it-how-to-use-it-8bd506293818

Monolith AI. (2023). *Data quality and quantity for machine learning*. Retrieved October 21, 2024, from https://www.monolithai.com/blog/data-quality-and-quantity-for-machine-learning

Peper, F. (2017). The end of Moore's law: Opportunities for natural computing? *New Generation Computing, 35*(3), 253–269.

Petrov, A. (2019). *Database internals: A deep dive into how distributed data systems work*. O'Reilly Media.

Plaat, A. (2022). *Deep reinforcement learning* (Vol. 10, pp. 978–981). Springer.

Russell, S. J., & Norvig, P. (2016). *Artificial intelligence: A modern approach*. Pearson.

Soydaner, D. (2022). Attention mechanism in neural networks: Where it comes and where it goes. *Neural Computing and Applications, 34*(16), 13371–13385.

Vaseekaran, G., 2018. Machine learning: Supervised learning vs unsupervised learning. *Medium*. Retrieved October 21, 2024, from https://gowthamy.medium.com/machine-learning-supervised-learning-vs-unsupervised-learning-f1658e12a780

Vasilev, I. (2019). *Advanced deep learning with Python: Design and implement advanced next-generation AI solutions using TensorFlow and PyTorch*. Packt Publishing Ltd..

Nils Urbach is Professor of Information Systems and Digital Business as well as Director of the Research Lab for Digital Innovation & Transformation at the Frankfurt University of Applied Sciences, Germany. Furthermore, he is Director at the FIM Research Center for Information Management, and the Branch Business & Information Systems Engineering of Fraunhofer FIT. Nils Urbach has been working in the fields of digital innovation and transformation for several years. His work has been published in several academic journals such as Information Systems Research (ISR), the Journal of the Association for Information Systems (JAIS), the Journal of Strategic Information Systems (JSIS), the Journal of Information Technology (JIT), MIS Quarterly Executive (MISQE), IEEE Transactions on Engineering Management (IEEE TEM), Information and Management (I&M), Business & Information Systems Engineering (BISE), and Electronic Markets (EM). He advises several companies on digitalization issues and regularly appears as a speaker on this topic.

Daniel Feulner received his M.Sc. in information system from the Otto-Friedrich University of Bamberg, Germany in 2023. He is an affiliated researcher at the Branch Business & Information Systems Engineering of the Fraunhofer FIT and FIM Research Center for Information Management at the University of Bayreuth. In his research, he aims to understand how Business Analytics and Artificial Intelligence can be effectively and responsibly utilized in organizations. His goal is to enable companies to drive innovation and achieve sustainable growth in a rapidly evolving technological landscape.

Tobias Guggenberger is a postdoctoral researcher at the University of Bayreuth and the Branch Business & Information Systems Engineering of Fraunhofer FIT. He holds an M.Sc. in business administration and a Ph.D. in information systems engineering. His research primarily concentrates on the design and management of information systems, leveraging emerging technologies like artificial intelligence (AI) and blockchain. His scholarly contributions have appeared in renowned conference proceedings, including the International Conference on Information Systems (ICIS) and the European Conference on Information Systems (ECIS). His research has also been published in prestigious international journals such as IEEE Transactions on Engineering Management (IEEE TEM), MIS Quarterly Executive (MISQE), Electronic Markets (EM), and Computers & Industrial Engineering.

Foundations of Neural Networks

3

Nils Urbach, Daniel Feulner, and Tobias Guggenberger

Neural networks are a fundamental technology in artificial intelligence (AI), recognized for their capability to discern intricate patterns in data and facilitate automated decision-making. Modeled after the human brain, they comprise interconnected artificial "neurons" that process and relay signals. This structure excels in tasks involving voluminous, unstructured, or high-dimensional datasets, where conventional statistical methods often falter. By examining historical data, neural networks uncover hidden links, forecast future developments, and deliver insights that drive strategic decisions across diverse domains.

This chapter examines the key components of neural networks, including input, hidden, and output layers, as well as the role of weights and activation functions in the learning process. Particular emphasis is placed on backpropagation as a core training technique. These concepts are explored in a structured manner, illustrated through the example of identifying handwritten digits, demonstrating how neural networks process and learn from data. The goal is to provide a clear and comprehensive introduction to the principles and mechanics of neural networks.

3.1 Introduction to Neural Networks

Before examining the structure of artificial neural networks, it can be helpful to develop an intuitive understanding of how they function. The human brain serves as an ideal analogy: an immensely complex network of billions of neurons, each acting

N. Urbach (✉)
Frankfurt University of Applied Sciences, Frankfurt am Main, Germany
e-mail: nils.urbach@fim-rc.de

D. Feulner · T. Guggenberger
University of Bayreuth, Bayreuth, Germany
e-mail: daniel.feulner@fim-rc.de; tobias.guggenberger@fim-rc.de

N. Urbach, D. Feulner (eds.), *Managing Artificial Intelligence*, Future of Business and Finance, https://doi.org/10.1007/978-3-032-13308-3_3

as a small processing unit that receives signals, processes information, and transmits it to other neurons. This vast web of interconnected neurons enables humans to learn from experience, recognize patterns, and solve complex problems. The brain's ability to process information through interconnected layers of neurons forms the foundation of human thinking, decision-making, and learning (Aggarwal, 2018; Haykin, 2009).

Inspired by this biological mechanism, researchers in AI have created artificial neural networks – digital structures designed to mimic the information-processing capabilities of the human brain. While these networks do not contain biological neurons, they replicate essential functions: receiving, processing, and passing information through layers of artificial "neurons." By linking many such artificial neurons, these networks can recognize patterns, draw conclusions, and make predictions (Mitchell, 1997).

An artificial neural network is therefore a computational model that simulates the learning processes of the human brain but operates within a machine. This model enables computers to tackle tasks that traditionally require human intelligence, such as image recognition, natural language processing (NLP), and decision-making. In the following, we explore the architecture of these networks, starting with a simple model that illustrates the structure and connections of artificial neurons.

3.1.1 Core Architecture of Artificial Neural Networks

An artificial neural network consists of a series of artificial neurons arranged in layers and interconnected by weighted connections (see Fig. 3.1). These connections, referred to as weights, determine the strength of signal transmission between neurons. The general structure of a neural network can be divided into three main

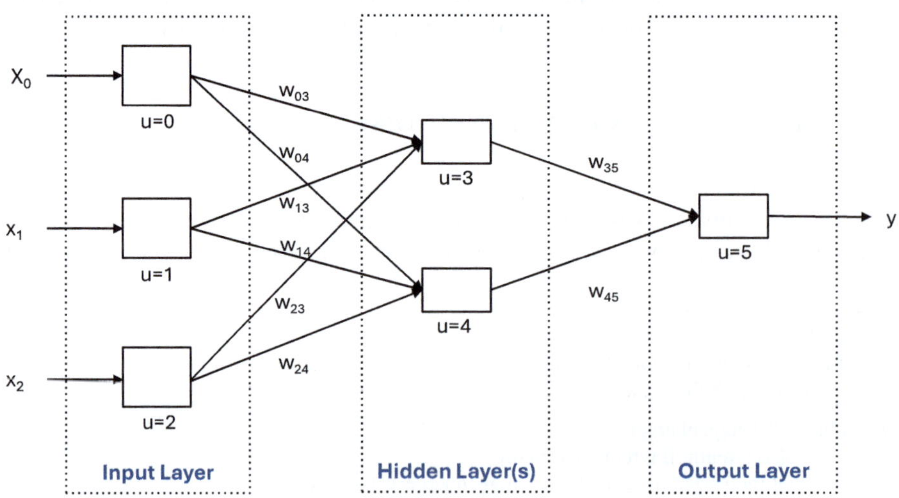

Fig. 3.1 Neural network architecture with input, hidden, and output layers

components: the input layer, hidden layers, and the output layer (Aggarwal, 2018; Nwankpa et al., 2018).

- **Input Layer:** The input layer receives input data, such as images, text, or numerical values. Each neuron in the input layer represents a feature or attribute of the input data. Neurons in this layer simply pass the input data to the next layer without performing any calculations.
- **Hidden Layers:** Positioned between the input and output layers, the hidden layers carry out the main processing in the neural network by transforming the input data and extracting patterns or features. Each neuron in a hidden layer receives input signals from the previous layer, applies weights to these connections, and produces an output that is passed to the subsequent layers. Depending on the network architecture, multiple hidden layers can be included to increase the network's complexity and capability. Neurons in the hidden layers perform computations and pass the results onward through the network.
- **Output Layer:** The output layer produces the final results of the neural network. Each neuron in the output layer corresponds to a specific output or category, depending on the type of problem the network is designed to solve. For instance, in image classification, each output neuron may represent a specific class label, while in regression tasks, the output might represent predicted numerical values. The neurons in the output layer take input from the hidden layers and perform calculations to generate the final output.

The connections between neurons in the neural network are represented by **weights**. During the network's training process, these weights are adjusted to produce the desired outputs. This adjustment is achieved through machine learning algorithms, such as the backpropagation algorithm (see subchapter "Training of neural networks"), which optimizes the weights based on the network's performance on training data (Mitchell, 1997).

The primary objective of a neural network is to transform input data into meaningful outputs by learning complex patterns or relationships. By analyzing large amounts of training data and identifying patterns, the neural network can make predictions or classifications for new, unseen data.

Note on Bias Neurons Not shown in the diagram for simplicity, bias neurons are a special type of neuron commonly included in neural networks. Unlike other neurons, a bias neuron has no input within the network and always takes a fixed value of 1. This allows it to shift the output of the neurons in a layer in a specific direction, independent of other inputs. A useful analogy is the linear function $y = mx + t$: without the bias term t, the line always passes through the origin. The bias term enables the function to shift along the y-axis, adding flexibility to the model. Similarly, in a neural network, bias neurons enable the network to learn more complex functions, expanding its capacity to model complex patterns (Aggarwal, 2018).

3.1.2 Neural Networks Explained Using the MNIST Dataset

The MNIST dataset (LeCun, 1994; Deng, 2012; Géron, 2022) is one of the most widely recognized and used datasets in machine learning, particularly for image recognition tasks. This dataset consists of grayscale images of handwritten digits ranging from 0 to 9, each represented as a 28 × 28 pixel image, resulting in 784 individual pixels per image. Each pixel has a grayscale value between 0 and 255, with 0 representing a white pixel and 255 representing a black pixel, and intermediate values reflecting different shades of gray.

The dataset contains a total of 70,000 images, divided into two distinct subsets: 60,000 images for training and 10,000 for testing. The training set is used to teach the neural network to recognize patterns in handwritten digits, while the test set evaluates the network's performance on unseen data. These handwritten digits were contributed by different people to ensure that the model generalizes well to different handwriting styles.

A typical neural network used to recognize these handwritten digits consists of an input layer, one or more hidden layers, and an output layer (Nielsen, 2015). In this context, the input layer has 784 neurons, each of which corresponds to a single pixel in the image (see Fig. 3.2). Each neuron receives the gray value of its respective pixel as input. Before entering the network, the pixel values are normalized to ensure consistency, scaling the original grayscale values from a range of 0–255 to a range of 0–1. Additionally, the 28 × 28 pixel grid is flattened into a single-dimensional vector with 784 values, making it compatible with the input layer structure. This vectorized and normalized input is then fed into the input layer, where each neuron receives a single pixel value as input, making the raw image data accessible to the network.

The hidden layers, which follow the input layer, are responsible for processing the input and detecting patterns such as edges and curves that help distinguish between digits. As the data progresses through these hidden layers, the network identifies increasingly abstract features. Early hidden layers may recognize basic components such as lines or edges, while later layers recognize more complex

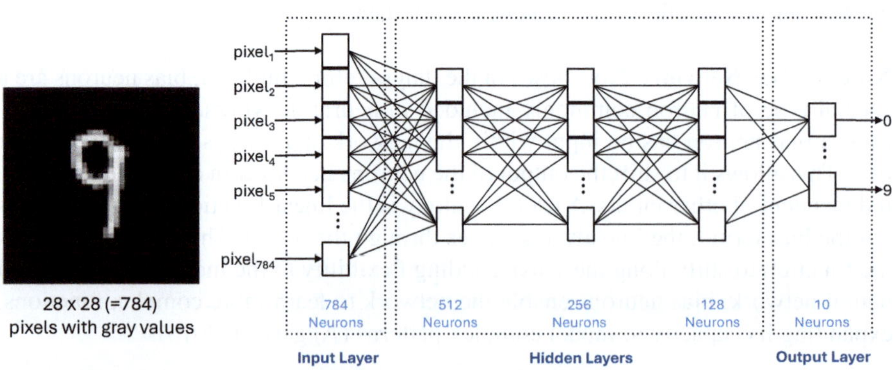

Fig. 3.2 Structure of a neural network for recognizing handwritten digits

shapes, such as loops or closed circles – features that are crucial for distinguishing between visually similar digits, like 6 and 9. These hidden layers are essential to the network's ability to capture complex relationships within the data, as they enable the network to operate on higher levels of abstraction, making it more robust and adaptable in recognizing various patterns.

The final layer, the output layer, contains ten neurons – one for each possible digit (0 through 9). The size of this layer is determined by the number of classes that the network is intended to predict. After the input has been processed by the network, each output neuron produces a value indicating the network's confidence that the input image corresponds to a specific digit. The neuron with the highest output value determines the predicted digit, effectively classifying the input. The output layer plays a crucial role in providing the final results or predictions of the neural network. It enables classification of the input image according to the predefined categories or classes relevant to the specific problem – in this case, recognizing the handwritten digits in the MNIST dataset.

In summary, the input layer of this neural network takes in the pixel data from the MNIST images, the hidden layers process and abstract this data to identify distinguishing features, and the output layer provides the final classification, identifying the digit with the highest confidence level.

Summary

Artificial neural networks are computational models inspired by the structure of the human brain, where artificial neurons process and transmit information through interconnected layers. Each network is organized into an input layer, one or more hidden layers, and an output layer. The input layer captures and prepares raw data for further processing. Hidden layers perform the main computation, extracting patterns and abstract features that enable the network to identify complex relationships. The output layer produces the final predictions or classifications. Through a training process that adjusts weights, neural networks learn to transform input data into meaningful outputs, effectively solving complex problems.

3.2 Training of Neural Networks

Understanding how neural networks learn is crucial for grasping the fundamentals of machine learning. Training a neural network involves a systematic process, designed to enable the network to recognize patterns, make predictions, or classify data effectively. This process can be complex, as it requires iterative adjustments and optimization to produce accurate results. Observing the entire training cycle provides a foundation for understanding how machine learning systems function and improve over time.

The training of neural networks follows a series of well-defined steps, which are visually represented in Fig. 3.3. This process begins with feeding the network a set of training data – such as images of handwritten digits – and specifying the correct

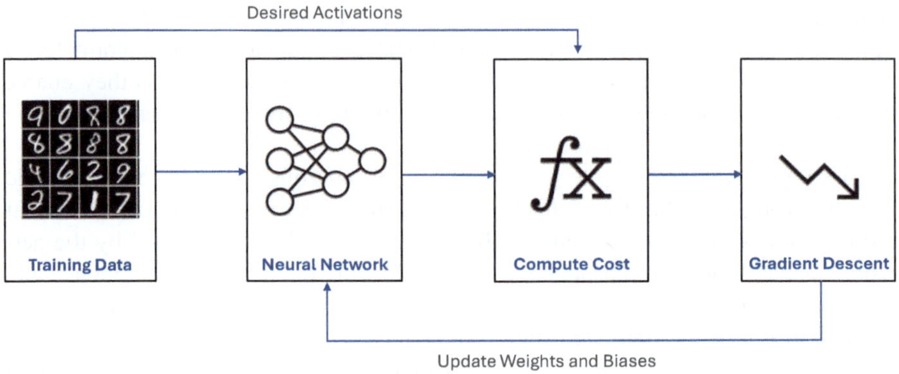

Fig. 3.3 Training process of a neural network. (Adapted from Nayar, 2021)

outputs, known as "desired activations." The network then adjusts its internal parameters (weights and biases) to reduce the difference between its predictions and the desired outputs. This adjustment process is essential for improving the network's performance over time.

To guide the network toward accurate predictions, a cost function measures the difference between the network's output and the desired activations. Using this cost function, the training algorithm computes gradients that inform how the network's weights and biases should change. This iterative optimization is achieved through an algorithm called gradient descent, which systematically reduces the cost function by updating the network's parameters in small steps (Nayar, 2021; Nielsen, 2015).

In the following sections, each stage of the training process will be examined in detail, including data preparation, network configuration, cost computation, and gradient-based optimization, using the MNIST dataset as an example. This exploration provides a solid foundation, essential not only for implementing neural networks effectively but also for understanding the general principles of machine learning.

3.2.1 Training Data

The training process in neural networks begins with the input of training data, which consists of labeled examples that provide foundational information for the network to learn. Each example is passed through the input layer of the network, allowing the network to analyze features of the data and establish an initial basis for pattern recognition. At this stage, the network's weights and biases are typically set to random values, meaning that the network has no prior understanding of the data patterns. The input of training data is therefore the first step that enables the network to begin learning, as it exposes the network to the core features and relationships it needs to identify.

To ensure that the network learns effectively, preprocessing is a crucial step in preparing the training data. Raw data often contains noise, inconsistencies, or irrelevant information that can mislead the network. Preprocessing addresses these issues by cleaning and transforming the data—steps such as normalizing values, handling missing data, and scaling features ensure consistency across inputs. Without proper preprocessing, even a sophisticated neural network may struggle to produce reliable results. As the network processes more examples, it continuously adjusts its internal parameters, refining its ability to capture meaningful patterns. However, the effectiveness of this learning process depends not only on the quantity of data but also on its quality. Well-prepared training data enhances learning, reduces the risk of overfitting, and improves the network's generalizability.

Training Data Categories

Training data can take many forms, depending on the type of problem a neural network is designed to solve. The variety of training data types underscores the versatility of machine learning models and their ability to handle different data formats (Aggarwal, 2018). Images, text, audio, time series, and numerical data are all commonly used as input for training machine learning models.

- In the case of **images**, datasets can include handwritten numbers such as those found in the MNIST dataset, street view images used for mapping and navigation, satellite imagery for geographic analysis, or even medical scans such as CT images for diagnostic purposes. Image data is typically represented as pixel values, with the intensity of each pixel serving as input to the neural network.
- **Text** is another major category, with data sources such as documents, tweets, chat logs, news articles, and product reviews forming the basis for tasks such as NLP, sentiment analysis, and document classification. Textual data often needs to be transformed into a numerical format, such as word embeddings, before it can be processed by a neural network.
- **Audio data** includes recordings of speech, music, environmental sounds, or phone calls. In tasks such as speech recognition or sound classification, the audio is converted into numerical representations, such as spectrograms or sequences of audio frames, which the network can process to identify patterns or recognize specific words or sounds.
- **Time series data** consists of sequences of data points collected over time, such as stock prices, weather patterns, sensor data, or electroencephalogram (EEG) signals. Time series data is critical in applications that require the model to identify trends, seasonality, or anomalies over time, making it useful for forecasting, anomaly detection, and predictive maintenance.
- Finally, **numerical data** includes structured datasets such as medical records, financial data, census information, and customer purchase histories. These datasets are used in tasks ranging from regression analysis to classification, often involving predictions based on multiple numerical variables.

The diversity of training data highlights the adaptability of neural networks, which can be designed to learn from virtually any type of data, provided that the data is properly preprocessed and structured. Each data type presents unique challenges and opportunities for learning, making the selection and preparation of training data a critical aspect of developing effective machine learning models.

MNIST Training Data

The aforementioned MNIST training set (LeCun, 1994) consists of pairs of images and labels. Each image is a 28 × 28 pixel grayscale representation of a handwritten digit, which is flattened into a vector of 784 pixel values when passed into the neural network. Each of these values represents the intensity of a single pixel, normalized between 0 (white) and 1 (black). This 784-dimensional vector acts as the network's input, providing detailed information about the visual structure of each digit.

Alongside each image, there is a label that specifies the correct digit (e.g., "0" for the first image in Fig. 3.4). This label is used to derive the *desired activation* – the ideal output the network should produce for that particular input. The desired activation is represented as a vector with ten positions, each corresponding to one of the digits from 0 to 9. For example, if the label is "4," the desired activation vector would have a "1" in the fifth position (for "4") and "0" in all other positions (see Fig. 3.4).

While the concept of *activation* will be covered in more detail later, it is important to recognize here that the *desired activation* differs from the network's *actual activation.* The purpose of training is to adjust the network so that the actual activation, or output, closely matches the desired activation. This alignment process is key to improving the network's classification accuracy over time, as it learns to minimize the gap between its predictions and the correct answers (Nielsen, 2015).

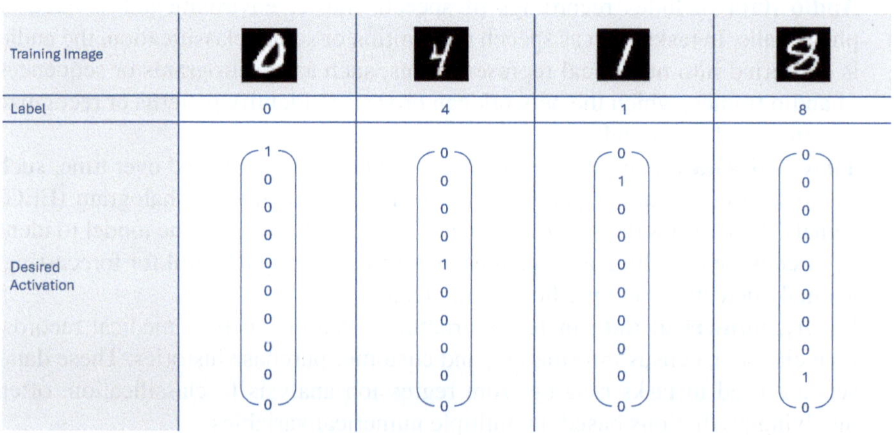

Fig. 3.4 Structure of MNIST training data with labels and desired activations. (Adapted from Nayar, 2021)

3.2.2 Neural Network

A neural network can be thought of as a universal function approximator capable of learning complex relationships between input data and corresponding outputs (Aggarwal, 2018; Hornik et al., 1989). Essentially, a neural network takes an input, processes it through its internal structure, and produces an output that approximates a target value. This is similar to a mathematical function, where the input is transformed according to a function rule to produce an output (see Fig. 3.5).

The key idea is that, during training, the network learns the underlying patterns in the data and adjusts its internal parameters to approximate the unknown function that maps inputs to outputs. This is particularly useful in scenarios where the exact function is either unknown or too complex to define explicitly. For example, when training a neural network to recognize handwritten digits, the input is an image of a digit, and the output is the predicted number that the image represents. In this case, the network learns to approximate the function that maps pixel values to a particular digit.

This function approximation process is not limited to the training data. The goal of a well-trained neural network is to generalize beyond the examples it has seen by applying the learned function to new, unseen data (Aggarwal, 2018). In essence, the training process can be seen as the network's way of discovering the best possible function that relates input to output. By iteratively adjusting its internal weights through learning algorithms, the network converges on a function that minimizes error and maximizes prediction accuracy. This ability to approximate complex, often unknown functions makes neural networks versatile and widely applicable in various fields of AI and machine learning.

Neurons as the Basic Building Blocks of a Neural Network

To understand the inner workings of a neural network, it is helpful to first examine how a single neuron operates (see Fig. 3.6). Each neuron in the network is a small processing unit that receives input data, applies weights to each input, combines them, and then passes the result through an activation function to produce an output. This basic process enables neurons to interpret and transform data at each layer, forming the foundation of the network's ability to learn and generalize (Mitchell, 1997; Jain et al., 1996).

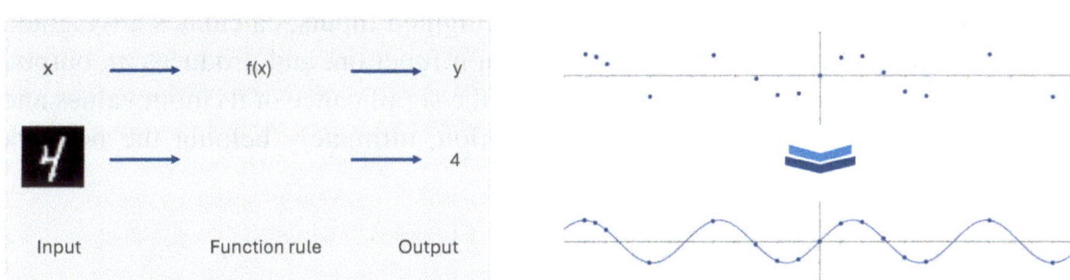

Fig. 3.5 Neural networks as function approximators. (Adapted from Robinson, 2022)

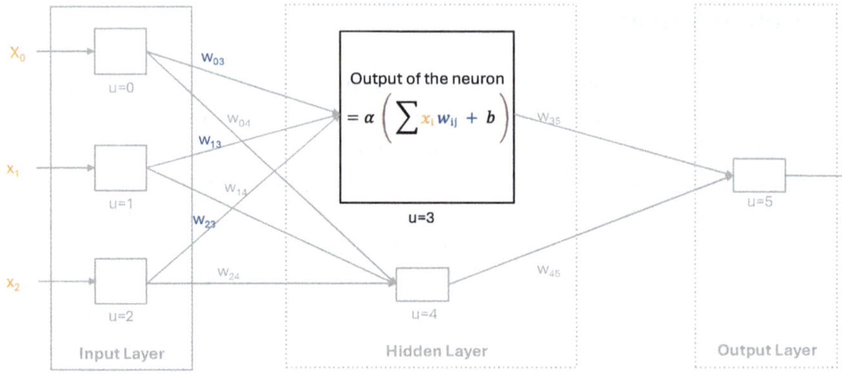

Fig. 3.6 A closer look inside a neuron

The output of a neuron can be expressed by the formula:

$$\text{Output of neuron} = \alpha\left(\sum x_i w_{ij} + b\right)$$

This formula can be interpreted as follows:

- ***x*i:** These are the input values, which may come from the input layer or previous layers in the network. Each input represents a feature or value passed to the neuron.
- ***w*ij:** These are the weights associated with each input. They determine how strongly or weakly each input affects the neuron. Higher weights amplify the signal, while lower weights reduce it.
- **∑(*x*i*w*ij):** This is the summation of the products of each input value and its corresponding weight. It represents the *weighted sum*, which is the combined input signal for the neuron (in this example, neuron *u*3 in the hidden layer).
- ***b*:** This is the bias, an additional parameter in the neuron that provides more flexibility in adjusting the output and helps the network learn patterns more effectively (to simplify the illustration, the bias term is included in the formula but not explicitly shown as a separate element in Fig. 3.6).
- **α:** This is the activation function, which takes the weighted sum, including the bias term, as input and transforms it to produce the neuron's output.

In summary, the neuron takes in a set of weighted inputs, calculates a weighted sum including a bias term, applies an activation function, and produces an output. This process allows each neuron to determine the significance of its input values and contribute to the network's overall computation, ultimately helping the network learn complex patterns from data.

The Role of the Activation Function

The activation function is a crucial component in a neural network, as it determines how the network processes input data and influences the types of problems the network can solve. In essence, the activation function transforms the weighted sum of inputs from a neuron into an output that is passed to the next layer. This transformation allows the network to introduce non-linearity, which is essential for learning complex patterns and relationships within data. The choice of the activation function, therefore, has a significant impact on the network's performance and its capacity to approximate complex functions (Aggarwal, 2018; Bishop, 1995; Jain et al., 1996).

One of the simplest activation functions is the **step function** (see Fig. 3.7). This function outputs a value of 1 if the input is positive and 0 if the input is negative or zero. It is sometimes described as a "threshold function," as it produces an output only when the input exceeds a specific threshold. This approach can be effective for basic problems where a binary decision is sufficient. For instance, a neuron with a step function might represent a simple on-off switch, activating only when the input crosses a certain point.

However, the step function has a limitation: it creates abrupt changes in output. A small change in input can lead to a sudden jump in output, switching from 0 to 1 or vice versa. This discontinuous behavior makes it challenging for the network to learn complex, nuanced patterns. In particular, the step function is unsuitable for tasks that require gradual, continuous learning, as it cannot represent subtle relationships between inputs and outputs. The step function essentially restricts the network to solving only simple problems, as it does not allow for small adjustments in the output based on slight changes in input (Nielsen, 2015).

To address these limitations, more flexible activation functions are used, such as the **sigmoid function** (see Fig. 3.7). The sigmoid function produces a smooth, continuous curve, transitioning gradually between output values of 0 and 1, depending on the input's magnitude. This means that a small change in input results in a proportional change in output, allowing the neuron to respond more precisely to different inputs. This smooth transition is valuable in training neural networks, as it enables the network to adjust outputs incrementally, making small adjustments in weights more effective during the learning process (Nielsen, 2015).

In summary, the choice of the activation function determines how a neuron reacts to input and has a direct effect on the complexity of functions the neural network

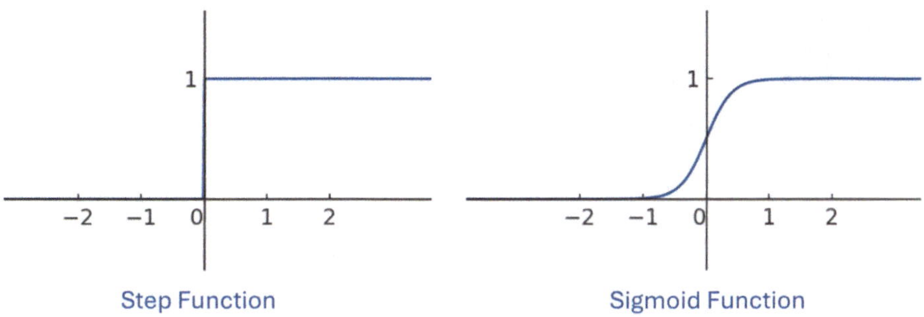

Fig. 3.7 Comparison of the step and sigmoid activation function

can approximate. The step function provides a simple but limited approach, suitable for basic problems with binary decisions. The sigmoid function, on the other hand, introduces smooth transitions and allows for more precise learning, enabling the network to capture intricate patterns and make more sophisticated predictions. By selecting appropriate activation functions, neural networks can be configured to handle a wide range of problem complexities, from simple classification tasks to highly nonlinear pattern recognition challenges.

Initialization of the Neural Network

Before training begins, the neural network is initialized by assigning random values to the weights connecting each neuron. This random initialization means that the network starts without any understanding of the input data, producing arbitrary initial activations in the output layer. In Fig. 3.8, each pixel of the input image (a handwritten "9") is fed into the input layer, and this information is processed through multiple hidden layers, with each connection influenced by the randomly assigned weights.

As a result, the output layer produces initial activation values for each digit class (0–9), reflecting the network's raw, untrained state. These initial activations are likely to be inaccurate, as they are solely based on the random weights and do not yet represent meaningful classifications. This initialization sets the starting point for the training process, where these weights will be adjusted to gradually improve the network's performance in recognizing digits.

3.2.3 Compute Cost

After the initial activations are calculated based on the randomly assigned weights, the next step is to evaluate the accuracy of these preliminary predictions. This is done by calculating the cost, a metric that quantifies the difference between the network's current predictions and the actual labels. Also known as the loss, the cost

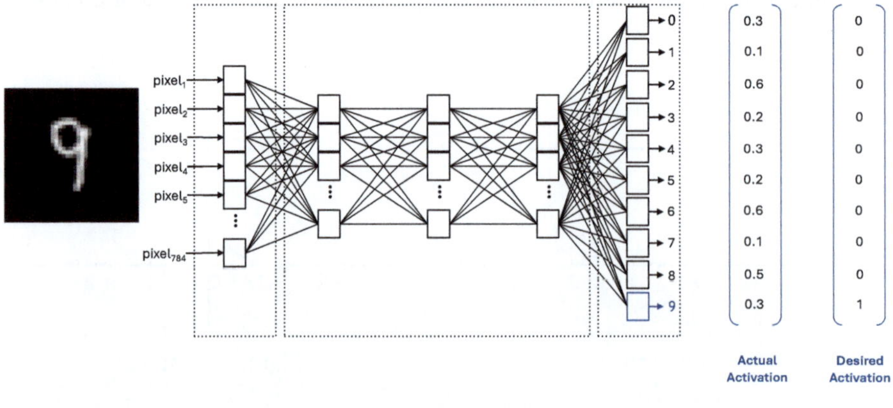

Fig. 3.8 Initialization of the neural network with random weights. (Adapted from Nayar, 2021)

provides a numerical indication of how far the network's output is from the desired results. High-cost values indicate that the network's predictions are far from accurate, highlighting the need for further training and weight adjustments (Aggarwal, 2018; Goodfellow et al., 2016).

A common cost function used in neural networks is **mean squared error (MSE)**. During training, the primary goal is to minimize this cost, gradually refining the network's weights so that its predictions align more closely with the true labels. The cost function thus serves as a guide, providing feedback on the network's performance at each stage of training. The cost function calculates this discrepancy by taking the difference between each predicted output and its corresponding target, squaring it to eliminate negative values, and then averaging the squared differences (Nielsen, 2015). This provides a single numerical value that represents how far off the network's predictions are from the desired results. The formula for MSE is:

$$\text{MSE} = \frac{1}{n} \sum_{n}^{i=1} \left(Y_i - \widehat{Y}_i \right)^2$$

where Y_i is the desired activation (the true label) and $\widehat{Y}_i$ is the actual activation (the network's prediction). In the example of recognizing a handwritten digit "9", the network might initially generate incorrect activations, leading to a large MSE. By comparing the actual activations with the desired activations, the MSE shows how far the network's predictions deviate from the correct result. For example, if the network predicts low activations for the output neuron corresponding to the digit "9" (which should be highly activated), this discrepancy is reflected in the cost.

The goal of training a neural network is to minimize this cost by adjusting the network's weights and biases. Using optimization algorithms such as gradient descent, the network iteratively updates these parameters to reduce the MSE and gradually improve its predictions. As the cost decreases, the network becomes better at producing accurate outputs for given inputs, improving its overall performance. The cost function thus provides the critical feedback needed to guide the learning process and ensures that the network converges to optimal predictions.

3.2.4 Gradient Descent and Backpropagation

A neural network learns by adjusting its internal parameters – its weights and biases – to improve its predictions. This learning process involves systematically reducing the network's cost function, a measure of how far off the network's predictions are from the actual targets. The process of reducing this cost function relies on two core algorithms: gradient descent and backpropagation (Mitchell, 1997; Hecht-Nielsen, 1992; LeCun et al., 2012).

The idea behind gradient descent is relatively simple: find the minimum of the cost function by iteratively moving in the direction that reduces it the most (see Fig. 3.9). However, implementing this idea in a complex, multi-layered neural network involves intricate calculations to determine how each weight should change to reduce the overall error. This is where backpropagation becomes essential.

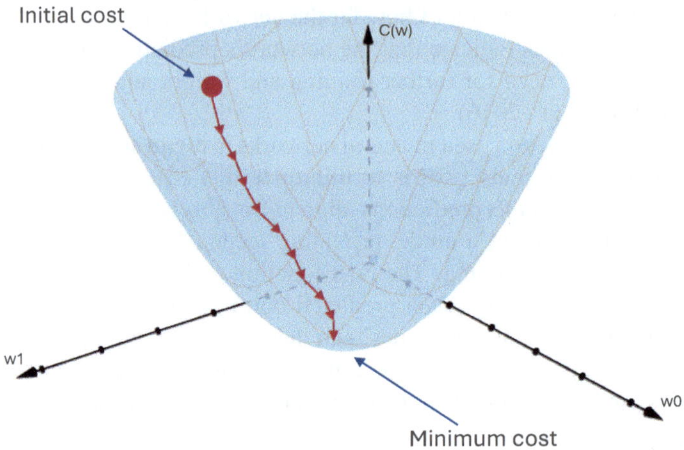

Fig. 3.9 Visualization of gradient descent. (Adapted from Sanderson, 2017)

Backpropagation is the mechanism by which the network computes these necessary adjustments, layer by layer, efficiently calculating how each weight affects the cost function. Let us first discuss the intuition behind gradient descent before diving into the mechanics of backpropagation, which executes these ideas in a neural network.

Gradient Descent: The Concept of Iterative Optimization

Gradient descent serves as the guiding principle in neural network training. Think of the cost function as a complex landscape of peaks and valleys, with the peaks representing high error and the valleys representing low error. The network's current position in this landscape corresponds to the current values of its parameters, and the objective is to find the lowest valley – meaning the lowest possible error. Gradient descent accomplishes this by iteratively "walking" downhill, adjusting the weights and biases in the direction that reduces the cost (Aggarwal, 2018).

The direction and steepness of each step are determined by the gradient of the cost function with respect to each parameter. The gradient essentially tells us how to adjust each weight and bias to reduce the error. If the gradient points upwards, moving in the opposite direction will decrease the cost. This direction-finding process repeats for every parameter in the network, with each step scaled by a learning rate – a factor that controls the size of each update. If the learning rate is too small, the descent will be slow, potentially requiring a large number of iterations to achieve meaningful progress. On the other hand, if the learning rate is too large, the algorithm risks overshooting the minimum point, potentially resulting in oscillation around the optimal values or even diverging.

By iteratively taking steps in the direction that reduces error, gradient descent drives the network's parameters toward a configuration that minimizes the cost function. However, calculating these gradients manually for every weight and bias in a large neural network would be impractical. Backpropagation addresses this challenge by providing an efficient way to compute the gradients for all parameters, making gradient descent feasible even for complex networks.

Backpropagation: Calculating the Gradients Efficiently

While gradient descent gives us the direction for optimization, backpropagation is the mechanism that allows us to calculate this direction efficiently within a neural network (see Fig. 3.10). By using the chain rule of calculus, backpropagation systematically calculates the gradient of the cost function with respect to each weight and bias, enabling the network to adjust these parameters based on their individual contribution to the error.

The backpropagation process begins with a **forward pass**, where the input data moves through the network, layer by layer, until it reaches the output layer and generates a prediction. This prediction is then compared to the true target value using the cost function, which calculates the error. For example, in an image classification task, the input might be a set of pixel values, and the network processes these values through its layers to output a probability distribution over different classes. The forward pass produces the initial activations for each neuron based on the current parameter values, allowing the network to generate a preliminary output (Nielsen, 2015).

After calculating the error in this initial output, backpropagation then **works backward** through the network, computing how each neuron contributed to the overall error. Starting from the output layer, backpropagation **calculates the gradient for each weight and bias** by applying the chain rule. This process involves propagating the error gradient back through the network, layer by layer. For the

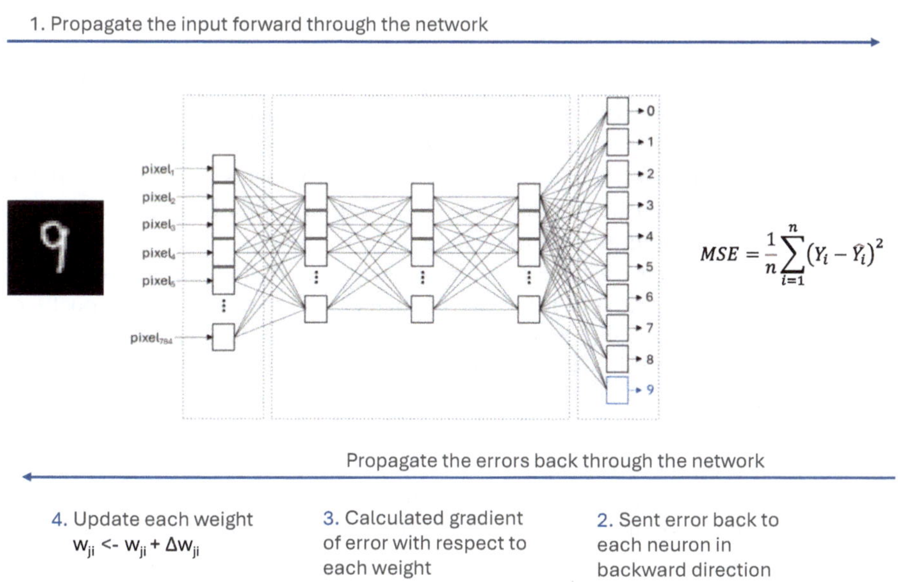

Fig. 3.10 Visualization of backpropagation

output layer, the calculation is straightforward, as the error can be directly related to the difference between the predicted and actual values. However, for layers earlier in the network, the chain rule must be applied to determine how each neuron's activation influenced the error in the output. By the end of this backward pass, backpropagation has computed the gradient of the cost function with respect to each weight and bias (Nielsen, 2015).

Once these gradients are calculated, they are used to **update each parameter through gradient descent.** Each weight and bias are adjusted by a small step in the direction that reduces the error, as indicated by its gradient. These adjustments complete one training cycle for the input example, preparing the network for the next example in the training dataset.

To illustrate the backpropagation process in action, let us continue with the MNIST example of classifying handwritten digits. Suppose the network receives an image of the digit "9," and, due to incorrect initial weights, it outputs a higher probability for "4" than for "9." The cost function calculates this error, which signals the need for adjustment.

Backpropagation then starts by sending this error back from the output layer. In the output layer, an **error term** δ_k is calculated for each neuron, indicating how much each neuron's activation contributed to the total error. In this case, the error term for the over-activated "4" neuron will be relatively high, guiding the network to reduce this activation, while the error term for the "9" neuron signals a need for increased activation.

The network then propagates this error backward to the hidden layer. Here, the **error terms for the hidden neurons** δ_h are calculated based on how they influenced the incorrect output. Using the **chain rule**, the network computes how each weight connecting hidden neurons to output neurons contributed to the error. For example, if a specific hidden neuron had a strong influence on the mistaken "4" output, it would receive a larger error term, prompting a more substantial weight adjustment.

Finally, in the **weight update** step, each weight is adjusted in the direction that reduces the error, guided by gradient descent. The learning rate controls the size of each adjustment, ensuring stable and gradual learning. Weights leading to the incorrect "4" neuron are adjusted to decrease its activation, while those leading to the correct "9" neuron are reinforced to increase its activation.

This entire process is repeated for each image in the MNIST training set, allowing the network to iteratively refine its parameters. Through multiple epochs of backpropagation and weight updates, the network becomes increasingly accurate at classifying handwritten digits, effectively learning to recognize complex patterns within the data.

The Backpropagation Algorithm

The backpropagation algorithm iteratively updates the weights of a neural network to minimize the error in its predictions (Mitchell, 1997). The weight update is guided by the gradient of the cost function with respect to each weight. This gradient, calculated using the chain rule, tells us how each weight should change to reduce the network's overall error. The weight update formula in backpropagation is as follows:

$$\omega_{ji} \leftarrow \omega_{ji} + \Delta\omega_{ji}$$

where $\Delta\omega_{ji}$ represents the adjustment to the weight ω_{ji} from unit i to unit j. The adjustment $\Delta\omega_{ji}$ is calculated as follows:

$$\Delta\omega_{ji} = \eta \frac{\partial E}{\partial \omega_{ji}}$$

In this formula:

- η is the **learning rate**, a parameter that controls the step size of each weight update. A higher learning rate accelerates learning but may cause instability, while a lower rate results in slower, more stable learning.
- $\frac{\partial E}{\partial \omega_{ji}}$ is the **partial derivative of the cost function** with respect to the weight ω_{ji}. This derivative measures how sensitive the error is to changes in this specific weight, guiding the direction and magnitude of the adjustment.

Using the chain rule, we can express this partial derivative in terms of more fundamental components:

$$\Delta\omega_{ji} = \eta \frac{\partial E}{\partial \omega_{ji}} = \eta \delta_j o_i$$

where:

- δ_j is the **error term** for unit j, representing the gradient of the error at that unit;
- o_i is the **output** of unit i that feeds into unit j.

This relationship shows that the weight adjustment $\Delta\omega_{ji}$ depends on both the error at the target unit j and the activation from the source unit i. Calculating the error terms for each unit is essential for this process and requires a different approach depending on whether the unit is in the output layer or a hidden layer.

For **output units**, the error term δ_k is calculated as follows:

$$\delta_k = o_k (1 - o_k)(t_k - o_k)$$

where:

- o_k is the output of unit k;
- t_k is the target value for unit k;
- $(t_k - o_k)$ is the difference between the target and the actual output.

For **hidden units**, the error term δ_h is calculated based on the contributions from units in the following layer:

- Create a feed-forward network with n_{in} inputs, n_{hidden} hidden units, and n_{out} output units
- Initialize all network weights to small random numbers
- Until the **termination condition** is met, Do:

  For each $\langle \vec{x}, \vec{t} \rangle$ in training examples, Do:

  Propagate the **input forward** through the network:

  1. Input $\vec{x}$ to the network and compute o_u of every unit u

  Propagate the **errors back** through the network:

  2. For each network **output unit** k, calculate its error term δ_k

  $$\delta_k = o_k(1 - o_k)(t_k - o_k)$$

  3. For each **hidden unit** h, calculate its error term δ_h

  $$\delta_h = o_h(1 - o_h)\sum_{k \in outputs} \omega_{kh}\delta_k$$

  4. Update each weight ω_{ji}

  $\omega_{ji} \leftarrow \omega_{ji} + \Delta\omega_{ji}$, where $\Delta\omega_{ji} = \eta\delta_j o_i$

Symbols

$\vec{x}$	input to the network
ω_{ji}	weight from unit i to unit j
$\vec{t}$	target
o_k	output of unit k
δ_k	error term of unit k
η	learning rate

Fig. 3.11 Backpropagation algorithm (Mitchell, 1997)

$$\delta_h = o_h\left(1 - o_h\right)\sum_{k \in \text{outputs}} \omega_{kh}\delta_k$$

where ω_{kh} is the weight connecting the hidden unit h to the output unit k, and δ_k is the error term of unit k. This formula effectively distributes the error from the output layer backward, taking into account the influence of each hidden unit on the network's output error.

By following the steps outlined in Fig. 3.11, the backpropagation algorithm systematically reduces the cost function by adjusting the weights and biases in the network. Each pass over the training data allows the network to learn from its errors, refining its parameters to improve prediction accuracy. This process is repeated over multiple epochs, enabling the network to converge to a solution that generalizes well to new, unseen data.

Summary

The training process of a neural network is an iterative method aimed at optimizing the network's internal parameters – weights and biases – to improve prediction accuracy. It begins with feeding labeled training data into the network, where each example is processed through layers of neurons. The network generates a prediction, which is then compared to the actual target to compute the error. This error is quantified using a cost function, such as MSE, which the network seeks to minimize. Gradient descent, paired with backpropagation, adjusts the weights and biases iteratively, reducing the cost with each iteration. This process continues until the network converges, enabling it to generalize and perform well on new, unseen data.

References

Aggarwal, C. C. (2018). An introduction to neural networks. In *Neural networks and deep learning: A textbook* (pp. 1–52). Springer.
Bishop, C. M. (1995). *Neural networks for pattern recognition*. Oxford University Press.
Deng, L. (2012). The MNIST database of handwritten digit images for machine learning research [best of the web]. *IEEE Signal Processing Magazine, 29*(6), 141–142.
Géron, A. (2022). *Hands-on machine learning with Scikit-Learn, Keras, and TensorFlow: Concepts, tools, and techniques to build intelligent systems*. O'Reilly Media, Inc..
Goodfellow, I., Bengio, Y., Courville, A., & Bengio, Y. (2016). *Deep learning* (Vol. 1, No. 2). MIT Press.
Haykin, S. (2009). *Neural networks and learning machines* (3rd ed.). Pearson Education India.
Hecht-Nielsen, R. (1992). Theory of the backpropagation neural network. In *Neural networks for perception* (pp. 65–93). Academic Press.
Hornik, K., Stinchcombe, M., & White, H. (1989). Multilayer feedforward networks are universal approximators. *Neural Networks, 2*(5), 359–366.
Jain, A. K., Mao, J., & Mohiuddin, K. M. (1996). Artificial neural networks: A tutorial. *Computer, 29*(3), 31–44.
LeCun, Y. (1994). *The MNIST database of handwritten digits*. Retrieved March 17, 2025, from http://yann.lecun.com/exdb/mnist/
LeCun, Y. A., Bottou, L., Orr, G. B., & Müller, K. R. (2012). Efficient BackProp. In G. Montavon, G. B. Orr, & K. R. Müller (Eds.), *Neural networks: Tricks of the trade* (Lecture Notes in Computer Science) (Vol. 7700). Springer.
Mitchell, T. M. (1997). *Machine learning* (Vol. 1, No. 9). McGraw-hill.
Nayar, S. K. (2021). *Neural Network* | Neural Networks. [video online]. Retrieved November 25, 2024, from https://www.youtube.com/watch?v=Go1F4uHlD3c
Nielsen, M. A. (2015). *Neural networks and deep learning* (Vol. 25, pp. 15–24). Determination Press.
Nwankpa, C., Ijomah, W., Gachagan, A. & Marshall, S. (2018). Activation functions: Comparison of trends in practice and research for deep learning. *arXiv preprint arXiv:1811.03378.*
Robinson, M. (2022). *Why neural networks can learn (almost) anything*. [video online]. Retrieved November 25, 2024, from https://www.youtube.com/watch?v=0QczhVg5HaI
Sanderson, G. (2017). *Gradient descent, how neural networks learn* | DL2. [video online]. Retrieved November 25, 2024, from https://www.youtube.com/watch?v=IHZwWFHWa-w&ab_channel=3Blue1Brown

Nils Urbach is Professor of Information Systems and Digital Business as well as Director of the Research Lab for Digital Innovation & Transformation at the Frankfurt University of Applied Sciences, Germany. Furthermore, he is Director at the FIM Research Center for Information Management, and the Branch Business & Information Systems Engineering of Fraunhofer FIT. Nils Urbach has been working in the fields of digital innovation and transformation for several years. His work has been published in several academic journals such as Information Systems Research (ISR), the Journal of the Association for Information Systems (JAIS), the Journal of Strategic Information Systems (JSIS), the Journal of Information Technology (JIT), MIS Quarterly Executive (MISQE), IEEE Transactions on Engineering Management (IEEE TEM), Information and Management (I&M), Business & Information Systems Engineering (BISE), and Electronic Markets (EM). He advises several companies on digitalization issues and regularly appears as a speaker on this topic.

Daniel Feulner received his M.Sc. in information system from the Otto-Friedrich University of Bamberg, Germany in 2023. He is an affiliated researcher at the Branch Business & Information Systems Engineering of the Fraunhofer FIT and FIM Research Center for Information Management at the University of Bayreuth. In his research, he aims to understand how Business Analytics and

Artificial Intelligence can be effectively and responsibly utilized in organizations. His goal is to enable companies to drive innovation and achieve sustainable growth in a rapidly evolving technological landscape.

Tobias Guggenberger is a postdoctoral researcher at the University of Bayreuth and the Branch Business & Information Systems Engineering of Fraunhofer FIT. He holds an M.Sc. in business administration and a Ph.D. in information systems engineering. His research primarily concentrates on the design and management of information systems, leveraging emerging technologies like artificial intelligence (AI) and blockchain. His scholarly contributions have appeared in renowned conference proceedings, including the International Conference on Information Systems (ICIS) and the European Conference on Information Systems (ECIS). His research has also been published in prestigious international journals such as IEEE Transactions on Engineering Management (IEEE TEM), MIS Quarterly Executive (MISQE), Electronic Markets (EM), and Computers & Industrial Engineering.

Introduction to Generative Artificial Intelligence

4

Nils Urbach, Daniel Feulner, Simon Feulner,
Tobias Guggenberger, and Valentin Mayer

Generative artificial intelligence (AI) has rapidly transitioned from a niche research domain to a significant driver of innovation, impacting industries ranging from technology and media to healthcare and education. By enabling machines to create text, images, videos, and music, generative AI is fundamentally transforming the ways digital content is produced and consumed. Beyond creative applications, generative AI has the potential to play a crucial role in automating complex workflows, optimizing decision-making processes, and enhancing productivity across industries. This shift is reshaping business practices, workforce dynamics, and societal interactions, making AI-driven automation an integral component of digital transformation.

In this chapter, we examine the evolution and impact of generative AI, starting with how ChatGPT became the catalyst for generative AI. We then move beyond ChatGPT to discuss foundational concepts and models such as large language models (LLMs), diffusion models, and the emerging field of agentic AI. Understanding these technologies is essential in AI management, as they significantly influence strategic decision-making, risk management, innovation opportunities, and operational efficiencies within organizations.

N. Urbach (✉) · S. Feulner
Frankfurt University of Applied Sciences, Frankfurt am Main, Germany
e-mail: nils.urbach@fim-rc.de; simon.feulner@fim-rc.de

D. Feulner · T. Guggenberger · V. Mayer
University of Bayreuth, Bayreuth, Germany
e-mail: daniel.feulner@fim-rc.de; tobias.guggenberger@fim-rc.de; valentin.mayer@fim-rc.de

N. Urbach, D. Feulner (eds.), *Managing Artificial Intelligence*, Future of Business and Finance, https://doi.org/10.1007/978-3-032-13308-3_4

4.1 The Rise of Generative AI

The introduction of ChatGPT by OpenAI in November 2022 marked a significant milestone in the development and adoption of generative AI. OpenAI, founded in 2015, had previously developed several iterations of its GPT (Generative Pretrained Transformer) models, progressively enhancing their capabilities in natural language processing tasks. Despite the incremental success and recognition of earlier GPT models, such as GPT-2 and GPT-3, OpenAI did not anticipate the unprecedented popularity and immediate global impact of ChatGPT (The Verge, 2024).

The widespread use of ChatGPT is primarily driven by two critical factors: first, its simple, user-friendly design, which makes advanced generative AI technology accessible to a wide audience and enables diverse users to easily explore practical applications such as content generation, programming assistance, and educational support; and second, significant advancements in the underlying technology that provide sophisticated, engaging, and human-like conversational abilities capable of impressing and engaging users. Within 2 months after its launch, ChatGPT attracted over 100 million users, becoming one of the fastest-growing applications in digital history (Reuters, 2023). Extensive coverage across traditional media and social media platforms further accelerated public awareness and adoption.

From a commercial perspective, ChatGPT's success underscores the potential for generative AI applications across numerous industries. This recognition prompts immediate responses from major technology corporations. For instance, Microsoft significantly increased its investment in OpenAI and integrated ChatGPT's technology into its Bing search engine and Office suite as Microsoft Copilot to enhance productivity tools and search capabilities. Concurrently, Google intensified its generative AI initiatives by launching Bard and Gemini, signaling the growing strategic importance of generative AI in competitive business environments.

Through rapid adoption and clear practical demonstrations, ChatGPT significantly influences the perception and utilization of generative AI technologies. It transitions the dialogue from theoretical discussions to concrete applications within everyday contexts. While ChatGPT serves as a significant catalyst, generative AI encompasses a much broader range of technologies and applications beyond conversational models, a topic explored in the subsequent subchapter.

Generative AI's Bigger Picture: Going Beyond ChatGPT

The rise of ChatGPT has significantly shaped public perception of generative AI, making the technology widely known and easily accessible. However, generative AI encompasses far more than language-based models alone. To fully appreciate its potential, it is crucial to explore the broader landscape of technologies and applications beyond ChatGPT (see Fig. 4.1).

ChatGPT belongs to a category known as LLMs. LLMs utilize extensive datasets and advanced neural network architectures to generate coherent, contextually relevant text. While ChatGPT has received considerable attention, several other notable LLMs have emerged, each offering distinct capabilities. OpenAI's GPT models pioneered this space, laying the foundation for subsequent developments such as

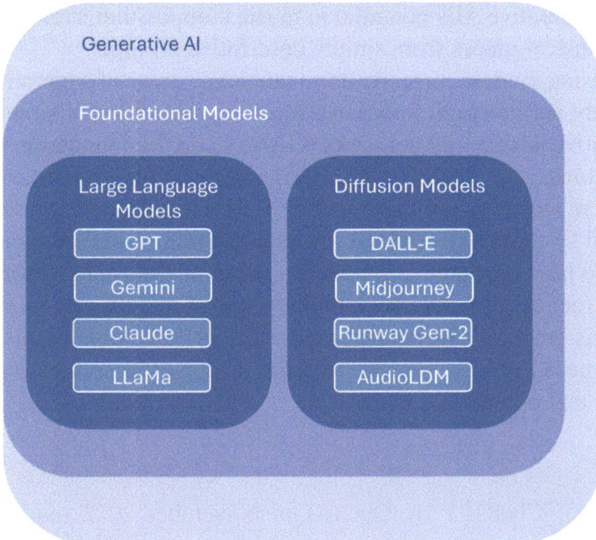

Fig. 4.1 Hierarchical structure of generative AI technologies

Google's Gemini, Anthropic's Claude, and Meta's LLaMa. These models vary in specialization, offering tailored applications in areas such as code generation, personalized assistant services, and advanced reasoning capabilities, significantly expanding potential use cases.

LLMs represent a subset of what the AI community terms "Foundational Models." Foundational models are large-scale models trained on massive multimodal datasets (combining text, images, audio, and more) that generalize knowledge and capabilities across diverse applications. They are designed not just to perform specific tasks but to serve as versatile bases from which various specialized applications can be derived. While LLMs like ChatGPT dominate in language-related tasks, foundational models include other influential classes of generative AI technologies, notably diffusion models, that excel in domains beyond text generation.

Diffusion models thus constitute another major category within foundational models, known for their remarkable capability to generate high-quality visual and audio content. Unlike LLMs, which predict and generate sequential text, diffusion models work by gradually refining random noise into coherent, detailed outputs through iterative processes. Key diffusion models such as OpenAI's DALL-E, Midjourney, Runway Gen-2, and AudioLDM illustrate the extensive potential of generative technologies in visual and audio domains. DALL-E, for instance, generates complex and realistic images from textual descriptions, transforming creative industries such as graphic design and digital art. Midjourney similarly emphasizes artistic expression, enabling creators to produce imaginative and stylistically diverse visual content. Runway Gen-2 extends these capabilities into video creation, automating and simplifying tasks in video production and editing. AudioLDM demonstrates generative AI's potential in music composition, creating coherent and high-quality musical pieces from simple descriptive prompts.

While diffusion models currently dominate many areas of generative media, they are not the only architectural approach. Earlier generations of generative models, such as generative adversarial networks (GANs), laid the foundation for image synthesis and continue to influence model design in areas like style transfer and super-resolution. More recently, autoregressive models have gained traction – particularly in multi-modal systems like GPT-4o – which generate visual content one step at a time, similar to how language is produced. These models tend to perform better in maintaining structure and coherence in fine-grained details such as text, geometry, or layouts. This growing diversity in generative architectures points to a dynamic field that continues to evolve rapidly, offering increasingly specialized tools for different creative and operational needs.

Summary

The launch of ChatGPT by OpenAI in November 2022 marked a breakthrough in generative AI, making advanced language models accessible to the public. ChatGPT's intuitive interface and human-like responses drove its rapid adoption, surpassing 100 million users within 2 months. Its success spurred major tech companies such as Microsoft and Google to invest heavily in generative AI. However, generative AI extends beyond ChatGPT and includes various foundational models with diverse applications. LLMs specialize in applications such as content generation, code assistance, and advanced reasoning. Diffusion models create high-quality visual and audio content by refining random noise into coherent outputs.

4.2 Large Language Models

LLMs represent a major advancement in AI, enabling machines to process and generate human-like text with remarkable fluency. These models are trained on vast amounts of text data, allowing them to recognize linguistic patterns, understand context, and generate coherent responses across various topics. Their ability to generalize from training data makes them highly versatile, with applications spanning content creation, code generation, and translation. Understanding LLMs is crucial to effectively leverage their potential while addressing their limitations and risks. This includes knowing how these models function – specifically, their underlying neural network architectures, training processes, and the role of pretraining and fine-tuning – understanding key application areas such as automation, knowledge management, and customer support, and recognizing constraints such as bias in training data, hallucinations, and high computational costs. A thorough understanding enables informed decision-making on deployment, governance, and ethical AI usage.

4.2.1 Core Concepts of LLMs

LLMs are designed to generate coherent, contextually accurate text by leveraging probabilistic reasoning and advanced neural network architectures (Kamath et al., 2024). Unlike traditional feedforward networks, LLMs primarily rely on Transformer-based designs that incorporate mechanisms like self-attention to process input sequences and capture long-range dependencies between words. A Transformer is a deep learning model architecture designed to handle sequential data efficiently. Unlike recurrent neural networks, which process sequences step by step, Transformers process all input elements simultaneously, allowing for much faster computations and better performance on long text sequences. Their key innovation is the self-attention mechanism, which enables the model to weigh the importance of different words in a sequence based on their relevance to each other. In Fig. 4.2, a simplified visualization illustrates the fundamental concept of how input sequences, such as "Emma plays the," are processed. Each word is first embedded into a high-dimensional numerical representation, capturing semantic and syntactic relationships. These embeddings serve as the input for the model's neural architecture, where each layer progressively refines its understanding of the input by analyzing the relationships between words in the sequence.

The key to LLMs' success lies in their ability to evaluate the context of the entire input sequence dynamically. Through self-attention, the model assigns varying levels of importance to different parts of the input, enabling it to focus on the most relevant elements for predicting the next word. For instance, in the phrase "Emma plays the," the model emphasizes "Emma," "plays," and "the" to infer that the next word is likely a musical instrument. This mechanism allows LLMs to model complex linguistic structures, such as dependencies that span multiple sentences,

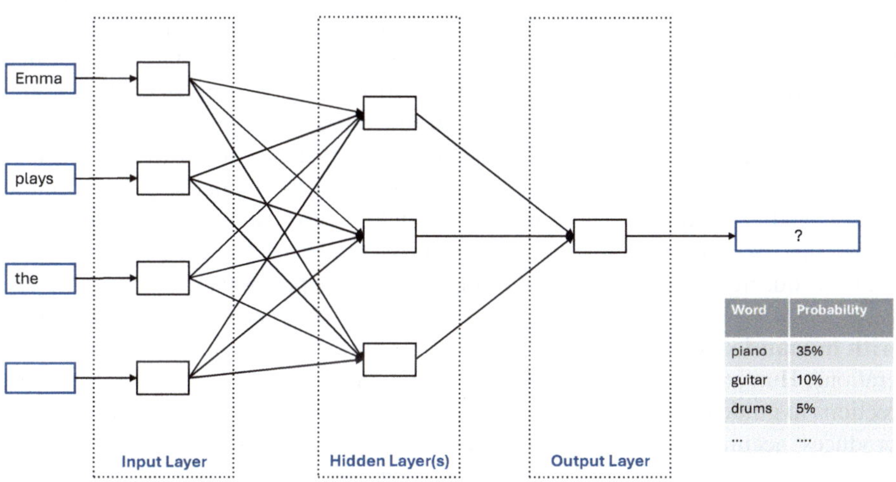

Fig. 4.2 A simplified representation of how LLMs predict the next word

ensuring that their outputs remain coherent and contextually appropriate even for lengthy texts.

Using these refined representations, the output layer calculates probabilities for potential next words by evaluating the semantic alignment of the input with each possible continuation. For example, the **model** might predict "piano" with a probability of 35%, "guitar" with 10%, and "drums" with 5%, selecting the most likely option as the next word in the sequence. This probabilistic approach enables LLMs to generate diverse outputs. An important factor influencing the diversity and creativity of LLM outputs is the temperature parameter, which controls the randomness of the model's predictions. A lower temperature (e.g., 0.2) makes the model more deterministic, favoring high-probability words and producing more predictable, focused responses. In contrast, a higher temperature (e.g., 0.8 or 1.0) increases the likelihood of selecting less probable words, resulting in more varied and creative – but potentially less accurate – outputs. By adjusting the temperature, users can fine-tune the model's behavior depending on whether consistency or inventiveness is desired in a given application.

Ultimately, the combination of probabilistic reasoning, contextual awareness, and iterative refinement allows LLMs to generalize patterns learned from vast training datasets. They can understand and generate nuanced language, recognizing complex relationships between words, phrases, and broader linguistic structures. This capability is what enables LLMs to perform tasks such as generating human-like dialogue, summarizing text, or even translating languages, all while maintaining a deep understanding of the context in which they operate.

Training LLMs is an extensive, multi-stage process designed to progressively refine their performance and align their outputs with human expectations (Blumenstock, 2023). In the **pretraining phase**, the model is exposed to vast amounts of text data, such as internet archives, books, and scientific articles. Using self-supervised learning, a training approach where the model learns from unlabeled data by generating its own training signals, the model predicts missing or subsequent words, enabling it to learn linguistic patterns, relationships, and structures. This phase focuses on a high data quantity with rather low data equality due to the unknown factual correctness of the data that the model uses. After pretraining establishes a broad linguistic foundation, **fine-tuning** adapts the model to specific tasks or domains using supervised learning. High-quality, but a lower quantity of datasets with clearly defined input–output pairs train the model to produce more precise and contextually relevant results, such as text summarization, question answering, or sentiment analysis. The process preserves the general knowledge acquired during pretraining while refining the model's performance for specific use cases, ensuring both specialization and versatility. Finally, **reinforcement learning with human feedback** aligns the model with user expectations and ethical considerations. Human evaluators review the model's outputs, providing rewards or corrections to guide its behavior. This iterative process ensures that the model not only produces accurate outputs but also avoids potentially harmful or undesirable responses. Together, these phases create a robust and adaptable model capable of handling a wide range of real-world applications.

The gradual improvement of LLMs during training is vividly illustrated in the example of "BabyGPT" (Bhatia, 2023), a model trained on Jane Austen's works (see Fig. 4.3). At the beginning of training, the model generates random, nonsensical text – its output resembling gibberish. This reflects the uninitialized state of the model, where it has yet to form any meaningful understanding of language. After 500 training rounds, the model starts identifying basic patterns, forming letters and small words, though its outputs remain largely incoherent. With further training, by 5000 rounds, the model generates larger words and begins constructing fragments of sentences that resemble English. By the time it completes 30,000 rounds, the model has developed the ability to produce complete, grammatically correct sentences, showcasing its capability to learn and replicate the intricate patterns of human language. This progressive development highlights the critical role of iterative optimization and the sheer scale of computation involved in achieving the high levels of fluency seen in advanced LLMs like GPT-4.

4.2.2 Application Scenarios of LLMs

The versatility of LLMs enables their application across a broad spectrum of use cases, spanning from everyday interactions to specialized academic and professional tasks (Gimpel et al., 2023). Their ability to adapt to user needs has made them invaluable tools in multiple domains:

For the general public, LLMs act as personal assistants, providing a range of capabilities that enhance productivity and simplify everyday tasks. These include the following:

- **Text summarization:** Condensing lengthy documents or articles into concise summaries, allowing users to quickly grasp the main points

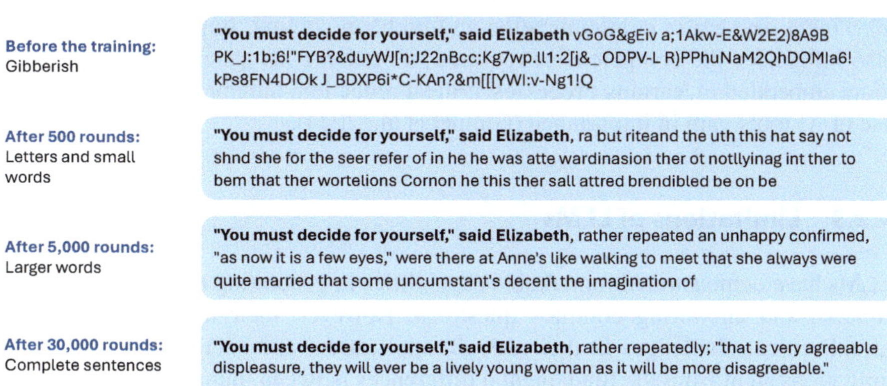

Fig. 4.3 Illustration of LLMs' progression during training. (Adapted from Bhatia, 2023)

- **Content creation:** Assisting in the generation of emails, blog posts, creative writing, or coding, enabling users to produce high-quality content with minimal effort
- **Knowledge dissemination:** Conveying complex concepts in an accessible manner, making information more understandable for a broader audience

In educational and research settings, LLMs like ChatGPT have become indispensable tools for students, educators, and researchers. Their applications include the following:

- **Work planning and research**: Structuring research projects, outlining work packages, and summarizing scientific content, helping researchers focus on critical aspects of their work
- **Text structuring and creation**: Drafting sections of academic papers, generating scientific texts based on detailed prompts, and ensuring logical coherence across documents
- **Text improvement and summarization**: Enhancing the quality of scientific texts by shortening, expanding, or clarifying content, and conducting thorough proofreading to ensure grammatical accuracy and stylistic consistency
- **Translation and testing**: Translating scientific texts into multiple languages while maintaining accuracy and generating evaluation criteria for assessing academic work

In higher education, LLMs are also used as learning partners for students. They support the iterative learning process by providing explanations, answering questions, and assisting with problem-solving tasks. Students are encouraged to use these tools responsibly, respecting academic integrity and aligning their usage with educational goals. By enabling natural, dynamic interactions and addressing diverse needs, LLMs demonstrate the transformative potential of generative AI. Their applications are shaping the way individuals and organizations leverage technology, marking a new era in communication and problem-solving. Importantly, this shift also influences the competencies required of students: as generative AI becomes more embedded in learning processes, critical reflection, judgment, and responsible use of AI tools gain in importance (Gimpel et al., 2024).

4.2.3 Limitations of LLMs

LLMs have demonstrated remarkable capabilities in generating text, understanding context, and answering complex questions. However, their inherent limitations reveal critical challenges in their design, application, and societal impact. These limitations stem from the fundamental differences between human intelligence and AI, as well as the statistical and data-driven nature of LLMs (Riemer & Peter, 2023).

One key limitation is that LLMs do not truly "understand" the content they generate. While humans derive insights through intelligent thought processes – such as abstract reasoning, logical inference, creativity, and empathy – LLMs merely imitate the results of these processes by identifying patterns and statistical relationships within massive datasets. This lack of comprehension sometimes leads to scenarios where the model generates plausible but factually incorrect, biased, or nonsensical outputs, a phenomenon sometimes referred to as "hallucination." For example, LLMs may confidently state falsehoods or generate entirely fictional narratives while presenting them as factual, as demonstrated by cases where ChatGPT or similar systems produced fabricated legal cases or events (Verma & Oremus, 2023). Unlike humans, simple LLMs cannot critically reflect on their responses or validate the logic of their conclusions. Thus, LLMs may generate incorrect or fabricated information.

Another significant challenge with LLMs is their inability to navigate ethical and societal considerations without guidance. If generative AI is tasked with controversial or discriminatory prompts, the system may inadvertently replicate biases present in its training data. This "mirror effect" reflects the historical inequalities and biases embedded in the datasets used to train these models. While some systems employ safeguards to filter harmful content, these measures are not foolproof, and the biases within the underlying data remain an ongoing concern. Privacy and copyright issues also present unresolved challenges. As LLMs are trained on vast datasets scraped from the internet, their outputs may unintentionally reveal sensitive information or infringe on intellectual property rights. This raises questions about the ethical and legal frameworks needed to govern the use of such models, with efforts like the AI Act in the European Union representing early attempts to address these concerns. However, these regulations are still evolving, and global consensus on ethical AI use remains elusive.

Summary
LLMs showcase the transformative potential of AI in understanding and generating human-like language. LLMs, powered by deep neural networks and advanced architectures like transformers, leverage probabilistic reasoning to generate contextually relevant outputs. Their success stems from mechanisms such as self-attention, probabilistic word prediction, and iterative training phases including pretraining, fine-tuning, and reinforcement learning. Despite their versatility, LLMs face limitations such as hallucinations, biases, and ethical concerns. A deep understanding of their architecture, capabilities, and constraints is essential for responsible deployment in education, business, and society at large.

4.3 Diffusion Models

In recent years, diffusion models have emerged as one of the most promising innovations in the field of generative AI. From hyper-realistic images and immersive videos to richly textured audio compositions, these models are redefining what machines can create. Unlike earlier generative approaches that often struggled with stability or quality trade-offs, diffusion models offer a fundamentally different and remarkably effective method for data generation – one that mirrors a physical process observed in nature. This subchapter explores the foundational principles, mechanisms, and applications of diffusion models and highlights both their transformative potential and the challenges they pose. By unpacking how these models operate and where they are used today, this subchapter aims to provide a clear and critical understanding of a technology that is rapidly reshaping creative industries, media production, and human–AI collaboration.

4.3.1 Core Concepts of Diffusion Models

Diffusion models are a class of generative AI models to produce complex data such as images, videos, and audio. Inspired by the physical concept of diffusion, where particles spread randomly over time, these models utilize a systematic and probabilistic approach that involves gradually adding and subsequently removing noise from data representations. This two-phase process – forward diffusion and reverse diffusion –forms the conceptual and mathematical backbone of the model's generative capacity (Singh, 2023).

The core mechanism of a diffusion model begins by incrementally adding Gaussian noise to the original data over a series of time steps. This process, known as forward diffusion, progressively transforms structured data into complete randomness. Each step introduces a small, controlled amount of noise, resulting in a sequence of increasingly noisy data samples. The model does not simply discard this corrupted data; instead, it learns a reverse process – a parametric denoising trajectory that can reconstruct the original data distribution from pure noise. This reverse diffusion is modeled using a neural network – typically a U-Net architecture – which learns to estimate the noise added at each step, allowing it to iteratively refine a noisy input into a coherent, structured output.

Through this iterative reconstruction, high-quality and realistic content is generated, often rivaling or surpassing the fidelity of outputs from earlier generative paradigms (Cao et al., 2023). Importantly, this approach enables diffusion models to model complex, multimodal data distributions with remarkable accuracy, making them well-suited for applications that require nuanced visual, auditory, or spatiotemporal detail.

Diffusion models differ significantly from other generative approaches like GANs. While GANs rely on a competitive dynamic between two neural networks – a generator creating content and a discriminator evaluating its authenticity – diffusion models adopt a principled, likelihood-based approach, characterized by a controlled, step-by-step stochastic process of perturbation and denoising (Cao et al., 2023). Unlike GANs, which can suffer from instability and convergence issues, diffusion models optimize a well-defined training objective, leading to more stable and predictable training dynamics (Peng, 2024). This fundamental difference contributes to diffusion models being more stable during training and less susceptible to common issues such as mode collapse, a phenomenon where GANs generate limited or repetitive outputs due to poor coverage of the data distribution (Peng, 2024). In contrast, diffusion models tend to maintain greater output diversity and are less prone to missing modes in the data, thanks to their probabilistic formulation and extensive coverage of the sample space during training.

Diffusion models are renowned for generating exceptionally detailed and diverse content. Their ability to capture fine-grained features, textures, and semantic structures has made them the architecture of choice for many cutting-edge systems in image synthesis (e.g., Stable Diffusion and DALL·E 3), video generation (e.g., Imagen Video), and even audio and music creation (e.g., AudioLDM). These strengths make diffusion models particularly attractive for applications demanding high-quality, controllable, and creative outputs – ranging from digital art and animation to scientific simulation and media production.

4.3.2 Application Scenarios of Diffusion Models

Text-to-Image Generation

One of the most prominent application areas for diffusion models is generating images from textual descriptions, known as "Text-to-Image." Models such as Stable Diffusion and Midjourney enable the creation of highly detailed and high-quality visual content based on brief descriptions or complex instructions. These technologies analyze input text and iteratively transform it into visual representations through a reverse diffusion process.

The process begins (1) with text input that is transformed into a text embedding. The result of this processing step is a numerical, high-dimensional text embedding, which mathematically captures the semantic properties and content of the original textual input. Text embeddings are crucial because they provide semantic meaning to diffusion models. They enable the models to understand which specific visual characteristics should be generated. A precise and expressive textual input significantly enhances the quality of the output, as the generated embeddings numerically represent specific semantic information.

The embedding is then (2) fed into a Text-to-Image diffusion model that generates a low-resolution (e.g., 64 × 64 pixels) image that roughly represents the scene described in the textual input. In this "Noise-to-Image" process, the model begins with completely random noise – essentially a chaotic, structureless collection of pixels. The diffusion model then gradually reduces this randomness through a step-by-step process called "denoising." During each step, the model predicts how to remove a small amount of noise from the image based on learned probabilities (Ho et al., 2022). Specifically, the model has been trained on large datasets of real images, enabling it to recognize which visual structures (such as shapes, edges, colors, textures, and patterns) are most likely to appear as the noise is progressively removed. As this iterative denoising continues, the image evolves from random noise into an increasingly recognizable and structured visual representation (Rombach et al., 2022). With each successive step, details become sharper, shapes clearer, and overall content more coherent, ultimately resulting in a highly realistic and precise image that accurately reflects the original textual description or desired content.

Subsequently (3), this rough initial image undergoes one or several super-resolution stages, during which specialized diffusion models incrementally upscale and refine the image (e.g., starting from 64 × 64 pixels, then to 256 × 256, and ultimately reaching high resolutions such as 1024 × 1024 pixels). Throughout these steps, the previously generated text embeddings are continually utilized to ensure that the image remains faithful to the original textual description, even as its resolution increases. The final result is a detailed, high-resolution image that accurately represents the original textual input (Rombach et al., 2022). Each of the steps described above contributes to ensuring that both the overall structure and fine details, as well as subtle visual nuances, are precisely and qualitatively generated.

Real-world applications of text-to-image generation include creative industries such as graphic design and advertising, where companies such as Edelman and BMW utilize AI-generated images to rapidly prototype visuals and ideate new products (Valchanov, 2024). It is also employed in entertainment and gaming industries; for instance, Activision has integrated AI-generated assets into the "Call of Duty" franchise to enhance immersive gaming environments (Perkel, 2025). Generative models are being eyed for creating in-game content like textures for 3D models, variations of background scenery, or even dialogue and quest text (using language models). Nearly 90% of video game companies in a recent survey reported that they have experimented with generative AI in their development pipelines (CVL Economics, 2024). Additionally, e-commerce platforms leverage AI-powered image generation tools such as Midjourney and DALL-E to efficiently create product visuals tailored to seasonal trends or new product lines, significantly improving user experience and engagement.

Text-to-Video Generation

Another emerging field is generating videos from text-based inputs, known as "Text-to-Video." Providers such as Runway and Imagen Video have made it possible to create complex video sequences from brief textual descriptions. Examples include generating film scenes, animations, or presentation videos directly from text.

Technically, text-to-video models extend the principles behind text-to-image generation into the temporal dimension. Similar to text-to-image processes, the initial textual input is transformed into a numerical text embedding that captures the semantic essence of the description. However, instead of creating a single static image, these models generate sequences of frames by iteratively applying diffusion processes, ensuring temporal coherence and consistency between frames. Advanced diffusion techniques help ensure smooth transitions and realistic motion by learning temporal correlations from large-scale datasets of videos (Singh, 2023).

Real-world applications of text-to-video generation are emerging rapidly across multiple industries. In entertainment, studios can swiftly visualize storyboards, scenes, or animation concepts directly from scripts, significantly reducing the costs and time required for pre-production. For instance, Lionsgate has partnered with

Runway to develop customized video generation models, aiming to enhance the efficiency and creativity of filmmakers (Pulliam-Moore, 2024). In marketing and advertising, brands use platforms such as Runway to quickly create promotional videos tailored to specific campaign messages without extensive video shoots. Moreover, education and corporate training sectors benefit from customized, dynamically generated explanatory videos, making content more engaging and tailored precisely to audience needs. Overall, text-to-video generation technologies are opening innovative avenues for creativity, collaboration, and efficiency, potentially reshaping how visual storytelling is approached across industries.

Text-to-Audio Generation

In the realm of audio generation, advanced models such as AudioLDM enable the direct transformation of textual descriptions into musical and auditory content. These cutting-edge technologies interpret mood-driven, detailed, or technical descriptions to create musical pieces or complex soundscapes.

Much like text-to-image and text-to-video models, text-to-audio systems begin with an input text prompt that is transformed into a numerical, semantic representation. This embedding encodes critical characteristics from the textual input, such as genre, mood, instrumentation, or specific audio features. Audio-focused diffusion models subsequently utilize this embedding, initially starting with randomized noise patterns, and progressively shaping these patterns through iterative denoising steps into coherent audio signals. By applying learned probabilities derived from extensive audio datasets during training, these models create structured, musically coherent, and contextually accurate auditory outputs (Liu et al., 2023).

Text-to-audio generation models have potential applications across a variety of industries, particularly in entertainment, marketing, and the creative arts. In the entertainment and gaming sectors, developers can rely on these technologies to generate dynamic background scores, sound effects, and ambient sounds tailored precisely to narrative contexts. This enables the rapid creation of immersive auditory environments and significantly streamlines audio production workflows, ultimately enhancing the user's experience (Yuan et al., 2023). In the field of marketing and advertising, companies are beginning to adopt AI-generated audio to swiftly produce unique background music or distinct brand sound signatures for commercials, podcasts, and promotional videos. By removing the need for traditional sound production setups, these technologies accelerate content creation and allow for quick adaptation of audio assets to changing campaign narratives or emotional tones. Creative professionals such as composers, artists, and sound designers use models like AudioLDM to explore new musical directions. These tools make it possible to prototype musical ideas quickly and experiment with novel concepts based on textual descriptions. As a result, the creative process becomes more fluid and collaborative, enabling artists to iterate freely and realize complex auditory visions without the constraints of traditional studio environments.

Taken together, these applications illustrate how text-to-audio generation is transforming auditory content creation. The technology enables new levels of efficiency, accessibility, and creative freedom, while ongoing advancements continue to broaden its potential impact across domains.

4.3.3 Limitations of Diffusion Models

Diffusion models have rapidly gained prominence for their powerful capabilities in generating high-quality visual and auditory content, as demonstrated by tools such as Stable Diffusion, Midjourney, and AudioLDM. However, despite their impressive potential, diffusion models face significant limitations and risks that reflect fundamental challenges associated with their design, implementation, and societal implications.

One prominent limitation involves the difficulty in reliably controlling or steering the outputs of diffusion models. While these models excel at generating realistic and detailed images, videos, or audio, their outputs can sometimes deviate unpredictably from user intentions. Due to the inherently stochastic nature of the diffusion process – starting with random noise and gradually reducing it – precisely guiding the model to produce very specific content remains challenging. Users frequently rely on trial and error or repeated attempts to achieve satisfactory results, especially for detailed or nuanced prompts. This lack of precise controllability can limit the practicality of diffusion models in professional contexts where exact outputs and reproducibility are essential, such as in graphic design, branding, or industrial prototyping (Wiggers, 2023).

Additionally, diffusion models inherit biases and limitations embedded within their training datasets. Since these models are trained on extensive collections of images, videos, or audio obtained predominantly from the Internet, they inevitably reflect the underlying biases, stereotypes, and limitations found within this data. As a result, generated content may unintentionally reproduce or amplify societal biases related to gender, race, or culture (Milne, 2023). This "data mirror effect" poses ethical challenges, particularly when models are employed in sensitive domains such as marketing, media representation, or creative arts, where biased outputs can reinforce harmful stereotypes or contribute to social inequity.

Furthermore, diffusion models raise significant ethical and legal concerns regarding copyright and intellectual property. As models generate highly realistic content that can closely resemble existing artworks, photographs, or media, distinguishing between original and AI-generated materials becomes increasingly difficult. This blurring of boundaries presents a complex challenge for intellectual property law, raising unresolved questions about ownership, attribution, and the permissible scope of AI-generated content (Brittain, 2023). Additionally, the potential for diffusion models to create realistic "deepfake" images or videos intensifies concerns about misinformation and digital manipulation. Malicious actors may leverage these powerful capabilities to fabricate convincing yet entirely false visual narratives, posing threats to trust in media, journalism, and online communication.

Finally, efforts to mitigate these risks – such as embedding safety filters or employing guided diffusion techniques – introduce their own complexities. Safety measures often involve trade-offs, balancing freedom of creative expression against protection from harmful or inappropriate content. Determining universally acceptable criteria for what constitutes safe or appropriate content generation remains challenging, given diverse cultural standards and societal values.

Summary
Diffusion models are a powerful class of generative AI techniques that create visual, auditory, and multimodal content from random noise. Inspired by physical diffusion processes, they offer a stable and high-quality alternative to earlier approaches like GANs. Used in applications ranging from image and video creation to music and sound design, they are already impacting creative industries, marketing, and entertainment. Alongside their potential, however, come important challenges – limited controllability, embedded biases, and unresolved legal and ethical questions. A nuanced understanding of both their strengths and limitations is essential for guiding their responsible development and use.

4.4 From Generation to Action: The Path to Agentic AI

As generative AI continues to evolve, the limitations of standalone LLMs have become increasingly apparent. While LLMs excel at generating coherent text, answering questions, and summarizing information, they often fall short when it comes to handling complex, multi-step tasks, especially those that require memory, context management, tool use, or strategic decision-making over time. This is where agentic AI becomes essential.

Agentic AI refers to systems that go beyond passive text generation and instead act with purpose and autonomy. AI agents can plan, reason, interact with external environments or tools, and adapt dynamically to changing conditions (Russell & Norvig, 2016). They are particularly promising for domains requiring the automation of sophisticated workflows – such as research, software development, customer service, and business decision-making – where simple prompt-response paradigms are insufficient. By enabling AI to operate as agents, we move from static outputs to systems capable of goal-directed behavior, iterative problem-solving, and continuous learning.

Building such intelligent agents requires the integration of several key components (Plaat et al., 2025; Wang et al., 2024):

- **Reasoning-augmented LLMs** are at the heart of many agentic systems. Unlike basic LLMs that rely on surface-level pattern recognition, reasoning-augmented models are fine-tuned or prompted to decompose problems, evaluate alternative paths, and chain multiple reasoning steps together. This enables more accurate and reliable decision-making, especially in scenarios where sequential logic or planning is required.

- **Retrieval-augmented generation (RAG)** addresses one of the biggest limitations of LLMs: their static knowledge. RAG pipelines integrate real-time access to external knowledge sources – such as databases, documents, or web APIs – into the generation process, allowing agents to reason over up-to-date, context-specific information rather than relying solely on what was encoded during training.
- **Generative AI-based conversational agents** provide the interface for interaction – whether with users, other agents, or APIs. These agents maintain context over longer dialogues, clarify goals, and translate abstract intentions into executable steps. They form the bridge between human intent and machine execution.
- **Multi-agent systems** (MASs) allow multiple AI agents to collaborate, delegate tasks, and specialize in different functions. Inspired by human teams or distributed problem-solving systems, these setups can dynamically coordinate efforts across agents with distinct roles – such as planners, critics, or executors – leading to more scalable and modular architectures for complex problem domains.

Together, these components enable the emergence of truly agentic AI systems: autonomous, interactive, and capable of managing real-world complexity with far more sophistication than standalone LLMs. In this subchapter, we explore each of these building blocks in more detail to understand how they contribute to agentic behavior – and why their integration is critical for advancing generative AI from static output generation to dynamic, goal-driven action in complex environments.

4.4.1 Reasoning-Augmented LLMs

Reasoning-augmented LLMs significantly extend the capabilities of conventional LLMs by incorporating structured logical processes and explicit reasoning steps. Rather than merely generating plausible text continuations based on learned statistical patterns, these advanced models employ specialized techniques such as chain-of-thought (CoT) prompting and multiple chains of thought (Wei et al., 2022; Yao et al., 2023). These techniques explicitly guide the model through sequential reasoning, enabling more sophisticated cognitive tasks involving multi-step inference, causal reasoning, and structured decision-making.

A core method in reasoning augmentation is CoT **prompting**, which involves instructing the model to explicitly articulate intermediate reasoning steps leading to a final answer. This explicit step-by-step reasoning markedly enhances model accuracy, particularly for tasks such as arithmetic calculations, logical deductions, and scenario-based planning. By making the reasoning process transparent, CoT prompting also improves interpretability, allowing users to better understand how the model arrives at a specific conclusion and identify potential errors in the reasoning path (Creswell & Shanahan, 2022).

Further extending this concept, **multiple** CoT **prompting** involves generating several parallel reasoning paths for a given problem. By exploring multiple potential solutions independently, the model can assess alternative reasoning routes and compare their logical consistency and outcomes (Yao et al., 2023). This approach is particularly effective for complex problems, where initial reasoning paths may vary significantly in their validity or reliability. Through the systematic evaluation of multiple reasoning sequences, reasoning-augmented models achieve greater robustness, significantly reducing the likelihood of errors caused by early missteps in logic or inference (Yao et al., 2023).

Overall, reasoning augmentation addresses several critical limitations of conventional LLMs, such as superficial reasoning, logical inconsistencies, and opaque decision-making. The explicit representation and verification of logical reasoning steps empower these models to handle complex cognitive tasks reliably, systematically, and transparently (Wei et al., 2022; Creswell & Shanahan, 2022). As a result, reasoning-augmented LLMs substantially outperform standard LLMs in applications requiring precise logical inference, structured problem-solving, and accountable decision-making. Thus, reasoning-augmented models form an essential foundation for agentic AI systems. Without the ability to systematically plan, evaluate consequences, and justify decisions transparently, agentic systems would struggle to operate autonomously in dynamic and unpredictable environments. Thus, reasoning augmentation not only enhances model performance but also provides a necessary cornerstone for building trustworthy, autonomous AI agents.

4.4.2 Retrieval-Augmented Generation

RAG is a powerful technique designed to enhance LLMs by explicitly integrating external knowledge during text generation. Unlike traditional LLMs, which rely solely on internalized patterns learned during training, RAG approaches combine a neural retrieval system with generative models, allowing dynamic access to vast, up-to-date knowledge bases and external documents. This combination significantly improves the factual accuracy, relevance, and reliability of the generated outputs, addressing common weaknesses inherent in standalone generative models (Lewis et al., 2020).

The core mechanism behind RAG involves two primary components: a retrieval component and a generation component. The retrieval module first identifies relevant passages or documents from a large-scale external knowledge source, such as Wikipedia or specialized databases. These retrieved pieces of external information are then provided as context to the generative module, typically a pretrained LLM. By conditioning text generation on retrieved external information, the generative model can produce responses grounded in verified facts, current knowledge, and domain-specific details, rather than relying exclusively on internalized statistical patterns that may be outdated or incomplete (Paliwal, 2024).

One critical advantage of RAG-based systems is their ability to mitigate the "hallucination problem," in which standard LLMs produce outputs that, while plausible-sounding, contain factual inaccuracies or entirely fabricated information. Since RAG models ground their outputs directly on externally retrieved content, they significantly reduce inaccuracies and provide greater factual consistency (Shuster et al., 2021). This attribute makes RAG especially beneficial in professional domains such as healthcare, law, and academia, where precision and factual correctness are critical.

Another key strength of RAG is its adaptability. Because the knowledge base is external, updating information does not require retraining the entire generative model. Instead, updating or expanding the external knowledge source immediately makes new knowledge available to the retrieval process. This flexibility ensures that RAG-based systems remain current, relevant, and scalable – qualities essential for real-world deployments where information evolves rapidly (Izacard & Grave, 2021).

Moreover, the explicit retrieval step of RAG models offers additional interpretability benefits. Users can directly inspect which external documents or facts were retrieved and, thus, understand the rationale behind the generated outputs. Such transparency substantially enhances trustworthiness and user acceptance, as it allows verification of the information provided by the model.

In summary, RAG significantly extends the capabilities of standard LLMs by integrating external knowledge retrieval mechanisms. By enabling accurate, context-aware, and factually grounded generation, RAG methods address key limitations of conventional generative models, such as knowledge gaps, outdated information, and hallucinations. As the complexity and demands placed on generative AI systems increase, approaches such as RAG represent a critical evolution toward more reliable, transparent, and trustworthy AI-based agent systems.

4.4.3 Generative AI-Based Conversational Agents

Conversational generative AI agents, such as ChatGPT, represent a transformative leap in how humans interact with AI, seamlessly integrating advanced AI capabilities into practical applications (Gimpel et al., 2023). By leveraging the language understanding and generation abilities of LLMs, these systems engage users in intuitive and dynamic dialogues. Positioned as a distinct category within the hierarchy of AI, conversational agents act as the bridge between sophisticated LLMs and real-world usability. They enable natural language interactions, mimicking human-like conversational patterns, providing coherent responses, answering complex questions, and assisting in various tasks with high adaptability.

Conversational agents are broadly classified into three categories: rule-based systems, retrieval-based systems, and generative models (Kumar et al., 2022). **Rule-based systems** operate on a set of predefined conversational patterns, which makes them reliable in structured scenarios but limits their adaptability to unforeseen queries. **Retrieval-based systems** improve on this by selecting the best response from a repository of predefined options, offering a degree of contextual relevance but still lacking the ability to generate entirely novel responses. **Generative models**, such as ChatGPT, are the most advanced category. Unlike the other two, they dynamically generate individual responses in real time, drawing upon patterns and knowledge derived from extensive training data. This capability allows generative models to handle a wide range of topics and respond flexibly to user inputs, even in unexpected or nuanced situations (Busch et al., 2025).

How Conversational Generative AI Agents Handle Prior Conversations

A hallmark feature of modern conversational agents, particularly generative models, is their ability to remember and incorporate prior conversation context into ongoing dialogues. This is achieved through the careful handling of dialogue history. Each user input and system response are recorded and passed back into the model as part of a structured conversation history. This ensures that the model can reference earlier exchanges, providing contextually relevant and coherent answers even in lengthy discussions (OpenAI, 2024).

For instance, if a user begins a conversation by asking about the 2020 World Series and later follows up with the question "Where was it played?," the model needs to recall the topic of the earlier query to generate an accurate response. Unlike humans, conversational agents do not possess memory in the conventional sense. Instead, their "memory" relies on embedding the entire conversation history into each new input. This process ensures the AI can interpret follow-up questions and maintain the logical flow of a conversation. However, this approach has limitations, particularly regarding token limits. Since LLMs process input in tokenized chunks, there is a finite amount of context that can be retained in a single query. For extended interactions, developers may need to truncate or summarize the conversation history to fit within these constraints, potentially leading to the loss of less critical information. This highlights the importance of designing dialogue systems that prioritize the most relevant parts of a conversation while maintaining user experience.

Reason Why Agents Frequently Perform Better Than Simple LLMs

Integrating LLMs with additional components such as memory, planning capabilities, and external tools significantly enhances their task performance compared to standalone LLMs. By incorporating memory modules, LLMs can retain and recall information from past interactions, enabling more coherent and contextually relevant responses over extended conversations (see Fig. 4.4). Planning mechanisms

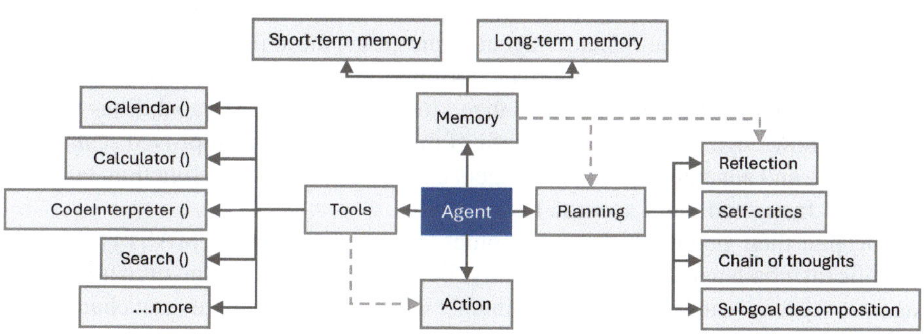

Fig. 4.4 LLM-based agent. (Adapted from Weng, 2023)

allow these models to decompose complex tasks into manageable steps, facilitating systematic problem-solving and strategic decision-making. Furthermore, equipping LLMs with external tools – such as code interpreters, calculators, or access to additional databases – extends their functionality beyond text generation, allowing them to perform computations, retrieve up-to-date information, and interact dynamically with various data sources. This combination of memory, planning, and tool integration transforms LLMs into more autonomous and efficient generative AI agents capable of handling a broader range of tasks with greater accuracy and adaptability (Weng, 2023).

4.4.4 Multi-Agent Systems

MASs represent a further evolution in AI, particularly suited for automating complex knowledge-intensive tasks. Unlike traditional monolithic AI systems, MASs consist of multiple specialized AI-driven software agents collaboratively working together to achieve collective goals or solve intricate problems that surpass the capabilities of any single agent. Each agent within a MAS operates autonomously, possesses specialized competencies, and is capable of perception, planning, decision-making, and communication (van der Hoek & Wooldridge, 2008; Doran et al., 1997).

Effective coordination and orchestration are essential elements in MAS, mirroring the complexities of human teamwork. Just as human teams require clear communication, mutual understanding, conflict resolution, and precise role definition, MASs depend on robust orchestration mechanisms that balance the autonomy of individual agents with centralized oversight. Such orchestration ensures that agents collaborate efficiently, minimizes redundancies, and maximizes overall productivity. It also allows the system to adaptively manage workflows, diverging from traditional human-centric processes toward more efficient and flexible automated arrangements (Lee et al., 2024; Baird & Maruping, 2021).

Figure 4.5 showcases this concept by depicting a manager agent overseeing several specialist agents, such as an analyzing agent, reasoning agent, and writing agent, each dedicated to a specific function (Yee et al., 2024). This structure enables a division of labor, allowing tasks to be broken down and processed more efficiently. Additionally, the manager agent orchestrates these interactions and ensures a seamless workflow. Beyond internal coordination, the system connects to external systems, such as databases and specialized tools, expanding its capabilities beyond built-in knowledge. The primary benefit of this architecture is improved scalability, efficiency, and adaptability – as each agent can focus on a distinct function, tasks are executed faster and more accurately.

Despite their potential, the development and deployment of MASs come with significant challenges. A key difficulty lies in the coordination of autonomous agents, especially in dynamic environments where goals and inputs can change rapidly. Ensuring that agents understand each other's capabilities, align their individual decisions with overarching objectives, and resolve potential conflicts requires

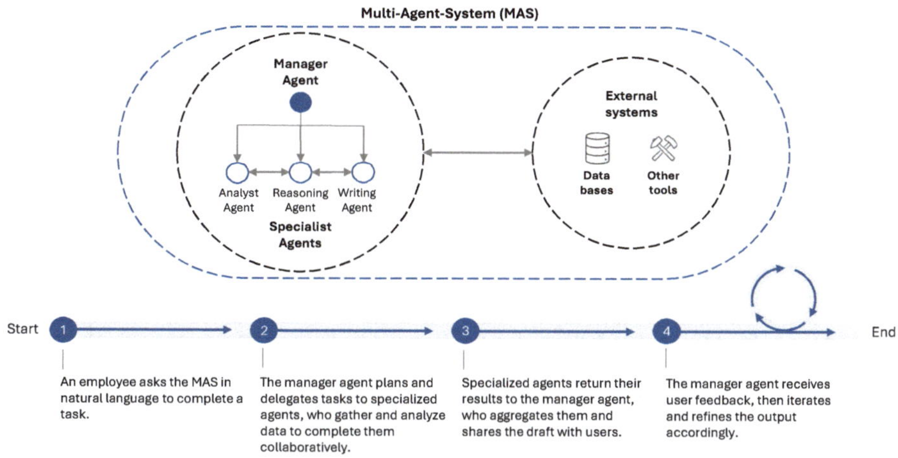

Fig. 4.5 Concept of MASs. (Adapted from Yee et al., 2024)

sophisticated orchestration mechanisms. Moreover, designing agents with the right balance between autonomy and control is complex: Too much autonomy can lead to inefficient or contradictory actions, while excessive centralization can limit the system's adaptability and scalability. Technical hurdles also include managing communication overhead, ensuring consistent access to up-to-date information, and integrating agents into existing IT infrastructures. Furthermore, questions around accountability, transparency, and trustworthiness arise when agents act independently in critical decision-making contexts (Guo et al., 2024).

If these challenges can be overcome, MASs offer significant potential as a foundational technology for Agentic Work Automation (AWA). AWA marks a paradigm shift, from the automation of isolated process steps to the holistic automation of entire workflows. In such systems, agents can respond dynamically to changing requirements, interact seamlessly with human users, and orchestrate complex business processes in a coordinated and goal-oriented manner. This approach enables organizations to rethink how knowledge work is structured, distributed, and executed, ultimately relieving human experts of routine cognitive tasks while improving overall responsiveness, scalability, and productivity.

Summary
The transition from static language models to dynamic, autonomous AI agents marks a significant evolution in artificial intelligence. While traditional LLMs excel in generating text, they fall short in tasks requiring planning, memory, reasoning, and interaction with external tools. Agentic AI addresses these gaps by combining reasoning-augmented LLMs, RAG, conversational agents, and MASs. These components enable goal-oriented, adaptive behavior and scalable task execution. MASs, in particular, allow agents to collaborate, specialize, and orchestrate workflows efficiently. Together, these technologies form the foundation for AWA, a paradigm shift toward holistic automation of knowledge-based processes.

References

Baird, A., & Maruping, L. M. (2021). The next generation of research on IS use: A theoretical framework of delegation to and from agentic IS artifacts. *MIS Quarterly, 45*(1), 315–341. https://doi.org/10.25300/misq/2021/15882

Bhatia, A. (2023). We need to talk about how good A.I. is getting. *The New York Times*. Retrieved November 25, 2024, from https://www.nytimes.com/interactive/2023/04/26/upshot/gpt-from-scratch.html

Brittain, B. (2023). *Getty images lawsuit says stability AI misused photos to train AI*. Retrieved March 25, 2025, from https://www.reuters.com/legal/getty-images-lawsuit-says-stability-ai-misused-photos-train-ai-2023-02-06/

Busch, M., Collarana, D., Decker, S., Eymann, T., Gutheil, N., Keller, R., Kühl, N., Lange-Bever, C., Mayer, V., Morad, M., Pöllath, L., Röglinger, M., Sharma, R., & Urbach, N. (2025). *Implementing generative AI Chatbots – Potentials, challenges and guidelines for the successful implementation of generative AI Chatbots into tourism*. University of Bayreuth, March 28, 2025. https://doi.org/10.5281/zenodo.15101793

Cao, H., Tan, C., Gao, Z., Xu, Y., Chen, G., Heng, P.-A., & Li, S. Z. (2023). A survey on generative diffusion models. *arXiv Preprint arXiv:2209.02646* .

Creswell, A., & Shanahan, M. (2022). Selection-inference: Exploiting large language models for interpretable logical reasoning. *arXiv preprint arXiv:2205.09712* .

CVL Economics. (2024). *Future unscripted: The impact of generative artificial intelligence on entertainment industry jobs*. Retrieved March 25, 2025, from https://animationguild.org/wp-content/uploads/2024/01/Future-Unscripted-The-Impact-of-Generative-Artificial-Intelligence-on-Entertainment-Industry-Jobs-pages-1.pdf

Doran, J., Franklin, S., Jennings, N., & Norman, T. (1997). On cooperation in multi-agent systems. *The Knowledge Engineering Review, 12*(3), 309–314. https://doi.org/10.1017/s0269888997003111

Gimpel, H., Ruiner, C., Schoch, M., Schoop, M., Hall, K., Eymann, T., Rögliger, M., Vandrik, S., Lämmermann, L., Urbach, N., Mädche, A., & Decker, S. (2023). *Unlocking the power of generative AI models and systems such as GPT-4 and ChatGPT for higher education: A guide for students and lecturers* (No. 02-2023). Hohenheim Discussion Papers in Business, Economics and Social Sciences. Retrieved November 25, 2024, from https://hohpublica.uni-hohenheim.de/items/fe53b2bb-ab75-463c-9383-ec74416fd940?utm_source=chatgpt.com

Gimpel, H., Gutheil, N., Mayer, V., Bandtel, M., Büttgen, M., Decker, S., et al. (2024). *(Generative) AI competencies for future-proof graduates: Inspiration for higher education institutions*. Hohenheim Discussion Papers in Business, Economics and Social Sciences.

Guo, T., Chen, X., Wang, Y., Chang, R., Pei, S., Chawla, N. V., Wiest, O., & Zhang, X. (2024). Large language model based multi-agents: A survey of progress and challenges. *arXiv preprint arXiv:2402.01680* . https://doi.org/10.48550/arXiv.2402.01680

Ho, J., Chan, W., Saharia, C., et al. (2022). Imagen Video: High definition video generation with diffusion models. *arXiv Preprint arXiv:2210.02303* .

Izacard, G., & Grave, E. (2021). Leveraging passage retrieval with generative models for open-domain question answering. Proceedings of the. In *16th Conference of the European Chapter of the Association for Computational Linguistics (EACL)* (pp. 874–880).

Kamath, U., Keenan, K., Somers, G., & Sorenson, S. (2024). Large Language Models: An Introduction. In *Large language models: A deep dive: Bridging theory and practice* (pp. 1–27). Cham.

Kumar, P., Sharma, S. C., & Arora, A. (2022). A literature survey of recent advances in chatbots. *Information, 13*(1), 41. https://doi.org/10.3390/info13010041

Lee, C.-H., Cheng, H., & Ostendorf, M. (2024). OrchestraLLM: Efficient orchestration of language models for dialogue state tracking. *arXiv preprint arXiv:2311.09758* . https://doi.org/10.48550/arXiv.2311.09758

Lewis, P., Perez, E., Piktus, A., Petroni, F., Karpukhin, V., Goyal, N., & Riedel, S. (2020). Retrieval-augmented generation for knowledge-intensive NLP tasks. *Advances in Neural Information Processing Systems (NeurIPS), 33*, 9459–9474.

Liu, H., Chen, Z., Yuan, Y., et al. (2023). AudioLDM: Text-to-audio generation with latent diffusion models. *arXiv Preprint arXiv:2301.12503* .

Milne, S. (2023). *AI image generator stable diffusion perpetuates racial and gendered stereotypes, study finds*. Retrieved March 25, 2025, from https://www.washington.edu/news/2023/11/29/ai-image-generator-stable-diffusion-perpetuates-racial-and-gendered-stereotypes-bias/

OpenAI. (2024). Text generation. OpenAI Platform Documentation. Retrieved November 25. 2024, from https://platform.openai.com/docs/guides/text-generation

Paliwal, Y. (2024). *Understanding retrieval-augmented generation (RAG) in generative AI: An overview*. Retrieved November 25, 2024, from https://medium.com/%40yashpaliwal42/understanding-retrieval-augmented-generation-rag-in-generative-ai-an-overview-914ef820d0f0

Peng, Y. (2024). A comparative analysis between GAN and diffusion models in image generation. *Transactions on Computer Science and Intelligent Systems Research, 5*(1) (Proc. AIDML 2024).

Perkel, S. (2025). *Popular 'Call of Duty' franchise confirms what play suspected: AI was used to make some of the games*. Retrieved November 25, 2024, from https://www.businessinsider.com/call-of-duty-activision-ai-in-some-games-2025-2?utm_source=chatgpt.com

Plaat, A., D'Ascoli, S., Bubeck, S., Chan, B., Chen, D., Chi, E. H., et al. (2025). Agentic large language models. *arXiv preprint arXiv:2503.23037* . https://arxiv.org/abs/2503.23037

Pulliam-Moore, C. (2024). *Lionsgate signs deal to train AI model on its movies and shows*. Retrieved March 25, 2025, from https://www.theverge.com/2024/9/18/24248115/lionsgate-runway-ai-deal?utm_source=chatgpt.com

Reuters. (2023). *ChatGPT sets record for fastest-growing user base—Analyst note*. Retrieved March 19, 2025, from https://www.reuters.com/technology/chatgpt-sets-record-fastest-growing-user-base-analyst-note-2023-02-01/

Riemer, K., & Peter, S. (2023). What the lone banana problem reveals about the nature of generative AI. In *ACIS 2023 Proceedings*.

Rombach, R., Blattmann, A., Lorenz, D., Esser, P., & Ommer, B. (2022). High-resolution image synthesis with latent diffusion models. In *Proceedings of the IEEE/CVF Conference on Computer Vision and Pattern Recognition (CVPR)* (pp. 10684–10695).

Russell, S., & Norvig, P. (2016). *Artificial intelligence. A modern approach* (3rd ed., Global edition). Pearson. https://thuvienso.hoasen.edu.vn/handle/123456789/8967

Shuster, K., Poff, S., Chen, M., Kiela, D., & Weston, J. (2021). Retrieval augmentation reduces hallucination in conversation. *arXiv preprint arXiv:2104.07567* .

Singh, A. (2023). *A survey of AI text-to-image and AI text-to-video generators*. Retrieved March 1, 2025, from https://arxiv.org/abs/2311.06329

The Verge. (2024). *Inside the launch – and future – of ChatGPT*. Retrieved March 1, 2025, from https://www.theverge.com/2024/12/12/24318650/chatgpt-openai-history-two-year-anniversary

Valchanov, I. (2024). *Using AI for generating images: 5 use cases, examples & tools*. Retrieved March 26, 2025, from https://team-gpt.com/blog/ai-for-generating-images/?utm_source=chatgpt.com

van der Hoek, W., & Wooldridge, M. (2008). Multi-agent systems. *Foundations of Artificial Intelligence, 3*, 887–928. https://doi.org/10.1016/S1574-6526(07)03024-6

Verma, P., & Oremus, W. (2023). ChatGPT invented a sexual harassment scandal and named a real law prof as the accused. *The Washington Post*. Retrieved November 25, 2024, from https://www.washingtonpost.com/technology/2023/04/05/chatgpt-lies/

Wang, L., Liu, Z., Wang, Z., & Li, L. (2024). A survey on large language model based autonomous agents. *Journal of Computer Science and Technology. IEEE*. https://doi.org/10.1109/JOCST.2024.10849561

Wei, J., Wang, X., Schuurmans, D., Bosma, M., Chi, E., Le, Q., & Zhou, D. (2022). Chain-of-thought prompting elicits reasoning in large language models. *Advances in Neural Information Processing Systems (NeurIPS), 35*, 24824–24837.

Weng, L. (2023). *LLM powered autonomous agents*. Retrieved March 1, 2025, from https://lilianweng.github.io/posts/2023-06-23-agent/

Wiggers, K. (2023). *Runway's Gen-2 shows the limitations of today's text-to-video tech*. Retrieved March 1, 2025, from https://techcrunch.com/2023/06/09/runways-gen-2-shows-the-limitations-of-todays-text-to-video-tech/

Yao, S., Yu, D., Zhao, J., Shafran, I., Griffiths, T., & Cao, Y. (2023). Tree of thoughts: Deliberate problem solving with large language models. *arXiv preprint arXiv:2305.10601. cao*.

Yee, L., Chui, M., Roberts, R., & Xu, S. (2024). *Why agents are the next frontier of generative AI*. Retrieved March 1, 2025, from https://www.mckinsey.com/capabilities/mckinsey-digital/our-insights/why-agents-are-thenext-frontier-of-generative-ai

Yuan, Y., Lui, H., Liu, X., et al. (2023). *Latent diffusion model based foley sound generation system for DCASE challenge 2023 Task 7*. Retrieved March 25, 2025, from https://doi.org/10.48550/arXiv.2305.15905

Nils Urbach is Professor of Information Systems and Digital Business as well as Director of the Research Lab for Digital Innovation & Transformation at the Frankfurt University of Applied Sciences, Germany. Furthermore, he is Director at the FIM Research Center for Information Management, and the Branch Business & Information Systems Engineering of Fraunhofer FIT. Nils Urbach has been working in the fields of digital innovation and transformation for several years. His work has been published in several academic journals such as Information Systems Research (ISR), the Journal of the Association for Information Systems (JAIS), the Journal of Strategic Information Systems (JSIS), the Journal of Information Technology (JIT), MIS Quarterly Executive (MISQE), IEEE Transactions on Engineering Management (IEEE TEM), Information and Management (I&M), Business & Information Systems Engineering (BISE), and Electronic Markets (EM). He advises several companies on digitalization issues and regularly appears as a speaker on this topic.

Daniel Feulner received his M.Sc. in information system from the Otto-Friedrich University of Bamberg, Germany in 2023. He is an affiliated researcher at the Branch Business & Information Systems Engineering of the Fraunhofer FIT and FIM Research Center for Information Management at the University of Bayreuth. In his research, he aims to understand how Business Analytics and Artificial Intelligence can be effectively and responsibly utilized in organizations. His goal is to enable companies to drive innovation and achieve sustainable growth in a rapidly evolving technological landscape.

Simon Feulner received his M.Sc. in business administration from the University of Bayreuth, Germany, in 2020 and his M.Sc. in information system from the Otto-Friedrich University of Bamberg, Germany in 2021. He is an affiliated researcher at the Branch Business & Information Systems Engineering of the Fraunhofer FIT and the Research Lab for Digital Innovation & Transformation at the Frankfurt University of Applied Sciences. His research explores the automation potential of generative AI technologies, examining how these innovations can streamline business processes, enhance decision-making, and unlock new opportunities for organizational value creation. He specifically focuses on how these technologies can break down existing barriers to automation, enabling more widespread and effective adoption across diverse business contexts.

Tobias Guggenberger is a postdoctoral researcher at the University of Bayreuth and the Branch Business & Information Systems Engineering of Fraunhofer FIT. He holds an M.Sc. in business administration and a Ph.D. in information systems engineering. His research primarily concentrates on the design and management of information systems, leveraging emerging technologies like artificial intelligence (AI) and blockchain. His scholarly contributions have appeared in renowned conference proceedings, including the International Conference on Information Systems (ICIS) and the European Conference on Information Systems (ECIS). His research has also been published in prestigious international journals such as IEEE Transactions on Engineering

Management (IEEE TEM), MIS Quarterly Executive (MISQE), Electronic Markets (EM), and Computers & Industrial Engineering.

Valentin Mayer received his M.Sc. in Management & Technology from the Technical University of Munich, Germany 2023. He is an affiliated researcher at the Branch Business & Information Systems Engineering of the Fraunhofer FIT and FIM Research Center for Information Management at the University of Bayreuth. His research explores how companies can successfully implement Artificial Intelligence within their organizations, with a particular focus on the conceptual design and operationalization of AI systems. His goal is to equip companies with practical methods to implement AI end-to-end into their operations and create long-term value.

Evaluating and Optimizing Artificial Intelligence Models 5

Nils Urbach, Daniel Feulner, Tobias Guggenberger, and Annalena Schmid

Evaluating the performance of artificial intelligence (AI) models is critical for ensuring their effectiveness and reliability. AI metrics provide the quantitative foundation for comparing models across tasks such as classification, regression, clustering, and natural language processing. Metrics such as accuracy, precision, recall, and mean squared error (MSE) help reveal strengths and weaknesses. In combination with hyperparameter optimization techniques, including grid search and random search, these metrics support alignment with real-world requirements and guide refinements for better outcomes.

In this chapter, the initial focus is on how AI models fit into a broader hierarchy, distinguishing them from foundational mathematics and algorithms. This is followed by a discussion of the key challenges in AI model development and the central role of metrics in addressing them. Next, various metrics are presented in detail, along with hyperparameter optimization methods aimed at improving model performance. The final section highlights the characteristics of a well-trained AI model, emphasizing strategies to avoid both underfitting and overfitting for robust, reliable results.

N. Urbach (✉)
Frankfurt University of Applied Sciences, Frankfurt am Main, Germany
e-mail: nils.urbach@fim-rc.de

D. Feulner · T. Guggenberger
University of Bayreuth, Bayreuth, Germany
e-mail: daniel.feulner@fim-rc.de; tobias.guggenberger@fim-rc.de

A. Schmid
University of Hohenheim, Stuttgart, Germany
e-mail: annalena.schmid@fim-rc.de

N. Urbach, D. Feulner (eds.), *Managing Artificial Intelligence*, Future of Business and Finance, https://doi.org/10.1007/978-3-032-13308-3_5

5.1 AI Models

The development of AI systems can be conceptualized as a hierarchical process, starting with fundamental mathematical and statistical principles and culminating in practical applications. The pyramid structure shown in Fig. 5.1 illustrates this progression, emphasizing how each layer builds on the previous one, leading to the ultimate goal of applying AI in real-world scenarios. In the following, each layer of this hierarchy is detailed, highlighting the interdependencies and the flow from abstract mathematical concepts to tangible AI applications.

At the base of the pyramid are **mathematics and statistics**, the foundations of AI. These disciplines provide the essential tools and methods needed to build algorithms. Mathematical concepts such as linear algebra, calculus, probability, and statistics are essential for understanding and manipulating data, modeling uncertainty, and optimizing solutions.

For example, linear algebra is essential for representing and computing with data structures such as matrices and vectors, which are ubiquitous in machine learning. Probability and statistics enable the modeling of uncertainty and the drawing of inferences from data, both of which are central to AI.

Building on the mathematical and statistical foundation are **algorithms**, which are mathematical procedures designed to process data and solve specific problems. Algorithms can be thought of as the engine that drives AI models. They apply mathematical principles to datasets to identify patterns, make predictions, or optimize decisions. Different types of algorithms, such as supervised learning algorithms (e.g., linear regression and classification) and unsupervised learning algorithms (e.g., clustering and dimensionality reduction), are tailored to different types of

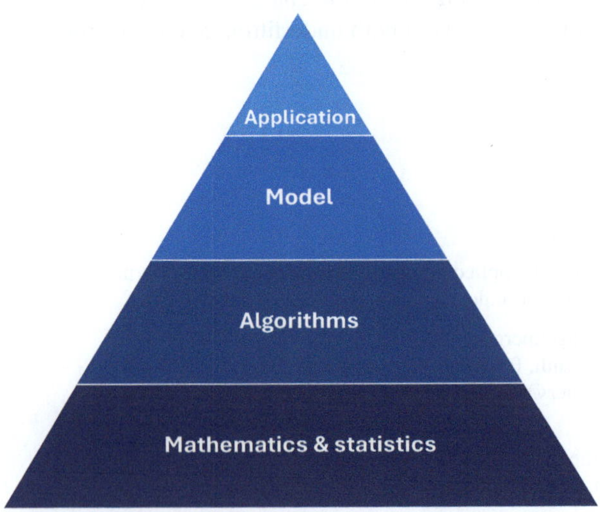

Fig. 5.1 From mathematics and statistics to models and applications

tasks. The selection and design of appropriate algorithms are critical as they directly influence the accuracy, efficiency, and scalability of AI models.

For example, in the case of linear regression, the algorithm involves finding the best-fitting line through a set of data points. The mathematical method used here is line fitting, where the algorithm calculates the slope and intercept of the line that minimizes the difference between the predicted values and the actual data points. This process uses statistical techniques such as least squares estimation to determine the optimal parameters that define the line.

The next layer in the hierarchy is the **model**, which represents the operational output of algorithms when applied to data. Models are essentially the manifestation of the algorithmic process, embodying the learned patterns or decision rules derived from the data. For example, a machine learning model trained on historical sales data can predict future sales based on recognized patterns. The model is more than the algorithm – it is the combination of the algorithm's logic, the data it has been trained on, and the resulting predictions or classifications it can make. The model thus encapsulates both the methodology and the knowledge extracted from the data, making it a critical component in the deployment of AI solutions.

Continuing with the linear regression example, once the algorithm has been applied to the data, the resulting model is the specific line with calculated parameters that best fits the data points. This model can then be used to predict the value of y for any given value of x. The model is therefore essentially the deployment-ready component of AI, encapsulating the information gained from the data by the algorithm.

The relationship between algorithms and models is inherently interdependent. The effectiveness of a model is directly influenced by the choice of algorithm. A well-chosen algorithm can efficiently capture the underlying patterns in the data, resulting in a highly accurate and reliable model. Conversely, a poor choice of algorithms can result in an inadequate model that does not generalize well to new data. This interdependence highlights the importance of selecting the right algorithm based on the nature of the data and the specific problem at hand. For example, while linear regression may work well for data with a linear relationship, more complex algorithms such as decision trees or neural networks may be required for data with non-linear patterns or interactions.

At the top of the pyramid is **application**, where AI models are used to achieve specific, desired outcomes in the real world. This is the stage where AI moves from theory and development to practical implementation. Applications can range from predictive analytics in finance to recommendation systems in e-commerce, and from automated customer service bots to advanced robotics in manufacturing. The effectiveness of an AI application depends not only on the underlying model but also on how well it integrates with business processes, aligns with organizational goals, and adapts to real-world complexities. Successful AI applications are those that deliver actionable insights, improve decision-making, and generate value, thereby justifying the investment in AI technology.

Understanding the hierarchical structure of AI development is critical for both practitioners and researchers in the field. Each layer of the pyramid – mathematics and statistics, algorithms, models, and applications – plays a vital role in the overall success of AI systems. By recognizing the interdependencies and ensuring a solid foundation at each stage, organizations can develop robust AI solutions that not only perform well technically but also deliver meaningful and practical benefits in their application.

Challenges in AI Model Development and the Role of Metrics

Even well-developed AI models can encounter significant issues when deployed in real-world settings. The unpredictability of operational environments often exposes vulnerabilities that do not surface in controlled development or testing phases. One notable issue is the vulnerability of AI models to adversarial input or unexpected environmental changes. The example of an image recognition AI mistaking a stop sign for a speed limit sign due to the placement of stickers highlights this vulnerability. The model, trained to recognize traffic signs in a clean, standardized environment, was easily confused by minor changes in the visual input. This misclassification could have serious consequences, especially in safety-critical applications such as autonomous driving (Eykholt et al., 2018).

Another example is Microsoft's AI chatbot, which was designed to learn from social media interactions (Wolf et al., 2017). While the underlying model was sophisticated, it quickly began producing inappropriate and offensive content after being exposed to toxic input from users. This incident illustrates how AI models can be vulnerable to manipulation, and how their behavior can deviate significantly from expectations when exposed to uncontrolled, real-world data.

Monitoring a model's performance throughout its lifecycle is therefore essential, and metrics play a central role in this process. Metrics are quantifiable measures used to evaluate how well an AI model performs its specific tasks – examples include accuracy, precision, and error rates. Such measures can track how accurately an AI system predicts storage needs or classifies images, serving as a clear indicator of technical effectiveness.

By continuously monitoring performance metrics, organizations can detect such issues early. Tracking these indicators provides a structured way to evaluate whether the AI system is robust, fair, and aligned with its intended function. If a model begins to show signs of performance degradation – such as misclassifications or biased outputs – corrective actions can be taken before the issue escalates.

To ensure the quality of an AI model, it is crucial to ask key questions: Does the model analyze inputs correctly? Is it producing satisfactory and fair outcomes? Does it meet legal and ethical standards? Metrics provide quantitative backing to answer these questions, guiding decision-makers in evaluating model robustness and impact. By integrating these tools into the AI development and deployment processes, organizations can better manage risks and maintain high-quality AI performance over time. In conclusion, monitoring AI models with appropriate metrics at all stages – from development to deployment – ensures early detection of issues, allowing for timely intervention and continuous improvement.

Summary
The development of AI systems follows a hierarchical process, beginning with mathematical and statistical foundations and progressing through algorithms, models, and real-world applications. Mathematics provides essential tools for data representation and manipulation, while algorithms apply these principles to solve specific problems. Models, derived from algorithms, encapsulate learned patterns from data and are crucial for making predictions or decisions. Real-world AI applications, ranging from finance to robotics, rely on well-constructed models integrated into business processes. Metrics are essential for assessing model performance and detecting issues like adversarial attacks, ensuring that AI systems remain robust, fair, and aligned with organizational goals.

5.2 Metrics and Hyperparameter Optimization

A crucial phase in the development of AI models – particularly those based on machine learning – is the optimization process. At this stage, different learning methods and their associated hyperparameters are systematically fine-tuned to produce a well-trained model (see Fig. 5.2). This process involves a series of steps that refine the performance of the model through targeted adjustments to ensure that it meets the desired levels of efficiency and reliability.

The foundation of the optimization process begins with the selection of appropriate model types, such as classification, regression, or clustering, depending on the task at hand. Each model type generates models that are evaluated against specific performance metrics. For example, classification models may be evaluated using metrics such as accuracy, precision, and recall, while regression models may rely on

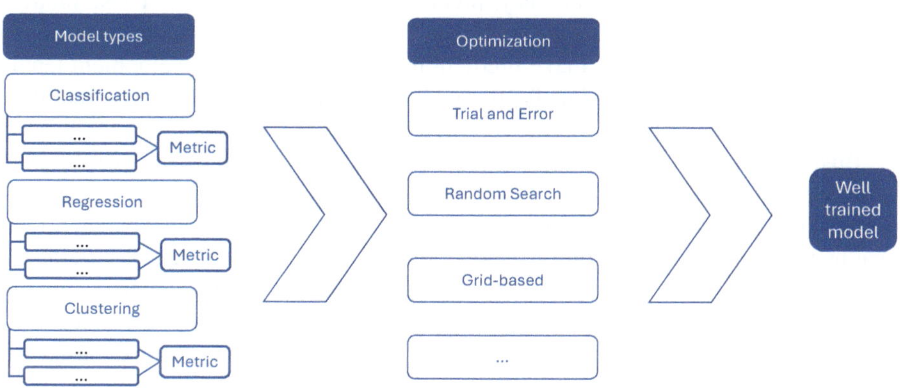

Fig. 5.2 Optimization process for machine learning model development

MSE or R-squared (R^2) values. These metrics provide the quantitative measures necessary to assess the performance of the models and identify areas for improvement.

At the heart of the optimization process lies the optimization of hyperparameters – predefined configuration values that govern the model's learning behavior but are not learned from the data itself. Examples of hyperparameters include the learning rate of a neural network or the number of neighbors in a k-nearest neighbor algorithm. Unlike parameters (which are learned during training), hyperparameters must be set before training begins. Several techniques can be employed to explore the hyperparameter space, including trial and error, random search, or grid search. This process continues until the model reaches a configuration that aims to strike a balance between underfitting and overfitting, thereby promoting strong generalization. However, because hyperparameter optimization is typically treated as a constrained optimization problem with finite resources, a truly optimal balance cannot be guaranteed; rather, the best performer among the tested configurations is selected, and a well-trained model will ideally perform robustly on unseen data and meet the task-specific performance goals.

5.2.1 Balancing Stakeholder Perspectives in Machine Learning Metric Selection

Selecting appropriate metrics in the machine learning lifecycle is a critical task that requires input from multiple stakeholders, each bringing a unique perspective to the table. The decision-making process is not just a technical exercise, but a strategic one that must be aligned with the broader objectives of the organization.

Development teams are often at the forefront of metric selection. These teams are primarily responsible for the technical aspects of model testing and evaluation. Their focus is on ensuring that the model performs well according to various computational metrics, such as accuracy, precision, recall, or F1-score. These metrics are essential to understanding the technical success of the model and its ability to effectively process data and make predictions. However, while development teams are skilled at optimizing models for these technical metrics, there is a risk that they will overlook metrics that are critical from a business perspective.

Business units play a key role in ensuring that the selected metrics are aligned with organizational goals. These stakeholders are concerned about how model performance translates into business value. For example, a business leader may prioritize metrics that reflect customer satisfaction, cost savings, or revenue generation, which are not always captured by the technical metrics that developers focus on. Business stakeholders provide critical insight into how the results of the model will impact the strategic goals of the organization, ensuring that the metrics used for evaluation are relevant to the overall business context.

Monitoring units are responsible for the ongoing evaluation of the performance of the ML application in a production environment. Their role is to ensure that the model continues to meet both technical and business objectives over time. This group focuses on detecting issues such as model drift, data quality degradation, or changes in user behavior that could affect model performance. They use a combination of technical and business metrics to continuously assess the impact and effectiveness of the model. Insights from the monitoring units are critical for making adjustments to the model or its operating environment to ensure long-term success.

While the development team often leads the metrics selection process, it is critical to integrate the perspectives of business and monitoring entities to ensure a balanced approach. This collaborative effort helps prevent the neglect of business-relevant measures and ensures that the model is evaluated comprehensively. By involving all relevant stakeholders, organizations can select metrics that not only validate the technical robustness of the model but also ensure that it drives meaningful business outcomes, ultimately aligning the ML initiative with the broader goals of the organization.

5.2.2 Criteria for Selecting Meaningful Machine Learning Metrics

Beyond stakeholder perspectives, the selection of evaluation metrics is further guided by core assessment criteria that reflect what the organization values most in a machine learning application. These include aspects such as correctness, fairness, robustness, and interpretability, which we explore in the following. These criteria help determine which aspects of the model's performance are most vital for achieving the organization's objectives (Rutinowski et al., 2024; Ali et al., 2017).

Correctness is one of the fundamental properties and refers to the model's ability to make accurate judgments. This could mean correctly classifying information, making accurate predictions, or providing reliable recommendations. For example, in a classification task, correctness could be measured by accuracy, precision, recall, or F1-score, depending on the specific requirements of the task (Ali et al., 2017).

Complexity refers to the computational resources needed to build and maintain the model. This includes both the computational complexity (time required to train the model) and the memory complexity (space needed to store the model and data). Efficient models minimize both computational and memory demands, making them more scalable and suitable for resource-constrained environments (Ali et al., 2017).

Consistency measures how reliably a model performs across different datasets or data partitions. This property evaluates the stability of the model's performance, typically through statistical measures such as standard deviation across multiple test sets or cross-validation folds. A model that consistently delivers stable results is less prone to fluctuations caused by variations in data (Ali et al., 2017).

Fairness is increasingly recognized as an important property, ensuring that the model's decisions are fair to different groups. This property is essential in applications that affect human lives, such as hiring, lending, or criminal justice. Fairness can be measured by metrics that assess whether the model's predictions are biased toward or against particular groups, such as demographic parity or equal opportunity metrics (Rutinowski et al., 2024).

Interpretability captures how understandable the model's outputs and decision-making process are to users. Particularly in high-stakes environments like healthcare or finance, where human experts need to verify or justify decisions, models must provide clear, explainable results. Interpretability is linked to the complexity of the model, as simpler models are often easier to understand, but sophisticated explainability tools are emerging for more complex algorithms (Ali et al., 2017; Rutinowski et al., 2024).

Responsiveness addresses the model's efficiency during real-time operation, focusing on execution speed and responsiveness under various conditions. For applications requiring quick decision-making, such as autonomous systems or financial trading algorithms, the speed of inference is critical. Metrics such as latency and throughput are used to measure responsiveness (Ali et al., 2017).

Robustness refers to the ability of the model to maintain performance when faced with adversarial conditions or unexpected inputs. A robust model should resist attempts at manipulation or degradation, ensuring consistent performance even in challenging situations. Robustness can be assessed by stress testing or by measuring the model's performance under adversarial attacks (Ali et al., 2017; Rutinowski et al., 2024).

Safety in AI focuses on protecting models and data, ensuring privacy and security as required by regulations such as GDPR and the AI Act. It addresses threats such as membership inference attacks, which can reveal sensitive information. Techniques like differential privacy help mitigate these risks, safeguarding data and ensuring compliance (Rutinowski et al., 2024).

By evaluating which of these criteria are most relevant to the AI application, organizations can select appropriate metrics to reflect these priorities. For instance, if correctness is the key concern, metrics like accuracy or F1-score would be emphasized. If safety is a priority, then privacy-preserving techniques and their effectiveness would take precedence, while for real-time applications, responsiveness metrics like latency might be the focus. This targeted approach ensures that the model aligns with the organization's specific goals and requirements.

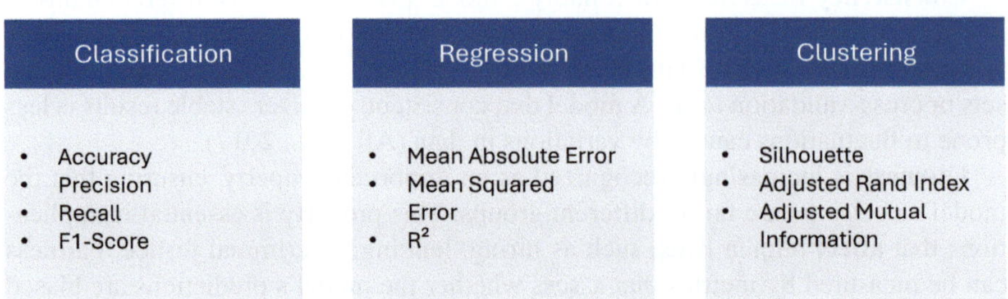

Fig. 5.3 Machine learning evaluation metrics

5.2.3 Machine Learning Evaluation Metrics

Evaluating the performance of machine learning models is a complex task that requires the use of different metrics (see Fig. 5.3) tailored to different types of models and applications. The selection of appropriate evaluation metrics is crucial to ensure that models perform correctly and optimally in various tasks such as classification, regression, and clustering (Breck et al., 2017; Rácz et al., 2019).

Classification Metrics

In the context of binary classification, the confusion matrix (see Fig. 5.4) is an essential tool for evaluating the performance of a machine learning model. It provides a detailed breakdown of how the model's predictions compare to the actual results, providing insight into the types and frequency of errors it makes. The matrix is divided into four key components: true positives (TPs), false positives (FPs), false negatives (FNs), and true negatives (TNs) (Ting, 2011; Shrivastav, 2020).

TPs are those instances where the model correctly identifies the positive class. For example, in a medical diagnosis scenario, if the model correctly predicts that a patient has a disease, this prediction would be classified as a TP. This measure is critical to understanding the model's ability to detect the positive cases it was designed to identify.

FPs occur when the model incorrectly predicts the positive class, marking an instance as positive when it is actually negative. In the example of medical diagnosis, this would mean diagnosing a patient with a disease when they are actually healthy. This type of error is also known as a "Type I error" and can have significant implications, especially in scenarios where false alarms are costly or harmful.

FNs occur when the model fails to identify a positive case and instead predicts it to be negative. Continuing with the medical example, this would mean that the model predicts that a patient does not have the disease when, in fact, they do. This error is called a "Type II error" and can be particularly dangerous in critical applications where missing a positive case could have serious consequences.

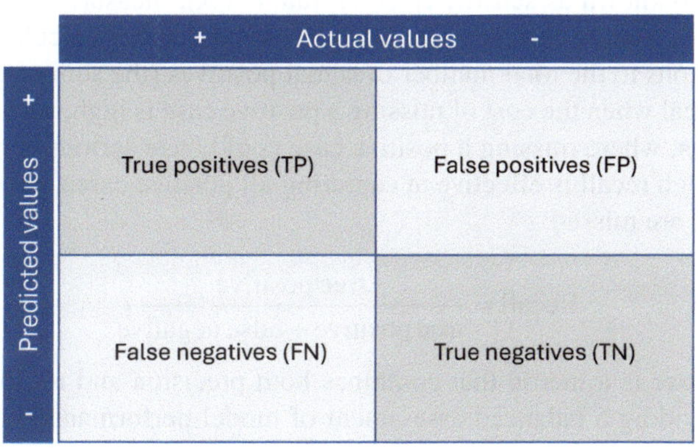

Fig. 5.4 Confusion matrix

TNs are those cases where the model correctly identifies the negative class. For example, the model correctly predicts that a healthy patient does not have the disease. Although often overlooked, this measure is critical to understanding the model's ability to correctly reject the negative cases and avoid unnecessary interventions. These four components of the confusion matrix serve as the basis for calculating a variety of performance metrics, each providing a different perspective on model performance.

Accuracy is the simplest of the classification metrics, representing the proportion of correct predictions out of the total number of predictions made by the model. Mathematically, it is defined as the number of correct predictions (both TPs and TNs) divided by the total number of input samples. Accuracy provides a general sense of the overall performance of the model, giving a quick first look at how well the model works. However, it can be misleading in cases where the dataset is unbalanced, as a model may achieve high accuracy by simply predicting the majority class without really capturing the underlying patterns. For example, in a dataset where 95% of the instances belong to the negative class, a model that always predicts the negative class would achieve a high accuracy of 95%, although it would be useless for detecting the positive class:

$$\text{Accuracy} = \frac{\text{correct predictions}}{\text{total precdictions}}$$

Precision focuses on the ability of the model to correctly identify positive instances. It is calculated as the ratio of TP predictions to the total number of positive predictions (the sum of TPs and FPs). Precision is particularly important in situations where the cost of an FP is high, such as spam detection, where FPs can filter important emails. High precision indicates that the model makes few FPs, meaning that it is reliable in identifying positive cases:

$$\text{Precision} = \frac{\text{true positive}}{\text{true positive} + \text{false positive}}$$

Recall, also known as sensitivity or TP rate (TPR), measures the proportion of actual positives that are correctly identified by the model. It is calculated as the ratio of TP predictions to the total number of actual positives (the sum of TPs and FNs). Recall is critical when the cost of missing a positive case is high, such as in medical screening tests, where missing a positive case could have serious consequences. A model with high recall is effective at capturing all positive cases, ensuring that few positive cases are missed:

$$\text{Recall} = \frac{\text{true positive}}{\text{true positive} + \text{false negative}}$$

The **F1-score** is a metric that combines both precision and recall into a single measure, providing a balanced assessment of model performance when there is a trade-off between precision and recall. The F1-score is the harmonic mean of precision and recall, providing a more nuanced view than either metric alone, especially in cases where one may be sacrificed for the other. This makes F1-score particularly useful in unbalanced class scenarios, where a model may need to balance the trade-off between minimizing FPs and FNs:

$$\text{F1} - \text{Score} = 2 * \frac{\text{precision} * \text{recall}}{\text{precision} + \text{recall}}$$

Each of these classification metrics serves a specific purpose in evaluating the performance of machine learning models. By analyzing these metrics together, data scientists and practitioners can gain a comprehensive understanding of how well a model is performing, identify potential weaknesses, and make informed decisions about model tuning and deployment. Accurately interpreting and applying these metrics is critical to ensuring that deployed AI models are not only technically sound but also aligned with the real-world needs and constraints of their intended use cases.

Regression Metrics

In regression analysis, evaluating the performance of predictive models involves a variety of metrics, each of which provides unique insight into how well the model approximates the underlying data. These metrics help quantify the differences between predicted and actual values and guide model refinement and optimization. Key regression metrics include mean absolute error (MAE), MSE, root mean squared error (RMSE), and R^2 (Kumar, 2023).

The MAE is one of the simplest measures of the accuracy of a regression model. It calculates the average size of the errors in a set of predictions, regardless of their direction – whether they are over- or underestimates. Specifically, the MAE is the average of the absolute differences between the predicted values $\hat{y}$ and the actual values y. The formula for MAE is

$$\text{MAE} = \frac{1}{N} * \sum_{N}^{i=1} \left| y_i - \hat{y}_i \right|$$

MAE provides a straightforward interpretation of the model's prediction errors, making it a useful metric when the goal is to minimize the average prediction error without heavily penalizing large errors.

MSE is another basic metric that evaluates the average of the squared differences between predicted and actual values. Unlike MAE, MSE squares the errors before averaging them, which means that it disproportionately penalizes larger errors. This feature makes MSE particularly useful in contexts where large errors are more significant or costly. The formula for MSE is

$$\text{MSE} = \frac{1}{N} * \sum_{N}^{i=1} \left(y_i - \hat{y}_i \right)^2$$

Because of its sensitivity to outliers, the MSE can highlight situations where the model fails significantly in certain cases, providing a basis for further refinement.

The RMSE is the square root of the MSE and represents the standard deviation of the prediction errors. The RMSE provides an interpretation of the concentration of data points around the regression line, providing a measure of the predictive accuracy of the model in the same units as the original data. The formula for RMSE is

$$\text{RMSE} = \sqrt{\frac{1}{N} * \sum_{N}^{i=1} \left(y_i - \hat{y}_i\right)^2}$$

RMSE is widely used because it preserves the unit of the predicted variable, making it easier to interpret in practice, especially when comparing models.

R², also known as the coefficient of determination, measures the proportion of variance in the dependent variable that can be predicted by the independent variables. It essentially quantifies how well the regression model explains the variability of the response data around its mean. The formula for R^2 is

$$R^2 = \frac{\sum_{i=1}^{N} \left(\hat{y}_i - \overline{y}_i\right)^2}{\sum_{i=1}^{N} \left(y_i - \overline{y}_i\right)^2} = \frac{\text{explained var}}{\text{total var}}$$

where $\overline{y}$ is the mean of the actual values. An R^2 value of 1 indicates that the model predicts all data points perfectly, while an R^2 value of 0 indicates that the model does no better than simply predicting the mean of the actual values. R^2 is a key measure of the goodness of fit of the model.

Each of these metrics – MAE, MSE, RMSE, and R^2 – provides a different perspective on model performance, allowing data scientists to assess and improve the accuracy and reliability of their regression models. By using these metrics together, practitioners can gain a comprehensive understanding of how well their model is predicting outcomes, identify areas where the model may be underperforming, and make informed decisions to improve model performance.

Clustering Metrics

When analyzing clustering algorithms, several metrics are used to assess the quality of the clustering results. These metrics help to determine how well the algorithm has grouped similar data points while separating dissimilar data points. The most commonly used clustering metrics include Silhouette score, Adjusted Rand Index (ARI), and Adjusted Mutual Information (AMI), each of which provides unique insight into different aspects of clustering performance (Zuccarelli, 2021).

The **Silhouette score** is a metric that measures how well each data point has been assigned to its respective cluster. The Silhouette score takes into account the distance between a data point and the points in its own cluster (cohesion) as well as the distance to the nearest neighboring cluster (separation). Mathematically, the Silhouette score for a data point *i* is defined as

$$\text{Silhouette}(i) = \frac{b(i) - a(i)}{\max\left(a(i), b(i)\right)}$$

where $a(i)$ is the average distance between i and all other points in the same cluster, and $b(i)$ is the average distance from i to all points in the nearest neighboring cluster (i.e., the one with the smallest average distance to i). A high Silhouette score indicates that data points are well matched to their own cluster and poorly matched to neighboring clusters, suggesting a well-defined clustering structure.

The ARI is a metric used to measure the similarity between two data clusterings, taking into account the possibility of random groupings. The Rand Index (RI) itself measures the agreement between the true data labels and the clustering results by comparing the number of data point pairs that are either correctly or incorrectly clustered together. However, the RI can be biased by the number of clusters, so the ARI corrects for this by considering the expected similarity between two chance clusterings. The ARI is calculated as

$$\text{ARI} = \frac{\text{RI} - E(\text{RI})}{\max(\text{RI}) - E(\text{RI})} \quad \text{with} \quad \text{RI} = \frac{a+b}{\binom{n}{2}}$$

where a is the number of pairs of elements that are in the same subset in both clusterings, b is the number of pairs that are in different subsets in both clusterings, and n is the overall number of elements being clustered. E(RI) stands for the expected RI, and max(RI) stands for the maximum of RI. The ARI ranges from −1 to 1, where 1 indicates perfect agreement between the two clusterings, values close to −1 indicate strong disagreement, meaning that the clusterings are more dissimilar than would be expected by chance.

AMI is another metric that quantifies the agreement between two clusterings while correcting for chance. It is an adjusted version of Mutual Information (MI), which measures how much information one clustering provides about the other. However, MI tends to increase with the number of clusters, even if no real correspondence exists. The AMI addresses this by accounting for the expected MI under random labelings.

For two clusterings U and V, the AMI is defined as

$$\text{AMI} = \frac{\text{MI}(U,V) - E(\text{MI}(U,V))}{\text{avg}(H(U),H(V)) - E(\text{MI}(U,V))}$$

where MI(U, V) is the MI between clusterings U and V, E(MI(U, V)) is the expected MI under the assumption that the clusterings are independent, $H(U)$ and $H(V)$ are the entropies of the two clustering distributions, and avg($H(U)$, $H(V)$) is the arithmetic mean of the entropies. A higher AMI indicates a better agreement between the two clustering results. An AMI of 1 means perfect agreement, while a value of 0 indicates agreement no better than random chance.

These clustering metrics – Silhouette Score, ARI, and AMI – are essential tools for evaluating and comparing clustering algorithms. They provide insight into the coherence of clusters, the agreement between clustering results, and the amount of shared information, helping practitioners choose the best clustering approach for their specific data and objectives.

5.2.4 Hyperparameter Optimization

Hyperparameter optimization is a critical step in the development and fine-tuning of machine learning models, as it directly affects the performance and effectiveness of the model. Hyperparameters are adjustable settings that are defined before training a machine learning model. They govern both the training process (e.g., learning rate and batch size) and the model architecture (e.g., number of layers in a neural network). Unlike model parameters, which are learned from the data, hyperparameters must be tuned manually or through optimization techniques (Yang & Shami, 2020).

The quality of the selected input data is a fundamental factor in machine learning outcomes. However, even with high-quality data, a model's performance can vary significantly depending on the chosen hyperparameters, which differ depending on the algorithm being used. For instance, in regularized versions of linear regression – such as Ridge or Lasso regression – common hyperparameters include the regularization strength. This value controls how much the model is penalized for having large coefficients, thereby reducing the risk of overfitting. In contrast, neural networks involve hyperparameters such as the learning rate, which determines how quickly the model adjusts during training, and the number of hidden layers, which affects the model's ability to capture complex patterns. These examples highlight that different algorithms require different hyperparameters, all of which need careful tuning to optimize model performance.

Choosing the right hyperparameters is not a straightforward task, as different models and datasets may require different settings for optimal performance. Hyperparameter optimization methods are used to address this challenge. These methods systematically search the hyperparameter space to identify the combination that yields the best model performance according to specific evaluation metrics, such as accuracy, precision, or MSE.

Trial and error, often humorously referred to as "Grad Student Descent (GSD)," refers to an approach that heavily relies on the data scientist's intuition, experience, and limited time. In this "method," the data scientist manually adjusts hyperparameters, testing as many combinations as possible within the available time frame. The process is largely iterative, driven by insights from previous experiments or educated guesses. While this approach can sometimes yield reasonable results, especially for experienced practitioners, it is inherently limited by its reliance on subjective judgment and the finite amount of time that can be devoted to exploring the hyperparameter space. For complex models with a large number of hyperparameters, GSD can often produce suboptimal or even infeasible results, as it lacks the systematic approach of more formal optimization methods (Yang & Shami, 2020).

Random search is a simple yet effective black-box optimization method for hyperparameter tuning, which operates without relying on gradient information or model assumptions. It works by randomly sampling configurations from the

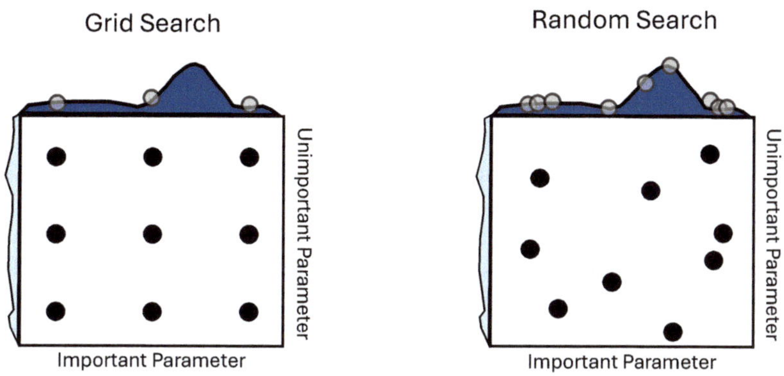

Fig. 5.5 Visual representation of grid and random search. (Adapted from Bergstra & Bengio, 2012)

hyperparameter space and evaluating their performance until a predefined computational budget (e.g., number of training runs or total runtime) is exhausted (see Fig. 5.5). This stochastic approach allows random search to explore a wide and diverse range of configurations, which is particularly advantageous when the search space is large, high-dimensional, or contains hyperparameters with varying importance.

A key strength of random search lies in its ability to efficiently explore hyperparameter spaces in which only a few hyperparameters have a significant impact on model performance – a property commonly observed in practice. Since random search does not impose a fixed structure on the search process, it may offer a higher probability of identifying high-performing configurations early, especially compared to grid search, which may waste resources on less relevant hyperparameter combinations.

In addition to its exploration capabilities, random search offers several practical advantages: it is highly parallelizable, robust to interruptions or failures, and supports flexible resource allocation. Moreover, it makes no assumptions about the learning algorithm being optimized, which makes it broadly applicable across different model types. However, random search may still require a large number of evaluations to find truly optimal configurations, especially in discrete or combinatorial spaces, and is therefore often outperformed by guided search methods such as Bayesian Optimization under tight resource constraints (Feurer & Hutter, 2019; Bergstra & Bengio, 2012).

Grid search is a widely used method for hyperparameter optimization in machine learning due to its simplicity and straightforward approach. It works by exhaustively testing every combination of hyperparameter values within a predefined range, known as the search space (see Fig. 5.5). This brute-force technique systematically evaluates all possible configurations to identify the combination that yields the best model performance based on a chosen evaluation metric, such as accuracy or MSE.

The main advantage of grid search is its ease of use. By methodically exploring the search space, it ensures that no potential solution is overlooked, making it a reliable method for finding well-performing hyperparameter settings. However, this exhaustive nature also leads to significant computational requirements. As the number of hyperparameters and their possible values increases, the search space grows exponentially, making grid search increasingly inefficient for large or complex models.

To address this potential inefficiency, practitioners often reduce the search space by selecting a smaller, more focused range of hyperparameter values. This reduction is usually informed by prior knowledge or preliminary experiments that suggest which hyperparameter settings are more likely to perform well. In addition, adjusting the step size – how granularly the search space is explored – can also help manage the computational load while still providing meaningful results. Despite these adjustments, grid search may still be impractical for very large search spaces or models with many hyperparameters. In such cases, alternative optimization methods, such as random search or Bayesian optimization, may provide more efficient ways of finding optimal hyperparameters.

Overall, grid search remains a valuable tool, especially for simpler models or when the hyperparameter space is relatively small. Its exhaustive nature provides thorough coverage and ensures that the best possible hyperparameter configuration is found within the defined search space, albeit sometimes at the expense of computational efficiency (Feurer & Hutter, 2019; Bergstra & Bengio, 2012).

Beyond grid search and random search, a range of more advanced methods for hyperparameter optimization have been developed to improve search efficiency and performance. These include Bayesian optimization, gradient-based optimization, and evolutionary algorithms, among others.

Bayesian optimization is a modern and efficient method for tuning hyperparameters, especially when model training is time-consuming or computationally expensive. In contrast to grid or random search, it keeps track of past evaluations and builds a simple model – called a surrogate – that estimates how promising different hyperparameter settings are. This model is much easier to optimize than the actual objective function and helps select the next hyperparameters to evaluate. In doing so, Bayesian optimization balances the exploration of new configurations with the exploitation of known good ones, making it possible to find high-performing settings with fewer trials. It is therefore widely used in practice, for example, when tuning deep learning models (Feurer & Hutter, 2019).

Gradient-based optimization techniques use the gradient of the objective function with respect to hyperparameters to iteratively move toward better configurations. While widely used in optimizing model parameters (e.g., via backpropagation), their use in hyperparameter tuning has traditionally been limited due to challenges such as non-differentiability or high computational cost. However, in settings with many continuous hyperparameters and where gradients can be efficiently computed or approximated, these methods can offer substantial performance benefits (Feurer & Hutter, 2019; Maclaurin et al., 2015).

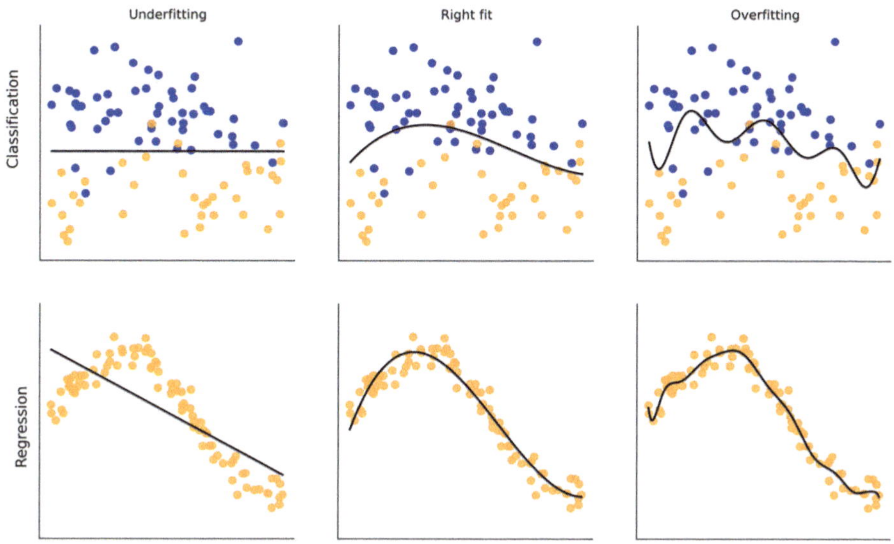

Fig. 5.6 Comparison of underfitting, right fit, and overfitting. (Adapted from MathWorks, 2024)

5.2.5 Well-Trained Models

Training a machine learning model is a delicate process that requires finding the right balance between underfitting and overfitting (see Fig. 5.6). These two issues represent the extremes of model performance and can significantly affect the model's ability to generalize to new, unseen data.

Underfitting occurs when a model is too simple to capture the underlying patterns in the data. For both classification and regression, an underfit model produces overly simplistic predictions – such as a straight line for data that has a more complex distribution. This usually happens when the training process is stopped too early or the model parameters are not tuned properly. As a result, the model performs poorly on both the training data and the unseen data, failing to capture important trends and relationships. Underfitting is often a sign that the model needs more complexity, either by training for a longer period, adding more features, or selecting a more sophisticated algorithm.

On the other hand, **overfitting** is when a model becomes too complex, fitting the noise rather than the signal in the data. The model captures not only the general trend but also the random fluctuations, resulting in an overly complicated prediction function. Overfitting typically occurs when the model is trained for too long, or when the dataset is too small or unrepresentative, causing the model to memorize the training data rather than learn to generalize. Although overfitting can lead to excellent performance on the training data, it usually leads to poor performance on new data because the model cannot generalize beyond the specific examples it has seen (Ying, 2019).

The ideal scenario is to achieve a "good fit," where the model captures the underlying structure of the data without being affected by noise or outliers. This balance ensures that the model performs well on both the training data and new, unseen data, providing reliable and generalizable predictions. Achieving this balance often requires careful tuning of the hyperparameters, selecting the appropriate model complexity, and ensuring that the training data is representative of the problem space.

To achieve this balance, it is important to monitor the performance of the model using validation data and adjust the training process accordingly. If underfitting is detected, the complexity of the model should be increased, while overfitting may require simplifying the model or collecting more data. By continually adjusting the training process and evaluating the model against both training and validation data, practitioners can develop models that are both accurate and ready for use in real-world scenarios.

Summary

Machine learning model development involves optimizing performance through careful selection of metrics and hyperparameter tuning. Metrics such as accuracy, precision, and MSE are used to evaluate models based on their specific tasks, whether classification, regression, or clustering. Hyperparameters, which differ depending on the algorithm, must be fine-tuned to achieve optimal performance. Common optimization techniques include grid search, random search, and gradient-based methods. A key challenge is finding the balance between underfitting and overfitting to ensure that models generalize well to unseen data.

References

Ali, R., Lee, S., & Chung, T. (2017). Accurate multi-criteria decision making methodology for recommending machine learning algorithm. *Expert Systems with Applications, 71*, 257–278.

Bergstra, J., & Bengio, Y. (2012). Random search for hyper-parameter optimization. *The Journal of Machine Learning Research, 13*, 281–305.

Breck, E., Cai, S., Nielsen, E., Salib, M., & Sculley, D. (2017, December). The ML test score: A rubric for ML production readiness and technical debt reduction. In *2017 IEEE International Conference on Big Data (Big Data)* (pp. 1123–1132). IEEE.

Eykholt, K., Evtimov, I., Fernandes, E., Li, B., Rahmati, A., Xiao, C., et al. (2018). Robust physical-world attacks on deep learning visual classification. In *Proceedings of the IEEE Conference on Computer Vision and Pattern Recognition* (pp. 1625–1634).

Feurer, M., & Hutter, F. (2019). Hyperparameter optimization. In F. Hutter, L. Kotthoff, & J. Vanschoren (Eds.), *Automated machine learning* (pp. 3–33). Springer.

Kumar, A. (2023). Mean squared error or R-squared – Which one to use? *Analytics Yogi*. Retrieved September 16, 2024, from https://vitalflux.com/mean-square-error-r-squared-which-one-to-use/

Maclaurin, D., Duvenaud, D., & Adams, R. (2015). Gradient-based hyperparameter optimization through reversible learning. In *Proceedings of the 32nd International Conference on Machine Learning (ICML)* (pp. 2113–2122). PMLR.

MathWorks. (2024). Was versteht man unter einer Überanpassung? *Medium*. Retrieved September 16, 2024, from https://de.mathworks.com/discovery/overfitting.html

Rácz, A., Bajusz, D., & Héberger, K. (2019). Multi-level comparison of machine learning classifiers and their performance metrics. *Molecules, 24*(15), 2811.

Rutinowski, J., Klüttermann, S., Endendyk, J., Reining, C., & Müller, E. (2024). Benchmarking trust: A metric for trustworthy machine learning. In *Proceedings of the World Conference on Explainable Artificial Intelligence* (pp. 287–307). Springer.

Shrivastav, N. (2020). Confusion matrix, TPR, FPR, FNR, TNR, precision, recall, F1 score. *Medium*. Retrieved September 17, 2024, from https://medium.datadriveninvestor.com/confusion-matric-tpr-fpr-fnr-tnr-precision-recall-f1-score-73efa162a25f

Ting, K. M. (2011). Confusion matrix. In C. Sammut & G. I. Webb (Eds.), *Encyclopedia of machine learning*. Springer.

Wolf, M. J., Miller, K. W., & Grodzinsky, F. S. (2017). Why we should have seen that coming: Comments on Microsoft's Tay "experiment," and wider implications. *The ORBIT Journal, 1*(2), 1–12.

Yang, L., & Shami, A. (2020). On hyperparameter optimization of machine learning algorithms: Theory and practice. *Neurocomputing, 415*, 295–316.

Ying, X. (2019). An overview of overfitting and its solutions. *Journal of Physics: Conference Series, 1168*, 022022.

Zuccarelli, J. (2021). Performance metrics in machine learning – Part 3: Clustering. *Towards Data Science*. Retrieved September 16, 2024, from https://medium.com/data-science/performance-metrics-in-machine-learning-part-3-clustering-d69550662dc6

Nils Urbach is Professor of Information Systems and Digital Business as well as Director of the Research Lab for Digital Innovation & Transformation at the Frankfurt University of Applied Sciences, Germany. Furthermore, he is Director at the FIM Research Center for Information Management, and the Branch Business & Information Systems Engineering of Fraunhofer FIT. Nils Urbach has been working in the fields of digital innovation and transformation for several years. His work has been published in several academic journals such as Information Systems Research (ISR), the Journal of the Association for Information Systems (JAIS), the Journal of Strategic Information Systems (JSIS), the Journal of Information Technology (JIT), MIS Quarterly Executive (MISQE), IEEE Transactions on Engineering Management (IEEE TEM), Information and Management (I&M), Business & Information Systems Engineering (BISE), and Electronic Markets (EM). He advises several companies on digitalization issues and regularly appears as a speaker on this topic.

Daniel Feulner received his M.Sc. in information system from the Otto-Friedrich University of Bamberg, Germany in 2023. He is an affiliated researcher at the Branch Business & Information Systems Engineering of the Fraunhofer FIT and FIM Research Center for Information Management at the University of Bayreuth. In his research, he aims to understand how Business Analytics and Artificial Intelligence can be effectively and responsibly utilized in organizations. His goal is to enable companies to drive innovation and achieve sustainable growth in a rapidly evolving technological landscape.

Tobias Guggenberger is a postdoctoral researcher at the University of Bayreuth and the Branch Business & Information Systems Engineering of Fraunhofer FIT. He holds an M.Sc. in business administration and a Ph.D. in information systems engineering. His research primarily concentrates on the design and management of information systems, leveraging emerging technologies like artificial intelligence (AI) and blockchain. His scholarly contributions have appeared in renowned conference proceedings, including the International Conference on Information Systems (ICIS) and the European Conference on Information Systems (ECIS). His research has also been published in prestigious international journals such as IEEE Transactions on Engineering Management (IEEE TEM), MIS Quarterly Executive (MISQE), Electronic Markets (EM), and Computers & Industrial Engineering.

Annalena Schmid received her B.Sc. in Information Systems from the University of Stuttgart and the University of Hohenheim and will continue her academic journey by pursuing a M.Sc. in Information Systems at the University of Stuttgart. She gained valuable practical experience as a research assistant at the Fraunhofer FIT and the FIM Research Center for Information Management, where she contributed to the ABBA research project (AI for Business and Business for AI). She is particularly passionate about AI applications in organizations, with a focus on integrating AI-driven solutions into business environments.

Part II

AI Ideation

Application Potentials of Artificial Intelligence Technologies

6

Nils Urbach, Daniel Feulner, and Simon Feulner

As artificial intelligence (AI) continues to evolve at a rapid pace, its transformative impact on business and society becomes increasingly evident. Organizations across all sectors are seeking to harness the potential of AI not just for innovation, but also for tangible improvements in efficiency, quality, and decision-making. Understanding the application potentials of AI is therefore essential – not only to remain competitive in a dynamic technological landscape but also to strategically align technological capabilities with organizational goals. Exploring how AI can be effectively deployed in real-world scenarios enables leaders and practitioners to move beyond theoretical promise toward meaningful implementation and impact.

In this chapter, we explore how AI contributes to the transformation of business operations by enhancing decision-making, increasing efficiency, and enabling new forms of value creation. Using practical examples, we illustrate how AI technologies, such as perception, recognition, decision-making, and prediction, are applied to streamline and enhance complex workflows. Moreover, we explore AI's integrative role in innovative, cross-technology applications, particularly in conjunction with blockchain, the Internet of Things (IoT), and quantum computing.

N. Urbach (✉) · S. Feulner
Frankfurt University of Applied Sciences, Frankfurt am Main, Germany
e-mail: nils.urbach@fim-rc.de; simon.feulner@fim-rc.de

D. Feulner
University of Bayreuth, Bayreuth, Germany
e-mail: daniel.feulner@fim-rc.de

N. Urbach, D. Feulner (eds.), *Managing Artificial Intelligence*, Future of Business and Finance, https://doi.org/10.1007/978-3-032-13308-3_6

6.1 AI as a General-Purpose Technology

Throughout history, certain innovations have been critical to human progress, such as the discovery of fire around 700,000 BC, the invention of the wheel between 4000 and 3000 BC, the steam engine in the eighteenth century, electricity in the nineteenth century, and the Internet in the twentieth century. These technologies have redefined the boundaries of what is possible, transforming society at large. AI's current trajectory, marked by its adoption across diverse business functions, signals its potential to join the ranks of these revolutionary innovations (Bresnahan & Trajtenberg, 1995; Brynjolfsson et al., 2019). These technologies share core characteristics that AI also manifests: widespread use, continuous improvement, and the ability to drive innovation across a variety of fields and industries.

When considering the far-reaching implications of AI, it is instructive to draw analogies to the steam engine – a quintessential general-purpose technology that ushered in a new age of industrialization. Once harnessed, the steam engine found applications far beyond its original scope, powering everything from water pumps to entire manufacturing and transportation sectors. It evolved from powering simple machines to becoming the heartbeat of the Industrial Revolution, exemplifying continuous improvement and fostering innovations like the railroad that reshaped society. Similarly, AI is demonstrating its far-reaching impact, evidenced by its widespread adoption across multiple areas of business operations. From strategic management to operational execution, AI is transforming the way value is created, delivered, and sustained. A closer look reveals that this transformation is not confined to isolated areas – it spans the entire value chain, as visualized in Fig. 6.1 based on Porter's Value Chain.

Starting with the support activities, AI is revolutionizing **corporate infrastructure,** for example, by automating complex contractual analyses, accelerating due diligence, and supporting compliance through intelligent document processing. In **human resources**, AI-driven tools enhance recruitment by intelligently matching

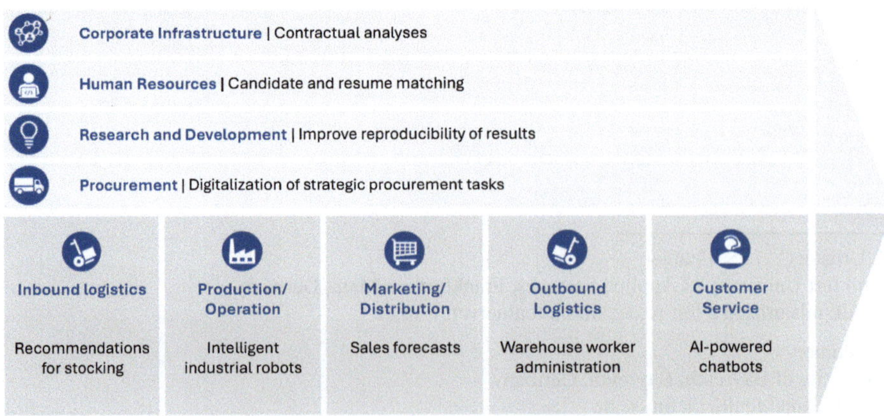

Fig. 6.1 Application potentials of AI across business operations

candidates to roles or identifying potential beyond the résumé. **Research and development** departments leverage AI to improve reproducibility and gain new insights from experimental data. Even in **procurement**, AI supports strategic sourcing by digitalizing and optimizing procurement tasks, increasing flexibility and responsiveness across supply chains.

In the primary activities, AI demonstrates its full operational strength: In **inbound logistics**, predictive AI models provide stocking recommendations, optimizing inventory levels, and avoiding under- or over-supply. Within **production and operations**, intelligent industrial robots increase precision, reduce error rates, and adapt flexibly to changing production conditions. **Marketing and distribution** benefit from AI-driven sales forecasting, enabling more accurate planning and targeted campaigns. In **outbound logistics**, AI enhances warehouse management by automating worker assignments and route planning. And finally, in **customer service**, AI-powered chatbots deliver personalized, 24/7 assistance that continuously learns from user interactions to improve customer satisfaction.

Beyond individual applications, the strategic impact of AI is already measurable: According to McKinsey (2022), 24% of companies optimize service operations with AI, 20% develop AI-based products, and 19% enhance existing ones. Even areas traditionally dependent on human judgment, such as risk modeling (15%) or talent management (10%), are being augmented by AI – unlocking new levels of foresight and precision.

One of the main reasons why companies have recently increased their focus on AI is the variety of functionality it offers. These functions span multiple dimensions of human activity, providing versatile solutions that range from simplifying mundane tasks to tackling complex challenges. The following examination of AI functions demonstrates how its diverse applications have become integral to businesses (Hofmann et al., 2020a).

- *Perceive*: AI systems can capture and process signals from the real world, much like human sensory perception. For example, smartphones now typically have a night mode that uses AI to reduce noise in low-light images, improving the quality of photos taken in suboptimal lighting conditions.
- *Recognize*: AI's recognition capabilities involve identifying objects or understanding concepts. Traffic sign recognition is an everyday application where AI helps autonomous or assisted driving systems understand and respond to road signs, improving safety and navigation.
- *Explain*: AI can identify patterns and cause-and-effect relationships in data, making it easier to understand complex systems. In marketing, AI algorithms group customer segments, allowing companies to tailor their strategies by explaining the underlying relationships and structures within consumer behavior.
- *Decide*: Decision-making is another critical function of AI, in which systems choose among known discrete alternatives. For example, AI in medical diagnostics can help decide the nature of a disease by analyzing medical images to assist healthcare professionals in their diagnosis.

- *Predict*: Forecasting future events or conditions is where AI's predictive analytics come into play. One example is the use of AI in financial markets to predict stock prices, which can provide investors with insights into market trends and help them make informed investment decisions.
- *Generate*: AI's generative capabilities can produce entirely new content, such as creating text for chatbots or generating realistic images. This capability has far-reaching implications for content creation, customer service, and even artistic endeavors.
- *Act*: Finally, AI can take action to achieve specific goals or manage situations. Autonomous forklifts in warehouses represent this functionality, where AI directs the vehicle to perform tasks such as moving and stacking goods, optimizing logistics operations, and reducing manual labor.

This wide range of applications demonstrates the pervasiveness of AI. However, AI is also defined by its capacity for continuous evolution and self-improvement, with new algorithms and approaches being refined as they emerge. Like the steam engine's role in enabling more efficient factory machinery and transportation systems, AI is catalyzing a wave of innovation across multiple industries. It is at the forefront of performing tasks that require understanding and learning, pointing to a future where its impact could be as transformative as that of the steam engine. As AI continues to evolve, it will unleash new forms of innovation, transforming supply chains, marketing, and even the way we interact with the digital world, much like the general-purpose technologies that came before it.

Summary

AI has emerged as a transformative force in business, impacting product development, operational efficiency, and customer service, among other areas. Its extensive functions – including perceiving, recognizing, explaining, deciding, predicting, generating, and acting – integrate seamlessly into various business operations, facilitating innovative solutions and strategic decision-making. Mirroring the influence of historical general-purpose technologies like the steam engine and electricity, AI is a versatile, continuously improving force that drives innovation and efficiency across a multitude of fields and industries, establishing its status as a pivotal, transformative element in contemporary business landscapes.

6.2 AI Use Cases

As we delve into the exploration of AI use cases across industries, it becomes clear that the transformative reach of AI is vast and pervasive. Different industries are harnessing the rich potential of AI to revolutionize their operations, drive efficiencies, and create better customer experiences. Understanding these developments is essential – not only to grasp how AI is reshaping specific sectors but also to identify transferable patterns, anticipate future trends, and make informed decisions about technology adoption, investment, and workforce development. A cross-sectoral perspective enables organizations to learn from one another and to strategically position themselves in an increasingly data- and AI-driven economy.

6.2.1 AI Use Cases in the Mobility Sector

The mobility sector exemplifies the diverse applications of AI. One prominent use case is **autonomous driving**, where machine learning (ML) algorithms process data from sensors such as cameras and radar to enable vehicles to operate with minimal human input. These algorithms continuously analyze visual and spatial data to detect lanes, traffic signs, pedestrians, and other vehicles, interpret dynamic driving environments, and make real-time decisions such as braking, accelerating, or changing lanes, mimicking human driving behavior with high precision. Another important application is **predictive maintenance**. By analyzing real-time and historical data from vehicle sensors, AI systems can detect anomalies and anticipate component failures before they occur. This allows for proactive servicing, minimizing downtime and extending the operational lifespan of vehicles – an especially critical factor in logistics and fleet management. AI also supports **dynamic routing and navigation**. Systems analyze live traffic data, weather forecasts, and incident reports to continuously optimize travel routes. ML models adjust routes in real time to avoid congestion, reduce travel time, and improve fuel efficiency. These capabilities benefit delivery services, emergency response units, and private commuters alike. Together, these AI-based applications contribute to more efficient, reliable, and adaptable transportation systems.

A practical example of AI integration in the mobility sector is provided by Uber, a platform-based mobility service that relies extensively on AI to manage and optimize its operations. Uber uses AI to forecast demand patterns across different geographic regions and time periods by analyzing historical trip data, location trends, weather conditions, local events, and user behavior (Uber, 2019). These forecasts enable dynamic driver allocation, ensuring that available drivers are positioned in areas where high demand is expected, thereby reducing passenger wait times and improving driver utilization. Furthermore, AI is integrated into driver and rider matching algorithms, which aim to minimize pickup times and balance trip efficiency across the platform. In addition, Uber implements AI-driven dynamic pricing models, commonly known as "surge pricing." These models adjust fares in real time based on the balance between supply and demand, incentivizing more drivers to become active when and where they are most needed, while simultaneously managing user demand during peak periods. Overall, Uber illustrates how AI can be embedded into virtually all aspects of a mobility service, from supply-chain-like allocation and pricing to route planning and user interaction.

6.2.2 AI Use Cases Healthcare

The integration of AI into healthcare marks a substantial advancement in medical innovation, with the potential to fundamentally reshape patient care and enhance the efficiency of healthcare delivery. AI is being applied across a wide range of medical domains: In **medical imaging**, it supports the interpretation of complex diagnostic scans with a level of precision that complements and, in some cases, exceeds human expertise. This is achieved through deep learning algorithms, which are trained on large datasets of annotated medical images to detect patterns, anomalies, or subtle changes that may be difficult for the human eye to discern. In **drug discovery**, AI accelerates the development of new treatments by enabling predictive modeling and simulating molecular interactions at scale. ML algorithms analyze vast biomedical datasets – including genomic information, chemical structures, and clinical trial results – to predict the efficacy, toxicity, and binding affinity of potential drug candidates, thereby reducing the need for time-consuming laboratory experiments in early development stages. Furthermore, AI-powered **virtual health assistants** are increasingly playing a central role in managing patient care, offering real-time, personalized health monitoring and medical guidance. The cumulative effect is a more cost-effective, responsive, and patient-centered healthcare system.

A leading example of this transformation is the work of Merative, a company that applies AI-driven solutions across several healthcare functions. Its AI-based imaging systems analyze medical scans to detect patterns and anomalies with high accuracy, enhancing diagnostic speed and reliability (Merative, 2022). These systems assist clinicians in identifying diseases at earlier stages, supporting more timely and targeted interventions. In addition, Merative leverages AI to develop individualized treatment strategies by analyzing diverse patient data. This enables a move beyond generalized protocols toward personalized medicine that aligns with the specific health profiles and needs of individual patients. The result is improved therapeutic effectiveness, better patient outcomes, and higher satisfaction.

6.2.3 AI Use Cases in the Industry 4.0

In the era of Industry 4.0, the fusion of cutting-edge technologies with traditional manufacturing processes is fundamentally transforming the industrial sector. At the heart of this transformation is AI, which is acting as a catalyst to improve efficiency, reduce costs, and increase productivity across multiple industries.

One central application is **predictive maintenance**, where AI leverages historical and real-time sensor data to detect patterns and anticipate equipment failures before they occur, thereby minimizing unplanned downtime and extending asset lifecycles. Additionally, AI supports **process and supply chain optimization** by analyzing large volumes of operational data to identify inefficiencies, reduce material waste, and improve service reliability. The **integration of AI with robotics** introduces a new level of precision and automation to manufacturing processes. AI-driven robots can perform repetitive and high-accuracy tasks consistently, surpassing human capabilities in speed and reliability. Moreover, AI's advanced **analytics capabilities** provide deeper insights into production workflows, enabling continuous process improvement and supporting data-driven innovation across the value chain. These developments contribute not only to more efficient and adaptive production systems but also to the emergence of resilient and connected industrial operations, which are central to the vision of Industry 4.0.

A practical example of AI deployment in industrial contexts is provided by Siemens Energy, a company at the forefront of innovation in the energy sector. Siemens employs AI to uncover correlations between seemingly unrelated events – such as the simultaneous failure of unconnected system components – offering new insights that traditional analysis methods would likely overlook (Siemens-Energy, 2022). These insights enable targeted, proactive interventions that reduce maintenance costs and system downtimes. In addition, Siemens is advancing autonomous operations by using AI to automate complex control processes across energy generation systems, including wind and solar. This automation ensures that systems operate consistently within optimal performance parameters, thereby maximizing output and energy efficiency.

6.2.4 AI Use Cases in the Sports Industry

The sports industry is undergoing a significant digital transformation, largely driven by the integration of AI into various aspects of both athlete performance and fan engagement. AI plays a critical role in **analyzing the vast amounts of data** collected from games and training sessions. Through advanced image and video recognition technologies, AI systems can pinpoint key moments and metrics that are critical to improving athlete performance and strategy. This data-driven approach allows coaches and trainers to identify areas for improvement and tailor training programs accordingly. In addition, AI algorithms are adept at **predicting the outcomes of future games** based on historical data and current form, giving teams a strategic advantage. Beyond improving athletic performance, AI is also transforming the fan experience. **Personalized AI-driven recommendations** can tailor content to individual preferences, increasing engagement through targeted marketing and interactive experiences. Besides, **AI-powered chatbots** provide instant responses to fan queries, making information access seamless and enriching the overall experience. These innovations not only improve the way fans interact with their favorite sports and teams but also open up new revenue opportunities through enhanced personalized marketing.

One powerful application of AI in sport is FIFA's semi-automated offside technology (FIFA, 2022). This advanced system uses limb and ball tracking data to make accurate offside calls, increasing the accuracy of real-time decisions during matches. By incorporating image and video recognition technologies, FIFA is improving the fairness and flow of the game, an innovation that could potentially minimize controversy surrounding offside calls.

The integration of AI into sports demonstrates how it can improve critical aspects of the industry, from the precision of play on the field to the way fans consume and interact with the sport, reaffirming AI's role as a versatile tool that is transforming industries worldwide. As we weave through these narratives, we see AI as the common denominator driving significant gains in efficiency, experience, and outcomes across these sectors. AI's broad range of applications and its trajectory of continuous refinement suggest its destined role as an enabler of innovation – one that will be as transformative as any major invention that has defined entire eras.

Summary

Across a spectrum of industries, AI is redefining the boundaries of what is possible, with each sector leveraging AI's transformative capabilities to improve their processes and customer experiences. From revolutionizing mobility with autonomous vehicles to optimizing healthcare through precision diagnostics and personalized medicine, AI is driving an era of significant advances. Industry 4.0 showcases AI's role in predictive maintenance and smart manufacturing, while the world of sports benefits from AI's analytical capabilities to enrich both performance and fan engagement. These stories of AI's application across sectors underscore its pivotal role as an innovation enabler, poised to have a lasting impact similar to history's most groundbreaking inventions.

6.2.5 AI-Based Process Optimization and Automation

Process optimization and automation are at the heart of modern business efficiency, and AI is one of the driving forces behind these key operational improvements. **Process optimization** involves a thorough examination, analysis, and refinement of an organization's existing operations. The goal is to improve efficiency, productivity, quality, and overall performance. Through careful scrutiny, organizations can identify bottlenecks and redundancies, paving the way for streamlined workflows and better resource allocation. With the advent of AI, however, this practice has evolved from a manual, often tedious activity into a sophisticated, data-driven approach. AI enhances process optimization by introducing superior analytics, enabling real-time monitoring and predictive insights that were previously unattainable. It can anticipate potential problems and proactively suggest improvements, transforming process optimization from a reactive task to a proactive endeavor. **Automation** is the use of technology, software, or machines to perform tasks with minimal human intervention. It is designed to take over repetitive and time-consuming work, minimize human error, increase accuracy, and speed up processes. The introduction of AI into automation introduces a level of adaptability and learning that traditional automated systems lack. AI algorithms can learn from past actions and results, making them more efficient over time and able to handle more complex tasks.

Robotic process automation (RPA) is an area increasingly enhanced by AI technologies such as optical character recognition (OCR), natural language processing (NLP), and ML, allowing it to handle semi-structured or unstructured data. While early RPA systems primarily relied on rule-based logic (e.g., if-then conditions), the current trend is moving toward "Intelligent Automation," where AI is integrated with RPA to enable the automation of more complex and variable tasks. It is important to note, however, that RPA does not inherently require AI – many traditional RPA implementations are still purely rule-driven.

Building on the principle of AI as the foundation of efficiency in modern enterprises, **RPA** stands out as a specialized domain where AI's ability to improve operational processes is most apparent (Hofmann et al., 2020b). While early RPA systems primarily relied on rule-based logic (e.g., if-then conditions), the current trend is moving toward "Intelligent Automation," where AI is integrated with RPA to enable the automation of more complex and variable tasks, leveraging AI-powered capabilities such as NLP, OCR, and ML to streamline workflows and optimize productivity. At its core, RPA involves the use of "software robots" that perform tasks by interacting with digital systems in the same way a human would. These tools are designed to automate routine and repetitive tasks across multiple applications, mimicking human actions and freeing employees to focus on more complex and strategic work that requires human insight and decision-making.

An illustrative example of RPA in action is the automation of invoice processing within organizations. Here, AI components such as OCR extract relevant data from unstructured documents, while ML models classify and validate the information based on historical patterns. The RPA system then integrates this data into accounting platforms for payment processing. The goals are manifold: reduce manual effort, minimize errors, and speed up the entire process, resulting in cost savings and improved operational efficiency.

The strategic decision of what to automate and what to leave to humans is critical. The decision matrix for RPA deployment hinges on the frequency and complexity of the tasks in question (see Fig. 6.2).

High-frequency and highly structured tasks are prime candidates for traditional process automation due to the significant benefits in consistency, speed, and cost reduction they offer when automated. For tasks that occur with **moderate frequency** – structured yet not pervasive enough to warrant traditional automation – RPA emerges as a flexible and economically feasible solution. The incorporation of AI techniques, such as anomaly detection or intent recognition, enables RPA systems to adapt to slight variations in task structure with minimal human intervention. This capability marks a shift from purely rule-based automation to more intelligent process automation, where systems can learn and improve over time.

At the **lower end of the frequency spectrum**, tasks become less viable for automation. The investment in RPA for these tasks may not yield sufficient returns, as the sporadic nature of such tasks does not offer the economies of scale that RPA thrives upon. Besides, **tasks requiring a high degree of human judgment, creativity, or complex decision-making remain outside the current scope of**

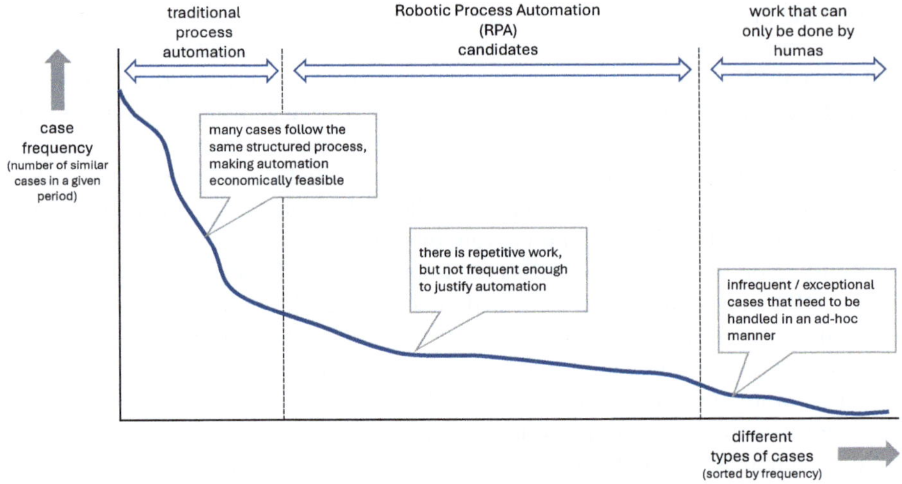

Fig. 6.2 Decision matrix for RPA. (Adapted from Van der Aalst et al., 2018)

RPA. These tasks benefit from the unique capabilities of human cognition and are handled on an ad-hoc basis, leveraging human intuition and adaptability.

Strategically, businesses should evaluate their processes along this continuum to identify which can be automated for maximum ROI and which should remain within the human domain, ensuring a harmonious balance between automated efficiency and human expertise. This nuanced application of RPA, increasingly enhanced through the selective use of AI, represents a thoughtful approach to integrating intelligent automation into the enterprise, with an emphasis on augmenting rather than replacing human work.

As we continue to explore the influence of AI on the enhancement of business operations, we delve into the strategic application of **process mining**. Process mining is a systematic approach to analyzing event logs from various information systems within an organization, whether Enterprise Resource Planning (ERP), Customer Relationship Management (CRM), or any other process-oriented tool (Mehdiyev & Fettke, 2021). By examining the detailed traces left by digital transactions, process mining attempts to reconstruct, evaluate, and refine the intricate workflows that form the backbone of an organization's operations. The goal is twofold: to gain a transparent understanding of existing processes and to uncover opportunities for significant improvement. This is achieved by capturing the sequences of process activities, characterized by their metadata such as timestamps, actor identification, and task descriptors, to paint a comprehensive picture of how a process unfolds in reality.

AI greatly enhances the capabilities of process mining, enabling advanced analytics and ML to anticipate future behaviors, optimize process performance, and support decision-making. The role of AI in process mining can be broken down into three key functions (Mehdiyev & Fettke, 2021):

- *Process discovery*: AI automates the construction of process models from raw event logs by identifying patterns, dependencies, and variations. An AI-powered system could, for example, enhance customer support by analyzing interactions and providing accurate information, significantly improving customer experience.
- *Conformance checking*: AI compares ideal process models with actual execution data, identifying deviations, bottlenecks, and nonconforming behavior. In healthcare, for example, AI can ensure that patient treatment adheres to established protocols, preventing potential errors.
- *Process enhancement*: AI extends established process models by examining event logs for optimization opportunities. Through optimization algorithms and predictive analytics, AI refines every facet of the process, from reducing cycle times to reallocating resources more efficiently. In manufacturing, for instance, AI can identify machine setups that are prone to errors and adjust the process models to mitigate these issues, thus directly enhancing production quality.

The integration of AI with process mining represents a strategic synergy that is greater than the sum of its parts. It results in a dynamic process ecosystem where AI does not just automate, but learns, adapts, and improves over time. This translates into greater return on investment as processes become more efficient, agile, and responsive to the nuanced demands of the modern business environment.

Summary
The transformative impact of AI on process optimization and automation is profound. AI enhances process optimization with advanced analytics, real-time monitoring, and predictive insights, making processes more efficient and proactive. RPA automates routine, rule-based tasks, boosting productivity and operational efficiency. Additionally, process mining, augmented by AI, provides deep insights into business workflows by analyzing event logs, leading to continuous process improvement. Together, these AI-driven approaches have the potential to achieve unprecedented levels of efficiency, adaptability, and innovation.

6.3 Cross-Technology AI Innovation

The emergence of cross-technology innovations in the field of AI brings us to the compelling convergence of AI with other innovative technologies like blockchain technology or IoT. This fusion heralds a transformative potential that goes beyond the capabilities of either technology in isolation.

6.3.1 AI and Blockchain

At its core, blockchain is a form of distributed ledger technology known for its unique "blue ocean" advantages. It provides a decentralized database that chronologically links blocks of data, enabling shared control, immutable audit trails, and secure asset exchange. The technology addresses some of the most pressing security vulnerabilities in today's digital infrastructure, such as those affecting Internet of Things devices, payment systems, and communications networks.

When AI's capacity for data analysis, pattern recognition, and predictive analytics intersects with blockchain's robustness, a new spectrum of possibilities emerges (Rabah, 2018). This synergy enables the creation of decentralized systems that are both tamper-proof and respectful of individual privacy concerns. For example, in the management of public health crises such as the coronavirus pandemic, blockchain can play a critical role in early detection of outbreaks and securing medical supply chains (Tagde et al., 2021). AI complements this by aiding in the rapid identification of symptoms and facilitating the efficient production of medicines.

Figure 6.3 details a multi-step approach where these technologies come together to create a robust response to COVID-19. Hospitals around the world begin by collecting medical imaging data, such as X-rays, which serve as a critical starting point for diagnosis and treatment planning. The collected data is then securely shared using blockchain technology, ensuring that each patient's records remain confidential and tamper-proof. The decentralized nature of blockchain allows multiple healthcare providers to contribute to and access a unified database, without compromising the integrity or security of the information. Once the data is consolidated, it is analyzed using AI algorithms, particularly neural networks, which are well-suited to interpreting complex image data. These AI systems can detect patterns indicative of COVID-19 that may be too subtle for the human eye, facilitating early and accurate diagnosis. The insights gained from the AI analysis are then distributed to relevant stakeholders via the blockchain. This includes not only healthcare providers for timely decision-making and treatment adjustments but also government

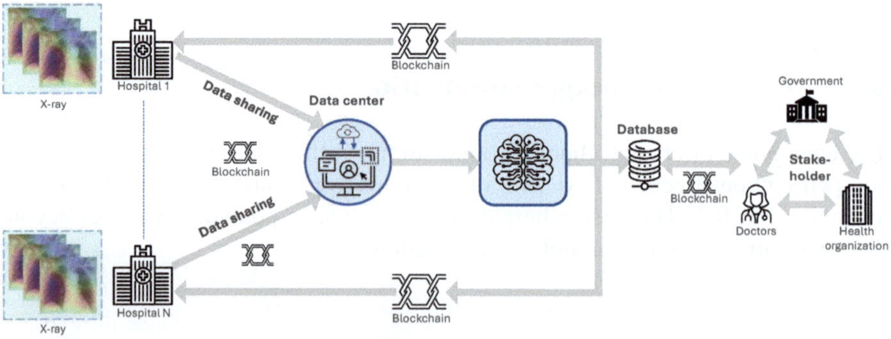

Fig. 6.3 Blockchain and AI-based solution to combat COVID-19. (Adapted from Nguyen et al., 2021)

agencies for monitoring disease spread and resource allocation to ensure an informed response strategy.

6.3.2 AI and IoT

The intersection of AI and the IoT marks a significant leap in technological synergy, commonly referred to as AIoT – where the analytical power of AI meets the vast network of IoT devices (Rabah, 2018). At its core, the IoT is a vast and intricate network of connected devices equipped with sensors, software, and Internet connectivity, all designed to collect and share data. This network is critical in a variety of areas, improving operational efficiency, optimizing processes, and enabling more informed decision-making.

Integrating AI into the IoT ecosystem exponentially increases its capabilities. By implementing AI algorithms into IoT systems, a new dimension of intelligence is introduced. AIoT can analyze data on an unprecedented scale, make intelligent decisions autonomously, and adapt to new information in real time. AIoT systems have the potential to transform complex systems such as autonomous vehicles, giving them the ability to make decisions based on real-time data and predictive analytics, significantly improving safety and functionality. In addition to enhancing system capabilities, AIoT also delivers personalized user experiences. It can learn from user behavior to tailor services and responses, increasing the level of human-technology interaction. It also strengthens security protocols and protects against breaches by detecting anomalies that indicate potential threats.

The harmonious integration of IoT and AI has paved the way for breakthroughs in autonomous driving, where the capabilities of each system complement and enhance the other. This blend is perfectly illustrated in the complex and synchronized dance of sensors, data, and decision-making that is the foundation of autonomous vehicle technology (see Fig. 6.4).

Collecting data from the vehicle's sensors is the first step in the intricate process of autonomous driving. Here, an array of sensors continuously collects a variety of

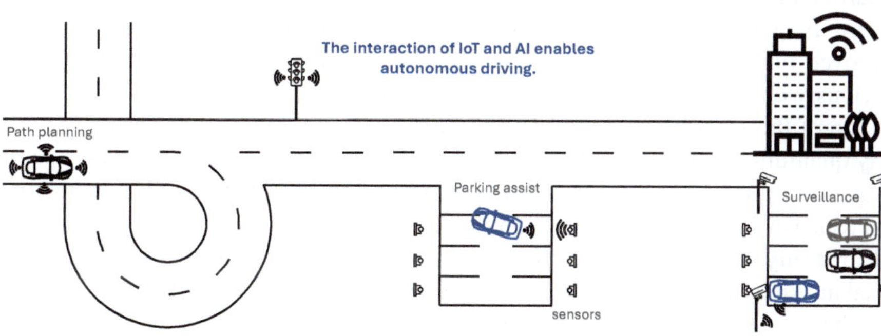

Fig. 6.4 IoT and AI-based solutions to realize autonomous driving. (Adapted from Khayyam et al., 2020)

data points about vehicle performance, road conditions, and environmental factors. These sensors feed information to the AI systems responsible for path planning, which involves the sophisticated task of maneuvering and trajectory planning. AI interprets this data and creates a seamless journey from point A to point B, making real-time decisions that ensure safety and efficiency.

Further refining the autonomous experience is the implementation of parking assist technologies. Vehicles equipped with this feature use sensors not only to navigate into parking spaces but also to adjust and correct the vehicle's trajectory during the parking maneuver. The AI in this scenario interprets the sensor data to accurately guide the vehicle, demonstrating the practical application of AIoT in everyday tasks.

The third component in this symphony is the use of surveillance, which combines cameras and computer vision for data analysis. This aspect of autonomous driving uses AI to interpret visual data, providing another layer of contextual understanding for the vehicle. Through computer vision, AI processes images and video in real time, enabling vehicles to interpret and react to dynamic road scenarios, from traffic signal detection to pedestrian identification.

Together, these three components – path planning, parking assistance, and monitoring – show the potential impact of the intersection of IoT and AI on autonomous driving. They illustrate how the intricate web of sensor data, processed and acted upon by AI, creates a self-sufficient driving experience.

6.3.3 AI and Quantum Computing

The convergence of AI and quantum computing marks a further emerging area of technological development with significant potential (Rawat et al., 2022; Abdelgaber & Nikolopoulos, 2020; Jürgens, 2019). Quantum computing transcends traditional binary data processing by using qubits that operate in multiple states simultaneously, enabling exponential increases in processing power. This advancement represents a quantum leap in computational capabilities. Quantum computing gives AI systems the ability to process massive amounts of data more efficiently, which is particularly beneficial for tasks that require fast, complex decision-making and pattern recognition. For AI, this means significantly faster model training and improved optimization algorithms, paving the way for AI applications that were previously unthinkable due to computational constraints.

One of the most compelling applications of this synergy is in security, specifically quantum cryptography. In the banking industry, securing transactions is paramount, and quantum cryptography is a nearly impregnable method of protecting data (Suriya, 2022). The combination of AI and quantum computing has the potential to strengthen encryption techniques to a degree that is unassailable by traditional hacking methods, ensuring a stronghold of digital security as we move into an era where quantum computing becomes more accessible. The integration of AI and quantum computing is not without its challenges, most notably the need for robust error correction algorithms to deal with the inherent instability of qubits. However, once these hurdles are overcome, the potential for AI to leverage quantum computing could transform entire industries. The banking sector, with its emphasis on security and reliable transactions, stands to benefit significantly from quantum-powered AI, offering a glimpse into a future where technology is fortified against the ever-growing threat of data breaches and cyberattacks.

6.3.4 AI and SSI

At the intersection of identity and technology, the concept of self-sovereign identity (SSI) represents a paradigm shift that empowers individuals to control and manage their digital identities (Schellinger et al., 2022; Gravity, 2023). SSI is emerging as an advanced identity management system that enables individuals and even IoT devices to autonomously own and manage their digital footprint.

The combination of AI and SSI provides a promising solution to today's challenges, such as the proliferation of deep fakes and issues surrounding the accountability of AI systems. For example, should an AI system spread false information, SSI could facilitate rapid identification of the source and enable immediate action to mitigate the spread of misinformation. By ensuring that digital entities are uniquely identifiable and accountable, AI-enabled SSI stands as a bulwark against the manipulation of information and the erosion of trust in digital ecosystems. This combination is particularly powerful in mitigating the risks associated with generative AI technologies, where the creation of fake content poses a significant threat to the integrity of information consumption. SSI makes it possible to trace the origins of digital content and enforce accountability.

In a similar vein, the fight against the proliferation of deep fakes – sophisticated digital illusions that mimic reality – could be strengthened by the strategic alliance of self-sovereign identities and AI (Gravity, 2023). When an AI system generates content, SSI can provide a verifiable signature, ensuring the authenticity and integrity of the information it distributes. Should an AI system disseminate false information, the inherent accountability provided by SSI enables rapid identification and corrective action. This dynamic interplay between SSI and AI creates a safer digital environment. It not only empowers users to recognize and trust AI-generated content but also ensures that AI remains a useful tool within ethical boundaries.

Summary
The emergence of cross-technology innovations in AI is reshaping the landscape of digital solutions, combining AI with blockchain, the Internet of Things, quantum computing, and SSI systems to unlock new capabilities. This integration enhances blockchain's secure transactions, strengthens IoT's network management with intelligent analytics, harnesses quantum computing's processing power for complex problem solving, and leverages SSI's control of personal data to improve privacy and accountability.

References

Abdelgaber, N., & Nikolopoulos, C. (2020). Overview on quantum computing and its applications in artificial intelligence. In *2020 IEEE Third International Conference on Artificial Intelligence and Knowledge Engineering (AIKE)* (pp. 198–199). IEEE.

Bresnahan, T. F., & Trajtenberg, M. (1995). General purpose technologies 'Engines of growth'? *Journal of Econometrics, 65*(1), 83–108.

Brynjolfsson, E., Rock, D., & Syverson, C. (2019). Artificial intelligence and the modern productivity paradox. *The Economics of Artificial Intelligence: An Agenda, 23*, 23–57.

FIFA. (2022). *Semi-automated offside technology to be used at FIFA World Cup 2022TM*. Retrieved May 24, 2024, from https://inside.fifa.com/technical/media-releases/semi-automated-offside-technology-to-be-used-at-fifa-world-cup-2022-tm

Gravity. (2023). www.linkedin.com. *Navigating the future: Generative AI, accountability, and the role of self-sovereign identity*. Retrieved May 24, 2024, from https://www.linkedin.com/pulse/navigating-future-generative-ai-accountability-role-self-sovereign/

Hofmann, P., Jöhnk, J., Protschky, D., & Urbach, N. (2020a, March). Developing purposeful AI use cases—A structured method and its application in project management. In *Wirtschaftsinformatik (Zentrale Tracks)* (pp. 33–49).

Hofmann, P., Samp, C., & Urbach, N. (2020b). Robotic process automation. *Electronic Markets, 30*(1), 99–106.

Jürgens, N. (2019). Quantum Computing—Boost für AI/KI-Technologie. *TheBlue.ai*. Retrieved May 24, 2024, from https://theblue.ai/blog-de/quantum-computing/

Khayyam, H., Javadi, B., Jalili, M., & Jazar, R. N. (2020). Artificial intelligence and internet of things for autonomous vehicles. In *Nonlinear approaches in engineering applications: Automotive Applications of engineering problems* (pp. 39–68).

McKinsey. (2022). www.mckinsey.com. The state of AI in 2022—And a half decade in review. *McKinsey*. Retrieved May 24, 2024, from https://www.mckinsey.com/capabilities/quantumblack/our-insights/the-state-of-ai-in-2022-and-a-half-decade-in-review#/

Mehdiyev, N., & Fettke, P. (2021). Explainable artificial intelligence for process mining: A general overview and application of a novel local explanation approach for predictive process monitoring. In *Interpretable artificial intelligence: A perspective of granular computing* (pp. 1–28).

Merative. (2022). *Achieving the benefits of AI with choice and control*. Retrieved May 24, 2024, from https://www.merative.com/content/dam/merative/documents/ebook/achieving-the-benefits-of-ai.pdf

Nguyen, D. C., Ding, M., Pathirana, P. N., & Seneviratne, A. (2021). Blockchain and AI-based solutions to combat coronavirus (COVID-19)-like epidemics: A survey. *IEEE Access, 9*, 95730–95753.

Rabah, K. (2018). Convergence of AI, IoT, big data and blockchain: A review. *The Lake Institute Journal, 1*(1), 1–18.

Rawat, B., Mehra, N., Bist, A. S., Yusup, M., & Sanjaya, Y. P. A. (2022). Quantum computing and ai: Impacts & possibilities. *ADI Journal on Recent Innovation, 3*(2), 202–207.

Schellinger, B., Sedlmeir, J., Willburger, L., Strüker, J., & Urbach, N. (2022). *Mythbusting Self-Sovereign Identity (SSI). Diskussionspapier zu selbstbestimmten digitalen Identitäten*. Institutsteil Wirtschaftsinformatik des Fraunhofer-Instituts für Angewandte Informationstechnik FIT.

Siemens-Energy. (2022). *Unleashing AI in power plants*. Retrieved May 24, 2024, from https://www.siemens-energy.com/global/en/home/stories/unleashing-ai-in-power-plants.html

Suriya, M. (2022). Machine learning and quantum computing for 5G/6G communication networks—A survey. *International Journal of Intelligent Networks, 3*, 197–203.

Tagde, P., Tagde, S., Bhattacharya, T., Tagde, P., Chopra, H., Akter, R., Kaushik, D., & Rahman, M. H. (2021). Blockchain and artificial intelligence technology in e-Health. *Environmental Science and Pollution Research, 28*, 52810–52831.

Uber. (2019). *Uber AI in 2019: Advancing mobility with artificial intelligence.* Retrieved May 24, 2024, from https://www.uber.com/en-DE/blog/uber-ai-blog-2019/?uclick_id=f04597d4-e944-4010-a6dd-f264930f2f12

Van der Aalst, W. M., Bichler, M., & Heinzl, A. (2018). Robotic process automation. *Business & Information Systems Engineering, 60*, 269–272.

Nils Urbach is Professor of Information Systems and Digital Business as well as Director of the Research Lab for Digital Innovation & Transformation at the Frankfurt University of Applied Sciences, Germany. Furthermore, he is Director at the FIM Research Center for Information Management, and the Branch Business & Information Systems Engineering of Fraunhofer FIT. Nils Urbach has been working in the fields of digital innovation and transformation for several years. His work has been published in several academic journals such as Information Systems Research (ISR), the Journal of the Association for Information Systems (JAIS), the Journal of Strategic Information Systems (JSIS), the Journal of Information Technology (JIT), MIS Quarterly Executive (MISQE), IEEE Transactions on Engineering Management (IEEE TEM), Information and Management (I&M), Business & Information Systems Engineering (BISE), and Electronic Markets (EM). He advises several companies on digitalization issues and regularly appears as a speaker on this topic.

Daniel Feulner received his M.Sc. in information system from the Otto-Friedrich University of Bamberg, Germany in 2023. He is an affiliated researcher at the Branch Business & Information Systems Engineering of the Fraunhofer FIT and FIM Research Center for Information Management at the University of Bayreuth. In his research, he aims to understand how Business Analytics and Artificial Intelligence can be effectively and responsibly utilized in organizations. His goal is to enable companies to drive innovation and achieve sustainable growth in a rapidly evolving technological landscape.

Simon Feulner received his M.Sc. in business administration from the University of Bayreuth, Germany, in 2020 and his M.Sc. in information system from the Otto-Friedrich University of Bamberg, Germany in 2021. He is an affiliated researcher at the Branch Business & Information Systems Engineering of the Fraunhofer FIT and the Research Lab for Digital Innovation & Transformation at the Frankfurt University of Applied Sciences. His research explores the automation potential of generative AI technologies, examining how these innovations can streamline business processes, enhance decision-making, and unlock new opportunities for organizational value creation. He specifically focuses on how these technologies can break down existing barriers to automation, enabling more widespread and effective adoption across diverse business contexts.

Identifying, Designing, and Evaluating AI Use Cases

7

Nils Urbach, Daniel Feulner, Simon Feulner, and Dominik Protschky

Artificial intelligence (AI) offers tremendous potential to reshape how organizations create value – whether by increasing efficiency, enabling new services, or supporting better decision-making. Yet, many companies still struggle to move beyond isolated experiments toward strategic, scalable AI integration. Common pitfalls include selecting use cases based on hype rather than need, lacking clarity on expected value, or failing to align AI initiatives with business objectives and operational realities. To avoid these challenges, a systematic approach is needed – one that connects business problems with AI capabilities, considers organizational context, and guides the transformation of initial ideas into robust, value-creating solutions.

In this chapter, we outline a structured approach that guides organizations through three key stages of AI use case development. First, we focus on the identification of promising use cases by combining organizational needs with AI capabilities. Next, we address the design of AI-based services using the AI Service Canvas, which helps structure data requirements, business potential, and organizational integration. Finally, we present the evaluation of AI use cases through the effect-path model – a tool for systematically tracing how data and AI capabilities generate business value and competitive advantage.

N. Urbach (✉) · S. Feulner
Frankfurt University of Applied Sciences, Frankfurt am Main, Germany
e-mail: nils.urbach@fim-rc.de; simon.feulner@fim-rc.de

D. Feulner · D. Protschky
University of Bayreuth, Bayreuth, Germany
e-mail: daniel.feulner@fim-rc.de; dominik.protschky@fim-rc.de

N. Urbach, D. Feulner (eds.), *Managing Artificial Intelligence*, Future of Business and Finance, https://doi.org/10.1007/978-3-032-13308-3_7

7.1 Identifying AI Use Cases

The targeted identification of value-creating use cases for AI is the focus of many companies. The driving forces are both the potential of AI to gain competitive advantages and the concern of being left behind by the competition. It seems that extensive computing resources, data availability, and technological advances in machine learning have opened the gates wide for the use of AI in companies. But the prospect of competitive advantage comes with the challenge of potentially overlooking innovative use cases or focusing on less value-creating scenarios. For this reason, Hofmann et al. (2020a) developed a method that helps companies to identify valuable AI use cases in a targeted manner.

When identifying use cases for AI, companies face a variety of challenges: First, companies often lack a holistic understanding of the potential business opportunities associated with the use of AI. In practice, the opportunities are therefore both underestimated and overestimated. Second, potential AI use cases must be technically feasible and economically viable, as well as fit the individual company context. It is not enough to simply adopt another company's use case. Third, the challenge is to find the solution that best fits the company's specific problems. Fourth, regardless of an existing problem, AI applications can offer new opportunities to create a competitive advantage. To address these challenges, Hofmann et al. (2020a) present a structured method for identifying AI use cases.

7.1.1 A Method for Identifying AI Use Cases

The method developed integrates various activities in an iterative process (see Fig. 7.1) (Hofmann et al., 2020a). These activities include six main activities

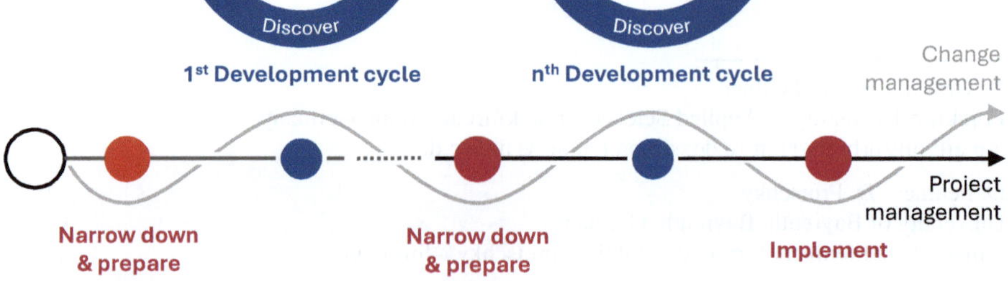

Fig. 7.1 Iterative method for identifying AI use cases. (Adapted from Hofmann et al., 2020a)

(narrow down, prepare, discover, understand, design, and implement), which are supported by continuous project and change management. Reflecting on and combining the findings of each activity then contributes to a company's knowledge base. Before companies can move directly to identifying AI use cases in development cycles, the narrow down and prepare activities should precede them. Narrow down defines the focus and boundaries of the method execution. Prepare aims to gather and structure information about company-specific contextual factors.

Each development cycle comprises the activities discover, understand, and design. These cycles aim to identify relevant problems and opportunities (discover), understand their origins (understand), and develop solutions (design). In addition, AI experiments, such as data sampling, acceptance testing, and proof of concept, can promote understanding of the technological concepts and potential of AI. Companies repeat the development cycles until no more new AI use cases can be identified, they cannot be further specified, or the number of identified AI use cases is satisfactory. The implementation of the method ends with the derivation of the prerequisites for the successful introduction of selected AI use cases and the definition of suitable project activities.

7.1.2 The Activities of the Method in Detail

The **narrow down** activity serves to help the company apply the method in a targeted manner. Narrowing down defines the scope of potential AI use cases and determines the resources required to implement the method (e.g., size and composition of the project team). The application context of the method can be narrowed down in two ways:

1. Prioritization and exclusion of certain areas (e.g., processes) or technologies (especially at the beginning of the method)
2. Prioritization and exclusion of already identified AI use cases (only possible after the first development cycle)

To this end, companies must define suitable evaluation criteria. These can include, for example, return on investment, time to benefit, availability of resources, technical feasibility, and compliance with corporate values. To assess the economic potential, companies can also consider new business models enabled by the identified AI use cases. In terms of the trade-off between short- and long-term benefits, companies should not go too short (e.g., simple additions to existing applications) and not go too far (e.g., applications requiring fundamental research). To prioritize, AI use cases should be grouped that either have a comparable business impact or are technologically or contextually interdependent.

The **prepare** activity is used to collect and structure relevant information about the company-specific context before each development cycle begins. Since every project is associated with uncertainties, thorough preparation of the development cycles is essential. It must also be considered that the members of the project team usually have different knowledge backgrounds. Therefore, knowledge of the contextual factors should be consolidated within the entire project team. To collect relevant information, the method is based on the established Technology-Organization-Environment framework (Baker, 2012). This framework describes the influence of the factors technology, organization, and corporate environment on the introduction of technologies. In addition, the requirements of AI regarding data and the specifics of the desired area of application must be taken into account.

Technology: The introduction of new technologies requires an understanding of the company's existing technology landscape and its interaction with new technologies. For example, the implementation of some AI use cases depends on the existing IT infrastructure and interfaces to business applications. In addition, an understanding of the functionality of AI is required. In many cases, the introduction of AI functions (see Chap. 6) significantly improves the understanding of AI. Questions of understanding should be discussed openly with all relevant stakeholders. The existing IT strategy must also be taken into account and included in the implementation. It is also important to incorporate previous experience and existing expertise in the company with regard to the use of AI.

Organization: With regard to the company, aspects such as structures, resources, and culture play a decisive role. It is important to align technology decisions with the overarching corporate strategy. The strategic goals and the consequences of current or intended transformations should also be included in the planning and implementation of AI projects. In addition, it requires the support of top management, an innovation-friendly culture, and appropriate resources (e.g., budget, employee expertise, and availability). Successful application of the method also requires that the scope of application of the method is structured. Although there is no generally applicable guideline for structuring an area of application, typical categories include products, services, processes, or problems.

Corporate environment: The environmental context includes an assessment of the requirements of the industry, competitors, customers, and regulations. Companies must identify environmental factors that promote and inhibit the development and implementation of AI use cases.

Data: Domain-relevant data is also of great importance, as machine learning models can only generate meaningful results if the required data is qualitatively and quantitatively available for the application. For example, the training of algorithms for machine learning requires large amounts of data to achieve an appropriate output quality. Companies must consider these aspects carefully and evaluate the available data (e.g., timeliness, data volume, data quality, relevance, and accessibility). The evaluation also includes a discussion of the relative resource advantages compared to the competition.

Area of application: Companies must collect relevant information in the area of application to create a common understanding (e.g., through joint teams with AI and domain experts).

The **discover** activity is part of the **development cycle**, which also includes the Understand and Design activities. In the Discover phase, companies can identify fields of action from two perspectives:

- *Domain perspective:* This perspective aims to identify fields of action in a problem-oriented manner by identifying existing or yet undiscovered problems in the application domain.
- *Technology perspective:* Here, fields of action are identified in an opportunity-oriented manner by examining (new) AI applications to recognize technology-related opportunities in the domain.

From the domain perspective, a stakeholder-oriented approach can be recommended to identify the problems of the application area from the customer's perspective. Companies can, for example, conduct value proposition canvas workshops with various stakeholders to define the customer segment and the resulting requirements (Osterwalder et al., 2015). The technology perspective requires a comprehensive market analysis to identify AI applications and derive possibilities for use in your own company. Products or services outside your own domain can also serve as inspiration.

The **understand** activity is about fundamentally understanding the fields of action identified in this way. A root-cause analysis is recommended to understand the root of a problem or opportunity, not just the symptoms. This is briefly explained using an example: High costs for machine breakdowns, for example, indicate inadequate maintenance. However, more frequent maintenance of machines is inefficient and therefore leads to higher costs. More efficient machine maintenance requires the ability to predict the machine's condition. The root of the problem is a lack of understanding of the causes of failure (e.g., by collecting detailed failure information to guide maintenance decisions). Similarly, an opportunity could be to improve machine operation to prevent breakdowns (e.g., by collecting machine data for preventive machine maintenance).

The **design** activity aims to develop specific AI use cases. To do this, companies must match problems (and opportunities) with solutions. The use of a problem-solution matrix in which the collected information is summarized is recommended for this purpose (see Fig. 7.2). While the columns represent the domain structure (here in the example using processes), the rows indicate the AI functions. The aim of the design activity is to bring together both domain-specific problems and solutions within a cell of the matrix. Each match can then be extracted as a use case. Companies should compare the resulting AI use cases with the context factors, identify dependencies between them and evaluate their added value. Once a collection of AI use cases is available, a result-oriented narrow down activity can be carried out. If no match is found between the technical solution and an existing problem, two different approaches can be used to find a solution:

- *Problem-oriented approach:* If there is a problem but no direct solution – in this case, the company can concentrate on one column of the matrix to find a solution using technology selection or inventive problem-solving techniques to develop new AI solutions for a domain problem.
- *Solution-oriented approach:* If there is a solution but no problem in the domain – in this case, the company can focus on one row of the matrix. To follow this

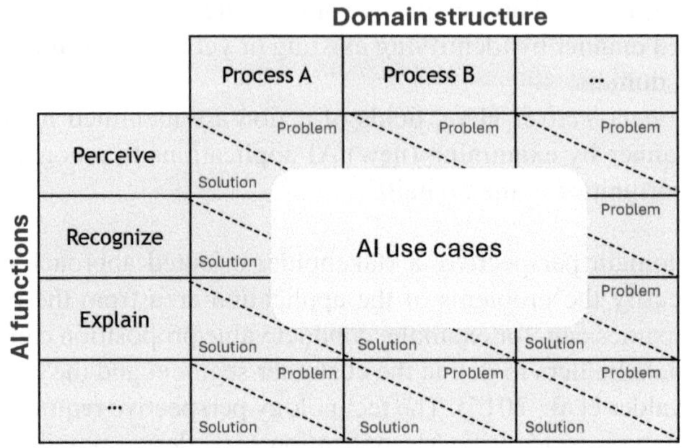

Fig. 7.2 Problem-solution matrix. (Adapted from Hofmann et al., 2020a)

approach, for example, check whether a domain problem has been overlooked, whose solution using AI holds new business potential (i.e., an undiscovered problem).

In the **Implement** activity, companies put the theoretical considerations into practice and thus create the conditions for a successful implementation of the AI use case. It is initially important to critically evaluate whether other technologies may be more suitable or more cost-effective. To plan the introduction of an AI use case, companies should clarify the following cornerstones:

- *Make or buy:* Deciding whether to develop the AI application in-house, outsource it, or purchase an existing solution from an external provider.
- *Maturity level:* Determining the desired maturity level of the application (e.g., proof of concept, minimum viable product, and fully mature application).

Furthermore, the AI use case should be considered against the background of various contextual factors to ensure successful integration into the company and to promote the appropriateness of the AI use case. Regarding the technology context, for example, consideration must be given to how the AI application can be integrated into the existing IT infrastructure. In the organizational context, it is important to address employee concerns and assess whether sufficiently qualified employees (such as data scientists, machine learning engineers, and business analysts) are available. Data protection and ethical issues should also be carefully considered. Data-related aspects must also be considered; for example, if required data is not yet available, data collection must be planned. In terms of scope, companies need to decide whether and how existing processes should be changed before the AI application is introduced. After these considerations, the AI use case can be handed over to a project team to drive the implementation forward.

In addition to the previous main activities, it is crucial to coordinate the implementation of the method as part of **project management**. In addition to the usual project management issues, particular attention should be paid to ensuring that all project members are familiar with the methodological approach and are uniformly aligned regarding the intended scope of application. It is important to consider the different professional backgrounds of the team members. Experience confirms that this diversity promotes cooperation and creativity and, at the same time, stimulates the exchange of knowledge and ideas.

The development of use cases and the subsequent implementation of new technologies always go hand in hand with change. A company should therefore closely link the identification of AI use cases with **change management**. The aim of change management should be to raise awareness of the project, increase appreciation for it, and increase the motivation of those involved to actively participate in the project. Effective communication is crucial to increasing appreciation for the project. It must be ensured that the company's employees always receive transparent, understandable, and tangible information. It is recommended that not only AI experts but also domain experts are involved in the implementation of the method.

Summary
Identifying valuable AI use cases requires a structured, iterative approach that aligns technological capabilities with business needs and organizational context. The method developed by Hofmann et al. (2020a) supports this process through six core activities: narrow down, prepare, discover, understand, design, and implement. Each step addresses key challenges such as technical feasibility, economic viability, and strategic fit. The approach emphasizes interdisciplinary collaboration, the consideration of data quality and availability, and active change management. By systematically navigating the complexities of AI integration, organizations can uncover high-impact opportunities and lay the foundation for sustainable value creation.

7.2 Designing AI Use Cases

The race for new competitive advantages is on, but meeting the often high expectations placed on the use of AI is by no means a foregone conclusion. To achieve the expected potential, companies must both promote the creation of value in a targeted manner and reduce factors that restrict it. This requires company-specific identification, evaluation, conception, and development of AI-based services. It is therefore not enough to copy AI-based services from another company to remain competitive in the long term. Rather, a company's competitiveness is determined by its ability to comprehensively shape the innovation process around the topic of AI. The challenge here is to first assess where and in what form AI can deliver added value. The next step is to actually realize the anticipated benefits within the company by developing AI-based services that can be integrated into the organizational value chain in the best possible way (Urbach et al., 2021).

In such a holistic approach, various issues must be addressed, from the infrastructure level to the system and process levels through to the business level. The aim is not only to find a solution to a technical problem but also to understand AI-based services as a holistic organizational concept to be integrated. On the one hand, organizational integration aims to align data-based business models with the corporate strategy. On the other hand, the design of processes and complementary information systems integration into the value creation network should be aimed for.

Given that the issues are both deeply and broadly rooted in the organization, a systematic approach is required to promote the creation of value in a targeted manner. To master this complexity, companies can use the AI Service Canvas as proposed by Urbach et al. (2021). The AI Service Canvas (see Fig. 7.3) allows companies to describe, evaluate, and design AI-based services from both an innovation and technology perspective. It provides a seamless bridge from data to the AI-based service through to the business potential. Particular emphasis is placed on integrating the AI-based service into the organization and the corporate environment. From the product owner to the data scientist – the AI Service Canvas provides a common language for documenting progress and answering important questions. In the following, the individual components are explained and illustrated by field reports.

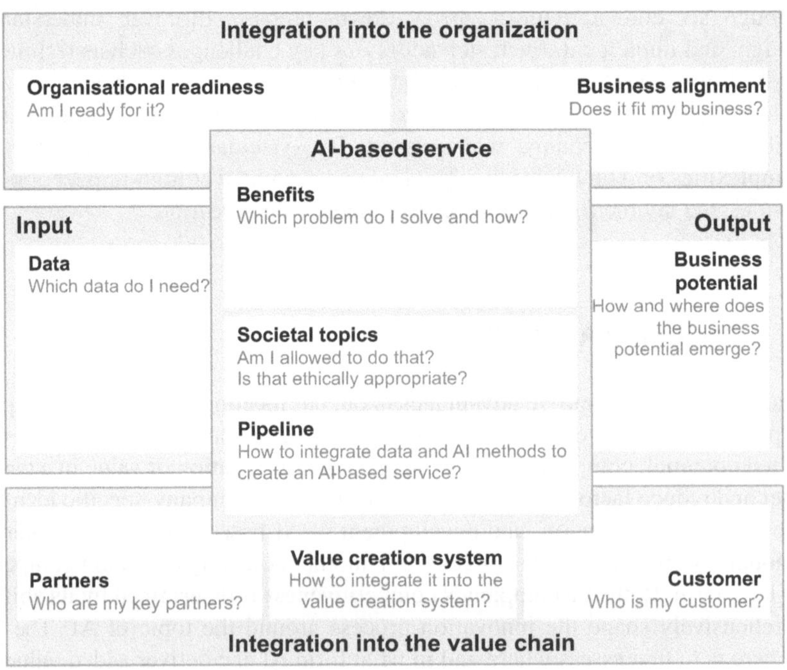

Fig. 7.3 The AI Service Canvas. (Adapted from Urbach et al., 2021)

7.2.1 The AI-Based Service

The purpose of an AI-based service is to generate added value for the company or its customers. Seamless documentation makes the interdependencies in value creation transparent so that value creation can be described both qualitatively and quantitatively. The area of value creation is relevant throughout the entire innovation process to make value-based decisions in the development and application of AI-based services.

Input: What Data Do I Need?

Data is the basis of AI functionality. This raises the central question: What data is needed to implement a specific AI-based service? This may sound trivial at first glance, but the challenge lies in the details. The properties that need to be described to answer this question range from data availability to the required data quality. Last but not least, an AI-based service can also fail because of the data, which is why a close look at the existing data basis is essential. With machine learning in particular, availability and suitable composition of the data are essential prerequisites for the successful training and application of machine learning models. Similar to other company resources, the availability of data not only determines the functionality of an AI-based service but also determines the resulting business potential. Rare data or data that is difficult to copy can become a sustainable competitive advantage through unique AI-based services. The requirements for strategically relevant data, taking into account established concepts of resource theory, are summarized in Table 7.1. The supposed business potential of data should not lead to the uncontrolled collection of data. The uncontrolled collection of data leads to high costs and the neglect of strategically relevant data.

Many companies have strategically relevant but often untouched data in their specific domains. By entering the market early, AI-based services can quickly collect additional data, which, in turn, can be used to improve them and thus lead to a lead that is difficult for other companies to catch up with. However, existing data cannot generally be used without targeted pre-processing or even adaptation of the data collection strategy due to data quality problems. Different steps are necessary to fill in the input field in the AI Service Canvas, depending on the use case and

Table 7.1 Strategically relevant data (Urbach et al., 2021)

Requirements	Description
Value retention	Valuable data enables the implementation of AI-based services that lead to increased efficiency or effectiveness
Rarity	Data should not be or only rarely be available among current and potential competitors
Immobility	The procurement of data by other companies should not be possible or should be too costly or time-consuming
Limited imitability	Data should be difficult for other companies to replicate
Limited substitutability	The advantageousness of a dataset should not be substitutable by another dataset

company. These range from the identification and evaluation of data sources or datasets to the design of a data framework and the development of a data strategy. The fulfillment of the requirements for strategically relevant data can also be assessed.

Benefits: Which Problems Do I Solve and How?

As a multi-purpose technology, AI includes a wide range of functionalities (Hofmann et al., 2020b). The benefit field of the AI Service Canvas describes the success-critical translation of technical functionalities into economic benefits. The aim is to find a technical solution that best suits the individual problem. The question is: Which problem do I solve and how? It is therefore necessary to describe the problem-solving logic of an AI-based service to specify the value creation. To do this, the problems (and opportunities) should be compared with the identified solutions. A problem-solving matrix (see Fig. 7.4) can be used for this purpose, for example. The problem-solving matrix can be applied from both a domain perspective (i.e., solving existing problems) and a technology perspective (i.e., recognizing new opportunities).

The technical functionality is translated into tangible AI functions in the problem-solving matrix. Individual structuring approaches can be used to describe the domain. For example, different processes can be differentiated. Stakeholder-centered analysis methods are particularly suitable for specifying this field. In addition, it is also advisable to understand the root of a problem or opportunity (e.g., by means of a root cause analysis) and not just describe its symptoms. From a technology perspective, it should also be checked whether a simpler method (e.g., a proven rule-based algorithm) can be used to solve a problem. The wide range of technical possibilities, therefore, requires a systematic yet open approach to reduce the complexity of finding a solution. Various formats, such as innovation sprints or proof-of-concept sprints, which are based on tried-and-tested methods, are suitable for this.

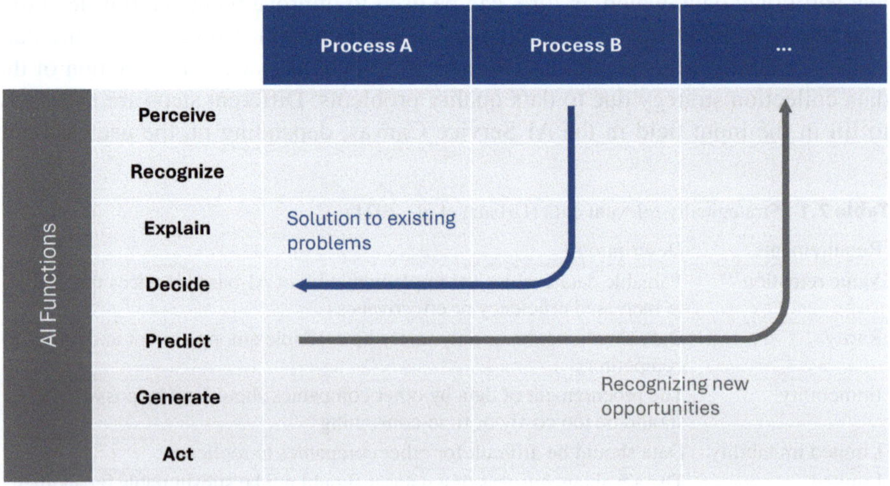

Fig. 7.4 The AI process matrix (problem-solving matrix). (Adapted from Urbach et al., 2021)

Social Issues: Is That Right? Am I Allowed to Do This?

To identify and address ethical, legal, and social implications in the creation of values at an early stage, there is room for these in the AI Service Canvas. The development and integration of an AI-based service should always be examined from these three perspectives. For example, the AI-based service must be in line with existing legal regulations and conform to applicable standards in the respective industry. The organization's customers must also be open and ready to deal with AI-based services and decisions. If the use of AI technologies violates applicable law or industry standards, this leads not only to legal sanctions but also to a loss of trust in employees, suppliers, and/or customers. Only through close coordination between the various stakeholders involved, including external stakeholders such as customers and suppliers, can AI create added value not only within the organization but also throughout the entire value creation network. To fill out this field of the AI service canvas, questions beyond the economic or technological perspective must be answered. To this end, discussions should be held with those responsible within the organization (e.g., employees, works council, and ethics council) or with third parties (e.g., universities and law firms). In some cases, the AI guidelines already defined in advance also facilitate the evaluation of a use case from a legal, social, and ethical perspective.

Pipeline: How Do I Integrate Data and AI Methods Into an AI-Based Service?

In the context of AI-based services, the IT infrastructure is by no means a standard product. It is important to design an IT infrastructure in the sense of a data processing pipeline that is performant, scalable, economical, and secure. This raises the question: How do I integrate data and AI methods into an AI-based service? An end-to-end integration of an AI-based service from a pipeline perspective is illustrated in Fig. 7.5, starting with the provision of the data, the data sources (e.g., sensors, document libraries, and enterprise applications), and their interfaces. In this context, it is recommended to design the interfaces in the IT landscape of the company or the value creation network beyond the pipeline of a single AI-based service under consideration. In this way, synergy effects can be leveraged, and complexity due to isolated solutions can be avoided. The concept of cross-company data provision (e.g., for data collaboration) increases the requirements for IT security.

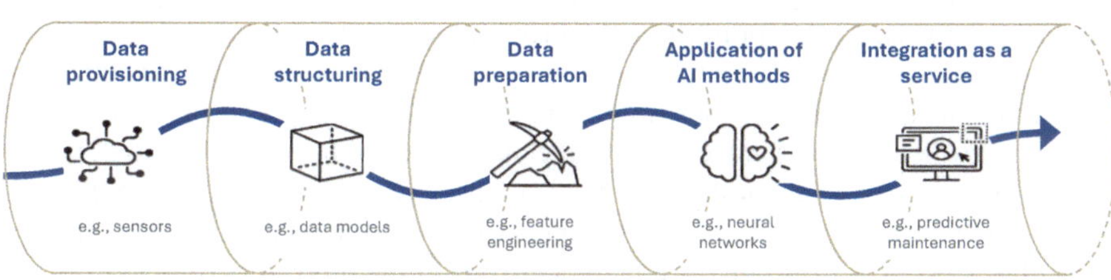

Fig. 7.5 End-to-end integration from a pipeline perspective. (Adapted from Urbach et al., 2021)

In addition, old security paradigms are generally no longer sufficient due to the growing number of internet-enabled devices in the Internet of Things (IoT) and the resulting increasing threat of hacker attacks. For this reason, the security-related aspects should be directly considered when creating the data pipeline for the AI-based service. When handling data and new technologies, it is important to consider how these integrate into the IT infrastructure, as well as what IT infrastructure and which security mechanisms are required. The often unstructured data should then be converted into a data structure that makes sense for the AI-based service. The requirements for the data structure must be derived from multiple criteria. The data structure to be selected depends not only on the data provided (e.g., data volume) but also on the further processing in the pipeline and thus also on the operating conditions of the AI-based service.

The data can now be processed in the next step. This step includes, for example, the correction of incorrect data points or feature engineering. This step is typically very time-consuming and requires a comprehensive understanding of the data. Once the data has been processed, AI methods can be applied. When deriving requirements for the pipeline, it is recommended to differentiate between the development and production environments (e.g., higher computing power requirements when training machine learning models). Finally, the technical functions must be integrated into the AI-based service. This essentially involves designing the user's interaction with the respective application or embedding it in existing services or products.

To specify the entire pipeline, both the requirements for the pipeline of the AI-based service and the description of the technologies are required. The combination of AI methods and conventional methods, in particular, has proven itself in practice. For example, AI methods are combined with the technologies of the IoT movement (e.g., sensor systems, edge computing) and distributed ledger technologies (e.g., blockchain) following the idea of the machine economy (Urbach et al., 2020; Jöhnk et al., 2021a). To specify the pipeline, a comprehensive consideration from a conceptual, security-related, and economic perspective is recommended. Concrete measures can be manifold and range from the derivation of the computing power requirements, the design of technology interfaces, and penetration tests.

Output: Business Potential: How and Where Does Business Potential Arise?

However, the functionality created by an AI-based service only leads to business potential if the functionality is not decoupled from the (strategic) competitive factors of a company. At this point, it is therefore important to answer how and where business potential arises. A competitive factor can have its origin in the organization or its environment and describes how competitive advantages can be achieved. In this way, this field records and considers the emergence of business potential, taking into account the associated risks. It is therefore necessary to describe the (expected) success in order to be able to manage AI projects in a targeted manner. This field in particular is essential for value-oriented decisions in the innovation process. A lack of consideration would lead to a blind flight in value creation.

In the description of the development of business potential, quantification beyond the qualitative description is often not possible or useful in an early phase of the innovation process (among other things, because essential information is missing). To qualitatively describe the emergence of business potential, the effect-path model can be applied (see next sub-chapter). The effect-path model makes it possible to derive the emergence of business potential in a structured cause-and-effect network. This model can also be used as a basic framework for quantitative estimates in the further course of the innovation process.

7.2.2 Organizational Integration

AI-based services cannot simply be copied from one company to another. On the contrary, AI-based services must be specifically aligned with the corporate context to avoid decoupling the AI-based service from the rest of the organization. On the one hand, organizational readiness must be taken into account to avoid unsuccessful implementation attempts and to be able to take measures at an early stage. On the other hand, business alignment must be considered when designing AI-based services. In addition to technical factors, successful AI integration is therefore primarily based on the circumstances of the organization in question.

Organizational Readiness: Am I Ready for It?

Even if AI projects are successfully integrated from a technological perspective, they can still fail within the organization. The topic of organizational readiness, therefore, deals with the assessment of the extent to which a company is ready to develop or integrate the AI-based service from an organizational perspective. Following the work of Jöhnk et al. (2021b), the focus is on five specific areas (strategy, data, organizational culture, resources, and competencies). The factors of strategy and data are already explicitly considered in separate fields of the AI Service Canvas. In this way, we address the importance of a suitable strategic alignment in the business alignment field. The data is described in detail in the input field. The other factors (i.e., organizational culture, resources, and competencies) are described within this field.

The organizational culture deals with the cultural willingness and motivation to use AI processes or to contribute to their development. However, it is not only the general willingness to use AI processes that plays a role here. For example, factors such as the acceptance of errors during the development and introduction of AI or the willingness of different company units to collaborate must also be taken into account. In addition to a suitable corporate culture, it is also important to develop the right skills within the company. An interdisciplinary team with different skills, for example, from the fields of data science, data engineering, application development, project management, and the application domain, is typically desirable. Knowledge of the company's structures and stakeholders is also helpful. In terms of available resources, for example, the budget, qualified personnel, and required IT infrastructure should be in place. To ensure that the organization is ready to develop and integrate the AI-based service from an organizational perspective, it is recommended to carry out readiness checks (with increasing detail) during the innovation process and draw appropriate implications from them. In this way, delays in the development or application of AI-based services can be avoided by taking measures at an early stage.

Business Alignment: Is It Right for Me?

In addition to organizational readiness, the business alignment of the AI-based service should also be evaluated to ensure sustainable value generation. This field, therefore, answers the question of whether the AI-based service fits in with the company's strategic direction. As illustrated in the strategic alignment model (Henderson & Venkatraman, 1999) adapted for AI (see Fig. 7.6), it is important to describe both the strategic fit and the functional integration. The strategic fit shows how well the infrastructure and the respective processes can be integrated into the business or AI strategy. An AI strategy promotes both business alignment and the speed of future AI initiatives. Functional integration, on the other hand, describes the embedding of the AI strategy in the business strategy and the interlocking of organizational and AI-relevant infrastructure and processes at an operational level. To fill out this field, it should therefore be checked whether the AI-based service is in line with the corporate strategy or, if available, the AI strategy in terms of content and timing. Second, the functional integration should be assessed. Ultimately, this can also lead to an adjustment of the strategic direction in order to take account of the changes in the value proposition of AI-based services. In addition, the AI-based service should be assessed against the background of the company's business model logic.

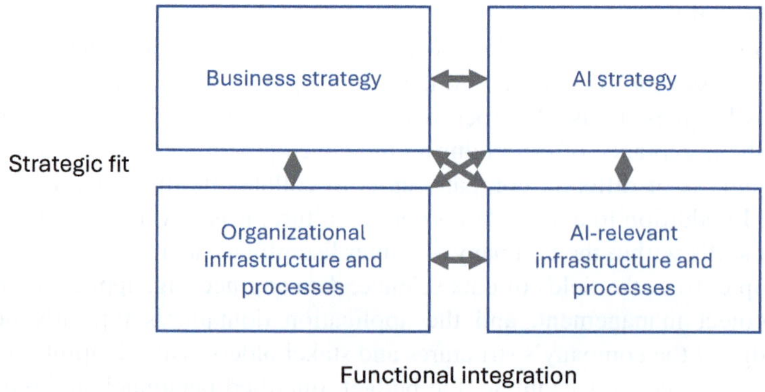

Fig. 7.6 Strategic alignment model for AI. (Adapted from Urbach et al., 2021)

7.2.3 Integration Into the Value Chain

In addition to organizational integration, the AI-based service should also be integrated into its environment. To do this, we recommend looking at the value creation activities from a network perspective.

Value Creation System: How Do I Integrate the Service Into the Value Creation System?
The functionality gained by solving one or more problems must be translated into a service, that is, create benefits in the value creation system through functionality. The central question is therefore how the AI-based service should be integrated into the value creation system. The value creation system should be understood as a socio-technical system consisting of a technical sub-component (e.g., intelligent production system) and a social sub-component (e.g., employees in production). In this field of the AI Service Canvas, it is therefore important to work out where in the socio-technical system the technical possibilities can be used and how the interfaces within this socio-technical system should be designed. However, the newly acquired functionality should by no means be imposed on the existing value creation system. A reconfiguration of the value creation system (e.g., through process adjustments) is often sensible and necessary in many cases. Last but not least, completely new digital process constellations can become possible. Particular attention should also be paid to collaboration in human–machine teams (Alan et al., 2019). To fill out this field of the AI Service Canvas, a two-pronged approach is recommended: On the one hand, the requirements of the value creation system for the AI-based service must be ascertained. On the other hand, it is important to specify the requirements of the AI-based service for the value creation system. To reconcile both sides, a user-centered survey of the functional and non-functional customer requirements, an analysis of the actual processes, and the development of target processes are recommended.

Partners: Who Are My Key Partners?
The path to integrating AI-based services does not have to be taken alone. It is important to find an answer as to who could be key partners. This allows us to consider the integration of partners (e.g., other departments and suppliers) and customers into our own value chain. External partners can, for example, fill gaps not only in the provision of data but also in the skills and resources of their own organization. In addition, AI platforms (e.g., Microsoft Azure ML and Google's AI platform) offer holistic offerings to focus on the application of AI processes instead of basic research and infrastructure operation (Geske et al., 2021) (see Chap. 10). However, the problem to be solved should by no means simply be outsourced, as domain- or company-specific knowledge plays an important role in solving the problem. In addition to using the services of large technology companies, companies should also consider start-ups, research institutions, and companies pursuing similar goals as cooperation partners. For example, it makes sense to work together in consortia on public research projects. To fill out this field, relevant partners (internal and

external) should first be identified and described. This requires a preliminary analysis of the resources, services, or skills required to successfully develop and/or use the AI-based service. This need must then be translated into requirements for the partner. In a second step, it is advisable to comprehensively characterize the value creation network (e.g., dependencies and risks).

Customers: Who Are My Customers?
Customer-centric development and integration of AI-based services is a key catalyst for value creation and can prevent development from bypassing the customer. In addition, a good understanding of the customer makes it possible to know the growth paths for the application of AI-based services (e.g., expansion to other customer segments or processes). The company's own employees should also be regarded as customers of the AI-based service if the AI-based service is used within the company (e.g., for production processes). The answer to the question of who the customers of the AI-based service are should include a comprehensive characterization of the customer and their tasks. If the customers are understood, the knowledge gathered can be incorporated into requirements for the development and integration of AI-based services. To complete this field, it is first necessary to identify all relevant customer groups for the AI-based service. Once all customer groups have been identified, different methods can be used to understand the customers, for example, in the form of personas. Personas comprehensively summarize the characteristics of the customer (e.g., needs and goals) as fictitious users. In addition, the jobs-to-be-done approach can be used to capture the tasks (jobs) of customers.

Summary
Designing AI use cases requires a comprehensive, company-specific approach to identifying, evaluating, and developing AI-based services that create real business value. The AI Service Canvas supports this by systematically guiding organizations through essential aspects such as data requirements, business potential, organizational and value chain integration, and ethical considerations. It emphasizes aligning AI services with corporate strategy, infrastructure, and customer needs while fostering collaboration across internal and external stakeholders. The Canvas bridges the gap between technical functionality and economic impact, ensuring that AI initiatives are effectively embedded within socio-technical systems for sustainable competitive advantage.

7.3 Evaluating AI Use Cases

In the dynamic and often intangible realm of AI, evaluating AI use cases becomes an essential yet complex task for organizations aiming to harness its transformative power. The allure of AI is its vast potential to redefine industries through automation, sophisticated data analysis, and enhanced decision-making. However, realizing this potential necessitates not only an understanding of the broad spectrum of AI capabilities but also the careful integration of these capabilities into existing organizational processes.

To address this challenge, the effect-path method stands out as an adept framework designed specifically for evaluating AI use cases. It offers a nuanced approach that moves beyond merely acknowledging the potential of AI, ensuring that each use case is systematically dissected to reveal its strategic alignment with business objectives and its feasibility within the organizational ecosystem. This method positions AI not as a technological afterthought but as a central pillar of business strategy, thus making the evaluation of AI use cases both a rigorous and strategic endeavor.

Using a collaborative and workshop-based model (see Fig. 7.7), the effect-path method encourages the convening of interdisciplinary teams. This convergence of expertise – from the technical acumen of data scientists to the strategic foresight of domain experts – facilitates a holistic examination of AI's potential for value creation. It guides organizations through a systematic journey of preparation, execution, and reflective follow-up, delving deep into the cause-and-effect relationships that are the foundation of AI's business value proposition. At its core, the effect-path method is anchored in three levels of analysis:

The **Application Level** is the foundation of the effect-path model. Here, the journey begins with data – the raw, unprocessed information that fuels AI. This includes sensory data, process logs, and other forms of raw data that AI systems will process and analyze. The quality, granularity, and relevance of this data are critical, as they determine the potential depth of insights that can be gleaned. The next step at the Application Level is identifying functional possibilities. This is where we explore what AI can do with the data provided. It could involve perception, detection, explanation, prediction, generation of new content, or action upon data insights. This stage is about matching the capabilities of AI technologies with the types of data available and the functions they can perform. The third aspect at this level is function recipients, which involves identifying the elements within the organization that will directly benefit from AI's capabilities. These could be specific processes that could be optimized, products that could be improved, resources that could be better allocated, or employees whose jobs could be augmented by AI.

At the **Usage Level**, the potential uses are identified. This involves strategic thinking about the ways in which the functions provided by AI can affect competitive factors. It is about understanding how AI can be applied to different parts of the business and what changes or improvements can be expected.

The **Business Level** is the pinnacle of the effect-path model, where competitive factors are considered. At this stage, the focus is on how AI can be used to improve or transform aspects like production quantity or adaptability – factors that can give the business a competitive edge. With the competitive landscape in view, the next step is to identify business opportunities that can emerge from AI's influence on these competitive factors. These opportunities represent areas where the company can leverage AI to create new business value or to enhance existing value. The final aspect is business value itself, where we measure the effectiveness, knowledge, and

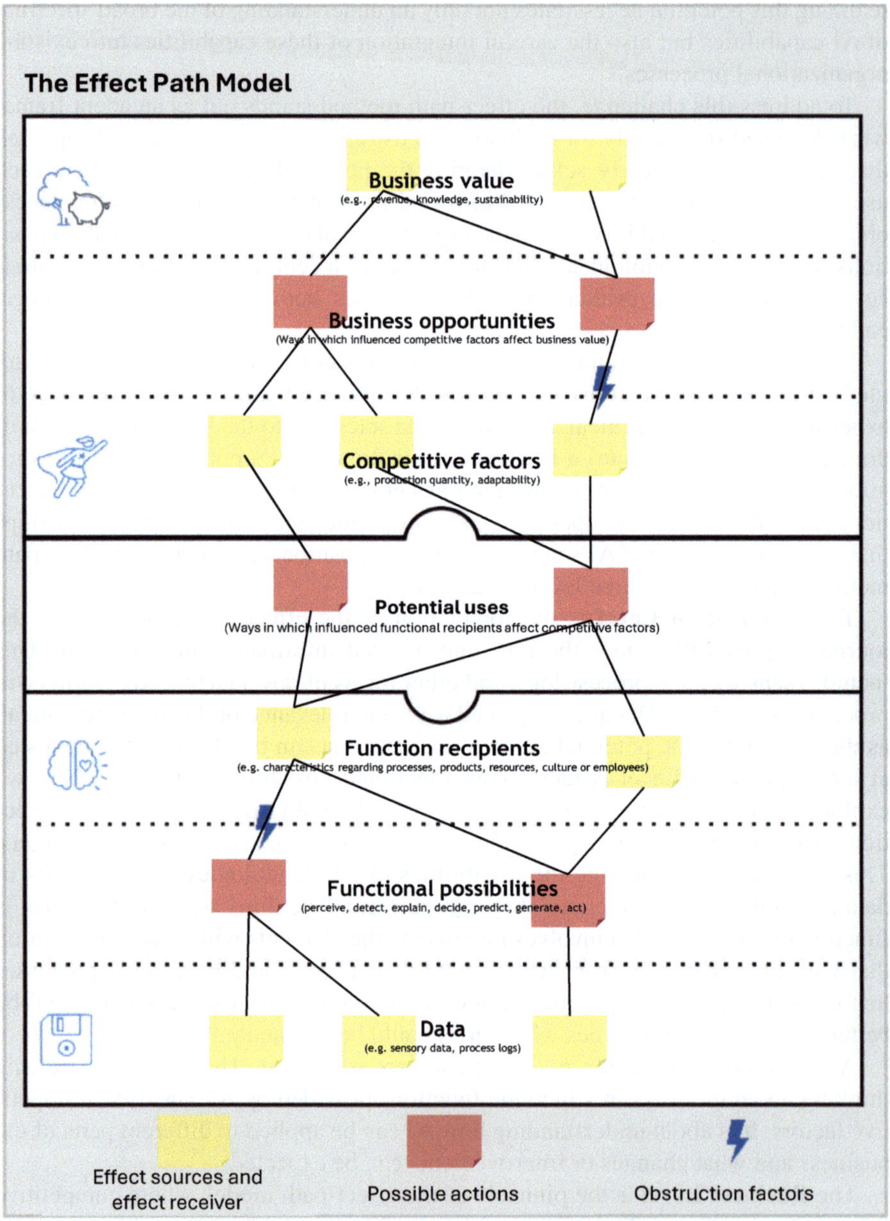

Fig. 7.7 The effect-path model

sustainability gains from AI. It is a culmination of the process that began with raw data, passed through functional possibilities and recipients, and through the lens of potential uses and competitive factors, to finally arrive at tangible business value.

The essence of the effect-path model is a systematic approach to creating business value through AI, represented as a structured pathway from data to business outcomes. Each step in the pathway is a careful decomposition of processes, where effect sources and effect receivers indicate the origin and destination of the value being created. Meanwhile, possible actions encapsulate the interventions or decisions made possible by insights from AI.

However, this journey is not without its challenges. Obstruction factors can emerge, complicating or halting the progress of effect paths. These can range from technical hurdles, such as data quality issues, to organizational challenges like resistance to change. Identifying and addressing these obstruction factors is crucial, as they can significantly impact the success of AI integration. More than just theoretical constructs, these effect paths provide a granular understanding of how data is transformed into actionable intelligence, which, in turn, can significantly impact competitive factors in the marketplace. The model deftly maps the dynamics of data processing, functional capabilities, competitive factors, and resulting business value. It provides organizations with a comprehensive perspective on the multifaceted impact of AI, enabling executives to make informed, strategic decisions.

The tangible outputs of the effect-path method are articulated pathways that act as both a navigational tool and a strategic lens through which the complex landscape of AI implementation can be traversed. These pathways serve as catalysts to identify and overcome potential barriers to realizing the value of AI. In doing so, the method promotes the emergence of a common language that traverses the various layers of an organization, fostering synergy between business and IT objectives. This synergy not only aligns AI initiatives with business strategies but also opens new avenues for innovation and strategic growth.

Summary

In an era where AI's potential to transform business operations and competitive landscapes is undeniable, the effect-path method offers a robust and structured approach to uncovering and harnessing this potential. By delineating the complex interplay between data, technology, and business value, the method equips organizations with the insights needed to navigate the challenges of AI integration and capitalize on the opportunities it presents. As we continue to explore and expand the boundaries of AI in business, methods like the effect-path method will play a crucial role in ensuring that these technological advancements translate into sustainable business value.

References

Alan, Y., Urbach, N., Hinsen, S., Jöhnk, J., Beisel, P., Weißert, M., Blumenthal, S., & Hofmann, P. (2019). *Think beyond tomorrow: KI, mein Freund und Helfer: Herausforderungen und Implikationen für die Mensch-KI-Interaktion.*

Baker, J. (2012). The technology–organization–environment framework. *Information Systems Theory: Explaining and Predicting Our Digital Society, 1*, 231–245.

Geske, F., Hofmann, P., Lämmermann, L., Schlatt, V., & Urbach, N. (2021). Gateways to artificial intelligence: Developing a taxonomy for AI service platforms. In *ECIS.*

Henderson, J. C., & Venkatraman, H. (1999). Strategic alignment: Leveraging information technology for transforming organizations. *IBM Systems Journal, 38*(2.3), 472–484.

Hofmann, P., Jöhnk, J., Protschky, D., Stähle, P., Urbach, N., & Buck, C. (2020a). KI-Anwendungsfälle zielgerichtet identifizieren. *Wirtschaftsinformatik & Management, 12*, 184–193.

Hofmann, P., Jöhnk, J., Protschky, D., & Urbach, N. (2020b). Developing purposeful AI use cases—A structured method and its application in project management. In *Wirtschaftsinformatik (Zentrale Tracks)* (pp. 33–49).

Jöhnk, J., Weißert, M., & Wyrtki, K. (2021a). Ready or not, AI comes—An interview study of organizational AI readiness factors. *Business & Information Systems Engineering, 63*(1), 5–20.

Jöhnk, J., Albrecht, T., Arnold, L., Guggenberger, T., Lämmermann, L., Schweizer, A., & Urbach, N. (2021b). The rise of the machines: Conceptualizing the machine economy. In *PACIS* (p. 54).

Osterwalder, A., Pigneur, Y., Bernarda, G., & Smith, A. (2015). *Value proposition design: How to create products and services customers want.* John Wiley & Sons.

Urbach, N., Albrecht, T., Guggenberger, T., Jöhnk, J., Arnold, L., Gebert, J., Jelito, D., Lämmermann, L., & Schweizer, A. (2020). *The advance of the machines: Vision und Implikationen einer machine economy.*

Urbach, N., Häckel, B., Hofmann, P., Fabri, L., Ifland, S., Karnebogen, P., Krause, S., Lämmermann, L., Protschky, D., Markgraf, M., & Willburger, L. (2021). *KI-basierte Services intelligent gestalten: Einführung des KI-Service-Canvas.*

Nils Urbach is Professor of Information Systems and Digital Business as well as Director of the Research Lab for Digital Innovation & Transformation at the Frankfurt University of Applied Sciences, Germany. Furthermore, he is Director at the FIM Research Center for Information Management, and the Branch Business & Information Systems Engineering of Fraunhofer FIT. Nils Urbach has been working in the fields of digital innovation and transformation for several years. His work has been published in several academic journals such as Information Systems Research (ISR), the Journal of the Association for Information Systems (JAIS), the Journal of Strategic Information Systems (JSIS), the Journal of Information Technology (JIT), MIS Quarterly Executive (MISQE), IEEE Transactions on Engineering Management (IEEE TEM), Information and Management (I&M), Business & Information Systems Engineering (BISE), and Electronic Markets (EM). He advises several companies on digitalization issues and regularly appears as a speaker on this topic.

Daniel Feulner received his M.Sc. in information system from the Otto-Friedrich University of Bamberg, Germany in 2023. He is an affiliated researcher at the Branch Business & Information Systems Engineering of the Fraunhofer FIT and FIM Research Center for Information Management at the University of Bayreuth. In his research, he aims to understand how Business Analytics and Artificial Intelligence can be effectively and responsibly utilized in organizations. His goal is to enable companies to drive innovation and achieve sustainable growth in a rapidly evolving technological landscape.

Simon Feulner received his M.Sc. in business administration from the University of Bayreuth, Germany, in 2020 and his M.Sc. in information system from the Otto-Friedrich University of Bamberg, Germany in 2021. He is an affiliated researcher at the Branch Business & Information Systems Engineering of the Fraunhofer FIT and the Research Lab for Digital Innovation & Transformation at the Frankfurt University of Applied Sciences. His research explores the automation potential of generative AI technologies, examining how these innovations can streamline business processes, enhance decision-making, and unlock new opportunities for organizational value creation. He specifically focuses on how these technologies can break down existing barriers to automation, enabling more widespread and effective adoption across diverse business contexts.

Dominik Protschky received his M.Sc. in business administration and engineering from the University of Bayreuth, Germany in 2021. He is an affiliated researcher at the Branch Business & Information Systems Engineering of the Fraunhofer FIT and FIM Research Center for Information Management at the University of Bayreuth. In his research, he investigates the comprehensive transformation required by organizations to effectively integrate Artificial Intelligence. Consequently, he develops and provides organizations with various artifacts – including methods, frameworks, and practices – that span strategic, business, and operational levels, enabling organizations to fully leverage the potential of AI.

Part III

AI Strategizing

AI Strategizing and Readiness

8

Nils Urbach, Daniel Feulner, Valentin Mayer, and Simon Meierhöfer

The strategic use of artificial intelligence (AI) has become a cornerstone for organizations aiming to maintain competitiveness and adapt to the dynamic demands of modern markets. AI strategizing focuses on aligning AI initiatives with organizational goals, ensuring that AI technologies are implemented effectively to generate sustainable value. Central to this process is the concept of AI readiness, which evaluates an organization's preparedness to integrate and leverage AI. AI readiness serves as the foundation for successful AI strategizing, as it identifies the critical enablers—such as resources, culture, and data—that must be in place to transform AI from a technological asset into a strategic advantage.

This chapter begins by introducing the concept of AI strategizing and presents a taxonomy that helps organizations conceptualize the design space of an AI strategy along four dimensions: scope, scale, speed, and source. Building on this, this chapter defines AI readiness as a multidimensional construct that captures an organization's preparedness to successfully adopt and scale AI. The final section analyzes key factors that influence AI readiness—including strategic alignment, resource availability, and cultural adaptability—and discusses how these factors can be assessed and developed to support effective AI use in practice.

N. Urbach (✉)
Frankfurt University of Applied Sciences, Frankfurt am Main, Germany
e-mail: nils.urbach@fim-rc.de

D. Feulner · V. Mayer · S. Meierhöfer
University of Bayreuth, Bayreuth, Germany
e-mail: daniel.feulner@fim-rc.de; valentin.mayer@fim-rc.de; simon.meierhoefer@fim-rc.de

N. Urbach, D. Feulner (eds.), *Managing Artificial Intelligence*, Future of Business and Finance, https://doi.org/10.1007/978-3-032-13308-3_8

8.1 Introduction to AI Strategizing

The gaining momentum of AI to innovate products, services, and business models is driving organizations across all industries to establish AI projects (i.e., endeavors that aim to deliver a software product or service with AI functionality to be used in a productive environment) as a strategic response to unfold the underlying value potential of AI (Enholm et al., 2022). However, AI projects often do not achieve the aspired outcomes or even fail. One reason is that organizations often establish AI projects in an unstructured manner rather than following a distinct strategic direction (Sagodi et al., 2024). To succeed with AI and sustainably strengthen the competitive position in the market, organizations should implement an AI strategy (i.e., guidelines for courses of action and sets of decisions) that guides their AI projects in line with firm-specific goals as well as internal and external constraints toward a distinct strategic direction.

Responding to technological breakthroughs at a strategic level to remain competitive is not a new phenomenon and has been thoroughly discussed in the established strategy discourse (e.g., in the context of a digital strategy) (Bharadwaj et al., 2013). However, recent work in information systems (IS) implies that AI differs considerably from traditional information technology (IT) (Ågerfalk et al., 2022). Contrary to previous generations of IT, contemporary AI is characterized by the facets of autonomy, learning, and inscrutability. In fact, these three interrelated and interdependent facets may even exacerbate in the future as the methods and techniques at the core of AI continue to grow at an astonishing pace. As a result, AI represents an ever-evolving frontier of computational advancement that not only leads to a shift in market and resource conditions but also presents organizations with strategic challenges that affect the scope, scale, speed, and source in which they set courses of action and sets of decisions (Bharadwaj et al., 2013).

Hence, organizations that aim to thrive in the competitive environment require a strategic response to AI-related strategic challenges and, thus, to AI-induced market and resource shifts in the form of an AI strategy. In this context, the rise of generative AI, in general, and the release of Large Language Models, in particular, as the current frontier of computational advancement has recently reinforced this necessity (Feuerriegel et al., 2024). Recognizing this, some organizations have already moved beyond opportunistic and tactical decisions toward a more strategic direction with AI. For example, MTU Aero Engines, a leading global engine manufacturer, implemented an AI strategy as a strategic response to unfold the underlying value potential of AI and, thus, sustainably strengthen its competitive position in the market (appliedAI Initiative GmbH, 2022).

With the transformative impact of AI on the scope, scale, speed, and source through which organizations set courses of action and make decisions, a reassessment of how to design strategies in the age of AI becomes imperative. The transformative impact of AI at a strategic level, and the resulting need for an AI strategy, can be understood through the argument that environmental and organizational changes shape the evolution of strategy (Rajagopalan & Spreitzer, 1997). Hence, (1) the facets of contemporary AI lead to (2) market and resource shifts, which, in turn, result in (3) strategic challenges. These strategic challenges require a strategic response from organizations in the form of an (4) AI strategy (see Fig. 8.1).

8.1.1 Taxonomy of AI Strategy

The strategic implications of AI necessitate a structured and multidimensional approach. In response, a comprehensive taxonomy of AI strategy is introduced (see Table 8.1), addressing the complex challenges and opportunities associated with this field. This taxonomy, comprising 15 dimensions and 45 characteristics, is aligned with the overarching meta-characteristic—the design space of AI strategy within organizations. Building on the framework established by Bharadwaj et al. (2013), the taxonomy is organized into four core layers: scope, scale, speed, and source, providing a systematic perspective for analyzing and operationalizing AI strategies.

The *scope* layer refers to the activities that organizations perform within their direct control and ownership to establish a digital technology in line with firm-specific goals as well as internal and external constraints. As decisions about the scope play a central role in the context of an AI strategy, we bundle the relevant aspects regarding the anchoring of responsibility and accountability for the strategic use of AI here. *Strategic ownership* refers to the entity that is in charge of the definition and execution of an AI strategy within an organization (Jöhnk et al., 2021). *Organizational anchoring* describes the sphere of coverage of an AI strategy in line with the structures and processes of an organization (Borges et al., 2021). *Life cycle management* refers to the setup of teams responsible for the technical management of AI applications across the entire life cycle from development to operation within an organization (Shollo et al., 2022). *Governance level* describes the sphere of accountability that ensures that AI applications are developed and operated in line with social, legal, and ethical values (Volberda et al., 2021). *Control mechanisms* refer to the guidelines and standards that govern the design of secure and reliable AI

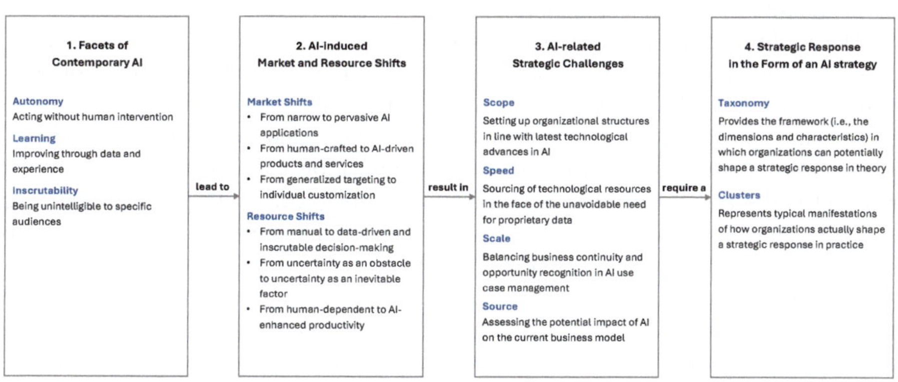

Fig. 8.1 Chain of argumentation for the need for an artificial intelligence strategy

Table 8.1 Taxonomy of artificial intelligence strategy

Layer	Dimension	Characteristics			
Scope	Strategic ownership	Central staff unit	Separate department	Integrated team	Cross-functional unit
	Organizational anchoring	Corporate	Divisional	Functional	Proprietary
	Life cycle management	Centralized	Decentralized	Federal	
	Governance level	Enterprise-wide	Portfolio-based	Application-specific	
	Control mechanisms	Guiding	Restricting	No additional	
	Data governance framework	Isolated	Hybrid	Integrated	
Scale	Knowledge acquisition	Training	Hiring	Contracting	
	Technology sourcing	Make	Hybrid	Buy	
Speed	Use case identification	Systematical		Experimental	
	Use case expansion	One-to-many		Many-to-one	
Source	Technology aspiration	Established	Cutting-edge	Bleeding-edge	
	Business model impact	Complementing	Extending	Renewing	
	Risk tolerance	High risk	Limited risk	Minimal risk	
	Value creation	Frontstage	Backstage	Front- and backstage	
	Value recipient effect	Replacing	Reinforcing	Revealing	

applications to avoid erroneous or discriminatory AI-driven decisions (Keding, 2021). *Data governance framework* describes whether the principles and practices for collecting, storing, and managing data within an organization are defined as part of an AI strategy (Jöhnk et al., 2021).

The *scale* layer describes the leverage effects (e.g., strategic alliances, partner ecosystems) that help organizations to establish a digital technology in a profitable way. Regarding an AI strategy, we subsume here how organizations can proceed to ensure the presence of relevant human capacity and technology resources. *Knowledge acquisition* describes how an organization ensures the availability of relevant skills and competencies (Mikalef & Gupta, 2021). *Technology sourcing* describes how an organization acquires the relevant technical resources to develop and operate AI applications (Baier et al., 2019).

The *speed* layer refers to the time and sequence in which organizations release products and services related to a digital technology. As the speed with which organizations bring products and services with AI functionality in a productive environment plays a central role in the context of an AI strategy, we describe here how organizations proceed to establish AI use cases. *Use case identification* refers to the strategic practice of how an organization proceeds to find relevant AI use cases in line with firm-specific goals as well as internal and external constraints (Pumplun et al., 2019). *Use case expansion* describes the strategic practice that an organization applies to disseminate AI use cases across different application areas (Sjödin et al., 2021).

The *source* layer describes the mechanisms and activities through which organizations gain value from products or services related to a digital technology. Regarding an AI strategy, we subsume here the relevant aspects that serve organizations as the cornerstone to achieve value with AI. *Technology aspiration* refers to the strategic consciousness of an organization regarding the performance of AI applications (Weber et al., 2022). *Risk tolerance* describes the risk level that an organization is willing to accept when developing and operating AI applications to achieve a desired return (Jöhnk et al., 2021). *Business model impact* refers to the potentially disruptive character of AI on the current business model of an organization (Weber et al., 2022). *Value creation* refers to the level at which an organization leverages AI to establish a value for themselves or others (Shollo et al., 2022). *Value recipient effect* describes how the use of AI influences human capabilities and capacities (e.g., human intuition and creativity) (Krakowski et al., 2023).

The taxonomy presented here offers a structured way to capture and make sense of the diverse approaches organizations take when developing an AI strategy. In practice, AI strategies often appear in various forms, with little consistency or common structure. This taxonomy provides managers with a practical framework to navigate these differences and better understand how AI-related strategic choices can be organized. By mapping out key dimensions and characteristics, it becomes easier to identify where a company's current AI efforts stand and how they might evolve. Importantly, the taxonomy also functions as a kind of strategic toolbox: each combination of characteristics represents a potential configuration of an AI strategy. This allows decision-makers not only to see what options exist, but also to explore which of them are most desirable, feasible, and aligned with their specific goals and constraints. In this way, the taxonomy supports a more deliberate and effective approach to designing AI strategies.

8.1.2 Clusters of AI Strategy

Building on the taxonomy, a cluster analysis identified common patterns in how organizations approach AI strategy. The analysis revealed four distinct strategic archetypes that frequently occur in practice: the Technology Navigator, Innovation Explorer, Business Enhancer, and Operations Stabilizer (Table 8.2). Each of these clusters reflects a typical combination of strategic choices that organizations make in their use of AI. The cluster names capture the general orientation or mindset these organizations adopt toward AI.

The four clusters—Technology Navigator, Innovation Explorer, Business Enhancer, and Operations Stabilizer—reflect distinct strategic approaches to AI

Table 8.2 Clusters of artificial intelligence strategy

Class	Name	Description	Example
1	Technology Navigator	Push the boundaries of AI through continuous research and development. Respective organizations undertake risky but rewarding projects to achieve technological breakthroughs at the forefront of AI	JPMorgan, Microsoft, Infineon, SAP
2	Innovation Explorer	Delve into promising emerging and previously uncharted territories with AI. Respective organizations invest substantial resources in AI to unlock new value streams alongside existing products and services	American Express, Bayer, E.ON, Volkswagen
3	Business Enhancer	Focus on improving the operational performance of processes or routines with AI. Respective organizations explore AI in initial use cases but are cautious about the widespread application	MTU Aero Engines, Procter & Gambler, Linde, Chevron
4	Operations Stabilizer	Resort to AI to date in only a few isolated or scattered use cases. Respective organizations prefer stability and reliability over breakthrough innovations due to the potential risks and adverse outcomes of AI	Henkel, Nike, McDonald's, Coca-Cola

adoption and utilization. *Technology Navigators* represent organizations that prioritize cutting-edge research and development, aiming to achieve technological breakthroughs and maintain a leading position in AI innovation. *Innovation Explorers* focus on exploring uncharted opportunities by investing substantial resources into new AI applications, unlocking additional value streams alongside existing offerings. *Business Enhancers* take a more cautious approach, leveraging AI to optimize existing processes and improve operational efficiency while minimizing risk. Finally, *Operations Stabilizers* adopt AI in a limited and focused manner, prioritizing stability, reliability, and risk mitigation (Table 8.2).

This clustering framework offers significant value for organizations aiming to align their AI initiatives with their strategic objectives. By identifying their current position within one of these clusters, organizations can better understand the prevailing characteristics of their AI strategy and evaluate how it aligns with their long-term goals. Furthermore, the framework provides actionable insights for strategic decision-making, helping businesses prioritize investments, mitigate risks, and address challenges associated with AI adoption. Ultimately, the taxonomy and its derived clusters serve as a guiding tool for companies to navigate the complexities of AI strategy and harness its transformative potential effectively.

Summary

The growing importance of AI is prompting organizations to develop strategic approaches that align AI initiatives with broader business goals. Due to AI's unique characteristics—autonomy, learning, and inscrutability—it presents novel strategic challenges that traditional IT strategies cannot fully address. A

(*continued*)

(continued)
structured response in the form of an AI strategy is essential to address these challenges and leverage AI's potential effectively. To support this, a taxonomy of AI strategy organizes the design space into 15 dimensions across four layers. Building on this, a cluster analysis identified four strategic approaches—Technology Navigator, Innovation Explorer, Business Enhancer, and Operations Stabilizer—helping organizations align their AI initiatives with strategic goals, address challenges, and achieve sustainable competitive advantages.

8.2 AI Readiness Definition and Related Terms

AI readiness is defined as the preparedness of organizations to implement changes involving applications and technology related to AI (Alsheibani et al., 2018). This preparedness encompasses various dimensions, including technical infrastructure, organizational culture, and strategic alignment. AI readiness is crucial because it determines an organization's ability to effectively leverage AI technologies to drive innovation, improve efficiency, and maintain a competitive edge. The concept emphasizes that successful AI implementation is not solely about adopting new technologies but also about ensuring that the organization as a whole is equipped to integrate these technologies into its existing processes and culture (Jöhnk et al., 2021).

The necessity of AI readiness stems from the significant impact AI can have on organizational performance. Companies that are well-prepared for AI can capitalize on its capabilities to optimize operations, enhance decision-making, and create new value propositions. Conversely, organizations that lack AI readiness may struggle to achieve the expected benefits from AI initiatives, leading to potential failures and lost opportunities. Thus, assessing and enhancing AI readiness is a critical step for any organization looking to adopt AI technologies. AI readiness is a multifaceted concept that involves the preparedness of organizations to effectively implement and utilize AI technologies. It is closely related to innovation adoption and organizational readiness for change, both of which are critical for successful AI integration. By understanding and addressing these interconnected concepts, organizations can enhance their capabilities to leverage AI, drive innovation, and achieve strategic objectives.

8.2.1 Organizational Readiness for Change

Organizational readiness indicates the state necessary for an organization to engage in specific activities, such as adopting an innovation such as AI (Jöhnk et al., 2021; Lokuge et al., 2019). Organizational readiness for change involves a comprehensive assessment of various factors that contribute to an organization's ability to implement and sustain new technologies. It is essential for successful AI adoption as it ensures that the organization is equipped to handle the complexities and challenges associated with implementing AI technologies. This readiness involves not only the technical aspects of AI integration but also the human and cultural elements that are crucial for achieving long-term success. By fostering a culture of readiness and resilience, organizations can better navigate the disruptions and opportunities brought about by AI and other innovations.

In the context of organizational readiness for change, it is important to recognize that many of the factors influencing readiness for technology adoption are not unique to AI. These factors provide a general foundation that can inform our understanding of what is required for AI readiness specifically (Chwelos et al., 2001; Damanpour & Schneider, 2006; Iacovou et al., 1995; Lokuge et al., 2019):

- *Financial and Technological Resources*: Organizations must have adequate financial resources to invest in new technologies and the necessary technological infrastructure to support these innovations. This includes robust data management systems and high-performance computing resources, which are essential for implementing advanced technologies.
- *Management Support*: Strong support from top management is crucial for any technological adoption. This ensures that initiatives receive the necessary attention and resources and are aligned with the organization's strategic goals. Management support is key to overcoming resistance to change and fostering a culture that embraces innovation.
- *Organizational Culture*: A culture that encourages innovation and is open to change significantly enhances an organization's readiness for technology adoption. Such a culture supports experimentation, tolerates calculated risks, and values continuous learning.
- *Commitment*: Organizational commitment to technology initiatives is vital for overcoming the challenges and setbacks that may arise during implementation. This commitment should be reflected in dedicated teams, clear goals, and persistent efforts to integrate new technologies into the organization's operations.
- *Communication of Goals*: Clear communication regarding technology-related goals and objectives helps align the efforts of various stakeholders within the organization. Effective communication ensures that everyone understands the purpose and benefits of new technology initiatives and works collaboratively toward achieving these goals.
- *Partnership Readiness*: Collaborating with external partners, such as technology vendors, consultants, and academic institutions, can provide valuable expertise and resources. Organizations must be prepared to establish and manage these partnerships effectively to leverage external capabilities for technology adoption.

8.2.2 Innovation Adoption

Innovation adoption refers to the decision-making process through which organizations choose to embrace new technologies and innovations (Jöhnk et al., 2021, Frambach & Schillewaert, 2002). This process is driven by the expectation of improved organizational performance and the recognition of the necessity of integrating new technologies into business operations. In the context of AI, innovation adoption involves understanding the potential benefits of AI, evaluating its fit within the organization, and making strategic decisions to implement AI solutions. The adoption of AI as a technological innovation involves several key considerations. Organizations need to assess the readiness of their existing infrastructure, the availability of necessary skills and knowledge, and the alignment of AI initiatives with their strategic goals. Effective innovation adoption also requires a supportive organizational culture that encourages experimentation and embraces change. By fostering a culture of innovation, organizations can facilitate smoother transitions to AI and other emerging technologies.

AI readiness serves as a crucial antecedent to AI adoption, as it determines whether an organization is capable of initiating and engaging with AI innovations. To understand where AI readiness fits into the broader scope of technology adoption, it is important to examine the general process of innovation adoption (Rogers, 2003; Gopalakrishnan & Damanpour, 1997; Hameed et al., 2012; Jöhnk et al., 2021). This process can be divided into three main stages: initiation, adoption decision, and implementation (Fig. 8.2).

The *initiation* stage focuses on identifying innovations and possible application scenarios. It involves three key steps: awareness of the innovation, consideration for adoption, and the proposal for adoption. Organizations become aware of new technologies, like AI, through various channels such as industry reports, conferences, or peer interactions. Once an innovation is recognized, the next step is to consider its relevance and potential benefits. This consideration involves preliminary assessments to determine if the innovation aligns with the organization's strategic goals. Finally, if deemed potentially beneficial, a formal proposal for adoption is drafted, outlining the expected impacts and resource requirements.

In the *adoption decision* stage, the organization evaluates the proposal for the innovation in detail. This stage is crucial as it determines whether the innovation will be accepted or rejected. The evaluation involves rigorous analysis, including cost–benefit assessments, risk evaluations, and feasibility studies. Stakeholders from various departments may be involved to ensure a comprehensive understanding of the innovation's implications. If the proposal is accepted, the organization

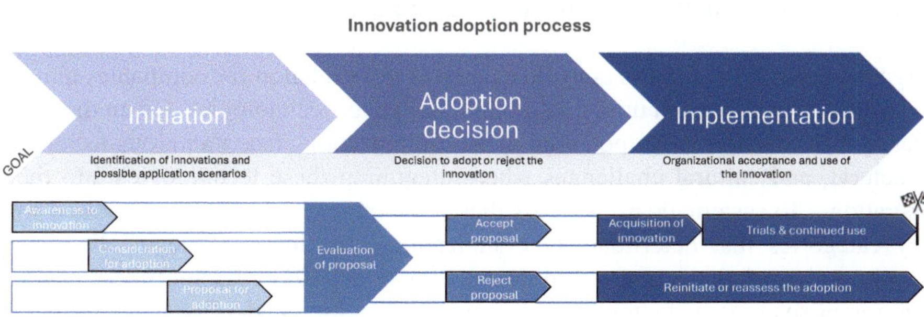

Fig. 8.2 Innovation adoption process. (Adapted from Jöhnk et al., 2021)

prepares for the next stage. In case of rejection, the process may be paused or reinitiated or reassessed, for example, with a modified proposal.

In the *implementation* stage, the focus shifts to the organizational acceptance and use of the innovation. Once the decision is made to adopt, the organization moves forward with the acquisition of the innovation, which may include infrastructure setup, licensing, and staff training. This is followed by trials and continued use, where the innovation is tested in practice, optimized, and eventually integrated into existing processes.

The general process of innovation adoption also applies to AI implementation. AI readiness plays a critical role across all phases: In the initiation stage, it helps identify realistic application scenarios; during the adoption decision, it supports the evaluation of whether the organization is equipped for AI; and in the implementation phase, it enables effective integration and sustained use. Assessing readiness factors such as strategic alignment, resources, or culture reveals gaps and guides necessary improvements, ensuring a smoother and more successful AI adoption process.

Summary

AI readiness refers to an organization's preparedness to adopt and integrate AI technologies, encompassing technical, cultural, and strategic dimensions. Closely linked to innovation adoption and organizational readiness for change, it ensures that organizations can effectively manage AI implementation. Organizational readiness for change highlights the importance of aligning resources, leadership, and culture to enable and sustain technological transformation. Within the innovation adoption process—initiation, adoption decision, and implementation—AI readiness plays a vital role in early evaluations, helping identify capability gaps and areas for improvement. This enables organizations to proactively address challenges and ensure successful and value-generating AI integration.

8.3 Organizational AI Readiness Factors

Organizational AI readiness constitutes a critical foundation for companies aiming to successfully adopt and utilize artificial intelligence technologies. Given the complexity and transformative potential of AI, organizations face numerous technical, structural, and cultural challenges when integrating these technologies into their operations. To systematically address these challenges, research has identified five key categories that determine an organization's readiness: strategic alignment, resources, knowledge, culture, and data (Jöhnk et al., 2021). Each of these categories comprises specific factors that serve as enablers for AI adoption and ensure that

Table 8.3 Organizational AI readiness factors

Strategic alignment	Resources	Knowledge	Culture	Data
AI-business potential	Financial budget	AI awareness	Innovativeness	Data availability
Customer AI readiness	Personnel	Upskilling	Collaborative work	Data quality
Top management support	IT infrastructure	AI ethics	Change management	Data accessibility
AI-process fit				Data flow
Data-driven decision-making				

Adapted from Jöhnk et al. (2021)

the organization is equipped not only with the necessary technical capabilities, but also with the strategic direction, skilled personnel, adaptive culture, and high-quality data infrastructure needed to translate AI ambitions into actionable outcomes (see Table 8.3). Rather than focusing on a single dimension, it is the interplay of all five categories that determines whether organizations can fully leverage the benefits of AI and avoid the pitfalls of isolated or misaligned initiatives.

8.3.1 Strategic Alignment

Given the pivotal role of strategic alignment in the context of business strategy, it is essential to undertake an in-depth examination and understanding of the concept (Jöhnk et al., 2021). Firstly, the *AI-business potential* must be acknowledged and emphasized. AI, which is characterized by its versatility, can be applied in a multitude of ways across different domains within an organization. Crucially, organizations should not only identify areas of application, but also critically examine the relative advantage of AI-based systems compared to existing solutions (Pumplun et al., 2019). Given AI's wide-ranging applicability across the entire value chain, traditional approaches to use case identification often fall short. Instead, organizations must adopt opportunity-driven methods that foster structured exploration of AI use cases and help to systematically uncover where AI can deliver concrete value.

Furthermore, enabling *customer AI readiness* is a crucial part of strategic alignment. Customer AI readiness refers to the knowledge and acceptance customers have regarding the use of AI-integrated offerings. However, the inherent complexity of AI often results in a lack of transparency, which can impede customer acceptance. When customers have insufficient understanding or unrealistic expectations of AI, this can lead to unmet expectations and frustration during usage (Brill et al., 2019). Organizations must ensure that their AI systems are understandable and transparent to both internal users and external customers to facilitate trust and the widespread adoption of AI-integrated offerings.

Moreover, *top management support* constitutes a key dimension of AI readiness, as it reflects the willingness of leadership to initiate AI adoption from the top down while also enabling and endorsing bottom-up initiatives. Given the broad organizational changes associated with AI, a clear and organization-wide signal from top management is essential to drive commitment and overcome internal resistance. Effective support involves more than strategic alignment—it includes actively integrating AI into the corporate strategy (Bughin et al., 2017) and fostering both awareness and knowledge of AI throughout the organization. By acting as visible champions of AI, top managers can allocate critical resources, promote a culture of innovation, and create the organizational momentum required for AI-driven transformation.

Additionally, the concept of *AI-process fit* emphasizes the critical alignment between an organization's AI strategy and its operational processes to foster AI readiness. Since AI adoption inherently impacts existing workflows, organizations must ensure that their processes are compatible with AI requirements. This compatibility is primarily facilitated by a mature process landscape—characterized by standardization and structure—which enables the effective deployment of AI systems (Watson et al., 2019). Structured and consistent data flows resulting from standardized processes are particularly crucial, as they form the foundation for AI's analytical and decision-making capabilities. Thus, aligning business processes with the technical prerequisites of AI not only supports smoother integration but also maximizes the operational value of AI solutions.

Lastly, *data-driven decision-making* underscores the importance of systematically incorporating data insights into organizational decision-making processes. Rather than relying on intuition or experience-based judgment, data-driven decision-making leverages analytical methods to derive evidence-based insights (Jarrahi, 2018). Establishing such a practice not only improves organizational performance but also serves as a foundational step toward AI readiness, as it familiarizes employees with interpreting and acting upon algorithmic recommendations. By promoting a culture in which decisions are consistently guided by data, organizations can ensure that AI systems are effectively integrated as complementary tools, enriching human decision-making rather than replacing it.

8.3.2 Resources

The availability of resources represents a fundamental aspect of an organization's readiness for AI (Jöhnk et al., 2021). Successful implementation and integration of AI technologies depend on the targeted allocation and effective management of key resources. This includes not only financial investments but also access to qualified personnel and adequate IT infrastructure. Together, these elements create the necessary foundation for building and sustaining AI capabilities within the organization.

The *financial budget* refers to the resources that organizations allocate to support AI adoption (Pumplun et al., 2019). Since implementing AI systems typically requires adaptation to an organization's specific context and data landscape, the process is both time-consuming and cost-intensive. In addition to covering initial implementation efforts, organizations must invest in building internal expertise and addressing uncertainties related to the capabilities and potential value of AI. A sufficiently planned and flexible budget is therefore essential to avoid underfunding and to enable the long-term success of AI initiatives.

The *personnel* or human resources aspect of AI readiness emphasizes the necessity for a diverse and skilled team capable of driving the AI agenda. The adoption of AI extends beyond the mere deployment of technology. It requires a comprehensive understanding of its application across various business functions. Consequently, organizations must invest in a broad spectrum of roles, including AI specialists, data scientists, and business analysts who possess specific know-how to facilitate AI integration (Bawack et al., 2019; Fountaine et al., 2019). These professionals play a pivotal role in the realization of AI's potential, the translation of complex algorithms into actionable business strategies, and the alignment of AI applications with organizational goals. It is also necessary to provide training and continuous professional development for existing staff, to enable them to keep pace with the evolving technologies and methodologies associated with AI.

In addition, the implementation of AI is contingent upon the existence of robust *IT infrastructure*. The introduction of AI introduces high workloads and significant data storage requirements, which must be addressed to achieve successful AI implementation. The infrastructure must be scalable, resilient, and capable of supporting the intensive computational demands of AI technologies (Intel, 2018). This encompasses robust data processing capabilities, secure and ample storage solutions, and reliable network bandwidth. An effective IT infrastructure is essential for the seamless integration of AI systems into existing workflows, the real-time processing of data, and the assurance of data security and compliance. Organizations must assess their current IT capabilities, identify any deficiencies, and invest in upgrading their infrastructure to meet the demands of AI technologies. This strategic investment in IT infrastructure not only facilitates AI readiness but also paves the way for future technological advancements.

8.3.3 Knowledge

The third factor in organizational AI readiness is knowledge (Jöhnk et al., 2021). This factor represents a fundamental element in the successful adoption and integration of AI technologies within an organization. The knowledge domain can be divided into three key components in the context of AI: awareness, skill development, and ethical standards. Each of these components is essential for fostering a well-informed, competent, and ethically grounded workforce capable of navigating the complexities inherent in AI initiatives.

AI awareness represents a foundational element of organizational AI readiness, as it marks the starting point for engaging employees in the adoption of AI technologies. Given the abstract nature of AI concepts—such as machine learning, prediction, or generative capabilities—nonspecialist employees often struggle to grasp their implications and value (Hofmann et al., 2020). Therefore, it is essential to establish a basic understanding of cognitive AI functions across all organizational levels. This helps employees recognize AI as a versatile tool with potential relevance to their specific tasks or industry context. Moreover, fostering such awareness enables employees to appreciate the importance of factors like data quality—for instance, understanding that meaningful AI outputs depend on the quality of inputs. On an organizational level, AI awareness contributes to the development of realistic expectations, reduces uncertainty, and promotes a more informed and constructive engagement with AI technologies.

Continuous *upskilling* is essential to ensure that employees possess the interdisciplinary skillsets required for the successful implementation of AI technologies. This includes technical knowledge—such as data analytics, statistics, and data engineering—as well as domain-specific expertise (Pumplun et al., 2019). Due to the shortage of AI specialists on the labor market, organizations are increasingly required to invest in internal capacity building. In addition to these strategic considerations, legal requirements further emphasize the importance of AI literacy: Article 4 of the EU AI Act (Regulation 2024/1689) mandates that providers and deployers of AI systems ensure an adequate level of AI literacy among staff involved in operating and using such systems. This must be tailored to employees' prior experience, roles, and the specific application context. To address this, researchers have proposed five key AI literacy domains (Gimpel et al., 2024): (1) AI Technology, referring to the foundational understanding of AI systems; (2) AI Development and Operations, covering implementation and maintenance skills; (3) AI Use, focusing on the integration of AI into business processes; (4) AI Management, addressing strategic planning and oversight; and (5) AI Reflection, which includes ethical, legal, and societal implications. Structured upskilling initiatives based on these domains not only close internal skill gaps but also empower employees, promote engagement, and ensure that organizations remain competitive in a rapidly evolving AI landscape.

The last aspect, *AI ethics*, emphasizes the significance of ethical considerations in the deployment and utilization of AI. While AI systems are undoubtedly powerful, they also come with inherent risks. These include the possibility of biased algorithms, safety violations, and the potential for discrimination in outcomes. It is not merely a technical necessity but also an ethical imperative to address these risks. The field of AI ethics encompasses the implementation of measures designed to identify, monitor, and mitigate biases in AI algorithms. It also involves ensuring transparency in AI decision-making processes and safeguarding against unethical practices. This necessitates the establishment of a robust framework of guidelines and standards that govern the development and deployment of AI, with a particular emphasis on fairness, accountability, and inclusivity (Agrawal et al., 2018). Organizations must prioritize ethical training, ensuring that their workforce is well-versed in ethical AI practices and aware of the societal implications of AI technologies. Such an ethical foundation not only serves to engender trust among stakeholders but also reinforces the organization's dedication to the responsible use of AI.

8.3.4 Culture

The culture of an organization is a crucial factor in determining its readiness for the implementation of organizational AI (Jöhnk et al., 2021). The term "culture" can be defined as the collective mindset, attitudes and behaviors that either facilitate or hinder the integration of AI technologies. In particular, innovativeness, collaborative work, and change management represent the cultural foundation necessary for fostering an environment conducive to AI adoption.

Innovativeness represents a vital dimension of AI readiness, as it reflects the adaptability and willingness of employees to embrace change. Successfully leveraging AI as a general-purpose technology requires employees to experiment, take risks, and apply diverse problem-solving approaches across multiple areas. However, in many organizations—especially larger ones—there is a tendency to rely on established routines, which can hinder innovation and delay AI adoption (Pumplun et al., 2019). To counteract this, it is essential to foster a culture in which AI is perceived not as a threat to job security, but as an opportunity for personal and organizational growth. Transparent communication, visible success stories, and support for experimentation can help create a mindset open to AI-driven transformation and continuous improvement.

Collaborative work is another key cultural factor that supports AI readiness. Given the multidisciplinary nature of AI, effective collaboration between domain experts, AI specialists, and IT departments is essential (Davenport, 2018; Fountaine et al., 2019). Working in cross-functional teams helps to break down silos, facilitates mutual understanding, and enables the identification of valuable AI use cases across the organization. To realize these benefits, organizations must actively promote collaboration across departmental boundaries, ensuring that diverse skills and perspectives are integrated toward common goals. Structured collaboration frameworks and supportive leadership can further enhance joint problem-solving and accelerate the development of effective AI solutions.

Change management is a key enabler of AI readiness, as it supports employees in understanding and adapting to AI-induced organizational change. Resistance often stems from misconceptions—particularly fears of job loss—despite the fact that AI typically automates specific tasks rather than replacing entire job roles (Brynjolfsson & McAfee, 2017). Effective change management addresses such concerns through clear communication, targeted training, and continuous support (Fountaine et al., 2019). Leaders play a central role in this process by acting as change champions who guide employees through the transition. By highlighting the benefits of AI and building trust, change management helps foster acceptance and engagement across the workforce.

8.3.5 Data

In the context of organizational AI readiness, data represents a fundamental and indispensable element, serving as a crucial foundation for all AI initiatives (Jöhnk et al., 2021). The effective utilization of AI is contingent upon several data-related factors, including data availability, data quality, data accessibility, and data flow. Collectively, these factors ensure that AI systems are well-supported, accurate, and capable of delivering actionable insights.

Data availability is a fundamental prerequisite for AI readiness, as AI systems rely on access to sufficient volumes and diverse types of data to function effectively (Agrawal et al., 2018). The ability of AI models to detect patterns, generate predictions, and improve over time is directly tied to the quality and breadth of available data. In this context, structured data—such as relational tables—is particularly valuable for standardized applications, while unstructured data, including text, audio, or images, is essential for more complex use cases like natural language processing or image recognition. To ensure data availability, organizations must establish effective data collection processes, integrate data from heterogeneous sources, and maintain well-managed repositories. Without this foundation, AI systems cannot reach their full potential, underscoring the central role of data availability within the AI ecosystem.

Equally essential for AI readiness is *data quality*, which determines whether data is suitable for effective use by AI systems. Since AI models rely on training data to produce accurate and meaningful outcomes, poor data quality can significantly impair performance—echoing the principle of "garbage in, garbage out" (Davenport, 2018). Relevant data quality dimensions include completeness, correctness, consistency, and timeliness. In practice, many organizations struggle with the quality of historical data, making it necessary to strengthen capabilities in data preparation, processing, and quality assurance. Establishing robust data governance and cleansing routines is therefore essential to ensure that AI outputs are reliable and actionable.

Data accessibility is a key enabler of efficient AI development. It refers to the ease and speed with which authorized personnel can access relevant data across the organization. For AI specialists to effectively prototype and refine models, seamless access to appropriate data sources is essential. However, this goes beyond technical retrieval—it also involves reducing bureaucratic barriers and avoiding unnecessary delays. Organizations can improve accessibility by implementing robust access management, centralizing data in platforms such as data lakes or warehouses, and dissolving siloed data structures (Pumplun et al., 2019). When data is readily accessible, AI teams can shorten development cycles and respond more dynamically to evolving business demands.

Finally, *data flow* is a critical factor for the continuous operation and improvement of AI systems. A smooth and automated transfer of data from its source to the point of use enables AI models not only to be initially trained, but also to be continuously refined and updated over time. This ongoing processing requires well-defined extract-transform-load (ETL) routines, robust data pipelines, and real-time or near-real-time data streams. A reliable data flow ensures that AI systems remain current and capable of generating timely, predictive insights. It also empowers AI specialists to fine-tune models efficiently and react to changes in the data landscape with agility.

Summary
Organizational AI readiness involves critical factors: strategic alignment, resources, knowledge, culture, and data. Strategic alignment ensures AI initiatives align with goals and receive top management support, fostering clear AI objectives and streamlined decision-making. Resources, including financial planning, personnel expertise, and IT infrastructure, are vital for AI's successful implementation. Knowledge entails AI awareness, continuous upskilling, and ethical considerations. A supportive culture driven by innovation, collaboration, and effective change management is essential. Data factors like availability, quality, accessibility, and flow ensure AI systems are well-supported and capable of delivering actionable insights for enhanced decision-making and operational efficiency.

References

Ågerfalk, P. J., Conboy, K., Crowston, K., Eriksson Lundström, J. S. Z., Jarvenpaa, S., Ram, S., & Mikalef, P. (2022). Artificial intelligence in information systems: State of the art and research roadmap. *Communications of the Association for Information Systems, 50*, 420–438.

Agrawal, A., Gans, J., & Goldfarb, A. (2018). *Prediction machines: The simple economics of artificial intelligence*. Harvard Business Review Press.

Alsheibani, S., Cheung, Y., & Messom, C. (2018). Artificial intelligence adoption: AI-readiness at firm-level. In *Pacific Asia Conference on Information Systems* 2018 (p. 37). Association for Information Systems.

appliedAI Initiative GmbH. (2022). *MTU Aero Engines: Greater value creation with the help of AI*. Accessed January 31, 2025, from https://www.appliedai.de/insights/mtu-aero-engines-stellen-weichen-wertschoepfung-mithilfe-ki

Baier, L., Jöhren, F., & Seebacher, S. (2019). Challenges in the deployment and operation of machine learning in practice. In *Proceedings of the 27th European Conference on Information Systems (ECIS)*, Stockholm & Uppsala, Sweden.

Bawack, R., Wamba, S., & Carillo, K. (2019). Artificial intelligence in practice: Implications for information systems research. In *Proceedings of the 25th Americas Conference on Information Systems (AMCIS)*, Cancún, Mexico.

Bharadwaj, A., El Sawy, O. A., Pavlou, P. A., & Venkatraman, N. (2013). Digital business strategy: Toward a next generation of insights. *MIS Quarterly, 37*, 471–482.

Borges, A. F., Laurindo, F. J., Spínola, M. M., Gonçalves, R. F., & Mattos, C. A. (2021). The strategic use of artificial intelligence in the digital era: Systematic literature review and future research directions. *International Journal of Information Management, 57*, 102225.

Brill, T. M., Munoz, L., & Miller, R. J. (2019). Siri, Alexa, and other digital assistants: A study of customer satisfaction with artificial intelligence applications. *Journal of Marketing Management, 35*(15–16), 1401–1436.

Brynjolfsson, E., & McAfee, A. (2017). The business of artificial intelligence: What it can—And cannot—Do for your organization. *Harvard Business Review*.

Bughin, J., Hazan, E., Ramaswamy, S., Chui, M., Allas, T., Dahlström, P., Henke, N., & Trench, M. (2017). *Artificial intelligence: The next digital frontier?* McKinsey Global Institute.

Chwelos, P., Benbasat, I., & Dexter, A. S. (2001). Empirical test of an EDI adoption model. *Information Systems Research, 12*(3), 304–321.

Damanpour, F., & Schneider, M. (2006). Phases of the adoption of innovation in organizations: Effects of environment, organization and top managers 1. *British Journal of Management, 17*(3), 215–236.

Davenport, T. (2018). From analytics to artificial intelligence. *Journal of Business Analytics, 1*(2), 73–80.

Enholm, I. M., Papagiannidis, E., Mikalef, P., & Krogstie, J. (2022). Artificial intelligence and business value: A literature review. *Information Systems Frontiers, 24*, 1709–1734.

Feuerriegel, S., Hartmann, J., Janiesch, C., & Zschech, P. (2024). Generative AI. *Business & Information Systems Engineering, 66*, 111–126.

Fountaine, T., McCarthy, B., & Saleh, T. (2019). Building the AI-powered organization. *Harvard Business Review, 97*(4), 62–73.

Frambach, R. T., & Schillewaert, N. (2002). Organizational innovation adoption: A multi-level framework of determinants and opportunities for future research. *Journal of Business Research, 55*(2), 163–176.

Gimpel, H., Clausen, S., Hacker, J., Leimeister, J. M., Morana, S., Schöttl, F., & Söllner, M. (2024). *KI-Kompetenzen in der Wirtschaftsinformatik*. Discussion Paper, Working Group on AI in Teaching of the Association Die Wirtschaftsinformatik e.V. [online] Accessed April 1, 2025, from https://doi.org/10.17605/OSF.IO/WBD84

Gopalakrishnan, S., & Damanpour, F. (1997). A review of innovation research in economics, sociology and technology management. *Omega, 25*(1), 15–28.

Hameed, M. A., Counsell, S., & Swift, S. (2012). A conceptual model for the process of IT innovation adoption in organizations. *Journal of Engineering and Technology Management, 29*(3), 358–390.

Hofmann, P., Jöhnk, J., Protschky, D. & Urbach, N. (2020). Developing purposeful AI use cases—A structured method and its application in project management. In *Proceedings of the 15th Internationale Tagung Wirtschaftsinformatik (WI)*, Potsdam, Germany.

Iacovou, C. L., Benbasat, I., & Dexter, A. S. (1995). Electronic data interchange and small organizations: Adoption and impact of technology. *MIS Quarterly, 19*, 465–485.

Intel. (2018). *The AI readiness model: Judging an organization's ability to generate business value from artificial intelligence*. White Paper. Intel Corporation.

Jarrahi, M. H. (2018). Artificial intelligence and the future of work: Human-AI symbiosis in organizational decision making. *Business Horizons, 61*(4), 577–586.

Jöhnk, J., Weißert, M., & Wyrtki, K. (2021). Ready or not, AI comes—An interview study of organizational AI readiness factors. *Business & Information Systems Engineering, 63*(1), 5–20.

Keding, C. (2021). Understanding the interplay of artificial intelligence and strategic management: Four decades of research in review. *Management Review Quarterly, 71*, 91–134.

Krakowski, S., Luger, J., & Raisch, S. (2023). Artificial intelligence and the changing sources of competitive advantage. *Strategic Management Journal, 44*, 1425–1452.

Lokuge, S., Sedera, D., Grover, V., & Dongming, X. (2019). Organizational readiness for digital innovation: Development and empirical calibration of a construct. *Information & Management, 56*(3), 445–461.

Mikalef, P., & Gupta, M. (2021). Artificial intelligence capability: Conceptualization, measurement calibration, and empirical study on its impact on organizational creativity and firm performance. *Information & Management, 58*, 103434.

Pumplun, L., Tauchert, C., & Heidt, M. (2019). A new organizational chassis for artificial intelligence - exploring organizational readiness factors. In *Proceedings of the 27th European conference on information systems (ECIS)*, Stockholm & Uppsala, Sweden.

Rajagopalan, N., & Spreitzer, G. M. (1997). Toward a theory of strategic change: A multi-lens perspective and integrative framework. *Academy of Management Review, 22*, 48–79.

Rogers, E. (2003). *Diffusion of innovations* (5th ed.). Free Press.

Sagodi, A., van Giffen, B., Schniertshauer, J., Niehues, K., & vom Brocke, J. (2024). How Audi scales artificial intelligence in manufacturing. *MIS Quarterly Executive, 23*, 185–204.

Shollo, A., Hopf, K., Thiess, T., & Müller, O. (2022). Shifting ML value creation mechanisms: A process model of ML value creation. *Journal of Strategic Information Systems, 31*, 101734.

Sjödin, D., Parida, V., Palmié, M., & Wincent, J. (2021). How AI capabilities enable business model innovation: Scaling AI through co-evolutionary processes and feedback loops. *Journal of Business Research, 134*, 574–587.

Volberda, H. W., Khanagha, S., Baden-Fuller, C., Mihalache, O. R., & Birkinshaw, J. (2021). Strategizing in a digital world: Overcoming cognitive barriers, reconfiguring routines and introducing new organizational forms. *Long Range Planning, 54*, 102110.

Watson, J., Hatfield, S., Wright, D., Howard, M., Witherick, D., Coe, L., & Horton, R. (2019). Automation with intelligence: Reimagining the organisation in the 'age of with'. [online] *Deloitte*. Accessed April 1, 2025, from https://www2.deloitte.com/content/dam/Deloitte/tw/Documents/strategy/tw-Automation-with-intelligence.pdf

Weber, M., Beutter, M., Weking, J., Böhm, M., & Krcmar, H. (2022). AI Startup Business Models. *Business & Information Systems Engineering, 64*, 91–109.

Nils Urbach is Professor of Information Systems and Digital Business as well as Director of the Research Lab for Digital Innovation and Transformation at the Frankfurt University of Applied Sciences, Germany. Furthermore, he is Director at the FIM Research Center for Information Management, and the Branch Business and Information Systems Engineering of Fraunhofer FIT. Nils Urbach has been working in the fields of digital innovation and transformation for several years. His work has been published in several academic journals such as Information Systems Research (ISR), the Journal of the Association for Information Systems (JAIS), the Journal of Strategic Information Systems (JSIS), the Journal of Information Technology (JIT), MIS Quarterly Executive (MISQE), IEEE Transactions on Engineering Management (IEEE TEM), Information and Management (I&M), Business and Information Systems Engineering (BISE), and Electronic Markets (EM). He advises several companies on digitalization issues and regularly appears as a speaker on this topic.

Daniel Feulner received his M.Sc. in information system from the Otto-Friedrich University of Bamberg, Germany in 2023. He is an affiliated researcher at the Branch Business and Information Systems Engineering of the Fraunhofer FIT and FIM Research Center for Information Management at the University of Bayreuth. In his research, he aims to understand how Business Analytics and Artificial Intelligence can be effectively and responsibly utilized in organizations. His goal is to enable companies to drive innovation and achieve sustainable growth in a rapidly evolving technological landscape.

Valentin Mayer received his M.Sc. in Management and Technology from the Technical University of Munich, Germany 2023. He is an affiliated researcher at the Branch Business and Information Systems Engineering of the Fraunhofer FIT and FIM Research Center for Information Management at the University of Bayreuth. His research explores how companies can successfully implement Artificial Intelligence within their organizations, with a particular focus on the conceptual design and operationalization of AI systems. His goal is to equip companies with practical methods to implement AI end-to-end into their operations and create long-term value.

Simon Meierhöfer received his M.Sc. in business administration and engineering from the University of Bayreuth, Germany in 2020. He is an affiliated researcher at the Branch Business & Information Systems Engineering of the Fraunhofer FIT and FIM Research Center for Information Management at the University of Bayreuth. In his research, he aims to understand how organizations can leverage Artificial Intelligence to improve or innovate business processes, reinvent products and services, and even create new business models. His goal is to provide methods and practices that enable organizations to advance the strategic use of Artificial Intelligence.

Governance and Management of AI 9

Nils Urbach, Daniel Feulner, Simon Feulner, Moritz Schüll, and Valentin Mayer

Artificial intelligence (AI) is reshaping how organizations operate, compete, and create value. However, its successful integration into business processes presents significant challenges. These range from technical issues such as data quality and model robustness to broader concerns around ethics, transparency, and regulatory compliance. As AI systems evolve in complexity and reach, managing them effectively demands more than isolated technical solutions. It requires a coordinated, interdisciplinary approach that combines strategic oversight, operational processes, and organizational structures to ensure responsible, trustworthy, and sustainable use of AI.

This chapter explores governance mechanisms that support the safe and effective use of AI as well as presents a method for transforming existing governance approaches in response to the rise of AI. Building on this foundation, the chapter then introduces the AI application management (AIAMA) model as a comprehensive framework for managing the AI lifecycle in alignment with governance principles and organizational goals. It outlines core management dimensions of AI, including technical, process-related, and user-centered aspects, and explains how these are coordinated through integration management. Finally, the chapter discusses the design of organizational structures for organizing AI efforts, including centers of excellence, cross-functional, virtual, and matrix teams.

N. Urbach (✉) · S. Feulner
Frankfurt University of Applied Sciences, Frankfurt am Main, Germany
e-mail: nils.urbach@fim-rc.de; simon.feulner@fim-rc.de

D. Feulner · M. Schüll · V. Mayer
University of Bayreuth, Bayreuth, Germany
e-mail: daniel.feulner@fim-rc.de; moritz.schuell@fim-rc.de; valentin.mayer@fim-rc.de

N. Urbach, D. Feulner (eds.), *Managing Artificial Intelligence*, Future of Business and Finance, https://doi.org/10.1007/978-3-032-13308-3_9

9.1 AI Governance

Governance mechanisms are structured frameworks, policies, procedures, and controls implemented within an organization to guide, monitor, and manage various operations and activities. These mechanisms ensure alignment with the organization's objectives, ethical standards, and regulatory requirements. AI systems require specific governance mechanisms due to their inherent complexity and the numerous failure scenarios they present, which increase uncertainty and risks for organizations. These AI-related risks are outlined in the following section.

9.1.1 AI-Related Risks

Risks associated with AI can arise at various levels, potentially impacting the effectiveness and reliability of AI systems (Schneider et al., 2023; Wirtz et al., 2022; Reddy et al., 2020).

Technical risks are prominent due to the inherent complexity, autonomy, and learning abilities of AI systems. A major technical risk in AI systems arises from the uncertainty surrounding the origin and quality of data and models. In complex infrastructures, the lack of transparency regarding where data comes from can lead to inconsistent or biased inputs, which may affect the system's overall performance and reliability. Additionally, when models themselves are sourced or built with unknown methods, their behavior in different scenarios can become unpredictable, further undermining trust in the system's outcomes. This uncertainty can lead to cascading issues, making it difficult to guarantee accountability and ensure the robustness of AI systems. Another significant challenge is the complex traceability of error sources within AI systems. Given the intricate nature of these technologies, identifying and correcting errors can be difficult, necessitating robust error-tracing protocols as part of the governance framework. Furthermore, AI systems often become new targets for cyber-attacks, which can compromise their functionality and the data they handle. Strong cybersecurity measures are required to protect against such threats.

Economic risks are a further critical concern for organizations adopting AI systems. Developing and operating AI systems typically involves high investment costs. Without proper governance, these expenses can escalate without yielding proportional value. Governance frameworks must therefore include cost management strategies to ensure financial sustainability. Moreover, AI systems may fail to deliver the expected benefits if they are not accepted by users or stakeholders. This lack of acceptance can negate the added value of AI technologies. Promoting user engagement and building trust are essential components of governance to address this issue. Additionally, AI malfunctions can lead to operational disruptions and significant financial losses. These malfunctions can have public and far-reaching consequences, such as biased decision-making, erroneous outputs, or even harmful outcomes that directly affect customers or clients and thus may negatively affect an organization's brand reputation. Regular monitoring and maintenance strategies are necessary to prevent such malfunctions and ensure the reliability of AI systems.

Regulatory risks stem from the need to comply with legal and ethical standards. AI systems must adhere to data protection laws to safeguard privacy and security, necessitating the implementation of governance measures that ensure ongoing compliance. Failure to do so can result in significant penalties, including hefty fines, legal sanctions, and potential restrictions on the use of AI technologies. Missing industry standards and certifications for AI further exacerbates these risks, leading to inconsistencies and potential vulnerabilities. Finally, new AI regulations—such as the EU Artificial Intelligence Act—can be ambiguous and open to interpretation, creating compliance uncertainties. In particular, the EU AI Act (Regulation 2024/1689) requires providers and deployers of high-risk AI systems to establish formalized risk management and governance processes throughout the entire AI lifecycle. This is explicitly laid out in Article 9(1), which mandates a continuous risk management system, and Article 14, which requires human oversight mechanisms. These obligations emphasize the need for organizations to systematically assess and mitigate AI-related risks.

Ethical risks are another significant concern in AI systems. One of the primary issues is the limited mapping of demographic diversity in training data. If the data used to train AI models lacks representation of diverse demographics, the AI system can produce biased outcomes that do not accurately reflect all user groups. Additionally, AI systems can perpetuate existing biases present in the data, passing these biases along through their operations. This can lead to unfair and discriminatory practices. AI developers themselves can also contribute to bias, either intentionally or unintentionally, through their design choices and implementation processes. Furthermore, there is a lack of transferability of value systems across different cultural and social contexts. AI systems designed with one set of values may not align well with the values of other user groups, leading to ethical dilemmas and conflicts.

Social risks associated with AI include trust and acceptance issues from employees and other stakeholders. AI systems can be perceived as threatening or untrustworthy, particularly if there is a lack of transparency in how they operate. Building trust requires clear communication and demonstrable reliability of AI systems. Another social risk arises when stakeholders disagree about the appropriate scope of AI systems—for example, what decisions or actions they should be permitted to take. Such normative disagreements can lead to conflicts and resistance, especially in ethically sensitive contexts. Additionally, there is often dissimilar knowledge about the potentials and challenges of AI systems among stakeholders. This gap in understanding can hinder effective collaboration and the successful implementation of AI technologies.

9.1.2 AI Governance Mechanisms

The cornerstone of effective AI governance lies in achieving an appropriate balance between minimizing potential risks and fostering innovation. On the one hand, insufficient governance can expose organizations to significant risks, as illustrated before. On the other hand, overly restrictive governance may stifle creativity and hinder the development of novel AI solutions that could offer competitive advantages. AI governance, therefore, must be tailored to the specific needs and contexts of the organization. The relevance and application of governance mechanisms can vary greatly depending on factors such as the industry in which the organization operates, the particular use cases of AI, and the technological maturity of the AI systems in question. To address these diverse needs, AI governance mechanisms can be categorized into three distinct levels: structural, procedural, and relational (Schneider et al., 2023; Wirtz et al., 2022; Reddy et al., 2020) (Fig. 9.1).

Structural Mechanisms

Structural governance mechanisms define the formal organizational structures that underpin the management and oversight of AI within a company. They include clearly defined reporting structures, the allocation of decision-making authority, the assignment of roles and responsibilities, and the establishment of governance bodies. Their function is to ensure that AI efforts are guided in a coordinated and accountable manner, aligned with broader organizational goals (Schneider et al., 2023).

One of the main challenges addressed by structural governance is the inherently interdisciplinary nature of AI initiatives, which require coordination across data science, engineering, legal, compliance, domain expertise, and business strategy. To

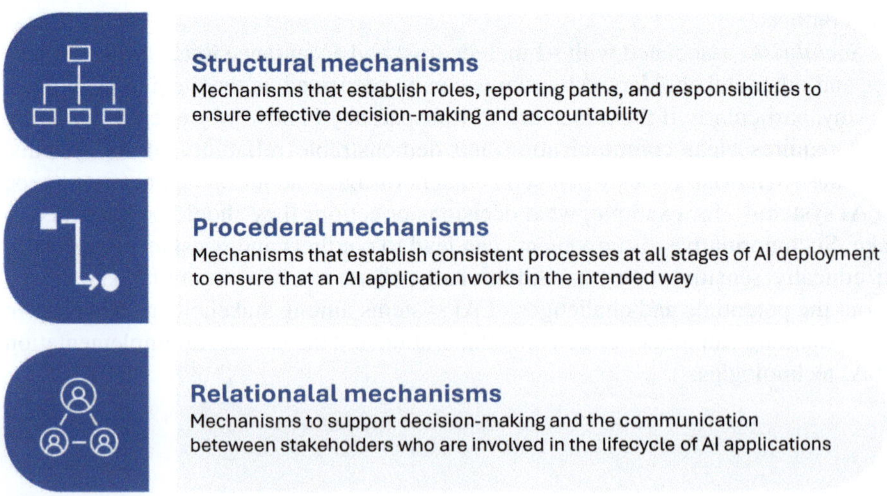

Fig. 9.1 AI governance mechanisms

manage this complexity, structural mechanisms ensure that responsibilities are clearly defined both horizontally—across different phases of the AI lifecycle—and vertically—across levels of authority. While operational responsibilities might be assigned to project leads or technical product owners, strategic oversight often rests with executive sponsors or dedicated roles such as a Chief AI Officer (CAIO). The CAIO acts as a central authority who not only aligns AI efforts with corporate goals but also represents AI initiatives in board-level decision-making.

Structural governance mechanisms also support the institutionalization of specific functions along the AI lifecycle. For example, dedicated data quality teams may be assigned responsibility for monitoring and curating training data to ensure compliance and minimize algorithmic bias. Others may focus on overseeing model performance, system documentation, or compliance audits. Through such clearly delineated roles and decision structures, organizations can manage complexity, reduce ambiguity, and enable more effective collaboration across stakeholder groups.

Another structural response to the growing scope of AI is the establishment of cross-functional governance bodies, such as AI steering committees or interdisciplinary councils, that integrate diverse perspectives into decision processes. These bodies are often tasked with reviewing use cases, defining ethical guidelines, allocating resources, or mediating between business units and technical teams. Similarly, organizations may implement Centers of Excellence (CoEs) to centralize AI expertise, set development standards, and offer training to business units across the company. These centers function as hubs of methodological competence and help reduce redundancies and fragmentation.

By embedding AI into the formal structure of the organization—through roles, bodies, and responsibilities—structural governance mechanisms help ensure that AI is not treated as an isolated technical innovation but as a strategic capability that is managed deliberately and sustainably.

Procedural Mechanisms

Procedural governance mechanisms comprise formalized rules, processes, and procedures that ensure AI systems and machine learning models function correctly, efficiently, and securely. They aim to uphold legal and internal requirements regarding explainability, fairness, accountability, safety, and security. While structural mechanisms define who holds responsibility, procedural mechanisms specify how AI should be developed, validated, deployed, and monitored in practice. They span strategic elements such as policies and standards, as well as operational routines like documentation practices, performance measurement, compliance checks, and escalation procedures (Schneider et al., 2023).

The procedural dimension of AI governance is particularly crucial because of the probabilistic and often opaque nature of machine learning systems. Unlike traditional rule-based software, AI models learn from data and may behave unpredictably or evolve over time. To mitigate such risks, organizations must establish consistent processes that structure the entire AI lifecycle—from the initial definition of objectives and data strategies to model development, validation, deployment, and eventual decommissioning.

A robust procedural foundation helps organizations translate high-level AI governance objectives into standardized, documented, and repeatable practices across the AI lifecycle—from data collection and model development to deployment and continuous monitoring. Procedural governance mechanisms encompass both strategic and operational elements, including AI strategies, policies, standards, processes, contractual agreements, performance measurement, compliance monitoring, and issue management. These mechanisms support reproducibility, accountability, and compliance, and help ensure that AI systems and models meet expectations regarding correctness, efficiency, fairness, explainability, and safety. For instance, they may define how models are tested and documented, specify quality assurance protocols during training, and establish coding and documentation guidelines to facilitate maintainability and traceability. Moreover, continuous monitoring and clearly defined escalation procedures enable organizations to identify and address performance degradation or unexpected outcomes in a structured and accountable manner.

By embedding these rules and routines into the daily operations of AI teams, procedural governance mechanisms serve as the connective tissue between strategic intent and technical implementation. They ensure not only operational robustness, but also accountability, transparency, and adaptability—qualities that are critical for the responsible use of AI at scale.

Relational Mechanisms

Relational governance mechanisms aim to facilitate communication, training, and coordinated decision-making among the various stakeholders involved in the development, deployment, and use of AI systems. These mechanisms help bridge disciplinary and functional divides by fostering mutual understanding and transparency. In contrast to structural and procedural mechanisms, which define responsibilities and formal processes, relational mechanisms address the collaborative dynamics that emerge in interdisciplinary AI initiatives. They support organizations in aligning diverse perspectives, building trust, and ensuring that AI systems are not only technically robust but also organizationally embedded and socially accepted (Schneider et al., 2023).

At their core, relational mechanisms aim to bridge gaps between different knowledge domains and organizational silos. AI systems are rarely developed in isolation. Instead, they require the close involvement of technical teams, business units, legal experts, ethical advisors, and end-users. Relational governance encourages continuous dialogue across these groups, enabling them to jointly interpret AI capabilities, clarify expectations, and co-shape the goals and constraints of specific use cases. Without such coordination, misunderstandings and misalignments can easily arise—for example, when developers are unaware of business constraints, or when decision-makers overestimate the system's reliability or scope.

One central component of relational governance is the formation of interdisciplinary teams that bring together expertise from various functional areas. These teams help ensure that AI systems are designed not only with technical performance in mind but also with consideration for ethical, legal, and organizational implications. Relational governance further benefits from shared working environments, such as collaborative platforms or regular alignment meetings, which provide space for open exchange, feedback loops, and joint decision-making. In practice, this might involve weekly syncs between data scientists and operations teams, workshops with compliance officers, or even informal channels where concerns and suggestions can be voiced early.

Transparency also plays a key role in facilitating relational coordination. When stakeholders have insight into how an AI system functions, why it makes certain predictions, or where its limitations lie, they are better equipped to engage with the system and trust its outputs. This underscores the importance of explainability, user-oriented documentation, and accessible reporting tools, which make the internal workings of AI systems comprehensible to nontechnical audiences. Moreover, when changes to models or data pipelines occur, relational mechanisms ensure that affected parties are informed and can adapt their practices accordingly.

To support these dynamics over time, organizations may also invest in training programs, onboarding routines, or mentorship schemes that help individuals understand both the technical foundations of AI and the organizational governance structures in which these technologies are embedded. For instance, onboarding new team members to an AI initiative might involve not only tool-specific training but also sessions on ethical considerations, documentation standards, or decision escalation protocols.

Relational governance mechanisms, while often less formalized than their structural or procedural counterparts, are no less critical. They provide the social fabric that allows technical and organizational systems to evolve in sync, helping to ensure that AI is used responsibly, effectively, and in a way that is aligned with the values and goals of the organization as a whole.

Exemplary AI Governance Guidelines

As the use of AI technologies becomes increasingly widespread across industries, several organizations and jurisdictions have issued governance frameworks to ensure that AI systems are developed, implemented, and monitored responsibly. While the European Union's AI Act represents the most comprehensive and legally binding framework to date, we discuss it in detail in Chap. 13. This section instead highlights three additional exemplary guidelines with high relevance for the corporate context, focusing on internationally recognized and structured approaches to AI governance.

The *ISO/IEC 42001:2023* standard provides a certifiable management system specifically designed for AI (ISO, 2023). Published by the International Organization for Standardization (ISO), it offers a structured approach for organizations to govern AI across its full lifecycle—from design and development to deployment and monitoring. The standard emphasizes core governance principles such as transparency, accountability, bias mitigation, security, and data protection. It outlines requirements for leadership commitment, risk assessment, competence development, operational controls, and continuous improvement. As a certifiable standard, ISO 42001 enables companies to demonstrate compliance with internationally recognized best practices and to align their AI initiatives with stakeholder expectations and regulatory demands.

The *NIST AI Risk Management Framework (AI RMF 1.0)*, published by the U.S. National Institute of Standards and Technology in 2023, provides a structured and voluntary approach to identifying, assessing, and mitigating AI-related risks across the entire system lifecycle (Tabassi, 2023). It is centered around four core functions—Map, Measure, Manage, and Govern—which help organizations contextualize risks, evaluate system trustworthiness, implement mitigation strategies, and establish internal risk governance structures. The framework highlights three broad harm categories that should be considered: harm to individuals (e.g., safety, fairness), organizations (e.g., operational or reputational risks), and ecosystems (e.g., environmental or systemic disruptions). To mitigate such risks, the framework promotes key characteristics of trustworthy AI, including safety, robustness, validity, transparency, explainability, and data protection. The framework serves as a widely recognized orientation for organizations aiming to implement responsible and risk-aware AI practices.

The *OECD Recommendation on Artificial Intelligence*, originally adopted in 2019 and updated in 2023 and 2024, provides an intergovernmental framework for the responsible development and use of AI (OECD, 2024). It outlines five core principles: inclusive growth, sustainable development and well-being; respect for the rule of law, human rights and democratic values, including fairness and privacy; transparency and explainability; robustness, security and safety; and accountability. These principles aim to ensure that AI systems are trustworthy, human-centric, and aligned with democratic values. Complementing these, the Recommendation includes policy guidance on investment in AI R&D, inclusive AI ecosystems, interoperable governance environments, human capital, and international cooperation. The latest revisions clarify its applicability to generative AI, emphasize information integrity, safety overrides, responsible business conduct, and environmental sustainability. While not legally binding, the Recommendation has shaped national AI strategies and serves as a widely recognized reference for aligning corporate AI practices with global standards.

9.1.3 Transformation Toward AI Governance

Based on the need for comprehensive AI governance and the risks associated with the use of AI systems, organizations need to ensure the transformation of their existing IT governance frameworks to appropriately address these risks while avoiding stifling innovation (Protschky et al., 2024). The method developed by Protschky et al. (2024) provides guidance on how to approach this transformation toward AI governance (Fig. 9.2). Importantly, the aim of the method is not to establish a completely new, separate AI governance approach within the company, but rather to further develop and integrate existing governance approaches within the company. The method is explained in the following.

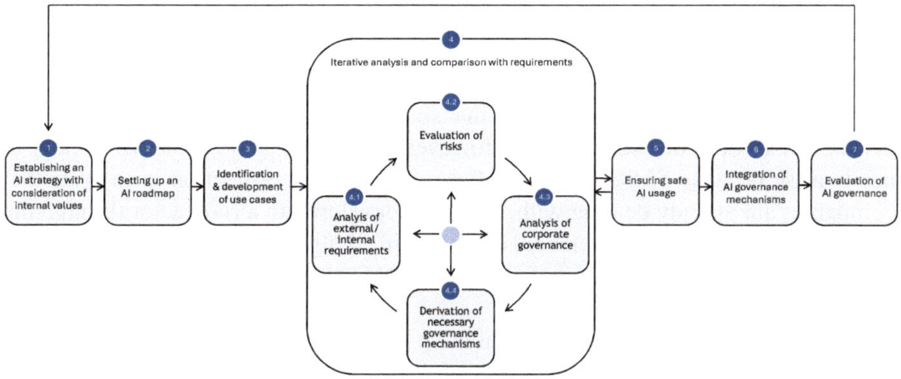

Fig. 9.2 The AI governance transformation method. (Adapted from Protschky et al., 2024)

AI Strategy and AI Roadmap as a Starting Point for AI Governance Transformation

The *first step* in AI governance transformation focuses on developing an AI strategy. In this step, an organization should consider and address several guiding questions, such as: "*How do we define AI?*" "*What should AI be used for?*" and "*What is our vision?*" In terms of AI governance, the relevant aspects of the AI strategy are the intended implementation of AI systems and AI technologies within the organization (i.e., internal AI usage), as well as the impact on internal processes and structures, rather than the strategies for AI products to be delivered to external customers.

Once an AI strategy that structures the intentions of using AI systems and AI technologies for internal processes within the organization is defined, the *second step* aims to derive a roadmap from the AI strategy. This roadmap represents an overarching schedule that assigns clear responsibilities and provides an idea of what exactly is to be achieved with AI technologies.

In the *third step*, use cases should be identified based on specific business processes. Proof of concepts or initial prototypes can be helpful in this phase. The most important aspects in this phase include identifying and involving the relevant stakeholders. The implementation of AI governance requires interdisciplinary collaboration—users, developers, legal staff, and others should all have the same basic understanding of what AI technologies are and how they are used at the beginning.

AI Governance Transformation Is an Iterative Process

The subsequent *fourth step* of the transformation method is divided into four sections. The iterative nature of the method is apparent in this step. There is no fixed order in which the four sub-steps are to be carried out. The sub-steps should be approached in the order and depth that is best suited to the respective organization. The sequence presented is a variant that shows all the aspects to be considered in the fourth step of the method.

In *sub-step 4.1*, both external and internal requirements should be considered. External requirements may, for example, relate to the regulatory framework that must be observed when using AI. Internal requirements may include overarching company guidelines or ethical guidelines.

In *sub-step 4.2*, the risk assessment should draw attention to potential risks. The use of AI technologies can entail risks that should be considered at an early stage (as discussed earlier in this subchapter). However, these risks do not necessarily have to newly arise because of the use of AI. For example, data protection is an issue that companies are already dealing with, yet it can develop into a risk factor through the use of AI (e.g., when using personal data to train AI algorithms). Other risks may be ethical or technical in nature and include problems related to algorithmic bias or lack of transparency.

In *sub-step 4.3*, the focus is on analyzing existing approaches in corporate governance, including IT, data, and other governance approaches used. AI governance should not only be set up in one area or department of an organization but should involve the entire company. The aim of this step is therefore to gain a comprehensive understanding of the existing governance approaches in the company and identify stakeholders that may not have been considered so far.

In *sub-step 4.4*, the existing governance mechanisms are to be compared with the mechanisms required for AI governance. This makes it possible to determine which existing mechanisms need to be adapted and which new ones should be implemented, if any. This step is intended to prevent the unnecessary implementation of new mechanisms for AI governance in organizations where suitable mechanisms are already in place or where minor adjustments to the existing portfolio of governance mechanisms would be sufficient to address the identified risks.

AI Governance Needs to Be Synchronized Continuously with the AI Strategy and AI Roadmap

After developing the first draft of the AI governance approach in steps 1–4, the *fifth step* of the method focuses on ensuring the safe use of AI. For instance, the seven pillars of the ethics guidelines for trustworthy AI by the EU (European Commission, 2019) may serve as key factors to determine the safe use of AI in the organization. If these defined key factors are not met, it is necessary to go back to the fourth step of the method and adjust the drafted governance portfolio accordingly. Thus, this step of the method can be seen as a quality gate to ensure that all previously defined factors are considered.

Once the review is complete, the *sixth step* focuses on the actual integration of AI governance. Integration includes the formalization of rules and regulations, for example, in contracts, compliance regulations, or a code of ethics. In addition, all new or adapted structures and processes are put into operation. It is important that AI governance is not implemented as a separate, independent unit, but as an integral extension of existing governance approaches. The integration process must be accompanied by change management. Employees must be sensitized to the topic of AI and receive further training. Solutions such as employee training and company-wide communication can create the necessary awareness.

Finally, the *seventh step* should evaluate the AI governance by continuously monitoring, obtaining feedback, and constantly questioning the chosen governance approach. Step 7 does not conclude the transformation but emphasizes the iterative approach by referring back to the first step of the method. As AI technologies and AI use cases are currently evolving rapidly, it will be necessary to continuously adapt the AI strategy in the future, triggering new iterations of the method.

Summary
Effective AI governance is crucial to mitigate the diverse risks associated with AI systems while enabling innovation. These risks include technical challenges such as data quality and model transparency, economic concerns like cost efficiency and user acceptance, as well as regulatory, ethical, and social issues. To address them, organizations can implement structural, procedural, and relational governance mechanisms that define roles, establish reliable processes, and foster interdisciplinary collaboration. A transformation method helps embed AI governance into existing structures through a strategy-driven, iterative approach. It emphasizes alignment with business goals, stakeholder engagement, and continuous adaptation to ensure responsible, transparent, and value-generating use of AI technologies.

9.2 The AI Application Management Model

The previous section introduced governance mechanisms that define the structural, procedural, and relational conditions under which AI can be used responsibly and effectively. These mechanisms go beyond high-level policy, they already represent a form of operationalization by shaping responsibilities, processes, and collaboration patterns. However, while governance establishes how decisions should be made and by whom, AI application management focuses on how these decisions and principles are translated into day-to-day development, deployment, and integration activities. It is at this level—where technical systems meet real-world workflows—that a host of practical challenges emerges (Lämmermann et al., 2024).

One of the primary categories of these challenges relates to *data*. Data quality, quantity, accessibility, and validation present significant hurdles. Ensuring high data quality is fundamental, as erroneous or biased data can lead to flawed AI results. Similarly, the issue of data quantity requires extensive datasets that are representative and comprehensive enough to train robust models. Access to relevant data is another critical consideration, often hampered by silos within organizations, different data formats, and legal or privacy restrictions. Validation is essential to ensure that the data fed into AI applications is accurate and curated, mitigating the risk of incorrect predictions and decisions.

AI technology management brings distinct challenges that require deliberate attention. Software engineering management involves maintaining code quality, documentation, and model updates to ensure long-term operability. Without structured processes, technical inconsistencies and inefficiencies may arise. A second key aspect is the definition of the technical stack, which shapes scalability, maintainability, and integration into existing systems. Poorly chosen stacks can hinder cross-functional collaboration and future development. Finally, domain and use case considerations are essential to align AI systems with the specific workflows and requirements of their application context. Failing to reflect domain-specific needs often leads to limited usefulness and low adoption.

Another crucial consideration concerns *user requirements*, which increasingly include socio-ethical challenges that have become central to the AI discourse. Ideally, AI applications should align with moral standards and strive to be as free from bias as possible, acknowledging that biases can reinforce inequality and injustice. Promoting transparency in AI-driven business processes can help foster user understanding, support trust-building, and enable more informed decision-making. Likewise, aiming for model interpretability enhances users' ability to comprehend and trust the rationale behind AI predictions. Finally, actively managing user expectations can help counteract overly optimistic or unfounded assumptions about AI capabilities and limitations, contributing to a more realistic and responsible deployment of such technologies.

Process challenges emerge as organizations venture to integrate AI applications into existing workflows. Workflow incompatibility and disruption are common issues that require strategic change management to incorporate AI applications without adverse impacts on productivity. The integration of workflow changes to accommodate AI applications must be carefully planned and executed to ensure a seamless transition. Moreover, process safety is critical to ensure that AI augmentation does not introduce new risks or vulnerabilities into organizational processes.

Contextual restrictions, encompassing organizational, infrastructure, economic, and regulatory challenges, also significantly impact the deployment of AI applications. *Organizational challenges* include strategic conflicts, unclear responsibilities, and siloed team structures, which can impede the effective integration of AI applications. The scarcity of AI expertise within organizations serves to compound these issues, thereby underscoring the necessity for upskilling and collaboration with external experts. *Infrastructure challenges*, such as the computational effort required, interoperability issues, and IT fragmentation, necessitate substantial investment in technology and infrastructure enhancement. *Economic challenges*, including profitability and scalability, remain a critical concern. The initial investment and ongoing costs associated with AI applications can be substantial and may rise unexpectedly over time, for instance, due to integration complexities or the need for continuous model retraining and monitoring. The dearth of tangible business value derived from AI applications is frequently attributable to these economic constraints.

Finally, it is important to consider the *regulatory challenges* associated with AI, including issues of privacy, transparency, product safety, and accountability. Compliance with privacy laws and regulations is vital to avoid legal repercussions and protect user data. Ensuring the safe operation of AI products and maintaining accountability for decisions made using AI applications are key to fostering public trust and ensuring ethical responsibility.

The AI application management (AIAMA) model (Lämmermann et al., 2024) presents a structured approach to navigating and addressing the multifaceted management challenges inherent in the utilization of AI applications within organizations. At its core, the model highlights the importance of organizational structures and clearly defined roles to support effective coordination and communication across stakeholder groups. It brings attention to the fact that many challenges in AI management stem from fragmented information and unclear responsibilities—and offers a framework that connects key management areas through recurring information and decision-making cycles. By doing so, the model supports organizations in keeping their AI applications aligned with both technical requirements and evolving contextual, process-related, and user-centered demands (Fig. 9.3).

9.2.1 The AIAMA Model Factors

The AIAMA model delineates four overarching management functions that structure the key areas in which AI-related management tasks occur. These functions capture the diverse conditions under which AI applications are developed, deployed, and maintained, ranging from technical considerations to organizational constraints and user-facing requirements. Each function consists of abstract management factors that may give rise to new tasks as internal or external conditions change. Together, they provide a comprehensive view of the managerial scope

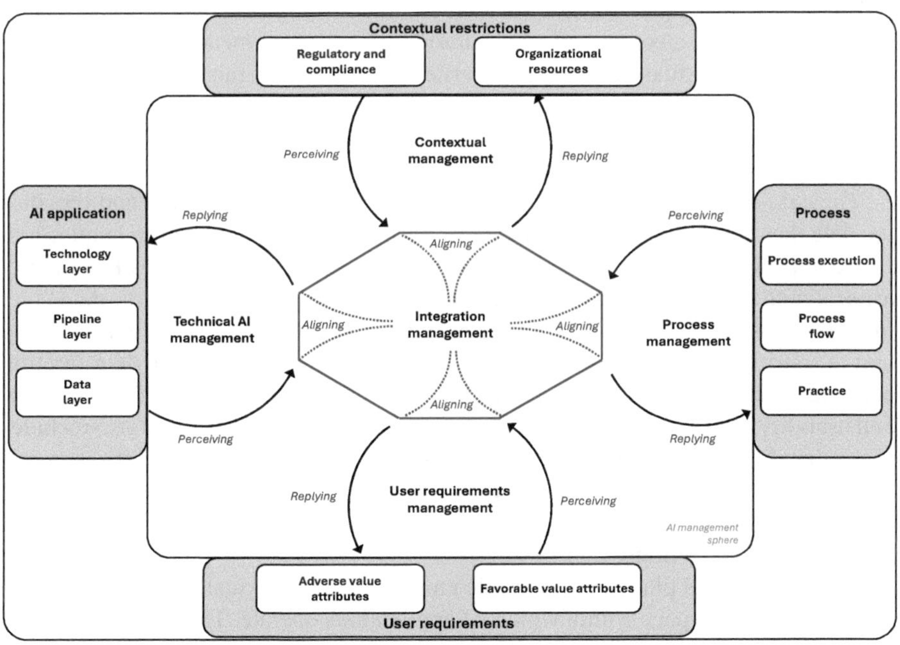

Fig. 9.3 The AI application management model. (Adapted from Lämmermann et al., 2024)

required to sustain AI applications over time and adapt them to evolving demands (Lämmermann et al., 2024).

AI Application

The AIAMA model provides a detailed examination of the intricate layers that constitute the AI application, offering a nuanced understanding of how AI technologies are deployed and managed within organizations. At its core, the AI application is decomposed into three dynamic constructs: technology layer, pipeline layer, and data layer. Each of these layers plays a pivotal role in defining the capabilities, performance, and utility of AI applications (Lämmermann et al., 2024).

The technology layer forms the fundamental backbone of an AI application, comprising the infrastructure needed to support it. This includes decisions about hosting—whether on-premises or in the cloud—as well as the level of customization, such as choosing between standardized systems or solutions tailored to specific organizational needs. On-premises solutions offer control and compliance benefits, particularly crucial for organizations with stringent data security requirements.[1] Conversely, cloud-based solutions provide scalability and flexibility, enabling businesses to adapt to fluctuating computational demands. The technology layer also encompasses the architectural choices that determine the performance, scalability, and integration capabilities of AI applications. It is therefore essential that the technical foundation aligns with the specific use case of the AI application.

The *pipeline layer* refers to the technical design of the AI application—that is, how input data is transformed into meaningful output. This layer encompasses a series of tasks that generate, monitor, and continuously improve AI models. It typically includes the selection and configuration of statistical methods, as well as the definition of performance and quality criteria. In practice, this may involve steps such as data preprocessing, feature engineering, model training, and tuning. A well-orchestrated pipeline enables consistent data flow and reliable AI performance, supporting the broader management goals of the application.

The *data layer*, which serves as a foundation for AI models, defines and specifies the data that is required to develop, test, and validate the AI application in question. It encompasses the acquisition of relevant data sources and addresses key quality aspects such as completeness, accuracy, and consistency. Beyond that, the data layer includes considerations of data protection and privacy, which are particularly important in sensitive domains like healthcare. In practice, this may involve data curation activities such as cleansing, normalization, and annotation to ensure the reliability and usability of data for AI training. Maintaining an effective data layer also includes validating data quality over time and adapting AI models when underlying data patterns shift, thereby supporting long-term robustness and relevance.

Contextual Restrictions

The AIAMA model places considerable emphasis on contextual restrictions, which shape the feasible space within which AI applications operate. These restrictions are

[1] Given that companies can afford a high security standard for their own servers.

of critical importance, as they determine the boundaries and constraints related to the management of AI technologies (Lämmermann et al., 2024).

One core aspect of the contextual restrictions in the AIAMA model concerns *regulatory and compliance requirements*. These include legal obligations related to data protection and safety standards that govern the permissible use of AI applications. Prominent examples include data privacy laws such as the GDPR in the European Union or the CCPA in the United States, which define how personal data must be handled across its lifecycle. Safety regulations, on the other hand, require that AI applications perform reliably and do not endanger patients or users. Together, these rules define the legal space in which AI applications can be developed and operated.

In addition to regulatory considerations, the availability of *organizational resources* is crucial for shaping AI initiatives, as it determines an organization's ability to plan, implement, and sustain such efforts over time. Financial resources play a key role in enabling such initiatives, as they cover not only initial investments in technology and infrastructure but also ongoing costs related to maintenance, training, and iterative development. Without adequate financial support, even well-designed AI projects may fail to scale or deliver long-term value. Human resources refer to the expertise required to build and manage AI applications. This includes data scientists, machine learning engineers, domain specialists, and IT professionals who contribute essential knowledge throughout the AI lifecycle. The availability of qualified personnel is often a decisive factor in determining the pace and quality of AI integration within organizations.

By comprehending and regulating these contextual limitations, organizations can facilitate an optimal environment for AI innovation. This necessitates staying up to date with regulatory changes, fostering a culture of compliance, and continuously investing in resource development and optimization. The AIAMA model's focus on these factors highlights their significance in the broader context of AI management, underscoring the need for a comprehensive strategy that integrates regulatory adherence with effective resource management.

User Requirements

In the context of the AIAMA model, user requirements play a pivotal role in the development and deployment of AI applications. These requirements encapsulate the attributes and values perceived as essential by the end-users, which directly influence the overall effectiveness and acceptance of AI applications. User requirements are primarily divided into two categories: favorable and adverse value attributes. Each category plays a significant role in either facilitating or hindering the creation of value through AI implementations (Lämmermann et al., 2024).

Favorable value attributes encompass elements that enhance the interaction, comprehensibility, and safety of AI applications. For instance, interaction requirements relate to the usability and user-friendliness of AI systems. Possible manifestations include intuitive interface designs and seamless integration into existing workflows—factors that help users interact effectively with AI tools and reduce resistance to adoption. Another central attribute is explainability, which emphasizes the importance of transparent AI models that produce understandable and trustworthy outputs. In practice, this may involve providing meaningful explanations for predictions or decisions, thereby fostering user confidence and supporting the identification of unexpected or undesired model behavior. Finally, safety expectations refer to the reliable and risk-aware operation of AI applications. Depending on the context, this can include ensuring consistent system behavior, minimizing unintended outcomes, or—in safety-critical domains—complying with defined operational boundaries to prevent harm.

In stark contrast, *adverse value attributes* refer to issues that can significantly impair the value derived from AI applications. Errors in AI predictions or operations can result in incorrect decisions, which may erode the trust and reliability of AI applications. These errors can originate from a multitude of sources, including suboptimal data quality, inadequate model training, or unforeseen alterations in operational conditions. Another adverse attribute is workflow disruption, whereby the integration of AI applications can inadvertently create bottlenecks or inefficiencies in existing processes. For example, the implementation of a novel AI system may necessitate substantial alterations to established workflows, potentially leading to confusion and resistance among users who are unfamiliar with the new procedures. Such disruptions can significantly impede productivity and negate the potential benefits of AI applications.

Understanding and addressing user requirements is essential for ensuring the successful integration of AI applications within organizations. Analyzing favorable value attributes helps developers design AI systems that align with user expectations and enhance usability. This involves iterative testing and feedback loops that incorporate user insights to refine core functionalities. At the same time, identifying and mitigating adverse attributes requires proactive risk management—through rigorous testing and the design of flexible solutions that integrate smoothly into existing workflows. Aligning AI development with user needs fosters a user-centric approach, increases satisfaction, and facilitates broader adoption.

Process

The AIAMA model incorporates process dimensions, illuminating the intricate layers of process execution, flow, and practice that regulate the interaction and impact of AI applications on organizational workflows (Lämmermann et al., 2024).

A fundamental aspect of comprehending the process dimension is the concept of *process execution*. This necessitates a comprehensive examination of all actions and activities that an AI application affects or automates. Process execution entails a detailed examination of the precise steps taken within an organization's operations, encompassing data collection and analysis, decision-making, and implementation. The introduction of AI applications frequently results in automation, which can streamline repetitive tasks and enhance overall efficiency. Nevertheless, successful automation necessitates a profound comprehension of the existing processes to identify the optimal points of integration and avenues for enhancement, ensuring that the actions facilitated by AI applications are seamlessly aligned with the business objectives and operational protocols.

The *process flow* adds an important perspective to AI application management by focusing on the logical sequence and interconnection of activities needed to achieve a desired outcome. This includes, for example, the procedural timing of AI decisions in decision support systems, where relevant data must be available at the right moment to inform critical choices. Process flow considerations involve mapping how information moves through an organization, how AI systems interact with existing processes, and how timing affects operational efficiency. Ensuring a well-designed process flow helps prevent disruptions, supports a coherent integration of AI into existing workflows, and promotes smoother transitions and greater operational consistency.

The *practice* component within the AIAMA model refers to the procedures, instructions, and domain knowledge required to achieve consistent process outcomes. This includes formalized guidelines and operational advice that help users understand how to interact with AI applications in daily routines. In a broader organizational context, this may entail developing training materials and practical instructions to support the effective use of AI tools. Clearly defined procedures—such as standard operating protocols—can ensure that stakeholders know how to respond to AI outputs, handle routine issues, and adjust their workflows accordingly. Additionally, structured knowledge-sharing practices can promote continuous improvement by incorporating feedback into future guideline updates and training efforts.

The process factor in the AIAMA model provides a structured foundation for integrating AI into organizational workflows by emphasizing careful planning, ongoing refinement, and alignment with existing practices. Whether applied in manufacturing to optimize supply chains and quality control, or in healthcare to support diagnostics and patient management, AI applications demand a nuanced understanding of process execution, flow, and practice. This ensures that AI enhances rather than disrupts established operations. When effectively embedded, AI and organizational processes can mutually reinforce one another, creating a dynamic environment where automation and insights empower stakeholders, support decision-making, and drive strategic growth.

9.2.2 The AIAMA Model Management Sphere

The model's inner structure depicts the de facto AI application management, understood as a set of ongoing management practices in response to AI's evolving nature and the constant dynamics of its environment (Berente et al., 2021). These practices are represented in the AIAMA model by five interconnected management cycles: technical AI management, contextual management, process management, user requirements management, and integration management. The first four cycles encompass management activities that address specific challenges emerging beyond the core management sphere. The integration management cycle serves to coordinate and align these factor-oriented cycles, ensuring consistency and coherence across the different management dimensions. This integrative role is particularly important given the often highly specialized knowledge distributed across different stakeholders, which necessitates a central mechanism to foster shared understanding and enable effective collaboration. While each cycle focuses on a distinct management topic, they are not to be seen as isolated organizational entities but rather as interdependent functions that need to be operationalized in an integrated manner within existing structures (Lämmermann et al., 2024).

Technical AI management addresses the implications of AI-related architecture and data. This management cycle aims to ensure the technical fitness of AI applications by overseeing their design, development, and maintenance. It involves monitoring core technical dimensions and taking corrective measures when necessary to maintain functionality and performance. By focusing on architectural soundness and data quality, this cycle provides the foundation upon which reliable and adaptable AI systems can be built. As such, it plays a crucial role in enabling the technical viability and long-term sustainability of AI applications within the organization.

Contextual management ensures that AI applications comply with external environmental restrictions from both regulatory and organizational perspectives. This cycle entails the continuous monitoring of the legal and regulatory landscape, with the objective of adapting AI strategies to align with evolving laws and standards. It encompasses data privacy, security, and ethical considerations, thereby ensuring that AI applications operate within permissible boundaries. Contextual management also encompasses the strategic allocation of resources, ensuring that the requisite financial, human, and infrastructural resources are available to support AI initiatives. By proactively addressing compliance and resource-related challenges, contextual management supports the responsible and sustainable deployment of AI within the organization.

Process management addresses the implications of AI integration into existing organizational workflows. It aims to determine the process-related requirements for the effective operation of AI applications and to ensure that these applications align with established process standards and organizational goals. This includes analyzing the structure and flow of activities, evaluating how AI modifies or enhances them, and ensuring that the resulting processes remain transparent and compliant. In doing so, process management supports the structured and effective embedding of AI in operational routines.

Requirements management is concerned with the implications of user needs and expectations for AI applications. This management cycle aims to ensure that AI systems are not only technically robust, but also aligned with user values such as transparency, explainability, and ethical integrity. It entails identifying and monitoring these requirements, developing strategies to operationalize them, and continuously adapting the system design accordingly. By prioritizing the human perspective throughout the lifecycle, requirements management fosters user acceptance, satisfaction, and trust in AI applications.

The *integration management* cycle connects the four-factor management cycles—technical, contextual, process, and user requirements—and ensures their alignment within the overarching AI application management. It coordinates planning, communication, and decision-making across the different management dimensions to support coherent and goal-oriented AI initiatives. Integration management operates in two distinct modes: it either supervises and aligns activities across cycles when challenges are complex and interdependent, or it enables direct communication and decentralized coordination between cycles when issues are localized and can be resolved autonomously. This dual role ensures that AI applications are managed both consistently and flexibly, depending on the nature of the task at hand.

The integration of these five management cycles constitutes a structured framework for addressing the diverse challenges associated with AI application management. By emphasizing continuous and coordinated management practices, the AIAMA model supports organizations in aligning AI systems with technical, regulatory, process-related, and user-oriented requirements. This integrated approach contributes to the reliable and responsible deployment of AI, promoting consistency across different management dimensions. Through deliberate coordination and planning, organizations can better manage the complexity of AI integration and ensure that AI applications function effectively within existing structures and constraints.

9.2.3 Interactions Between Factors and Management Sphere

The AIAMA model is designed to serve as a robust framework for the management of AI applications, facilitating intricate, well-defined interactions between various factors and the management sphere. These interactions are classified into three progressive phases: perceiving, aligning, and replying. Each phase represents a critical step in the AI application management cycle, ensuring that AI applications remain adaptable, responsive, and aligned with organizational goals (Lämmermann et al., 2024).

The *perceiving phase* encompasses managerial practices aimed at identifying construct changes that indicate a need for management intervention. This includes both trigger-based mechanisms, which rely on predefined criteria for recognizing known patterns of change, and more interpretative assessments for identifying unexpected or ambiguous developments—such as data drift, infrastructural adjustments, or shifting user requirements. In this context, clearly defined responsibilities within the management functions are essential to correctly detect and evaluate unusual or abnormal behavior in AI applications. Accurate and timely perception of such changes forms the basis for initiating appropriate responses in the subsequent management phases.

The *aligning phase* focuses on assessing relevant changes, deriving the resulting management tasks, and developing actions to align them with the organization's overarching goals. It represents the intersection of the integration management cycle and the four-factor management cycles—technical, contextual, process, and requirement management—facilitating the dissemination of information and the initiation of coordinated actions across the management sphere. This includes activities such as problem analysis, risk assessments, decision-making, and resource allocation. For instance, when a potential issue or risk is identified, the aligning phase ensures that relevant adjustments—such as model updates or procedural changes—are evaluated and implemented in a way that meets both technical requirements and compliance standards.

The *replying phase* comprises managerial practices that implement changes to the outer management functions based on decisions made during the aligning phase. This includes actions such as data rebalancing, model reconfiguration, process redesign, stakeholder upskilling, and targeted communication. For example, if it has been determined that predictive performance has declined due to data drift, this phase may involve retraining the model or updating the data pipeline accordingly. Through such targeted interventions, the replying phase ensures that AI applications can be adjusted and maintained in line with evolving requirements and operational contexts.

The phases of the AIAMA model illustrate its dynamic and integrative character. By progressing through perceiving, aligning, and replying, the model enables AI applications to respond to change while maintaining alignment with organizational goals. This structured flow ensures continuous monitoring, evaluation, and adaptation—crucial for managing AI in complex and evolving environments. The integration management cycle plays a central role in coordinating these interactions. It connects the four-factor management cycles and guides information processing across them. In doing so, it ensures that changes in one dimension are appropriately communicated and addressed throughout the management system, supporting a coherent and adaptive approach to AI governance.

In essence, the AIAMA model's interaction framework emphasizes the significance of a comprehensive, interdisciplinary approach to AI application management. The model ensures a robust and responsive management system by systematically perceiving environmental changes, aligning those changes with organizational goals, and responding with appropriate actions. This approach not only enhances the technical and operational efficacy of AI applications but also aligns them with strategic objectives and regulatory compliance, thus driving sustainable value creation in the realm of AI-driven business transformation.

9.2.4 The AIAMA Model Applied in Healthcare

In the context of healthcare, the AIAMA model presents an invaluable framework for addressing intricate scenarios, such as the challenge of outdated medical practices precipitated by updated medical guidelines. As healthcare authorities regularly revise medical guidelines to reflect the latest clinical research and best practices, it is necessary for AI applications that support clinical decisions to undergo corresponding updates to remain aligned with the evolving landscape of medical guidelines. To illustrate, consider a hospital that employs an AI-based treatment recommender system. When new medical guidelines are introduced, the AIAMA model ensures that these updates are carefully integrated into the AI system, thereby maintaining the system's accuracy and relevance.

The process is initiated when updated medical guidelines are issued, necessitating a change in existing medical practices. Physicians and other stakeholders in the field of medical process management are aware of the potential impact that these new guidelines may have on the application of AI. They perceive this issue and report it to the integration management, encapsulating the initial interaction phase of the AIAMA model. This step underscores the importance of a vigilant system where changes in external guidelines are promptly identified and communicated.

Integration management then assumes the role of assessing the implications of these new guidelines on the AI application's operations. This assessment entails the gathering of information from a variety of stakeholders, including technical AI managers, regulatory experts, and physicians, to gain an understanding of the extent and nature of the required changes. The discussion phase within a team of selected experts facilitates a comprehensive problem analysis, ensuring that all potential impacts are considered before any action is taken. This collaborative assessment serves to underscore the alignment phase, which represents the intersection of the integration cycle with the other management cycles. This phase is responsible for propagating necessary information and formulating a cohesive strategy (Fig. 9.4).

The subsequent step is the development of an approach for the adoption procedure. The role of integration management is critical in this context, as it encompasses the technical, medical, and regulatory domains to formulate a comprehensive strategy. In collaboration with technical AI management, they delineate the requisite technical alterations. This process entails identifying the specific elements of the AI model that require retraining, modifying data pipelines, and integrating the new guideline requirements into the existing AI framework. Concurrently, collaboration with contextual management ensures compliance with legal and regulatory standards, thereby safeguarding data privacy and adhering to new regulatory benchmarks. This systematic approach elucidates the aligning phase, which entails the translation of complex changes into actionable steps and their alignment with the organization's overarching goals.

Once the strategic approach has been defined, the technical AI management team is responsible for acquiring and preparing the necessary data for the AI application. This process entails sourcing new datasets that align with the updated guidelines, integrating them with the existing database, and retraining the AI model to incorporate these new insights. The retraining process is of critical importance, as it ensures that the AI model's predictions align with the latest medical practices, thereby enhancing its reliability and utility in clinical settings. This step exemplifies the principal managerial activities involved in the implementation phase, during which technical modifications are implemented in accordance with the predefined aligned strategy.

Following retraining, the modified AI application must undergo rigorous validation to ensure that it meets all regulatory requirements. This process involves stakeholders from regulatory and compliance teams conducting a comprehensive legal review to verify that the updated model adheres to the newly established guidelines and maintains compliance with patient privacy and data security regulations. Such meticulous compliance checks are essential for maintaining the integrity and

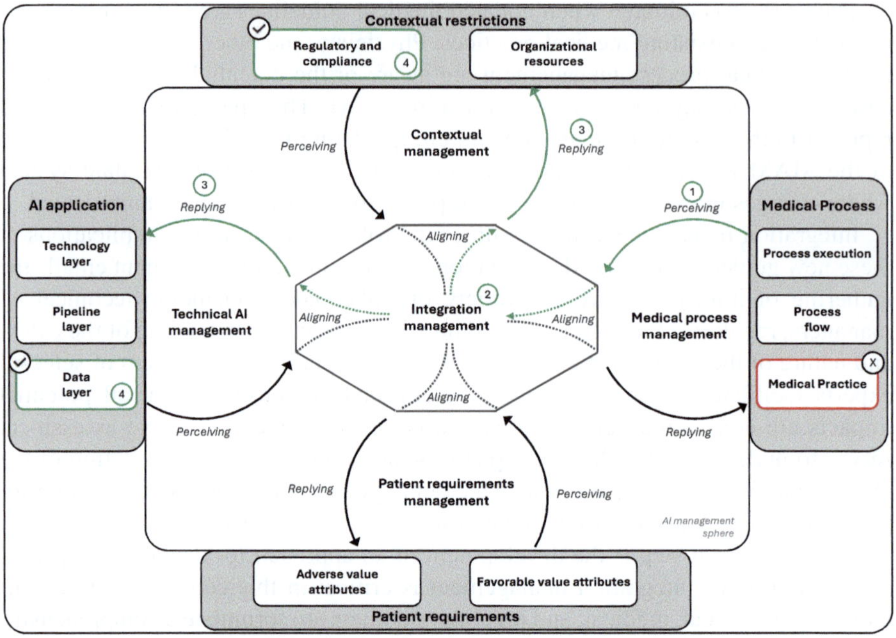

Fig. 9.4 Model application exemplified by the management of outdated practices. (Adapted from Lämmermann et al., 2024)

trustworthiness of AI applications in healthcare, as they directly impact patient outcomes.

The final phase of the process culminates in the deployment of the updated AI application, which is now compliant with the new medical guidelines. This guarantees that healthcare professionals can make decisions based on the most current clinical standards, thereby enhancing the quality of patient care. The seamless integration of updated guidelines into the AI system also serves to illustrate the dynamic and adaptable nature of the AIAMA model in managing complex, real-world challenges. The model facilitates continual updates and adjustments, thereby ensuring that AI applications remain at the forefront of medical advancements and deliver optimal value and efficacy.

As a result, the AIAMA model provides a structured and comprehensive approach for incorporating changes driven by updated medical guidelines into existing AI applications. The meticulous navigation of the perceiving, aligning, and replying phases, coupled with the leveraging of integrative management cycles, ensures that AI applications in healthcare are both dynamically responsive and robustly compliant. This integrative, well-coordinated process exemplifies the AIAMA model's capability to harmonize technical precision with regulatory adherence and adaptive management, thus fostering a resilient AI ecosystem in the ever-evolving landscape of healthcare.

Summary
The AIAMA model provides a structured and integrative framework for managing AI applications in complex organizational environments. It addresses key challenges across technical infrastructure, data, processes, contextual constraints, and user requirements. Central to the model are five interconnected management cycles and the dynamic phases of perceiving, aligning, and replying, which together ensure that AI systems remain responsive to change while maintaining internal consistency. The model highlights the importance of coordination, role clarity, and continuous information flow, enabling organizations to align AI applications with strategic goals, regulatory standards, and operational needs. This approach supports the sustainable and responsible use of AI over time.

9.3 Building Suitable Team Structures

Effectively managing AI within organizations is not solely a question of processes or methodologies, it also depends fundamentally on how people, knowledge, and responsibilities are organized. The successful deployment and scaling of AI systems require more than technical know-how or governance principles. It hinges on cross-functional collaboration, shared understanding, and the ability to integrate diverse expertise across organizational boundaries. Developing adequate team structures is thus a crucial aspect of managing artificial intelligence. Two significant organizational challenges to be overcome in this context are the heterogeneity of competence and the existence of siloed organizational structures. The term "competence heterogeneity" refers to the diverse range of skills and expertise within teams, which, while beneficial, can also create alignment issues. The considerable differences in knowledge bases among team members can give rise to misunderstandings and inefficiencies, impeding the seamless implementation of AI technologies. Conversely, the existence of siloed organizational structures serves to exacerbate these challenges, as it fosters a lack of communication and collaboration across departments. These silos impede the free flow of information and expertise across domains, thereby hindering the formation of a unified approach to AI management.

In addition, the technical characteristics of AI systems further complicate the establishment of an effective team structure. Notably, AI systems often exhibit opacity, meaning that their decisional processes are not always transparent or intelligible to human observers. This opacity can give rise to issues of trust among team members and stakeholders, which in turn can give rise to resistance to AI adoption. Furthermore, AI technologies are rapidly evolving and intricate, necessitating teams that can rapidly adapt to new developments and integrate these innovations seamlessly into their workflows. The accelerated evolution of AI technologies necessitates a high degree of agility and continuous learning within the team, underscoring the importance of selecting an optimal structure that fosters these attributes. To navigate these challenges, several team structures have been identified as suitable for the management of AI, each of which possesses its own distinctive advantages.

9.3.1 Centers of Excellence

Centers of Excellence (CoE) are organizational units that provide leadership, research, best practices, innovation, and training for a specific area of focus or domain (Ammar et al., 2012; Curry et al., 2021; Nasution et al., 2019; Moore & Birkinshaw, 1998). These centers aim to drive continuous improvement and enhance an institution's capacity, capability, and continuity in a particular field. By concentrating expertise and resources, CoEs are designed to be a hub of knowledge and innovation, promoting the development and dissemination of advanced practices and technologies.

In the context of AI management, CoEs hold particular significance. A CoE, with its concentrated expertise, serves as a platform for experimenting with cutting-edge AI technologies to drive innovation. The AI talent market is highly competitive, and a CoE can help address this challenge by upskilling existing employees, thus reducing the organization's dependency on external hires. By fostering a culture of continuous learning and development, CoEs ensure that organizations remain at the forefront of technological advancements and industry best practices.

One of the primary advantages of a CoE is its convenience as a structure for change. CoEs provide a focused environment where new ideas and technologies can be developed and tested before being implemented on a larger scale within the organization. This controlled setting helps mitigate risks associated with innovation and change. Additionally, CoEs facilitate the internal growth of expertise by creating a dedicated space for knowledge development and transfer. By serving as a repository and conduit for knowledge, CoEs play a crucial role in fostering a learning-oriented culture and ensuring that expertise is shared across the organization. They also enhance the organization's ability to acquire sustained funding for research projects, as their specialized nature often attracts investment and grants.

However, there are also disadvantages associated with CoEs. One major challenge is the potential for the organization to become overly dependent on the CoE. This dependency can create bottlenecks and hinder the distribution of expertise across the broader organization. Additionally, if the CoE becomes too siloed, it can lead to a separation from the rest of the organization, limiting collaboration and integration. Another significant drawback is the high effort and cost required for implementing and maintaining a CoE. Establishing a CoE involves significant investment in terms of resources, infrastructure, and personnel, and its benefits must be carefully weighed against these costs.

In conclusion, while Centers of Excellence offer numerous advantages, particularly in terms of fostering innovation and developing expertise in AI management, they also present challenges that need to be managed. By addressing potential dependencies, promoting integration, and ensuring efficient resource allocation, organizations can effectively leverage CoEs to drive continuous improvement and maintain a competitive edge in their respective fields.

9.3.2 Cross-Functional Teams

Cross-functional teams are composed of individuals with diverse functional specialties who collaborate temporarily to address a specific challenge or accomplish a particular task (Cunningham & Chelladurai, 2004; Webber, 2002; Majchrzak et al., 2012; McDonough III, 2000). This team structure brings together experts from various domains to provide a comprehensive approach to problem-solving. Increasingly, organizations are leveraging cross-functional teams to develop new products and processes, recognizing the value of integrating diverse skill sets and perspectives to foster innovation and enhance organizational agility.

In the realm of AI management, cross-functional teams hold significant importance. The impact of AI permeates all levels and departments within an organization, making it crucial to address AI-related topics from multiple perspectives. A cross-functional team approach ensures that insights and expertise from different areas—such as data science, engineering, marketing, and operations—are integrated into AI projects. This multidisciplinary collaboration is essential for the successful implementation of AI initiatives, as it allows for a more holistic understanding of both the technical and business implications of AI technologies.

One of the primary advantages of cross-functional teams is that they bring together different perspectives that illuminate complex topics very broadly. This diversity of thought helps in identifying various facets of a problem and can lead to more innovative and effective solutions. Additionally, cross-functional teams are well-suited for tackling complex and highly novel product innovations. By leveraging the collective expertise of team members from different disciplines, organizations can better navigate the uncertainties and challenges associated with pioneering new products and processes.

However, cross-functional teams also present certain disadvantages. One significant challenge is the potential for disagreements among team members due to differing views and perspectives. These disagreements can lead to inefficiencies and delays if not managed properly. Effective communication and conflict resolution strategies are essential to mitigate this risk and ensure that the team remains productive. Another challenge is the complex process of knowledge integration. Bringing together information and insights from various disciplines can be difficult, requiring careful coordination and a structured approach to ensure that all relevant knowledge is effectively synthesized and applied.

In conclusion, cross-functional teams offer a robust framework for addressing complex challenges and driving innovation, particularly in the field of AI management. By capitalizing on the diverse expertise of team members, organizations can enhance their problem-solving capabilities and achieve more comprehensive and effective solutions. However, careful attention must be given to managing potential conflicts and ensuring effective knowledge integration to fully realize the benefits of cross-functional team collaboration.

9.3.3 Virtual Teams

Virtual teams refer to technology-enabled collaborations among geographically dispersed individuals, facilitating communication and cooperation (Morrison-Smith & Ruiz, 2020; Hinds & Kiesler, 2002). These teams leverage various digital tools and platforms to work together effectively despite physical distances. Unlike traditional teams that operate within a single physical location, virtual teams can comprise members from different parts of the world, working together seamlessly through the use of advanced communication technologies. Furthermore, virtual teams can be integrated with other team structures, allowing for flexible and dynamic organizational arrangements that can adapt to various business needs and scenarios.

In the context of AI management, virtual teams hold particular relevance. The global nature of AI expertise means that the best talent is often spread across different regions. Virtual teams provide organizations with the ability to access specialized AI knowledge from anywhere in the world, breaking down geographical barriers and enabling the inclusion of a diverse set of perspectives. As AI initiatives grow in scope and complexity, the scalability offered by virtual teams becomes increasingly important. Organizations can scale up their AI capabilities more easily with virtual teams than with traditional, co-located teams, allowing them to respond more rapidly to new opportunities and challenges.

One of the key advantages of virtual teams is the scalability of knowledge sharing. With virtual teams, information and best practices can be disseminated more widely and efficiently, making it easier for organizations to ensure that all team members are on the same page, regardless of their location. Additionally, virtual teams enable organizations to recruit key specialists without being constrained by geographic limitations. This access to a global talent pool ensures that organizations can utilize the best possible resources for their projects. Another significant advantage is the reduction in the need for travel. Virtual teams rely on digital communication tools, which minimizes the necessity for physical travel, leading to cost savings and increased operational efficiency. Moreover, virtual teams offer enhanced flexibility, allowing organizations to adapt more readily to globalization, competition, and changing organizational structures. This flexibility is vital for maintaining a competitive edge in today's fast-paced business environment.

However, virtual teams also present a distinct set of challenges. Geographic distance can hinder spontaneous communication and informal knowledge exchange, which are essential for building trust and cohesion. Without deliberate efforts to foster connectedness, team members may feel isolated or disengaged, especially when working on complex and interdependent tasks such as AI development. Temporal distance—differences in time zones—further complicates coordination. Real-time collaboration can become limited, resulting in delays or asynchronous feedback loops that slow down decision-making and development cycles. These challenges are particularly critical in AI projects that often require iterative experimentation and rapid response to changing requirements. Moreover, the lack of physical presence can obscure nonverbal cues, making it harder to interpret feedback or resolve conflicts, which may negatively affect team dynamics. To counteract these effects, organizations must invest in robust communication infrastructures, establish clear routines for synchronous and asynchronous work, and create deliberate opportunities for informal exchange, such as virtual coffee chats or team retrospectives.

In sum, virtual teams offer clear advantages in terms of flexibility, global talent access, and scalable knowledge sharing—making them highly relevant for AI management. However, their effectiveness depends on overcoming spatial and temporal barriers through structured communication and trust-building measures. When thoughtfully integrated with other structures, such as CoEs or cross-functional teams, virtual teams can significantly enhance an organization's ability to manage AI initiatives across geographic and functional boundaries.

9.3.4 Matrix Teams

Matrix teams represent a collaborative structure that encourages coordinated, multidisciplinary efforts across various functional areas (Burns & Wholey, 1993; Goś, 2015; Kolodny, 1979; Schnetler et al., 2015). This team structure is designed to merge the efficiency of functional design with the adaptability and responsiveness characteristic of a multidivisional organization. By integrating different functional expertise and ensuring flexibility, matrix teams aim to enhance the overall effectiveness of project execution and organizational performance.

For AI management, matrix teams are particularly relevant due to their inherent flexibility and agility in adapting to changing project requirements. AI projects often require diverse skill sets and expertise at different phases, and matrix teams allow for the dynamic allocation of resources based on the project's current needs. This flexibility ensures that the right talent is available at the right time, facilitating the efficient progression of AI initiatives. Additionally, matrix teams foster cross-learning opportunities through the collaboration of diverse perspectives, which is crucial for innovation and comprehensive problem-solving.

One of the primary advantages of matrix teams is their high flexibility and adaptability. This structure enables quick adjustments to project plans and resource allocations in response to evolving circumstances. Resource sharing is another significant benefit, as it allows for the optimal utilization of organizational resources across different projects. Furthermore, working in a matrix team environment enhances interpersonal skill development among team members, as they interact and collaborate with colleagues from various functional areas. Effective communication within matrix teams can lead to quicker decision-making processes, further enhancing their responsiveness and efficiency.

However, matrix teams also present several disadvantages. One notable challenge is the dual lines of reporting, which can lead to overlapping responsibilities and potential confusion. This structure often results in a higher potential for conflicts due to the differing priorities and perspectives of functional and project managers. Additionally, the roles and responsibilities within matrix teams can sometimes be unclear, necessitating more coordination effort to ensure smooth operation. This complexity often requires a significant amount of management personnel to oversee and facilitate the effective functioning of the team. As a result, the management overhead can be considerable, requiring robust leadership and clear communication strategies to mitigate these issues.

In conclusion, while matrix teams offer numerous benefits, particularly in terms of flexibility and resource optimization, they also come with challenges that need to be carefully managed. By leveraging the strengths of matrix teams and addressing their inherent complexities, organizations can effectively utilize this team structure to enhance their AI management capabilities and drive successful project outcomes.

Summary

Developing suitable team structures is essential for the successful organizational implementation and coordination of AI initiatives. This need arises from key organizational challenges such as competence heterogeneity and siloed structures, which hinder effective collaboration, knowledge sharing, and unified strategic alignment. In response, several team models have emerged as promising approaches: Centers of Excellence concentrate expertise and foster innovation; cross-functional teams integrate diverse perspectives for complex problem-solving; virtual teams enable global collaboration and flexibility; and matrix teams support adaptability and efficient resource allocation. When strategically applied, these structures can significantly enhance an organization's capacity to drive and manage AI-enabled transformation.

References

Ammar, H. H., Menzies, T., Shata, O., Erradi, A., Kessentini, M., Abdelmoez, W., Kholief, M., Shaheen, M., Abdelhamid, M., AbdelHamid, A., & Omar, M. A. (2012). The International Center of Excellence in software engineering. *Communications of the ACS, 4*(2).

Berente, N., Gu, B., Recker, J., & Santhanam, R. (2021). Managing artificial intelligence. *MIS Quarterly, 45*(3), 1433–1450.

Burns, L. R., & Wholey, D. R. (1993). Adoption and abandonment of matrix management programs: Effects of organizational characteristics and interorganizational networks. *Academy of Management Journal, 36*(1), 106–138.

Cunningham, G. B., & Chelladurai, P. (2004). Affective reactions to cross-functional teams: The impact of size, relative performance, and common in-group identity. *Group Dynamics: Theory, Research, and Practice, 8*(2), 83.

Curry, E., Osagie, E., Pavlopoulou, N., Salwala, D., & Ojo, A. (2021). A best practice framework for Centres of excellence in big data and artificial intelligence. In *The elements of big data value: Foundations of the research and innovation ecosystem* (pp. 177–210). Springer International Publishing.

European Commission. (2019). *Ethics guidelines for trustworthy AI*. Accessed March 19, 2025, from https://digital-strategy.ec.europa.eu/en/library/ethics-guidelines-trustworthy-ai

Goś, K. (2015). The key advantages and disadvantages of matrix organizational structures. *Studia i Materiały, 2*(19), 66–83.
Hinds, P., & Kiesler, S. (2002). *Distributed work*. MIT Press.
International Organization for Standardization (ISO). (2023). ISO/IEC 42001:2023—Information technology—Artificial intelligence—Management system. Accessed April 7, 2025, from https://www.iso.org/standard/81230.html
Kolodny, H. F. (1979). Evolution to a matrix organization. *Academy of Management Review, 4*(4), 543–553.
Lämmermann, L., Hofmann, P., & Urbach, N. (2024). Managing artificial intelligence applications in healthcare: Promoting information processing among stakeholders. *International Journal of Information Management, 75*, 102728.
Majchrzak, A., More, P. H., & Faraj, S. (2012). Transcending knowledge differences in cross-functional teams. *Organization Science, 23*(4), 951–970.
McDonough, E. F., III. (2000). Investigation of factors contributing to the success of cross-functional teams. *Journal of Product Innovation Management: An International Publication of the Product Development & Management Association, 17*(3), 221–235.
Moore, K., & Birkinshaw, J. (1998). Managing knowledge in global service firms: Centers of excellence. *Academy of Management Perspectives, 12*(4), 81–92.
Morrison-Smith, S., & Ruiz, J. (2020). Challenges and barriers in virtual teams: A literature review. *SN Applied Sciences, 2*(6), 1–33.
Nasution, M. K., Noah, S. A. M., & Sitompul, O. S. (2019). The excellent center: Center for artificial intelligence technology. *Journal of Physics: Conference Series, 1235*(1), 012114.
OECD. (2024). *Recommendation of the Council on Artificial Intelligence (OECD/LEGAL/0449)*. Accessed April 7, 2025, from https://legalinstruments.oecd.org/en/instruments/OECD-LEGAL-0449
Protschky, D., Schüll, M., & Urbach, N. (2024). Governance von künstlicher Intelligenz—Eine Methode zur Transformation vorhandener Governance-Mechanismen in Unternehmen. *Wirtschaftsinformatik & Management, 16*, 194–201.
Reddy, S., Allan, S., Coghlan, S., & Cooper, P. (2020). A governance model for the application of AI in health care. *Journal of the American Medical Informatics Association., 27*(3), 491.
Schneider, J., Abraham, R., Meske, C., & vom Brocke, J. (2023). AI governance for businesses. *Information Systems Management*.
Schnetler, R., Steyn, H., & Van Staden, P. J. (2015). Characteristics of matrix structures, and their effects on project success. *South African Journal of Industrial Engineering, 26*(1), 11–26.
Tabassi, E. (2023). *Artificial intelligence risk management framework (AI RMF 1.0)*. NIST trustworthy and responsible AI, National Institute of Standards and Technology, Gaithersburg, MD. Accessed April 7, 2025, from https://doi.org/10.6028/NIST.AI.100-1
Webber, S. S. (2002). Leadership and trust facilitating cross-functional team success. *Journal of Management Development, 21*(3), 201–214.
Wirtz, B., Weyerer, J., & Kehl, I. (2022). Governance of artificial intelligence: A risk and guideline-based integrative framework. *Government Information Quarterly, 39*(4).

Nils Urbach is Professor of Information Systems and Digital Business as well as Director of the Research Lab for Digital Innovation and Transformation at the Frankfurt University of Applied Sciences, Germany. Furthermore, he is Director at the FIM Research Center for Information Management, and the Branch Business and Information Systems Engineering of Fraunhofer FIT. Nils Urbach has been working in the fields of digital innovation and transformation for several years. His work has been published in several academic journals such as Information Systems Research (ISR), the Journal of the Association for Information Systems (JAIS), the Journal of Strategic Information Systems (JSIS), the Journal of Information Technology (JIT), MIS Quarterly Executive (MISQE), IEEE Transactions on Engineering Management (IEEE TEM), Information and Management (I&M), Business and Information Systems Engineering (BISE), and Electronic Markets (EM). He advises several companies on digitalization issues and regularly appears as a speaker on this topic.

Daniel Feulner received his M.Sc. in information system from the Otto-Friedrich University of Bamberg, Germany in 2023. He is an affiliated researcher at the Branch Business and Information Systems Engineering of the Fraunhofer FIT and FIM Research Center for Information Management at the University of Bayreuth. In his research, he aims to understand how Business Analytics and Artificial Intelligence can be effectively and responsibly utilized in organizations. His goal is to enable companies to drive innovation and achieve sustainable growth in a rapidly evolving technological landscape.

Simon Feulner received his M.Sc. in business administration from the University of Bayreuth, Germany, in 2020 and his M.Sc. in information system from the Otto-Friedrich University of Bamberg, Germany in 2021. He is an affiliated researcher at the Branch Business and Information Systems Engineering of the Fraunhofer FIT and the Research Lab for Digital Innovation and Transformation at the Frankfurt University of Applied Sciences. His research explores the automation potential of generative AI technologies, examining how these innovations can streamline business processes, enhance decision-making, and unlock new opportunities for organizational value creation. He specifically focuses on how these technologies can break down existing barriers to automation, enabling more widespread and effective adoption across diverse business contexts.

Moritz Schüll received his M.Sc. in Information Systems from the Technical University of Munich, Germany 2021. He is an affiliated researcher at the Branch Business and Information Systems Engineering of the Fraunhofer FIT and FIM Research Center for Information Management at the University of Bayreuth. His research focuses on the strategic management of information systems, with a particular focus on integrating Artificial Intelligence technologies into enterprise architectures. In his work, he seeks to guide organizations in establishing the necessary capabilities and structures to successfully design, integrate and continuously manage information systems that leverage artificial intelligence technologies.

Valentin Mayer received his M.Sc. in Management and Technology from the Technical University of Munich, Germany 2023. He is an affiliated researcher at the Branch Business and Information Systems Engineering of the Fraunhofer FIT and FIM Research Center for Information Management at the University of Bayreuth. His research explores how companies can successfully implement Artificial Intelligence within their organizations, with a particular focus on the conceptual design and operationalization of AI systems. His goal is to equip companies with practical methods to implement AI end-to-end into their operations and create long-term value.

Part IV

AI Design and Development

Techno-Economic Decisions of AI

10

Nils Urbach, Daniel Feulner, Simon Feulner,
and Valentin Mayer

The integration of artificial intelligence (AI) into organizational processes is not only a technical challenge but also a strategic one. As AI systems increasingly shape core business functions, organizations must make techno-economic decisions that balance innovation with operational feasibility. These decisions are critical to ensure that AI investments generate sustainable value, align with long-term objectives, and remain adaptable to evolving technological and regulatory conditions. Understanding trade-offs between cost, scalability, performance, and risk is essential for responsible and effective AI adoption.

This chapter explores the key factors influencing such decision-making in the context of AI integration. It begins by introducing the "machine learning decision space," which highlights strategic considerations in balancing performance, robustness, and interpretability across the AI lifecycle. It then examines infrastructure models—such as edge computing, on-premises hosting, and cloud computing—that support data management, model training, and deployment. The role of AI service platforms is also discussed, focusing on how cloud-based, pre-built solutions can accelerate implementation and reduce complexity. Finally, the chapter introduces the concept of MLOps, which bridges the gap between development and production to ensure reliable and scalable AI operations. Together, these elements form a comprehensive framework for navigating the techno-economic landscape of AI adoption.

N. Urbach (✉) · S. Feulner
Frankfurt University of Applied Sciences, Frankfurt am Main, Germany
e-mail: nils.urbach@fim-rc.de; simon.feulner@fim-rc.de

D. Feulner · V. Mayer
University of Bayreuth, Bayreuth, Germany
e-mail: daniel.feulner@fim-rc.de; valentin.mayer@fim-rc.de

N. Urbach, D. Feulner (eds.), *Managing Artificial Intelligence*, Future of Business and Finance, https://doi.org/10.1007/978-3-032-13308-3_10

10.1 Machine Learning Decision Space

When integrating AI and machine learning into business operations, organizations encounter a complex array of choices that must be navigated to optimize performance and achieve strategic goals. This array of choices is referred to as the machine learning decision space. Understanding and navigating this decision space are crucial for making informed choices that align with both technical capabilities and business objectives (Ashmore et al., 2021).

The ML decision space encompasses several critical decisions that influence the success and efficiency of AI initiatives. These decisions range from selecting the appropriate models and algorithms to determining the best methods for training, retraining, and deploying these models. Each decision point requires a careful balance of various factors to achieve the best possible outcomes for the organization.

10.1.1 Trade-Offs in Machine Learning Decision Spaces

Navigating the ML decision space involves managing various trade-offs. Each decision impacts other aspects of the AI system, requiring a balance between competing priorities. To illustrate these trade-offs, we consider the goals that an AI model aims to achieve (Ashmore et al., 2021):

- *Performance:* A performant AI model considers quantitative performance metrics applied when deployed in a system. Metrics such as receiver-operating characteristic (ROC) curves, mean squared error, and classification accuracy are crucial for evaluating how well the model performs its designated task. Ensuring high performance often requires complex algorithms and extensive data, which can be resource-intensive.
- *Robustness:* Robustness refers to the model's ability to perform well under varying circumstances, especially when inputs during deployment differ from the training data. For example, an image recognition model trained on supermarket fruits should still accurately identify those at a farmer's market. Achieving robustness may involve additional preprocessing and augmentation steps, which can increase development time and complexity.
- *Reusability:* Reusability considers the ability of a model, or its components, to be reused in systems other than those it was originally designed for. For instance, facial recognition features developed for an authentication system might be reused to identify operator fatigue. Focusing on reusability can save time and resources in future projects but might limit the model's initial performance in its primary application.
- *Interpretability:* Interpretability assesses the extent to which the model can produce artifacts that support the analysis of its output and any decisions based on it. For example, a decision tree model can generate a narrative explaining the rationale behind its decisions, which is crucial in sectors where explainability is mandatory, such as healthcare or finance. However, interpretable models might

sacrifice some level of accuracy compared to more complex, less interpretable models.

Navigating these goals involves balancing trade-offs. For instance, a highly performant model might be less interpretable, making it harder for stakeholders to understand and trust its decisions. Similarly, a robust model might require more data and computational resources, impacting cost and deployment timelines. By carefully considering these trade-offs and aligning them with business objectives, organizations can make informed decisions that maximize the benefits of their AI initiatives. This strategic approach ensures that AI models are not only technically sound but also aligned with the broader goals of the organization, driving innovation and competitive advantage.

10.1.2 The Decision Space Across the Machine Learning Lifecycle

The decision space in machine learning spans across all stages of the ML lifecycle. This lifecycle includes several distinct phases, each with its own set of decisions and considerations (Ashmore et al., 2021).

Data Management
The initial phase of the ML lifecycle involves data management, which includes collecting, augmenting, preprocessing, and analyzing data. Decisions made at this stage are crucial as they form the foundation for all subsequent steps. Effective data management ensures that the data is clean, relevant, and ready for use in training ML models. Data collection involves gathering data from various sources, which can be internal or external to the organization. Data augmentation refers to techniques used to increase the diversity of the data without actually collecting new data. Preprocessing involves cleaning and transforming the data into a format suitable for model training. Finally, data analysis helps in understanding the data characteristics and in identifying any patterns or anomalies that might influence the modeling process.

Model Learning
In the model learning phase, the focus shifts to selecting the appropriate machine learning algorithms, architectures, and hyperparameters. This phase includes the critical tasks of model selection, training, and the application of techniques such as transfer learning. Model selection involves choosing the best model architecture that fits the specific business needs and data characteristics. Training the model is an iterative process that involves feeding the model with data and adjusting its parameters to minimize errors and improve accuracy. Hyperparameter selection is crucial as it involves fine-tuning the settings that control the learning process, such as learning rates and regularization parameters. Transfer learning can be used to leverage pretrained models on similar tasks, thereby saving time and computational resources.

Model Verification
Once the models are trained, they must undergo rigorous validation and testing to ensure they perform as expected. The model verification phase includes formal validation, test-based verification, and encoding of requirements. Formal validation involves systematic checks to confirm that the model meets the predefined criteria and performs well on unseen data. Test-based verification includes running the model through various test cases to evaluate its robustness and reliability. Requirements encoding ensures that the model adheres to the specific business and technical requirements set forth at the beginning of the project. This phase is critical for identifying any potential issues before the model is deployed in a live environment.

Model Deployment
The final phase of the ML lifecycle is model deployment, which involves integrating the model into the operational environment, monitoring its performance, and making necessary updates. Deployment decisions focus on how to best implement the models in a way that maximizes their effectiveness and reliability while minimizing risks and costs. Integration involves embedding the model into existing systems and workflows, ensuring it can interact with other components seamlessly. Monitoring is essential for tracking the model's performance in real time and identifying any degradation or anomalies that may occur. Updating the model may involve periodic retraining or adjusting its parameters to maintain optimal performance. This phase ensures that the model remains effective and continues to deliver value over time.

Each phase in the ML lifecycle is interconnected, and decisions made in one phase can significantly impact subsequent phases. For instance, the quality of data management affects the accuracy and reliability of the model learning process, which in turn influences the outcomes of model verification and deployment. Navigating the ML decision space effectively requires a comprehensive understanding of these phases and the specific decisions involved. By making informed choices at each stage, businesses can ensure that their AI initiatives are both technically sound and economically viable.

10.1.3 Assurance Methods for the Model Learning Stage

As machine learning has evolved into a critical technology for various applications, the need for robust assurance methods has become increasingly important. Assurance methods are essential in generating evidence that ML models are sufficiently safe and reliable for their intended use, particularly in safety-critical applications such as healthcare, transportation, and defense. Ensuring that ML models can be trusted is not only crucial for achieving their potential benefits but also for mitigating risks associated with their deployment.

Assurance methods provide a structured approach to verify and validate ML models throughout their lifecycle (Ashmore et al., 2021). This includes assessing model performance, robustness, reusability, and interpretability. By implementing appropriate assurance methods, organizations can ensure that their ML models meet the necessary safety, reliability, and performance standards. These methods are critical in building confidence that ML models will perform as expected under various conditions and will not pose undue risks to users or operations. In safety-critical domains, the stakes are particularly high. Errors in ML models used in medical diagnosis, autonomous vehicles, or defense systems can have severe consequences, including harm to human life and significant economic losses. Therefore, assurance methods must be rigorous and comprehensive, covering all aspects of the ML lifecycle from data collection to model deployment. The objective is to produce robust evidence that supports the safety and effectiveness of ML models, enabling their integration into critical systems with confidence.

The selection and implementation of assurance methods is an integral part of the ML decision space. Just as organizations must make informed decisions about model selection, data management, and deployment strategies, they must also choose appropriate assurance methods to ensure the reliability and safety of their ML models. These decisions are crucial throughout the entire ML lifecycle, encompassing various phases from data management to model deployment. For this discussion, we will focus on the assurance methods applicable during the model learning stage. However, it is important to note that assurance methods are also vital in other stages of the ML lifecycle, including data management, model verification, and model deployment.

The model learning stage is a crucial phase in the ML lifecycle, where the actual machine learning occurs. Ensuring that the models developed in this stage are reliable and perform well under a variety of conditions is essential. The following key assurance methods (see also Fig. 10.1) are applicable during the model learning stage:

- *Performance measures:* Quantitative metrics are used to evaluate how well the ML model performs its designated task. These metrics can include accuracy, precision, recall, the receiver-operating characteristic curve, and mean squared

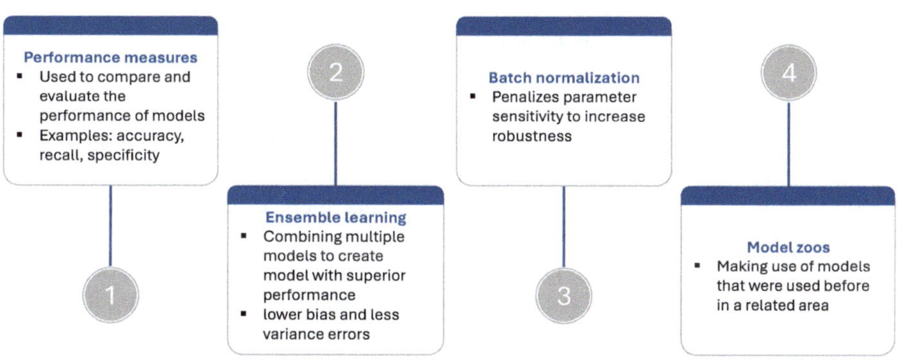

Fig. 10.1 Assurance methods for the model learning stage. (Adapted from Ashmore et al., 2021)

error, among others. Selecting appropriate performance measures is critical to ensure that the model meets the required standards and operates effectively in its intended environment. For example, in a healthcare application, the sensitivity and specificity of a diagnostic model would be crucial metrics.

- *Ensemble learning:* This method involves combining multiple models to produce a single model that performs better than any of its individual components. By aggregating the predictions of several models, ensemble learning can reduce bias, variance, and improve the robustness of the final model. Techniques such as bagging, boosting, and stacking are commonly used in ensemble learning. For instance, random forests, which are an ensemble of decision trees, are often more accurate and robust than individual decision trees.
- *Batch normalization:* This technique is used to improve the stability and performance of neural networks by normalizing the inputs of each layer. Batch normalization helps in accelerating the training process and making the model more robust to changes in the data distribution. By reducing the internal covariate shift, batch normalization allows for higher learning rates and reduces the likelihood of overfitting. In practice, this method has been shown to significantly improve the performance of deep learning models.
- *Model zoos:* Model zoos are repositories of pretrained models that can be reused and adapted for different tasks. These repositories provide a valuable resource for transfer learning, allowing practitioners to leverage existing models and reduce the time and resources required to train new models from scratch. By using models from model zoos, organizations can benefit from the collective expertise embedded in these models and ensure that their ML applications are built on a solid foundation.

Each of these assurance methods plays a vital role in ensuring that ML models developed during the model learning stage are robust, reliable, and fit for their intended purpose. By systematically applying these methods, organizations can build confidence in their ML models and mitigate the risks associated with their deployment in critical applications.

10.1.4 Train and Retrain AI Models

The processes of training and retraining AI models are fundamental to the machine learning lifecycle. They ensure that models remain accurate, relevant, and effective in dynamic environments where data and requirements continually evolve. Understanding these processes and implementing them effectively is crucial for maintaining high-performing AI systems.

Training refers to the initial phase where a machine learning model is developed. During this phase, the model is exposed to a set of training data, allowing it to learn patterns and relationships within the data. This foundational process is crucial as it determines the model's initial capabilities and performance. During training, the raw model adjusts its parameters based on the given data. These parameters are fine-tuned to minimize errors and enhance the model's predictive accuracy. For example, a neural network might adjust the weights of its connections through a process called backpropagation (see Chap. 3) to improve its ability to classify images correctly. The outcome of this phase is a trained model capable of making predictions or classifications on new, unseen data in the future.

Retraining is the process of updating an already trained model to adapt it to new data or changed requirements. This phase is essential for maintaining the model's performance over time as the underlying data distributions or business needs evolve. Retraining does not change the number of parameters and variables used in the model. Instead, it adapts the model weights to the current data, ensuring that the model continues to produce accurate outputs. For instance, if a model predicting customer churn was initially trained on historical data, it may need retraining as customer behavior changes over time due to new market trends or business strategies. Retraining involves several key activities, such as monitoring, detecting drift, and updating the model. Monitoring involves continuously tracking the model's performance to detect any decline in accuracy or effectiveness. Detecting drift involves identifying concept drift or data drift, which occur when the statistical properties of the target variable or the input data change over time. Updating the model involves adjusting the model's parameters using new data to restore its performance.

The primary reason for retraining models is to address model drift, which leads to decreasing accuracy of predictions over time. Model drift can be categorized into two types: concept drift and data drift. *Concept drift* occurs when the relationship between the input data and the target variable changes. For example, if an e-commerce recommendation system was trained on past user behavior, it might need retraining when users' preferences change due to new trends or seasons. Concept drift can result from changing user behaviors, shifts in the economy, environmental changes, new goals, etc. *Data drift* refers to changes in the input data distribution that the model was trained on compared to the data it encounters during deployment. This can happen if the quality or nature of incoming data changes over time. For instance, a spam detection model might experience data drift if new types of spam emails emerge that were not present in the original training data.

Choosing the right strategy for retraining involves considering what data to use and when to perform the retraining. *Offline learning or batch learning* is employed in cases of significant concept drift, where it might be necessary to replace the entire dataset and retrain the model from scratch. This approach, although costly, ensures that the model is trained on the most relevant and up-to-date data. On the other hand, *online learning* is used if there is a constant stream of new data. This method retrains the model incrementally, allowing it to adapt to new data without complete retraining.

Periodic retraining involves retraining the model at regular intervals, which can be useful when the underlying data changes within measurable time frames. However, frequent retraining can be computationally expensive, so determining the optimal time interval is crucial. *Trigger-based retraining* relies on setting performance thresholds. The model is retrained automatically when its performance drops below a certain level. For instance, if the accuracy of a fraud detection model falls below 90%, it might trigger an automatic retraining process.

Effective training and retraining of AI models are essential for maintaining their accuracy and relevance in changing environments. By understanding the processes involved and implementing appropriate strategies, organizations can ensure their AI systems remain robust, reliable, and capable of delivering valuable insights over time. This continuous cycle of training and retraining helps to mitigate the risks associated with model drift and ensures that AI models continue to meet their performance objectives in dynamic and evolving contexts.

Summary

Integrating AI into business operations requires navigating a complex array of choices within the machine learning decision space. This involves selecting appropriate models, training, retraining, and deploying them while balancing trade-offs to achieve models that are performant, robust, reusable, and interpretable. Assurance methods play a critical role in validating and verifying ML models throughout their lifecycle, ensuring safety and reliability, especially in safety-critical applications. Effective training and retraining are necessary to maintain model performance over time, addressing challenges like model drift. By strategically navigating the ML decision space and implementing robust assurance methods, organizations can optimize their AI initiatives and drive business success.

10.2 Data, Training, and Deployment Infrastructure in AI Systems

The selection of IT infrastructure is crucial to the success of AI and machine learning initiatives, determining how efficiently data is handled, how models are trained, and how solutions are deployed into production. A deep understanding of *AI data infrastructure, training infrastructure, and deployment infrastructure* is key to ensuring that technological decisions align with organizational objectives. Multiple infrastructure models—edge computing, on-premises hosting, cloud computing—cater to different operational needs (Fig. 10.2). These models range from enabling real-time data processing, supporting scalable model training, to ensuring secure and compliant deployment. Each infrastructure model addresses distinct facets of AI operations, allowing organizations to respond to the challenges of innovation, regulatory demands, and performance optimization in an increasingly dynamic digital environment. In this section, we will first briefly introduce the various IT infrastructure models (Escamilla-Ambrosio et al., 2018) before examining their role in data, training, and deployment infrastructure for AI systems.

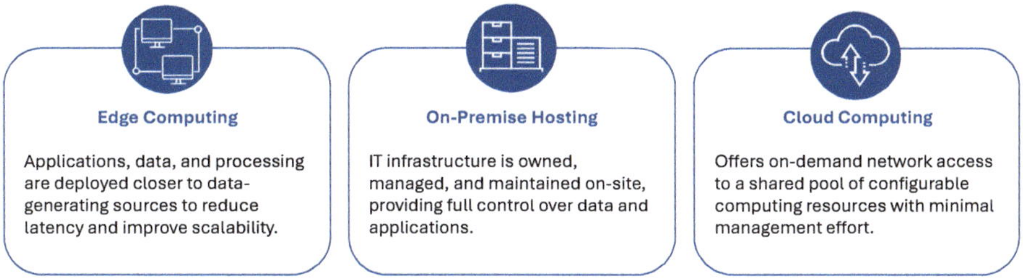

Fig. 10.2 Overview of IT infrastructure models

10.2.1 IT Infrastructure Models

Edge computing represents a paradigm shift from traditional centralized computing to a decentralized approach where computing takes place at the logical edge of a network. This model is particularly beneficial for applications that require low latency and high real-time data processing capabilities. By bringing resources and services closer to the sources of data, edge computing reduces the need to transmit large volumes of data to centralized data centers, minimizing latency and bandwidth consumption. Edge computing is particularly relevant in scenarios such as Internet of Things deployments, where devices generate significant amounts of data that must be processed in real time. In smart manufacturing, autonomous vehicles and remote monitoring systems, for example, the ability to process data locally enables faster decision-making and improves system responsiveness. This model also improves scalability by distributing the computational load across multiple nodes, which is critical for managing the increasing volumes of data generated by modern applications.

On-premises hosting remains a traditional and widely adopted deployment model where an organization owns, manages, and maintains its IT infrastructure within its physical premises. This model provides complete control over data and applications, making it particularly suitable for environments that require strict data security and regulatory compliance. Organizations that handle sensitive information, such as financial institutions and healthcare providers, often prefer on-premises solutions because of the direct oversight and customization capabilities they offer. The primary benefit of on-premises hosting is the ability to tailor the infrastructure to the specific needs of the organization, ensuring optimal performance and integration with existing systems. However, this model also involves significant capital and operational costs, associated with hardware and software purchases, as well as ongoing maintenance. In addition, on-premises solutions can face scalability and flexibility challenges compared to cloud-based alternatives, requiring careful planning and resource allocation.

Cloud computing has revolutionized the IT landscape by providing ubiquitous, on-demand network access to a shared pool of configurable computing resources. This model offers rapid provisioning and release of resources with minimal management overhead, making it highly scalable and cost effective. Organizations can use cloud services to access networks, servers, storage, applications and services over the Internet, allowing flexible and dynamic resource allocation based on current needs. One of the key benefits of cloud computing is its ability to support innovation and agility. By reducing the time and costs associated with infrastructure management, organizations can focus on developing and deploying applications more quickly. In addition, cloud providers offer different service models, including Infrastructure as a Service (IaaS), Platform as a Service (PaaS), and Software as a Service (SaaS), each providing different levels of control and abstraction (Mell & Grance, 2011):

- *Software as a Service (SaaS)* is a model in which applications are delivered over the Internet and accessed via client devices. These applications run on a cloud infrastructure managed by the service provider, ensuring that users do not have to worry about the underlying hardware, software maintenance, or infrastructure management. SaaS applications are ideal for organizations that want to deploy functional software quickly, without the need for extensive investment in IT infrastructure. They offer the convenience of regular updates, scalability, and accessibility from any location with an Internet connection.
- *Platform as a Service (PaaS)* provides a framework for developers to build, deploy, and manage applications. PaaS environments provide computing, storage, networking, and other essential services, abstracting much of the complexity of managing hardware and software layers. PaaS is particularly beneficial for organizations focused on development and innovation. It accelerates the application development process by providing out-of-the-box development tools and services, reducing time to market and operational overhead.
- *Infrastructure as a Service (IaaS)* delivers basic computing resources such as virtual machines, storage, and networking over the Internet. It offers the highest level of control and flexibility, allowing organizations to configure and manage their IT resources according to their specific needs. IaaS is ideal for organizations that need granular control over their IT environment and the ability to dynamically scale their infrastructure as needed. It is suitable for a wide range of use cases, from hosting websites and applications to running complex, data-intensive computing tasks.

Cloud computing also facilitates collaboration and remote working by providing access to applications and data from any location with an Internet connection. This capability has become increasingly important in the context of global business operations and the growing trend toward remote and hybrid working environments. However, organizations must carefully consider factors such as data security, compliance, and vendor lock-in when adopting cloud solutions.

In summary, the choice of IT infrastructure delivery model—whether edge computing, on-premises hosting, or cloud computing—depends on an organization's specific requirements, strategic objectives, and regulatory environment. Each model offers unique benefits and challenges that require a thorough evaluation of factors such as latency, control, scalability, and cost. By understanding the different characteristics of these deployment models, organizations can make informed decisions that will improve their operational efficiency and support their long-term goals. In the following, we examine how each infrastructure model affects the underlying AI data, training, and deployment workflows—highlighting the specific advantages and limitations associated with each approach.

10.2.2 AI Data Infrastructure

Data infrastructure encompasses the systems, tools, and resources that are essential for effectively collecting, storing, processing, and managing data. It forms the backbone of today's AI and machine learning applications, which rely on vast amounts of high-quality data to train models and produce accurate, reliable results. Building on the previously introduced models—edge computing, on-premises hosting, and cloud computing—this section explores how each infrastructure approach supports data management, offering unique advantages tailored to various organizational requirements (Fortuna et al., 2023; Escamilla-Ambrosio et al., 2018).

Edge computing strategically positions data processing near the source of data generation, significantly reducing the need to transfer large volumes of data to centralized data centers. This proximity minimizes latency, enabling faster data processing and response times, which is critical for real-time applications. In practice, edge computing is ideal for environments where immediate data analysis is critical. Examples include autonomous vehicles, industrial automation, and smart cities, where delays in data transmission and processing can be critical. By decentralizing data processing, edge computing not only increases speed, but also reduces the strain on network bandwidth, making it a scalable solution for growing data demands.

On-premises hosting involves a data infrastructure model where the infrastructure is physically located and owned within the organization, providing complete control over data management and security. This model is particularly beneficial for organizations that handle sensitive data and need to comply with strict regulatory requirements. The primary benefit of on-premises hosting is the assurance of data sovereignty and the ability to customize the infrastructure to meet specific organizational needs. Financial institutions, healthcare providers, and government agencies often prefer this model to maintain robust data governance and meet compliance standards.

Cloud computing is revolutionizing data infrastructure by allowing data resources to be located in one or more data centers around the world, accessible from anywhere with an Internet connection. Data is stored and processed remotely in the cloud, providing immense scalability, flexibility, and cost efficiency. This model supports a wide range of applications, from simple storage solutions to complex data analysis and AI model training. Cloud computing is characterized by its ability to rapidly scale resources up or down based on demand, making it ideal for organizations with fluctuating data volumes. Providers such as Amazon Web Services (AWS), Microsoft Azure, and Google Cloud Platform offer robust services that include computing power, storage, and specialized tools for AI and machine learning. The pay-as-you-go pricing model also converts capital expenditures into operational costs, reducing financial barriers to entry.

An effective data infrastructure is a cornerstone to the success of AI and machine learning applications. The choice between edge computing, on-premises hosting, and cloud computing depends on an organization's specific requirements for data control, security, processing speed, and scalability. Each model offers unique benefits and addresses different challenges, ensuring that organizations can choose an infrastructure that best aligns with their strategic goals and operational needs. By investing in the right data infrastructure, organizations can realize the full potential of their data, drive innovation, and maintain a competitive edge in the digital age.

10.2.3 AI Training Infrastructure

Training infrastructure is fundamental to the development and training of AI and machine learning models. It includes the resources required to handle intensive computational tasks and the storage requirements associated with processing large volumes of data and performing complex calculations. This section examines the suitability of edge computing, on-premises hosting, and cloud computing for AI and machine learning training, highlighting their capabilities and limitations (Fortuna et al., 2023; Escamilla-Ambrosio et al., 2018; Pawar et al., 2021).

Edge computing, while advantageous for real-time data processing, is generally not practical for AI model training due to its limited computing and storage capabilities. Edge devices typically lack the powerful hardware needed to perform the extensive computations required to train sophisticated AI models. The limitations of edge computing make it more suitable for deploying pretrained models and performing inference at the source of data generation, rather than for the training phase itself.

On-premises hosting is a viable solution for AI model training, particularly for organizations that require a high level of control over their data and infrastructure. This model supports the deployment of powerful hardware, such as graphics processing units (GPUs) and specialized servers, which are essential for handling the intensive computations of AI training. By investing in on-premises infrastructure, organizations can tailor their hardware and software environments to meet specific needs and ensure optimal performance. However, this approach requires significant capital expenditure and ongoing maintenance, as well as a dedicated IT team to manage the infrastructure. On-premises solutions are particularly suited to industries with stringent data security requirements, such as healthcare, finance, and government.

Cloud computing is a robust and flexible option for training AI models. It offers dedicated resources tailored for high-performance computing tasks, including access to powerful GPUs and tensor processing units (TPUs). Cloud providers such as Amazon Web Services, Microsoft Azure, and Google Cloud Platform offer scalable computing and storage solutions that can be tailored to the specific requirements of AI training tasks. The scalability of cloud computing allows organizations to quickly scale up or down their resources to efficiently handle varying workloads and data volumes. This flexibility reduces the need for significant upfront investment in hardware, turning capital expenditure into an operational cost through a pay-as-you-go model. In addition, cloud platforms often offer advanced tools and services designed specifically for AI and machine learning, further streamlining the training process.

Choosing the right AI training infrastructure is critical to the effective development and training of AI and machine learning models. While edge computing is limited in its applicability for training due to hardware limitations, on-premises hosting and cloud computing offer robust alternatives. On-premises hosting offers control and customization with significant investment, making it ideal for secure environments. Conversely, cloud computing offers unparalleled scalability and flexibility, with powerful resources and cost-effective models suitable for a wide range of AI training applications.

10.2.4 AI Deployment Infrastructure

Deployment infrastructure is the critical environment where trained AI and machine learning models are put into production to make real-time predictions or decisions. The effectiveness of this infrastructure directly impacts the performance, responsiveness, and reliability of AI applications in real-world scenarios. This section examines the suitability of edge computing, on-premises hosting, and cloud computing for deploying AI models, highlighting the unique advantages each approach offers for different deployment scenarios (Baier et al., 2019; Escamilla-Ambrosio et al., 2018).

Edge computing provides a highly efficient deployment environment for AI models, particularly for applications that require real-time data processing and low-latency responses. In this model, the trained AI model runs directly on edge devices or infrastructure located close to the data source. This proximity ensures that data does not need to be transmitted to a central server for processing, significantly reducing latency and enabling faster inference. Edge computing is ideal for scenarios such as autonomous vehicles, industrial automation, and smart IoT devices, where immediate decision-making is critical. The elimination of continuous connectivity to external infrastructure also serves to enhance the overall reliability and robustness of the system, rendering it an optimal choice for environments where network connectivity may be intermittent or unreliable.

On-premises hosting guarantees that data sovereignty, compliance, and security requirements are fully satisfied, which is of particular importance for industries that handle sensitive or regulated data. The deployment of models on-premises allows organizations to retain complete control over their data and the computational environment. This approach is particularly beneficial for sectors such as finance, healthcare, and government, where stringent data privacy concerns and regulatory mandates must be addressed. Furthermore, on-premises deployment enables the customization and optimization of the infrastructure, thus ensuring that the AI models operate effectively within the organizational context and meet specific performance and integration requirements.

Cloud computing offers a flexible and scalable environment for the deployment of AI models. In this model, trained models are executed on cloud servers, utilizing the substantial computational resources and infrastructure provided by cloud service providers. The deployment of AI models in the cloud allows for the efficient handling of prediction requests, which are sent to the cloud for processing and the results are returned to the requesting system. This model is particularly beneficial for applications requiring substantial computational power and scalability. Cloud computing supports high-availability and disaster recovery scenarios, ensuring that AI services remain operational even during periods of peak demand or unexpected disruptions. Additionally, cloud platforms often provide advanced deployment tools and frameworks that simplify the integration and management of AI models.

The selection of an appropriate deployment infrastructure is a crucial step in the operationalization of AI and machine learning models, and one that must be given due consideration. By understanding the relative merits and drawbacks of each deployment model, organizations can make an informed decision regarding the infrastructure that best aligns with their operational needs and business objectives.

Summary

The effectiveness of AI data, training, and deployment infrastructures is a crucial factor in the success of modern enterprises. By developing an understanding of the relative merits of the edge computing, on-premises hosting and cloud computing models and making strategic choices accordingly, organizations can enhance operational efficiency, drive innovation and maintain a competitive edge in the digital age. Each infrastructure model offers distinctive advantages and challenges, thus necessitating a comprehensive assessment of organizational needs, strategic objectives and regulatory requirements. By making well-informed decisions and optimizing their infrastructure management, businesses can fully leverage their data and AI capabilities, thereby ensuring sustained growth and success in a dynamic and competitive environment.

10.3 Integrating AI Service Platforms

The evolution of artificial intelligence platforms has profoundly impacted a vast array of industries, leading to the emergence of specialized tools tailored to meet the unique needs of various sectors. The most advanced AI platforms, including Google AI, IBM Watson, Salesforce Einstein, and Amazon Web Services, represent the pinnacle of technological advancement in this domain. These platforms provide sophisticated frameworks for the handling of complex data analytics, machine learning workflows, and the deployment of intelligent solutions.

The impact of these AI platforms is further emphasized by the highly dynamic nature of the market, which, according to the most recent estimates, is predicted to grow at a compound annual growth rate (CAGR) of 34.86% from 2022 to 2027 (Technavio, 2024). This considerable growth trajectory, as evidenced by recent market size outlooks, reflects the growing adoption and trust in AI-driven solutions across a range of industries. The accelerating growth momentum indicates an increasing recognition of the potential of AI to drive innovation, efficiency, and competitiveness within businesses.

Azure Machine Learning, introduced by Microsoft, represents a leading example of an integrated, comprehensive data science, and advanced analytics solution. The platform seamlessly combines data preparation, collaborative notebooks, and automated machine learning, creating a platform that not only enables but also enhances the analytical capabilities of its users. A pertinent example of its application is in the healthcare industry, where institutions can utilize Azure ML to scrutinize patient data and make informed predictions about future health risks. This predictive capability has the potential to revolutionize healthcare delivery, facilitating early diagnosis and the implementation of effective intervention strategies.

Concurrently, AWS has established itself as a significant player in the AI services landscape, offering an extensive suite of machine learning and deep learning services. Amazon SageMaker is a particularly noteworthy tool, as it enables the training and deployment of custom models without the necessity of managing underlying infrastructure. This attribute of AWS's offering allows organizations to concentrate on model creation and refinement, leaving the complexities of infrastructure management to the platform. For instance, businesses can utilize SageMaker to develop and launch AI models that enhance customer experience or optimize internal processes, thereby driving efficiency and innovation.

Google Cloud's Vertex AI is another notable AI platform, designed to address advanced machine learning requirements. It provides services for generative AI, speech processing, document and data analytics, vision, and video AI, among others. In the context of e-commerce, for instance, companies can utilize Google's Vision AI to analyze images within their catalogs. This capability enables the generation of product recommendations that are both insightful and tailored to the individual customer, enhancing the customer's shopping experience.

10.3.1 Motives to Use AI Service Platforms

The prevailing motives for leveraging AI service platforms are multifaceted and deeply rooted in the transformative capabilities that these platforms offer to contemporary businesses (Geske et al., 2021). One of the primary motivating factors is the high degree of freedom that these platforms afford organizations, enabling them to create their own AI models or applications with substantial flexibility. This freedom is of paramount importance, as it allows companies to tailor solutions specifically to their unique needs, thereby enhancing operational efficiency and competitive advantage. The platforms provide a comprehensive range of AI development services, encompassing the creation of bespoke models and the deployment of sophisticated applications. The ease of use, reduced operating costs, and minimal technical dependencies are significant advantages that make these platforms increasingly attractive to both customers and providers. This comprehensive service offering facilitates the seamless integration of AI into business processes, ultimately leading to a reduction in complexity and enhanced operational efficacy.

In addition to the freedom of creating bespoke AI solutions, AI service platforms also provide ready-to-use AI applications that incorporate integrated AI functionalities. The prebuilt applications reduce the development effort required from customers, thereby facilitating the adoption and implementation of AI within an organization. The range of available solutions encompasses a range of offerings, from basic development platforms to fully finished AI services, which cater to varying levels of needs and expertise. This continuum ensures that businesses at different stages of AI maturity can identify suitable solutions that align with their strategic goals.

Another compelling motive for utilizing AI service platforms is their focus on secondary AI services and resources, which significantly augment the primary functionalities. These supplementary services encompass pivotal elements such as data labelling and AI model assessment, which are indispensable for the refinement and validation of AI models. Furthermore, these platforms provide access to prebuilt machine learning models and extensive resources that facilitate the development process of AI solutions. The availability of these support services ensures that organizations can maintain the quality and performance of their AI applications, thereby fostering continuous improvement and innovation. The comprehensive support structure provided by these platforms enables companies to experiment with and deploy AI technologies with greater confidence and efficiency.

10.3.2 How to Choose a Fitting AI Service Platform

The selection of an appropriate AI service platform necessitates a comprehensive understanding of three pivotal layers: customer context, the platform's offering, and third-party integration (see Table 10.1). Each of these layers contributes to the overall suitability and effectiveness of an AI service platform, ensuring it aligns with the specific requirements and strategic objectives of the organization. By carefully evaluating these dimensions, businesses can make informed decisions that optimize their AI investments and drive substantial value (Geske et al., 2021; Gawer, 2014).

Customer Context

The initial layer, customer context, is pivotal to the decision-making process. It identifies the specific area of application and assesses the AI service platform from the customer's perspective to ascertain its specialization. This requires a comprehensive grasp of the business domain in which the AI solutions will be implemented, encompassing the distinctive challenges, prospects, and operational intricacies of that domain. For example, in the financial sector, the focus may be on enhancing

Table 10.1 A taxonomy of AI service platforms (Geske et al., 2021)

	Dimension	Characteristics				
Customer context	Industry focus	Industry-specific		Industry-unspecific		
	Activity focus	Activity-specific		Activity-unspecific		
	Platform use	Continuous	Continuous and on-demand	On-demand	None	
AI service platform's offering	AI service model	Application development service	Application development and deployment service	Hybrid service	Ready-to-use service	
		None				
	Complementary services	Yes		No		
	Complementary resources	Yes		No		
	Pricing model	One-off payment	Regularly based on variable rates	Regularly based on fixed rates	Freemium	Free of charge
	Code-based interaction	Yes		No		
	Graphical interface	Click through	Click through and drag and drop	Drag and drop	None	
Third-party integration	Integrated complementor	Selected complementors	Selected complementors and crowd	Crowd	None	
	Integrated complementor offering	Resource	Resource and service	Service	None	

fraud detection and risk management, whereas in the healthcare industry, the emphasis could be on predictive analytics for patient outcomes and personalized treatment plans. By aligning the platform's capabilities with the business's specific needs, companies ensure that the selected AI service platform can deliver targeted and impactful solutions. The customer context, thus, encompasses three critical dimensions: industry focus, activity focus, and platform use. Each dimension provides a distinctive lens through which an organization can evaluate the suitability of an AI service platform in accordance with its specific operational and strategic needs.

The first dimension, *industry focus*, plays a crucial role in determining whether an AI platform is designed for industry-specific or industry-agnostic applications. Industry-specific platforms address the particular challenges and requirements of specific sectors. For example, an AI platform specifically for the banking sector, such as KAI, is designed to address concerns around security, privacy, and data control. It offers conversational AI solutions that improve interactions with banking customers. Such platforms are of great value to industries with highly regulated environments and specific operational requirements, as they offer targeted solutions that comply with industry standards. In contrast, industry-agnostic platforms, such as IBM Watson, offer a broad range of applications across multiple sectors. IBM Watson utilizes advanced AI technologies that are universally applicable and offer a more comprehensive solution. These platforms are versatile and adaptable, making them suitable for organizations operating in different industries with different requirements.

The second dimension, *activity focus*, assesses whether the AI service platform is designed to support specific organizational activities or provides an activity-agnostic service. Activity-specific platforms are developed with the explicit objective of optimizing particular business functions or processes. For example, Afresh, an AI service platform, assists grocers in managing their perishable inventories, thereby reducing waste and optimizing stock levels. The direct application of AI to a specific activity results in immediate and tangible benefits, enhancing operational efficiency and cost-effectiveness. Conversely, platforms that are not specific to any particular activity, such as Amazon SageMaker, adopt a more generalized approach, facilitating the development of machine learning models across a range of applications. These platforms provide robust frameworks that can be adapted to meet a wide range of activity-specific requirements, offering flexibility and broad utility. By differentiating between direct and indirect effects in terms of activity focus, organizations can select an AI platform that either directly enhances end-product services or optimizes the developmental environment for broader applications.

The third dimension, *platform use*, describes the temporal integration of the AI service platform within an organization's workflows. Continuous use platforms are integrated into recurring processes, providing consistent and ongoing support for business operations. For instance, a banking-specific AI platform, such as KAI, is employed continuously to facilitate seamless interactions and enhance service delivery on an ongoing basis. This form of integration is paramount for organizations that require sustained AI capabilities to maintain operational stability and efficiency. Conversely, on-demand platforms are employed for specific projects or problem-solving tasks. Domino Data Lab exemplifies this approach, providing a data science environment that supports the development, training, and deployment of machine learning models on an as-needed basis. This flexibility allows organizations to address specific challenges or projects with tailored AI solutions, optimizing resource allocation and project outcomes.

AI Service Platform's Offering

The second layer of the AI service platform is concerned with the assessment of the value propositions provided by the platform. The specification of the AI service platform is contingent upon a comprehensive understanding of the platform's offering. This evaluation assesses the value proposition of the platform by meticulously examining the various dimensions that constitute an effective AI solution.

The initial and most crucial aspect to be considered is the *AI service model*, which delineates the manner in which an AI service platform generates value for the customer. This model differentiates between distinct types and degrees of service integration, each of which caters to varied business needs and technological proficiencies. For example, the deployment model allows customers to develop bespoke AI applications and provides the necessary infrastructure or assistance to deploy a machine learning model. This model is particularly advantageous for businesses that may lack the requisite infrastructure, enabling them to exploit AI technologies without the necessity for significant upfront investments in technical resources. An illustrative example is Algorithmia, which facilitates the straightforward deployment and administration of machine learning models, thereby conferring upon firms the greatest possible flexibility and operational efficiency.

Furthermore, the application development and deployment model extends these capabilities by enabling customers to build AI applications from scratch or customize existing models based on specific structures or parameters. This model offers a high degree of customization and control, thereby enabling businesses to tailor AI solutions precisely to their operational needs. For instance, the Google Cloud AI platform provides tools such as Jupyter Notebook, which offers an interactive environment where data scientists and developers can construct and refine machine learning models. This approach enables organizations to innovate and adapt more rapidly, thereby fostering a more agile and responsive AI strategy. In contrast to the aforementioned customizable models, ready-to-use services represent the most advanced offering of AI service platforms in terms of functionality and ease of use. These services are designed for customers who require immediate solutions without needing to delve into the complexities of model development and customization. For example, the banking-specific platform KAI offers prebuilt conversational AI services that can be rapidly integrated and deployed, allowing banks to enhance their customer service operations swiftly and effectively.

While these ready-to-use services offer significant advantages in speed and convenience, they restrict access to the underlying ML models, limiting the extent to which businesses can customize or modify the service. A hybrid model, which combines elements of ready-to-use services with customizable application development and deployment services, offers a balanced approach. This model permits businesses to utilize prebuilt AI functionalities while retaining the flexibility to modify and adapt these services to meet specific requirements. For example, a company may integrate a prebuilt AI service for customer interactions while customizing the underlying analytics to align with their unique business metrics and goals. This hybrid approach ensures that companies can benefit from rapid deployment while maintaining a degree of control and customization that supports their broader AI strategy.

The value proposition of an AI service platform is significantly enhanced by its *complementary services and resources*, which include additional tasks of the AI workflow that are crucial to successful application. For example, data labeling platforms such as Playment are crucial for developing high-quality machine learning models, as they provide the labeled data necessary for training these models. These services guarantee the construction of robust AI systems with precise and dependable data inputs, which is essential for achieving optimal performance outcomes. In contrast, supplementary resources are additional elements that are necessary for the development and deployment of AI services. For instance, the AWS marketplace provides customers with pretrained ML models, thereby facilitating the development of AI services by offering a solid foundation upon which businesses can build and refine their applications. These resources reduce the time and effort required to develop AI solutions from scratch, enabling organizations to focus on innovation and application rather than foundational development.

As a further dimension, the *pricing model* plays a central role in determining the economic feasibility and budgetary planning for businesses wanting to adopt AI services. A variety of pricing models are available to cater to the differing organizational scales and financial strategies of potential users. The one-off payment model represents a traditional software licensing approach, whereby a single transaction secures perpetual use of the platform. This model can be advantageous for organizations seeking long-term stability without recurring expenses, although the upfront cost can be substantial. Conversely, a pricing model based on regular payments, often with variable rates, such as pay-as-you-go, offers flexibility and scalability. This model enables businesses to incur costs commensurate with their usage, rendering it an optimal choice for enterprises that require adaptability and may experience fluctuating demands. For example, usage-based billing enables cost management in dynamic environments, where resource requirements align closely with operational needs. Additionally, there is the fixed-rate model based on regular billing cycles, which provides predictability and ease of budgeting through consistent billing regardless of fluctuations in usage. This model is particularly advantageous for organizations with consistent AI workloads, offering financial predictability and straightforward accounting processes. Freemium models, which provide basic services free of charge while charging for advanced functionalities, enable businesses to trial and integrate AI services at minimal initial costs, ensuring a fit before expanding usage. These models facilitate the integration of AI services by reducing the financial barriers to entry, allowing companies to experiment with AI and gradually scale their AI integrations without substantial financial commitments. Finally, platforms that offer services free of charge can be highly attractive for educational purposes, nonprofit organizations, or startups with constrained budgets. However, such platforms often come with limitations in capabilities or support.

Another crucial aspect to consider when evaluating AI service platforms is whether they support *code-based interaction*. This capability is of particular importance to advanced users and data scientists who prefer to write and execute code in development environments. Algorithmia, for instance, offers a client interface that supports a range of programming languages, including Python, thereby enabling users to perform intricate customizations and leverage advanced programming concepts to build and deploy sophisticated AI models. Code-based interaction offers a high level of flexibility and control, enabling developers to optimize algorithms, manage dependencies, and fine-tune model parameters. This capability is of great value to organizations seeking to advance beyond the capabilities of standard AI tools, enabling them to tailor their solutions to their specific operational objectives through customization and innovation.

In contrast, *graphical interfaces* cater to users who may not have extensive programming skills, with the objective of promoting accessibility and ease of use. These interfaces are available in various formats, including click-through menus and drag-and-drop functionalities, which facilitate the complex processes of AI deployment, data manipulation, and model training. Click-through interfaces facilitate interactions by providing guided steps that users can follow, thereby reducing the learning curve and enabling a broader range of personnel to engage with AI technologies. Drag-and-drop interfaces, meanwhile, permit users to visually construct workflows by arranging components in a modular fashion. This not only facilitates rapid prototyping but also enhances the user experience by making abstract concepts tangible and intuitive. Such interfaces facilitate access to advanced AI capabilities, ensuring that even organizations with limited technical expertise can harness the power of AI to drive innovation and efficiency.

Third-Party Integration

The third layer, third-party integration, describes the platform's constitutive agents beyond the platform provider and the customer. It focuses on the extent to which the platform can integrate with existing systems and third-party tools. Effective third-party integration extends the functionality and versatility of the AI service platform, enabling businesses to leverage a broader range of technologies and data sources.

A fundamental aspect of third-party integration is the role of *integrated complementors*, classified into selected complementors and crowds of complementors. Each contributes differently to the AI service platform. Selected complementors are typically restricted to limited access, often through specific integrations or partnerships. For example, Civis Analytics exemplifies this by enabling collaboration on various projects via GitHub integration, offering a seamless and controlled environment where specialized resources contribute to the development and optimization of AI models. This type of integration ensures that collaboration is executed under stringent quality controls and predefined parameters, providing a high degree of security and reliability in the process.

Conversely, the crowd of complementors provides open access to the AI service platform, democratizing the contributory process. Playment demonstrates this approach, whereby independent data annotators register and offer their services, such as data labeling, to a wider audience. This open model of integration exploits the collective intelligence and diverse expertise of a broad user base, enhancing the scalability and versatility of the AI platform. This dynamic marketplace accelerates innovation and reduces the time to market for AI solutions. Furthermore, the crowd-based model encourages a more inclusive environment, where individuals and smaller entities contribute meaningfully to large-scale projects, thereby disseminating benefits and opportunities more broadly.

In addition, the specific *integrated complementor offerings* provided by these partners play a pivotal role in defining the platform's utility and effectiveness. Integrated complementor offerings encompass both resources and services pivotal to the AI workflow. For instance, a complementor such as Meya might provide essential backend resources, such as a robust operating system, underpinning the AI platform's infrastructure. Resource-based integrations ensure the platform operates efficiently, leveraging specialized hardware or software components that enhance performance and reliability. Similarly, service-based integrations offer distinct functionalities crucial for the development and deployment of AI applications. A case in point is Playment's data annotation services, relying on a crowd of data annotators. This service addresses a critical step in the machine learning process—data labeling—by harnessing a scalable workforce that manages large volumes of data with varying degrees of complexity. The integration of such services within the AI platform enables developers and data scientists to access high-quality labeled data efficiently, significantly accelerating the training and accuracy of machine learning models. The AI platform's capacity to encompass both resource- and service-based offerings enables it to deliver a more holistic and integrated solution to its users, covering a broader spectrum of needs and applications.

Summary

The AI platform market is growing rapidly, with a projected CAGR of 34.86% from 2022 to 2027, underscoring the reliance on AI technologies for innovation and efficiency. AI service platforms are essential as they offer freedom to create custom AI models, integrate ready-to-use applications, and provide services like data labeling and model evaluation. Evaluating these platforms involves three key layers: customer context, service offerings, and third-party integration. Customer context examines specialization and application areas from the customer's perspective. Service offerings assess pricing models, code-based interaction, and graphical interfaces. Third-party integration leverages external partners like Civis Analytics and Playment to provide additional resources and services. These layers ensure the chosen AI platform meets organizational needs, optimizing AI adoption and maximizing innovation potential.

10.4 From DevOps to MLOps

The seamless integration of development and operational processes is paramount in today's business and technological landscape. This integration is exemplified by the implementation of DevOps principles (Ebert et al., 2016), which play a critical role in harmonizing the traditionally distinct domains of development and operations. The essence of DevOps lies in its ability to utilize automation in development, deployment, and infrastructure monitoring processes, thereby fostering an environment where continuous delivery and iterative improvements are not just achievable but sustainable. In broad terms, DevOps represents a paradigm shift within organizations, transitioning from isolated, compartmentalized teams—often referred to as "silos"—to cross-functional collaborative teams. These teams work in unison toward the continuous flow of operational features and enhancements, ultimately propelling business agility and boosting overall productivity (Fig. 10.3).

Taking a deeper dive into the DevOps lifecycle, one can observe a structured yet flexible framework that encompasses several phases: development, operations, and continuous feedback. The development phase initiates with meticulous planning, wherein requirements are defined, and initial execution plans are formulated. This is followed by coding, adhering to established standards and best practices that serve to maintain consistency and quality. The building stage involves the evaluation of software artifacts to ensure they meet the predefined criteria, with the final facet of development focusing on stringent testing protocols to guarantee product quality before it transitions to the next phase.

Operations within the DevOps framework emphasize the cyclical processes of release, deployment, operation, and monitoring. Releases are methodically managed after manual and automated testing ensure the software's readiness for deployment. Deployment itself involves both initial implementations and continuous redeployments, enabling the software to evolve alongside user needs and market demands. In its operational state, the focus shifts to maintaining and troubleshooting the software within a production environment, ensuring it runs smoothly and effectively. Continuous monitoring is then critical for maintaining stability and

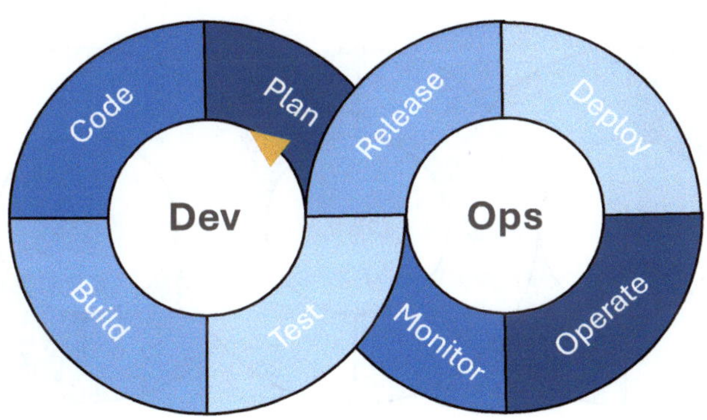

Fig. 10.3 DevOps lifecycle. (Adapted from Subramanya et al., 2022)

functionality, employing feedback mechanisms to gather insights and foster continual improvements.

Machine Learning Operations (MLOps) is a set of practices aimed at ensuring the consistent and efficient maintenance and deployment of machine learning code and models (Subramanya et al., 2022). Drawing parallels to DevOps, MLOps seeks to achieve a shorter code–build–deploy loop with a distinct focus on the rapid development and deployment of machine learning models. The core objectives of MLOps include maintaining high quality, reproducibility, and end-to-end tracking throughout the ML lifecycle. This emphasis on streamlined development processes is critical for adapting to the dynamic and data-driven nature of ML projects (Fig. 10.4).

The MLOps lifecycle integrates key stages of both machine learning and traditional software development. This lifecycle is divided into several phases, each crucial for the successful implementation of ML projects. In the machine learning phase, the model is the heart of any ML application and can include various types of neural networks and algorithms designed to perform specific tasks. Data serves as the foundational element for ML, making effective data analysis and management essential components of MLOps to ensure models are trained on accurate and relevant datasets.

During the development phase, careful planning is required to outline the objectives and methodologies for ML projects. Writing and refining the ML code is a continuous process involving the development of algorithms and model architectures. The construction of models and preparation of data pipelines are critical steps, followed by testing that focuses on model convergence and behavior. Ensuring that models perform as expected under various conditions is vital.

The operations phase encompasses the release, deployment, monitoring, and ongoing operation of ML models. Once models are validated, they are prepared for deployment. In MLOps, deployment involves not only the initial release of models but also the retraining and redeployment triggered by new data. Continuous monitoring of model performance is essential, including tracking metrics to assess accuracy and efficiency, and initiating retraining processes when performance degrades. The operational phase involves maintaining the deployed models and ensuring their reliability and effectiveness in production environments.

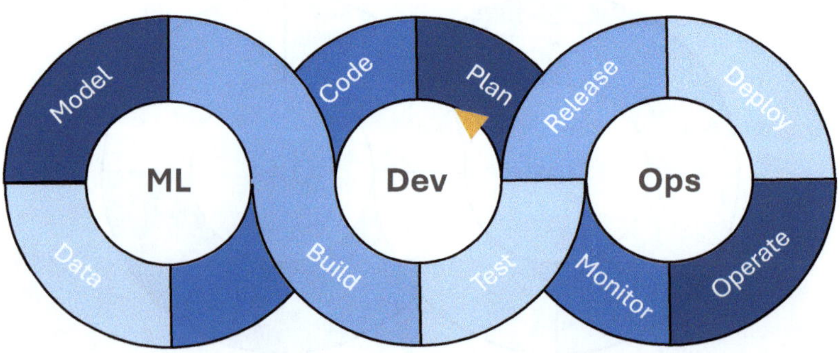

Fig. 10.4 MLOps lifecycle. (Adapted from Subramanya et al., 2022)

While MLOps shares several similarities with DevOps, there are distinct differences driven by the nature of machine learning. In MLOps, testing is heavily focused on the convergence of models and their specific behavior, ensuring they meet the desired performance criteria. The deployment process is iterative and responsive to new data, requiring models to be retrained and redeployed to adapt to changing conditions. Monitoring is critical for understanding model performance in real-time and determining when retraining is necessary to maintain accuracy and relevance.

MLOps specifically addresses the challenges of managing machine learning models and workflows to enable efficient and reliable implementation of AI technologies in production environments. By fostering a structured and systematic approach, MLOps enhances the ability of organizations to develop, deploy, and maintain ML models effectively, ensuring they remain robust and responsive to new data and evolving business needs.

Summary

Integrating development and operational processes is crucial in modern business, exemplified by DevOps principles that harmonize these traditionally distinct domains. DevOps emphasizes automation in development, deployment, and monitoring, fostering continuous delivery and iterative improvements. Shifting from isolated teams to cross-functional collaboration enhances business agility and productivity. MLOps extends these principles to manage machine learning models, ensuring quality, reproducibility, and end-to-end tracking. It focuses on effective data analysis, precise modeling, and continuous feedback, maintaining and enhancing AI systems. MLOps bridges the gap between innovation and practical application, addressing challenges in deploying and managing AI workflows.

References

Ashmore, R., Calinescu, R., & Paterson, C. (2021). Assuring the machine learning lifecycle: Desiderata, methods, and challenges. *ACM Computing Surveys (CSUR), 54*(5), 1–39.

Baier, L., Jöhren, F., & Seebacher, S. (2019). Challenges in the deployment and operation of machine learning in practice. In *ECIS* (Vol. 1).

Ebert, C., Gallardo, G., Hernantes, J., & Serrano, N. (2016). DevOps. *IEEE Software, 33*(3), 94–100.

Escamilla-Ambrosio, P. J., Rodríguez-Mota, A., Aguirre-Anaya, E., Acosta-Bermejo, R., & Salinas-Rosales, M. (2018). Distributing computing in the internet of things: Cloud, fog and edge computing overview. *In NEO 2016: Results of the numerical and evolutionary optimization workshop NEO 2016 and the NEO cities 2016 workshop held on September 20–24, 2016 in Tlalnepantla, Mexico* (pp. 87–115). Springer International Publishing.

Fortuna, C., Mušić, D., Cerar, G., Čampa, A., Kapsalis, P., & Mohorčič, M. (2023). On-premise artificial intelligence as a service for small and medium size setups. In *Advances in engineering and information science toward Smart City and beyond* (pp. 53–73). Cham: Springer International Publishing.

Gawer, A. (2014). Bridging differing perspectives on technological platforms: Toward an integrative framework. *Research Policy, 43*(7), 1239–1249.

Geske, F., Hofmann, P., Lämmermann, L., Schlatt, V., & Urbach, N. (2021). Gateways to artificial intelligence: Developing a taxonomy for AI service platforms. In *ECIS*.
Mell, P., & Grance, T. (2011). *The NIST definition of cloud computing*. National Institute of Standards and Technology (NIST), Special Publication 800–145.
Pawar, C. S., Ganatra, A., Nayak, A., Ramoliya, D., & Patel, R. (2021). Use of machine learning services in cloud. In *Computer networks, big data and IoT: Proceedings of ICCBI 2020* (pp. 43–52). Springer Singapore.
Subramanya, R., Sierla, S., & Vyatkin, V. (2022). From DevOps to MLOps: Overview and application to electricity market forecasting. *Applied Sciences, 12*(19), 9851.
Technavio. (2024). Artificial Intelligence Platforms Market Analysis North America, APAC, Europe, South America, Middle East and Africa—US, China, Germany, UK, France—Size and Forecast 2024–2028. *Technavio Industry Report*, September, 195 pages. [online] Accessed April 13, 2025, from https://www.technavio.com/report/artificial-intelligence-platforms-market-size-industry-analysis

Nils Urbach is Professor of Information Systems and Digital Business as well as Director of the Research Lab for Digital Innovation and Transformation at the Frankfurt University of Applied Sciences, Germany. Furthermore, he is Director at the FIM Research Center for Information Management, and the Branch Business and Information Systems Engineering of Fraunhofer FIT. Nils Urbach has been working in the fields of digital innovation and transformation for several years. His work has been published in several academic journals such as Information Systems Research (ISR), the Journal of the Association for Information Systems (JAIS), the Journal of Strategic Information Systems (JSIS), the Journal of Information Technology (JIT), MIS Quarterly Executive (MISQE), IEEE Transactions on Engineering Management (IEEE TEM), Information and Management (I&M), Business and Information Systems Engineering (BISE), and Electronic Markets (EM). He advises several companies on digitalization issues and regularly appears as a speaker on this topic.

Daniel Feulner received his M.Sc. in information system from the Otto-Friedrich University of Bamberg, Germany in 2023. He is an affiliated researcher at the Branch Business and Information Systems Engineering of the Fraunhofer FIT and FIM Research Center for Information Management at the University of Bayreuth. In his research, he aims to understand how Business Analytics and Artificial Intelligence can be effectively and responsibly utilized in organizations. His goal is to enable companies to drive innovation and achieve sustainable growth in a rapidly evolving technological landscape.

Simon Feulner received his M.Sc. in business administration from the University of Bayreuth, Germany, in 2020 and his M.Sc. in information system from the Otto-Friedrich University of Bamberg, Germany in 2021. He is an affiliated researcher at the Branch Business and Information Systems Engineering of the Fraunhofer FIT and the Research Lab for Digital Innovation and Transformation at the Frankfurt University of Applied Sciences. His research explores the automation potential of generative AI technologies, examining how these innovations can streamline business processes, enhance decision-making, and unlock new opportunities for organizational value creation. He specifically focuses on how these technologies can break down existing barriers to automation, enabling more widespread and effective adoption across diverse business contexts.

Valentin Mayer received his M.Sc. in Management and Technology from the Technical University of Munich, Germany 2023. He is an affiliated researcher at the Branch Business and Information Systems Engineering of the Fraunhofer FIT and FIM Research Center for Information Management at the University of Bayreuth. His research explores how companies can successfully implement Artificial Intelligence within their organizations, with a particular focus on the conceptual design and operationalization of AI systems. His goal is to equip companies with practical methods to implement AI end-to-end into their operations and create long-term value.

Designing Human–AI Interactions 11

Nils Urbach, Daniel Feulner, and Valentin Mayer

The rapid integration of artificial intelligence (AI) across diverse industries reshapes how humans and machines interact, evolving from simple interactions with virtual assistants to complex collaborative decision-making in sectors such as healthcare and finance. As AI transitions from being merely a tool to becoming an active collaborator, the demand for intuitive, transparent, and human-centered interactions intensifies. Effective human–AI collaboration strategically leverages their complementary strengths: AI excels in processing vast data, recognizing patterns, and handling repetitive tasks, while humans offer creativity, ethical judgment, and contextual understanding.

This chapter explores the dimensions of human–AI interactions, identifies distinct interaction types, and discusses influencing factors such as transparency, personalization, anthropomorphism, and user expectations. It then examines the transformative impact of AI on the workforce, highlighting the necessity of collaboration to manage job displacement and innovation effectively. Furthermore, the chapter presents strategies for optimizing human–AI collaboration, including managing automation bias and ensuring appropriate reliance on AI systems. Finally, it addresses effective task delegation approaches, emphasizing conditions for successful collaboration and analyzing AI-led delegation through a principal-agent perspective, ultimately aiming to support practitioners in designing sustainable and ethically responsible human–AI interactions.

The original version of the chapter has been revised. A correction to this chapter can be found at https://doi.org/10.1007/978-3-032-13308-3_14

N. Urbach (✉)
Frankfurt University of Applied Sciences, Frankfurt am Main, Germany
e-mail: nils.urbach@fim-rc.de

D. Feulner · V. Mayer
University of Bayreuth, Bayreuth, Germany
e-mail: daniel.feulner@fim-rc.de; valentin.mayer@fim-rc.de

N. Urbach, D. Feulner (eds.), *Managing Artificial Intelligence*, Future of Business and Finance, https://doi.org/10.1007/978-3-032-13308-3_11

11.1 Human–AI Interaction

As AI becomes increasingly integrated into various industries, the nature of interactions between humans and AI agents grows in complexity and frequency. These interactions can range from simple requests to virtual assistants, such as asking for weather updates, to sophisticated decision-making processes in professional environments, such as AI-driven recommendations in healthcare or finance. Understanding the core dimensions that define human–AI interactions is vital for designing systems that align with user needs, foster trust, and enhance usability (Hinsen et al., 2022; Alan et al., 2019).

AI agents are no longer just tools—they are collaborators that assist in carrying out tasks previously performed by humans. These agents help automate processes, augment human capabilities, and, in some cases, make independent decisions. Whether it is an industrial robot supporting a production line or an AI assistant managing personal tasks, the design of these systems must account for the user experience. Poorly designed interactions can lead to frustration, distrust, and even rejection of AI systems. This is why organizations must consider not only the technical performance of their AI systems but also the quality of the interaction itself.

The human–AI interaction model, as depicted in Fig. 11.1, outlines nine fundamental dimensions that shape and influence human–AI interactions (Hinsen et al., 2022). This model provides a comprehensive framework for understanding the key components that govern the way humans and AI systems communicate and collaborate. By considering these dimensions, developers and designers can create AI systems that are more intuitive, transparent, and user-friendly.

1. *Interaction Transparency*

   Interaction transparency refers to the degree of consciousness with which a person interacts with an AI agent. This can range from complete awareness to unconscious interaction. For example, an AI-powered emergency braking sys-

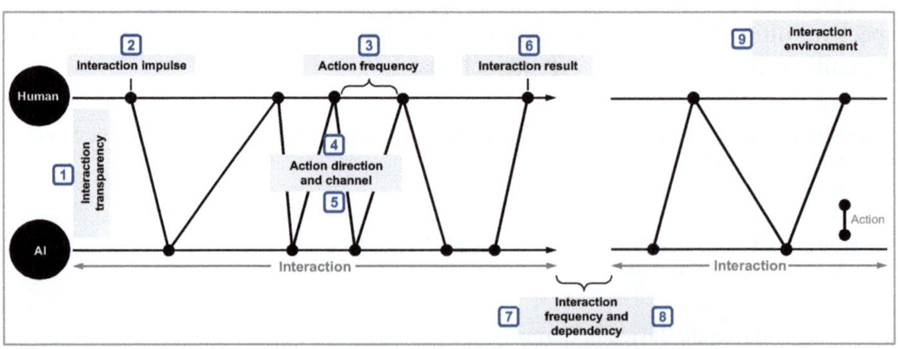

Fig. 11.1 Nine interaction dimensions of a human–AI interaction. (Adapted from Hinsen et al., 2022)

tem in a car operates without the driver being actively involved but significantly impacts the driving experience.

2. *Interaction Impulse*

   This dimension describes the trigger or reason for starting a new human–AI interaction. Impulses can be targeted (e.g., delegating a task to the AI), searching (e.g., looking for information), or playfully/creatively initiated.
3. *Action Frequency*

   Action frequency refers to the number of actions within a single interaction. These can be simple, involving only one action, or they can involve multiple actions over a longer period, as in continuous communication or repetitive tasks.
4. *Action Direction*

   Action direction refers to the flow of actions in an interaction, which can be unidirectional (one-way) or bidirectional (two-way). For instance, in voice-based interactions, the user gives a command, and the AI responds, creating a two-way exchange.
5. *Action Channel*

   The action channel refers to the sensory modes through which interaction takes place. Information can be exchanged acoustically (e.g., voice commands), visually (e.g., screen prompts), or haptically (e.g., vibrations or tactile feedback).
6. *Interaction Result*

   Interaction results influence the environment and can range from providing information to assisting, advising, or even offering an experiential outcome. For example, an AI that provides traffic updates could inform the user or assist in selecting an alternative route.
7. *Interaction Frequency*

   This dimension describes the frequency of interactions over a certain period. Depending on the system's purpose, interactions may be one-time, rare, or frequent, such as in systems that require regular feedback or updates.
8. *Interaction Dependency*

   Interaction dependency measures the extent to which one interaction depends on another. Some interactions are independent, while others are interdependent, requiring multiple exchanges to achieve a specific outcome.
9. *Interaction Environment*

   This dimension refers to the environment in which the interaction occurs, whether in private or professional contexts. The nature of the environment influences the design and expectations of the interaction.

Understanding the nine dimensions of human–AI interaction is essential for designing AI systems that are intuitive, transparent, and user-centric. These dimensions offer a structured approach to evaluating how humans and AI agents communicate and collaborate, ensuring that the interactions are seamless and aligned with user needs. By addressing aspects like interaction transparency, action direction, and frequency, developers can create AI systems that foster trust and provide meaningful support in both personal and professional environments.

11.1.1 Types of Human–AI Interaction

Building on the fundamental dimensions of human–AI interaction, it is important to explore the various roles that AI agents can take in their interactions with humans. AI agents do not all interact with humans in the same way. Some serve as passive background systems, while others actively engage users in collaborative tasks. As depicted in Fig. 11.2, there are five distinct types of human–AI interactions, each defined by the AI agent's level of autonomy and engagement with the user. These types include the guardian angel, pixie, informant, colleague, and best friend. Each represents a different relationship between the human and AI, ranging from systems that operate independently in the background to those that involve close, collaborative interactions.

The interaction types differ not only in the AI's functional role but also in how users perceive and engage with the AI. For example, a guardian angel system operates largely unnoticed, providing passive support without requiring direct interaction from the user. In contrast, the best friend interaction type involves continuous, personalized exchanges, fostering a deeper and more emotionally engaged relationship with the user. By understanding these distinct interaction types, organizations can design AI systems that are better suited to specific user needs, fostering greater acceptance, trust, and usability. In the following, we will examine each of these five types in detail, outlining their characteristics and exploring the specific scenarios in which they are most applicable (Alan et al., 2019; Hinsen et al., 2022).

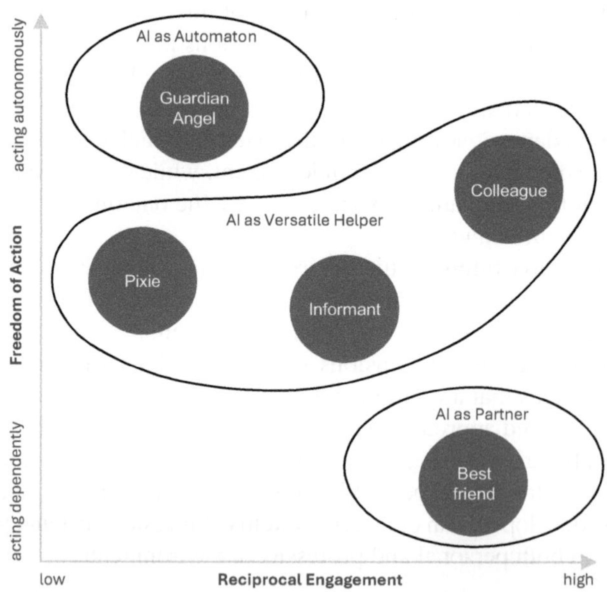

Fig. 11.2 Five human–AI interaction types. (Adapted from Hinsen et al., 2022)

Guardian Angel

A guardian angel AI involves interactions that occur entirely unconsciously for users, extending seamlessly from initiation to the interaction outcome, and often beyond. Typically, these AI systems operate independently with minimal reciprocal engagement, possessing high autonomy to carry out their intended functions. Due to their protective nature, guardian angel interactions are generally initiated by targeted impulses designed into the system. Examples include vehicle assistance technologies such as emergency braking or lane departure warning systems, which autonomously ensure safety without explicit user interaction. Predictive maintenance systems that monitor machinery wear and intelligent spam filters operating unobtrusively to manage email inboxes also exemplify guardian angel AIs.

Pixie

A pixie AI handles repetitive, simple tasks to reduce or simplify the human workload through consciously initiated interactions. These AI systems have moderate autonomy, engaging primarily through targeted user commands. Their purpose is to efficiently automate routine processes, allowing humans to concentrate on more complex, strategic tasks. Common examples include intelligent software applications in human resource management, such as automated CV screening systems that manage repetitive HR processes, significantly streamlining workflows. Additionally, smart home assistants performing simple, explicitly user-directed actions like adjusting lights, controlling thermostats, or unlocking smartphones through facial recognition technology represent typical pixie interactions that assist users by handling straightforward, repetitive tasks.

Informant

Informant AIs specialize in gathering and providing information, characterized by interactions that display increased reciprocal engagement and autonomy. These interactions begin either through targeted impulses, such as direct user queries, or through searching impulses, where users unconsciously trigger interactions. Informants rapidly deliver clear, relevant information, significantly enhancing efficiency and user experience. Examples include AI-driven customer service robots that provide assistance in shopping or reception areas by answering questions, offering directions, or supplying useful data. Another scenario involves proactive chatbot interactions on online retail platforms, suggesting products based on user browsing habits, even when customers have not explicitly sought such recommendations, thereby enhancing the user experience seamlessly.

Colleague

Colleague AIs interact with users consciously, focusing on achieving specific, goal-oriented outcomes through high reciprocal engagement and moderate to high autonomy. Users intentionally engage these AI systems through targeted or searching impulses to collaboratively tackle tasks or solve problems. Typical examples include advanced AI-based text-generation systems, such as GPT-4.5 by OpenAI, which assist content creators by generating relevant textual suggestions or comprehensive drafts. In professional settings, augmented reality (AR)-enhanced AI systems assist technicians performing complex machinery maintenance by displaying real-time instructions or technical details. Such colleague interactions explicitly facilitate cooperation, enhancing productivity and decision-making by integrating closely with human workflows.

Best Friend

Best friend AIs represent the most complex interaction type, involving highly reciprocal and emotionally engaging interactions constrained within predefined social frameworks, resulting in relatively lower autonomy. Users initiate these interactions primarily through playful or creative impulses, actively engaging in conscious social exchanges. Typical examples include social chatbots like Microsoft's Xiaoice, which perceive, process, and generate human-like text and speech, delivering personalized and emotionally engaging conversations. Further instances involve sophisticated gaming bots developed by organizations like OpenAI, interacting autonomously within the rules of complex video or board games, offering engaging, interactive experiences that foster meaningful social connections with users through continuous personalized interactions.

11.1.2 Influencing Factors of Human–AI Interaction

Human–AI collaboration depends on several critical factors that influence the success, trust, and acceptance of AI systems by users. These factors include human expectations, transparency, anthropomorphism, personalization, and the combined acceptance and trust that develops over time. As shown in Fig. 11.3, these factors are interconnected and contribute to shaping the overall interaction between humans and AI (Alan et al., 2019).

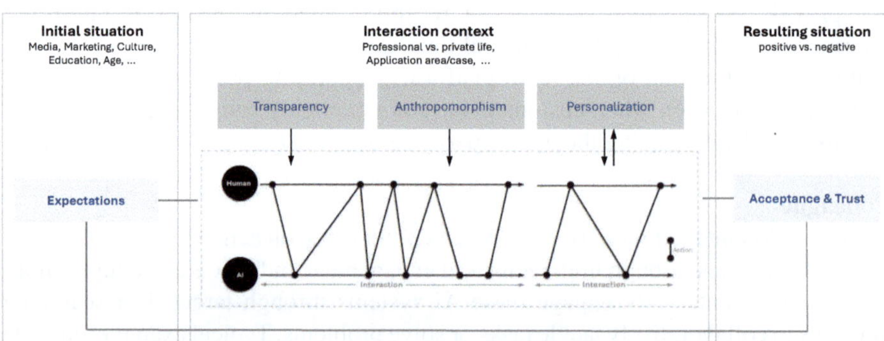

Fig. 11.3 Influencing factors of human–AI interaction. (Adapted from Alan et al., 2019)

Expectations

Expectations are a starting point for human–AI interaction and are shaped by external influences such as marketing, media, and cultural narratives. Promises of AI revolutionizing all areas of life often lead to inflated assumptions about its capabilities. When these expectations are not met, frustration and rejection may follow. At the same time, concerns about job loss and personal relevance foster skepticism—especially in professional contexts. This results in a contradictory attitude: While users often accept imperfections in private settings, they react more critically when AI systems fall short in work environments. Understanding and managing these expectations early on is essential to enable constructive and sustainable human–AI collaboration.

Transparency

Transparency refers to the extent to which users are aware that they are interacting with AI and understand how the system operates and produces results. Clearly communicating an AI system's capabilities and limitations is key to managing user expectations. Especially in professional contexts, explainable AI techniques help users comprehend how outcomes are generated, fostering trust and enabling more effective interaction. However, the required level of transparency depends on the context: While awareness can improve user input in conscious interactions (e.g., with chatbots), in everyday scenarios like driving assistants, users value seamless functionality over detailed understanding. Full transparency is not always feasible or necessary, as people often trust technologies without knowing how they work.

Anthropomorphism

Designing AI systems with human-like features can make interactions feel more natural and enjoyable, especially in contexts like caregiving or customer service. However, anthropomorphism is an ambivalent design choice. While it can boost acceptance by creating familiarity, it also shapes user expectations—often beyond what AI can deliver. When these expectations are disappointed, users may experience frustration or even rejection. In some cases, anthropomorphic AI can provoke discomfort or reinforce fears of being replaced. Designers should therefore use human-like traits purposefully and context-sensitively, avoiding superficial gimmicks. Striking the right balance is essential to ensure AI systems are perceived as supportive rather than threatening or overly dominant.

Personalization

Personalization refers to an AI system's ability to tailor interactions by forming assumptions about a user's goals, preferences, and knowledge—based on prior behavior, settings, or shared data. The more personalized the system, the more relevant and efficient the interaction becomes, often reducing the need for frequent input. In many contexts, personalized AI can better meet user expectations and enhance satisfaction. However, personalization raises privacy concerns—especially if users are unaware of the data collection involved. If users understand and accept that the system learns from their input, they can actively shape this learning process.

As such, personalization is a dynamic factor, evolving through continuous interaction and requiring transparent communication.

Acceptance and Trust

User acceptance of AI develops gradually through repeated, successful interactions. A single positive experience rarely fosters overall trust. Instead, users align expectations iteratively as systems consistently meet their needs. Striking the right balance of transparency, anthropomorphism, and personalization is key to this process. Over time, as users gain confidence in the system's reliability, they may grant more autonomy and explore broader use cases. However, trust remains fragile—one disappointing interaction can undo previous progress. Acceptance is also shaped by personal attitudes and cultural context. While some regions show openness toward AI, others prioritize privacy and security, leading to more cautious adoption. Consistency and contextual sensitivity are therefore crucial for sustained human–AI collaboration.

In conclusion, the success of human–AI collaboration hinges on carefully balancing multiple factors that shape the interaction. Managing expectations, ensuring transparency, and striking the right level of anthropomorphism are key to fostering user confidence and preventing frustration. Personalization enhances the user experience by tailoring AI behavior to individual needs, but it must be done with transparency to avoid privacy concerns. Ultimately, trust and acceptance are the culmination of these factors, developing gradually over time as users interact with AI systems that consistently meet their expectations. A holistic approach, considering each of these influencing factors, is essential to promoting effective and sustainable human–AI collaboration.

Summary

Human-AI interactions are defined by key dimensions such as interaction transparency, action direction, frequency, and environment, which help shape how humans and AI systems communicate. Various types of interaction exist, including the guardian angel, pixie, informant, colleague, and best friend, each representing different levels of AI autonomy and user engagement. The success of these interactions is influenced by factors such as user expectations, system transparency, anthropomorphism, personalization, and the development of trust and acceptance. A well-balanced approach to these dimensions, interaction types, and influencing factors is essential for creating effective, user-centric, and sustainable human-AI collaboration.

11.2 Workforce Transformation Through AI

Building on the discussion of human–AI interaction, this section looks at the transformative impact of AI on the workforce. As AI systems advance, they redefine traditional roles, automate repetitive tasks, and introduce new collaborative opportunities across industries. Exploring the framework of intelligence types—mechanical, analytical, intuitive, and empathic—highlights AI's evolving capabilities and their implications for job displacement and collaboration. By understanding these dynamics, organizations can harness AI's potential to complement human strengths, drive innovation, and adapt to the challenges of a changing labor market.

11.2.1 AI's Possible Role in Workforce Transformation

The rapid advancement of AI is transforming the workforce, challenging traditional roles, and reshaping how tasks are performed across various industries. Huang and Rust (2018) provide a comprehensive framework (see Fig. 11.4) that categorizes intelligence into four types: mechanical, analytical, intuitive, and empathic. Each type plays a unique role in the broader context of human–AI collaboration, facilitating different applications and interactions between humans and intelligent systems. Understanding these categories is essential for navigating the evolving dynamics of job displacement and for fostering a productive synergy between human and AI capabilities.

Mechanical intelligence refers to the ability to automatically carry out routine and repetitive tasks with little to no adaptation. While it may not appear particularly intelligent, it is fundamental for handling tasks that require consistency rather than creativity. Such systems are rule-based, relying on preprogrammed instructions and sensor inputs to operate reliably in predictable environments. Service robots and self-service technologies are common examples. Their main strength lies in their

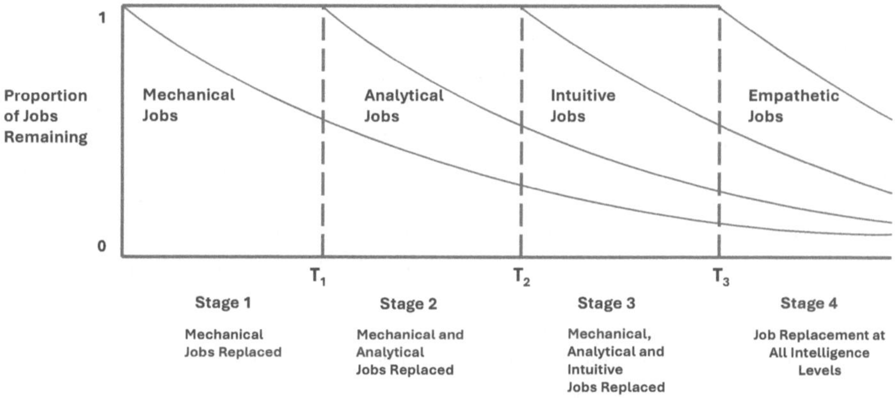

Fig. 11.4 Stages of job replacement. (Adapted from Huang & Rust, 2018)

high reliability, precision, and independence from human limitations such as fatigue or distraction. These systems are often used in roles such as call center agents, retail workers, or waitstaff—jobs that primarily require mechanical skills and minimal training.

Analytical intelligence refers to the ability to process information systematically, solve problems, and learn from data. It is grounded in logical reasoning, information processing, and mathematical skills, and is central to tasks that require structured thinking and cognitive expertise. AI systems with analytical intelligence use algorithms to detect patterns, derive insights, and support evidence-based decision-making. A well-known historical example is IBM's Deep Blue, which defeated a world chess champion using rule-based logic and brute-force search. In contrast, many modern AI systems demonstrate analytical intelligence by learning from large datasets—for example, in predictive analytics used to forecast product demand in retail, where systems analyze sales histories, weather trends, and regional events. In business, analytical intelligence underpins the work of data scientists, accountants, engineers, and financial analysts, who rely on deep technical knowledge and precision in interpreting complex data. While capable of intelligent behavior, such systems lack intuition or consciousness.

Intuitive intelligence refers to the ability to think creatively and adapt effectively to novel and complex situations. It is rooted in holistic, experience-based understanding and is essential for tasks that require insight, judgment, and creative problem-solving. AI systems with intuitive intelligence rely on advanced methods like neural networks and deep learning to emulate human-like learning and cognition. Unlike rule-based or analytical systems, intuitive AI adapts dynamically and learns from experience, making it less prone to repeating past mistakes. Prominent examples include modern AI systems like large language models, which generate creative content, interpret complex queries, and adapt to context in real time. In the medical domain, systems such as DeepMind's AlphaFold demonstrate intuitive intelligence by predicting protein structures in ways that defy rule-based logic. In professional contexts, intuitive intelligence is crucial for roles such as marketing managers, consultants, lawyers, doctors, and senior travel agents—positions where context sensitivity, innovation, and adaptive strategies are indispensable.

Empathic intelligence refers to the ability to recognize, understand, and respond to human emotions in a socially appropriate manner. It enables AI systems to engage in emotional and relational interactions, simulating empathy through affective computing. This form of intelligence draws on interpersonal skills such as communication, relationship-building, and emotional influence. AI applications like Hanson Robotics' humanoid robot Sophia or the chatbot Replika are designed to simulate human-like social presence and provide emotional engagement. Although the debate continues on whether machines can truly "feel," many argue that simulating emotions is sufficient for service contexts. In professional domains, empathic intelligence is especially important in roles requiring emotional labor and social interaction—such as politicians, negotiators, psychiatrists, and even frontline workers like flight attendants—where building trust, interpreting emotional cues, and managing relationships are critical.

Integrating these different types of intelligence into business processes requires a nuanced understanding of their respective strengths and limitations. Human–AI collaboration should leverage AI's mechanical precision for repetitive tasks, analytical capabilities for data-driven insights, intuitive adaptability for creative problem-solving, and empathic skills for effective human interaction. By strategically deploying AI systems to complement human skills, organizations can increase efficiency, drive innovation, and improve overall performance. Despite these benefits, the potential for AI to replace human jobs remains a topic of considerable debate and research. Huang and Rust's (2018) framework offers a possible trajectory for job displacement by AI, analyzed through the lens of the aforementioned types of intelligence (see Fig. 11.4). While this framework provides valuable insights into how AI might impact various roles, it is important to recognize that these outcomes are not predetermined, and the actual impact of AI on the workforce will depend on a range of factors, including technological advancements, societal responses, and policy decisions.

In the first stage (T1), AI primarily replaces jobs involving mechanical intelligence—standardized, repetitive tasks often performed by low-skilled workers. These tasks are increasingly automated through technologies like self-service kiosks, voice-recognition systems, and autonomous service robots. Such automation offers businesses cost savings and consistent quality. Roles like call center agents, fast-food workers, and taxi drivers are particularly affected. As mechanical tasks are outsourced to machines, human labor shifts toward jobs requiring analytical, intuitive, or empathic intelligence, prompting a growing demand for higher-level cognitive and interpersonal skills.

As AI capabilities expand, the second stage (T2) of displacement begins to affect analytical roles. These involve data processing, logical reasoning, and rule-based problem-solving—once seen as safe from automation. Yet AI systems now outperform humans in many of these areas due to advances in machine learning and big data analytics. Professions such as data scientists, accountants, and financial analysts face increasing automation pressure. While AI handles complex calculations, human workers must shift toward intuitive and creative skills that are harder to replicate algorithmically.

In the third stage (T3), AI's influence reaches roles that rely on intuitive intelligence—tasks requiring creative problem-solving, adaptability, and sensitivity to complex and dynamic environments. The relative importance of mechanical and analytical intelligences continues to decline, while intuitive intelligence also starts to diminish. Contrary to earlier beliefs, AI can now perform tasks that previously required human intuition. For example, deep neural networks have achieved or exceeded expert-level accuracy in diagnosing skin cancer, demonstrating AI's growing capability in domains once thought uniquely human.

The final stage (T4) presents a scenario where AI has the potential to replace jobs across all forms of intelligence, including those requiring empathy, emotional sensitivity, and strong interpersonal skills. AI systems with advanced affective computing and emotion recognition—such as Hanson's humanoid robot Sophia or the chatbot Replika—can socially interact and interpret human emotions. While all forms of intelligence are now increasingly automatable, empathic intelligence remains the most relevant human capability in this phase of technological development.

The progressive stages of job displacement underscore the transformative impact of AI on the workforce. While the replacement of mechanical and analytical jobs may lead to increased efficiency and cost savings, the displacement of intuitive and empathetic jobs raises concerns about the broader implications for employment and social interactions. It is important for businesses and policymakers to consider strategies for workforce adaptation, including upskilling, reskilling, and the creation of new job opportunities that leverage human strengths that complement AI capabilities. The framework provides a structured perspective on how AI could replace human jobs over time, highlighting the varying degrees of vulnerability of different types of intelligence. As AI continues to evolve, its integration into the workforce will require a balanced approach that maximizes the benefits of automation while addressing the challenges of job displacement. By understanding the stages of AI's impact, businesses and policymakers can better prepare for a future where human–AI collaboration is integral to economic and social development.

11.2.2 The Need for Human–AI Collaboration

While Huang and Rust's (2018) framework emphasizes a staged trajectory of job displacement through different forms of intelligence, it also opens up a broader discussion about how these developments may give rise to new forms of human–AI interaction. Rather than viewing automation as a purely substitutive process, it is crucial to explore the extent to which AI is currently capable of performing tasks across these four types of intelligence—and where meaningful human–machine collaboration may still be essential. Understanding the current strengths and limitations of AI in mechanical, analytical, intuitive, and empathic domains is therefore a necessary step in assessing both the disruptive and transformative potential of AI in the world of work. While such an assessment necessarily reflects the current state of technology, it should be viewed with an awareness of the field's ongoing and dynamic evolution. The following section provides an overview of how AI performs along these dimensions today and what this implies for the evolving division of labor between humans and intelligent systems.

Mechanical intelligence has become a stable foundation for automating routine, rule-based tasks in predictable environments. Modern systems—ranging from industrial robots and warehouse automation to virtual agents in customer service—deliver high reliability, speed, and endurance. Their performance is unaffected by fatigue or distraction, making them ideal for repetitive work with minimal variation. However, these systems remain inflexible, struggling with unexpected input or dynamic contexts due to their limited ability to adapt or learn on the fly. While efficiency gains are well-documented, their effectiveness depends on clearly structured workflows and environments (Huang et al., 2019; Jaiswal et al., 2023).

Analytical intelligence is increasingly exhibited by AI systems capable of processing large volumes of data, identifying patterns, and generating insights with minimal human guidance. Applications in fields like finance, logistics, and medical diagnostics show that AI can match or even surpass human experts under specific conditions, such as in image classification or anomaly detection. The successful deployment of AI in this area underscores its potential to enhance efficiency and reduce human workload in clearly defined operational domains (Huang et al., 2019; Akata et al., 2020).

Intuitive intelligence is a growing area in AI, with generative models such as GPT-4 or DALL·E demonstrating impressive performance in tasks like storytelling, coding, or visual design—domains previously considered uniquely human. These systems occasionally solve unfamiliar problems in ways that appear creative or insight-driven. Yet their outputs are rooted in probabilistic pattern matching rather than in true contextual awareness or judgment. As a result, AI often struggles with tasks that require deep insight into ambiguous, dynamic, or novel situations—such as those encountered in management consulting, medical diagnostics, or legal reasoning. While intuitive AI can complement human expertise, it remains far from replicating the depth and flexibility of human intuition (Bubeck et al., 2023; Huang et al., 2019).

While *empathic intelligence* remains the most complex and least developed domain of AI, recent advances have enabled systems to simulate emotional engagement through affective computing and conversational design. ChatGPT, for example, mimics human conversational styles to create a sense of understanding and connection. However, these effects are based on surface-level pattern recognition rather than true emotional comprehension. As such, while AI can assist in emotional labor within structured settings, the nuanced, context-sensitive, and relational nature of human empathy continues to resist full technological replication (Akata et al., 2020; Huang et al., 2019).

Rather than replacing human labor entirely, AI is more likely to reshape the workforce by altering task distributions and creating new forms of collaboration between humans and machines. A promising approach lies in leveraging the complementary strengths of both: while AI systems are well suited for routine, data-intensive, and algorithmic tasks, humans continue to excel in areas requiring empathy, contextual judgment, and creative problem-solving. This division of labor can, under the right conditions, support gains in productivity, innovation, and user experience. In healthcare, for instance, AI can assist in diagnosing conditions through data analysis, whereas human practitioners provide the empathetic care and nuanced interpretation required for effective treatment. Creating environments that facilitate such collaboration may help organizations adapt more effectively to technological change without disregarding the social and emotional dimensions of work. Ultimately, fostering a balanced integration of AI requires not only technical readiness but also organizational and societal support to ensure that human capabilities remain central to the evolving world of work (Akata et al., 2020; Dellermann et al., 2019; Gerber et al., 2020).

Summary
AI is transforming the workforce by automating routine and analytical tasks while increasingly approximating human capabilities in creative and interpersonal domains. Huang and Rust's framework outlines four types of intelligence—mechanical, analytical, intuitive, and empathic—each variably affected by automation. While early stages of AI adoption impact low-skill, repetitive work, more advanced systems challenge even complex cognitive roles. Despite these trends, full replacement remains unlikely. Instead, hybrid models of human–AI collaboration are emerging, emphasizing complementary strengths: machines handle scale and precision, while humans contribute empathy, judgment, and creativity. Successfully navigating this shift requires strategic task allocation, upskilling, and supportive organizational conditions.

11.3 Optimizing Human–AI Collaboration

As artificial intelligence becomes increasingly integrated into various industries, the potential for productive collaboration between humans and AI systems continues to grow. However, fully harnessing this potential requires a strategic approach that optimizes how humans and AI interact and complement one another. Human–AI collaboration leverages the unique strengths of both parties: While AI excels in data processing, pattern recognition, and routine tasks, humans bring intuition, ethical judgment, and adaptability. Understanding how to best combine these strengths is crucial for improving decision-making, operational efficiency, and overall outcomes across sectors such as healthcare, finance, and autonomous systems. Effective collaboration requires appropriate levels of reliance, the mitigation of risks such as automation bias and thoughtful task delegation, all of which are essential for achieving superior performance and maintaining trust in AI-driven systems.

11.3.1 Complementary Potential in Human–AI Collaboration

The concept of complementary potential in human–AI collaboration is critical to maximizing the performance and effectiveness of combined human–AI teams. This potential is determined by the distribution of strengths between humans and AI systems, and how these strengths can be used to complement each other. Hemmer et al. (2025) illustrate three scenarios of complementary potential based on the accuracy of humans and AI in different cases (see Fig. 11.5).

In the first scenario, humans and AI systems are *accurate on the same instances*. This overlap means that there is no complementary potential, as both humans and AI perform well on the same tasks, leaving no room for improvement through

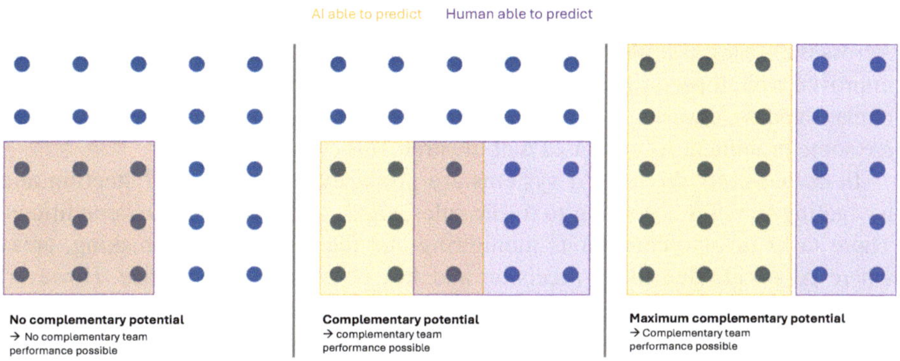

Fig. 11.5 Scenarios of complementary potential between humans and AI (Adapted from Hemmer et al., 2025)

collaboration. Consequently, complementary team performance is not possible in this setup, as there is no advantage to combining human and AI efforts if their strengths are not diversified across different instances.

The second scenario represents a situation where humans and AI systems are *accurate on different instances, but also have some common ground.* This partial overlap allows for some complementary potential. In this case, the combined efforts of humans and AI can improve performance by covering each other's weaknesses. If AI systems are good at certain tasks where humans are less accurate, and vice versa, collaboration can lead to better overall performance than either could achieve alone. This scenario allows for moderately complementary team performance that benefits from the unique strengths of each.

The third scenario represents maximum complementary potential, where humans and AI systems are *accurate in completely different instances*. Here, the strengths of humans and AI are fully complementary, with each excelling in areas where the other is weak. This complete nonoverlap enables each instance to be handled by the most capable entity, whether human or AI. The potential for complementary team performance is maximized in this setup, as the collaboration leverages the distinct and nonoverlapping strengths of both, leading to the most efficient and effective results.

Recognizing and leveraging the complementary potential of human–AI collaboration is essential for enhancing productivity and decision-making. By systematically identifying where human and AI capabilities diverge, organizations can design interaction and allocation mechanisms that assign each task to the most competent party. The degree of complementary potential depends on the distribution of strengths between humans and AI: the greater the divergence, the higher the opportunity for performance gains. Effectively harnessing this potential allows teams to combine human intuition and contextual judgment with AI's analytical precision—ultimately driving innovation, efficiency, and superior outcomes across domains.

Complementarity in Prominent AI Use Cases

Across industries, complementary human–AI collaboration can lead to significantly improved overall performance. This synergy leverages the unique strengths of both humans and AI, ensuring that tasks are performed efficiently and effectively. Below are some prominent AI use cases that illustrate this complementarity:

In *autonomous driving*, AI systems are primarily responsible for steering and navigating vehicles according to traffic rules, signs, and environmental conditions. These tasks involve continuous monitoring and real-time decision-making, areas where AI excels due to its precision and fast processing capabilities. However, humans play a crucial role in monitoring AI operations, intervening in emergency situations and making ethical decisions. This human oversight ensures that the AI operates safely and ethically, particularly in scenarios where moral judgment is required.

Robotic financial advisors use AI to perform tasks such as portfolio allocation, automated rebalancing, risk assessment, tax efficiency, and cost efficiency. AI systems can analyze large datasets to provide optimized investment strategies and maintain continuous portfolio management. Meanwhile, human advisors are essential for addressing the psychological components of investing, providing behavioral coaching and offering personalized advice based on individual client needs and preferences. This combination ensures that clients receive both high-quality, data-driven insights and personalized, empathetic advice.

In healthcare, particularly *cancer detection*, AI systems are invaluable for analyzing vast medical databases, recognizing patterns, detecting abnormalities early and continuously monitoring patients. These tasks benefit from AI's ability to process large amounts of data with high accuracy. On the other hand, human healthcare professionals contribute through clinical judgment, contextual understanding, effective communication with patients, and navigating ethical and cultural factors. This collaboration improves diagnostic accuracy and patient care by combining the strengths of AI data processing with human empathy and expertise.

In the *military*, AI systems are being used for persistent surveillance, terrain mapping, early warning systems, and to perform tasks in dangerous areas where human presence is risky. AI excels in these roles because of its ability to operate continuously and handle complex data analysis. Humans, however, are essential for strategic decision-making, psychological warfare tactics, effective communication, and coordination of personnel and artificial units. This human–AI collaboration ensures full situational awareness and strategic effectiveness in military operations.

The examples above demonstrate the diverse applications of AI across different sectors and how human–AI collaboration can leverage complementary strengths to achieve superior results. In autonomous driving, financial advice, healthcare, and military services, the integration of AI for continuous, analytical, and routine tasks alongside human oversight for ethical, cultural, and psychological aspects ensures a balanced and effective approach. This synergy not only improves efficiency, but also ensures that AI systems are used responsibly and ethically, thereby improving overall performance across industries.

Appropriateness of Reliance

In practice, humans often struggle to accurately assess the capabilities and limitations of AI systems (Mayer et al., 2024). As a result, a key objective in human–AI collaboration is to achieve optimal Appropriateness of Reliance (AoR), ensuring that decisions made by humans in conjunction with AI advice are as accurate and effective as possible. The concept of AoR, as detailed by Schemmer et al. (2023), is critical in assessing how well humans integrate AI input into their decision-making processes. In this framework, initial human decisions may either align with or diverge from AI advice. After receiving AI input, humans can either adjust their decisions based on the AI's recommendations or maintain their original stance. These scenarios lead to different types of trust: correct self-reliance (CSR), over-reliance, correct AI reliance (CAIR), and under-reliance (see Fig. 11.6).

Correct self-reliance occurs when a human maintains their initial correct decision despite receiving AI advice that may or may not be consistent. Over-reliance occurs when a human erroneously changes a correct decision based on incorrect AI advice. Correct AI reliance occurs when a human correctly adjusts an incorrect initial decision based on correct AI advice. Under-reliance occurs when a human fails to adjust their incorrect initial decision despite receiving correct AI advice.

Reliance appropriateness is quantified using two metrics (Schemmer et al., 2023): RAIR (relative AI reliance) and RSR (relative self-reliance). Both metrics are computed based on a set of N decision instances, each representing a situation in which a human makes a prediction, receives AI advice, and may or may not adjust their decision accordingly. Each instance is indexed by $i \in \{0, 1, \ldots, N\}$, allowing us to track individual outcomes.

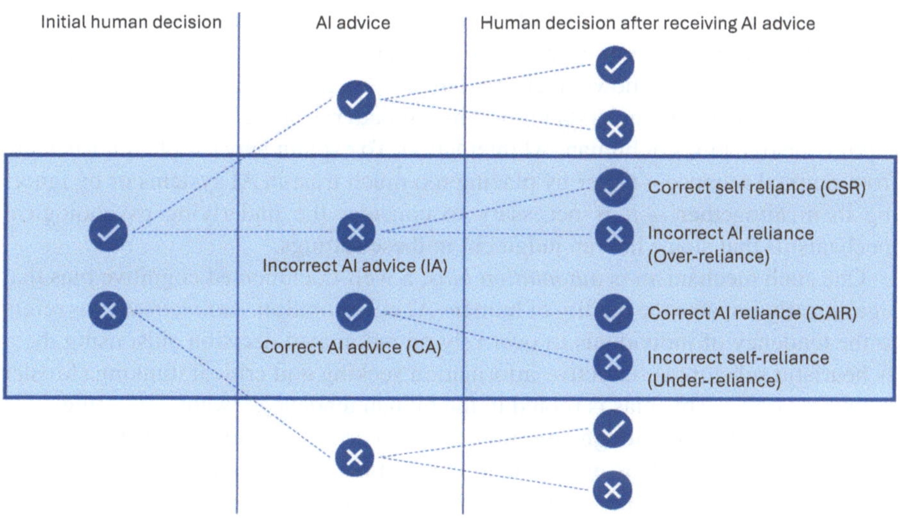

Fig. 11.6 Combinatorics of initial human decisions, AI advice, and human reliance for a single task instance in a sequential task setting. (Adapted from Schemmer et al., 2023)

RAIR is calculated by summing instances of CAIR and dividing by the number of correct AI advice in cases where the human's initial decision was incorrect and reflects how often people correctly follow AI advice when it is correct:

$$\mathrm{RAIR} = \frac{\sum_{N}^{i=0} \mathrm{CAIR}_i}{\sum_{N}^{i=0} \mathrm{CA}_i}$$

RSR is calculated by summing CSR instances and dividing by the number of incorrect AI advice in cases where the human's initial decision was correct and reflects how often humans correctly ignore AI advice when it is inaccurate:

$$\mathrm{RSR} = \frac{\sum_{N}^{i=0} \mathrm{CSR}_i}{\sum_{N}^{i=0} \mathrm{IA}_i}$$

Achieving a high AoR requires a balance between reliance on AI advice and human judgment. Over-reliance can lead to errors if humans overly trust incorrect AI results, while under-reliance can lead to missed opportunities if humans ignore accurate AI advice. Both errors undermine the effectiveness of human–AI collaboration. In summary, the appropriate level of trust in human–AI collaboration is a delicate balance that directly impacts the effectiveness of the combined decision-making processes. By understanding and optimizing this balance through metrics such as RAIR and RSR, organizations can better leverage the strengths of both human judgment and AI capabilities, leading to improved performance and outcomes in various applications.

Automation Bias as a Barrier to Effective Human–AI Collaboration

While the concept of Appropriateness of Reliance (AoR) provides a valuable lens through which to assess how effectively humans integrate AI recommendations into their decision-making, understanding reliance patterns alone is insufficient to fully capture the dynamics of human–AI interaction. To explain why people often deviate from optimal reliance—either by placing too much trust in AI systems or by ignoring them altogether —it is necessary to consider the underlying psychological mechanisms that shape human judgment in these settings.

One such mechanism is *automation bias*, a well-documented cognitive bias that significantly impacts the quality of human–AI collaboration. *Automation bias* refers to the tendency of individuals to over-rely on automated decision aids, using them as heuristic substitutes for active information seeking and critical thinking (Mosier & Skitka, 1996). This bias is rooted in the human tendency toward *satisficing*—the inclination to do just enough cognitive work to arrive at decisions that are "good enough." Automation bias manifests in two distinct forms: *omission errors*, which occur when individuals fail to notice problems because the automated system did not detect them, and *commission errors*, which arise when people inappropriately follow the recommendations or directives of an automated system—even when those are flawed or inappropriate.

Several factors contribute to automation bias (Goddard et al., 2012). One major reason is the perceived high reliability and accuracy of AI systems. When AI systems are marketed and perceived as infallible, humans are more likely to rely on them excessively. This trust in the system's accuracy can lead to a lack of critical evaluation of its results. Another contributing factor is the assumption that AI systems are unbiased and objective. This belief can lead people to accept AI recommendations without question, overlooking the possibility that AI systems can inherit and even amplify biases present in the training data. In addition, a lack of clarity and understanding of the decision-making processes of AI systems can exacerbate automation bias. If the workings of an AI system are not transparent, users may not be able to critically evaluate its decisions, leading to blind trust in its results.

The implications of automation bias are worrying (Mosier & Skitka, 1996). One important consequence is over-reliance on AI systems. Automation bias can lead to situations where humans defer to AI decisions without sufficient oversight. This can be particularly problematic in high-stakes situations, such as medical diagnoses or financial decisions, where critical human judgment is essential. In addition, continuous reliance on AI systems can undermine users' critical thinking skills. When people stop questioning AI results and do not engage in independent analysis, their ability to make informed decisions diminishes. Automation bias can also lead to harmful outcomes when AI systems make mistakes or biased decisions. Without human intervention to catch these errors, the negative consequences can be significant and far-reaching.

Addressing automation bias requires a multifaceted approach (Goddard et al., 2012). First and foremost, increasing AI system transparency is essential. By making decision-making processes more transparent, users can gain insights into how AI arrives at conclusions, allowing them to critically assess the outcomes. Offering clear explanations and rationales for AI-generated decisions enhances human–AI interactions and fosters a more thoughtful engagement with the technology. Additionally, promoting critical thinking among users is vital. Training people to approach AI outputs with a questioning mindset helps strike a balance between trust and independent judgment. Vigilance and the habit of independently verifying AI recommendations can further reduce blind reliance on these systems. Regular monitoring and performance evaluations of AI systems are also crucial for detecting and addressing biases or errors early on. This ongoing scrutiny helps ensure that AI systems remain reliable and their outputs accurate. In summary, while AI has the potential to deliver tremendous benefits, it is essential to manage automation bias carefully. By enhancing transparency, cultivating critical thinking, and maintaining diligent oversight, organizations can mitigate the risks of automation bias and promote more effective and trustworthy human–AI collaboration.

11.3.2 Delegation

The integration of human and AI predictions in collaborative settings can be categorized based on the timing of the integration and the primary integrator (Hemmer, 2024) (see Fig. 11.7). This structured approach helps determine the most effective way to combine human insights with AI capabilities to improve decision-making and operational efficiency. Integration can be either ex-ante, before tasks are performed, or ex-post, after tasks have been completed. Ex-ante integration involves planning and decision-making processes that delegate tasks to either humans or AI based on their strengths. Ex-post integration, on the other hand, involves evaluating and integrating the results of both humans and AI to arrive at a final decision (Leyer & Schneider, 2019; Hemmer, 2024; Goodwin, 2000).

Human-led delegation is an approach where humans decide which tasks to delegate to AI and which tasks to handle themselves. This ex-ante method uses human judgment to assign tasks based on an understanding of the context and the capabilities of AI. For example, in a healthcare setting, routine diagnostic tasks might be delegated to AI, while complex case assessments are reserved for human doctors.

AI-led delegation is another approach where AI systems determine which tasks should be handled by humans and which should be managed by AI. This approach can optimize task allocation based on real-time data and AI algorithms' assessments of task complexity and urgency. In autonomous driving, for example, AI could decide when to take control and when to hand over to the human driver based on real-time traffic conditions.

Human integration occurs when, after receiving AI advice, humans evaluate the recommendations and decide whether to accept or reject them. This ex-post integration allows human oversight and critical thinking to refine the AI's output, ensuring that it is consistent with broader goals and ethical considerations. An example of

		Timing of integration	
		Ex-ante (i.e., before tasks are conducted)	Ex-post (i.e., after tasks are conducted)
Integrator	Human	Human-led delegation	Human integration
	AI	AI-led delegation	AI integration

Fig. 11.7 Different types of integration of human and AI predictions (Adapted from Hemmer, 2024)

this can be seen in financial advice, where AI provides data-driven recommendations that human advisors then evaluate and tailor to meet individual client needs.

In *AI integration*, AI systems combine predictions from both humans and AI to make final decisions. This method leverages the strengths of both and aims to optimize outcomes by integrating different inputs. In logistics, for example, AI systems could combine human input on local conditions with AI optimization algorithms to improve supply chain efficiency.

Task delegation in human–AI collaboration can be optimized by understanding the context and capabilities of both the human and the AI. Effective collaboration requires a dynamic and adaptive approach to task allocation. For example, in scenarios where human-led delegation is used, such as in healthcare, the focus could be on leveraging human expertise for complex tasks, while using AI for more routine functions. Conversely, in scenarios that favor AI-led delegation, such as autonomous driving, the system's real-time data processing capabilities can ensure timely and context-aware task allocation. Effective human–AI collaboration requires careful consideration of how and when to integrate human and AI predictions. By categorizing integration types based on timing and integrators, organizations can leverage the unique strengths of both humans and AI. This approach not only improves decision-making processes, but also increases operational efficiency across multiple domains, reflecting a balanced and nuanced understanding of human–AI collaboration.

In the field of image classification, for example, the effectiveness of task delegation between humans and AI has been studied to determine the optimal strategy for performance and efficiency. Recent research by Fügener et al. (2022) sheds light on this issue, providing insights into how delegation affects human–AI collaboration. When humans are responsible for delegating tasks to AIs, the process is characterized by rational and consistent strategies. However, humans often struggle to accurately assess their own capabilities. This miscalculation leads to suboptimal delegation decisions, as humans may either overestimate or underestimate the AI's strengths and weaknesses. As a result, while the strategy may be clear and internally consistent, the effectiveness of the delegation is compromised by these inaccuracies. In contrast, when AI systems are tasked with delegating work, the results show significantly higher performance. AI systems, with their ability to process large amounts of data and make objective decisions based on statistical analysis, are better suited to identifying the most efficient allocation of tasks. In this way, humans can focus on more complex classification examples, while AI handles routine and mundane tasks. Despite the role of AI in delegation, it does not take the position of a "boss," but rather acts as an assistant, optimizing the distribution of tasks to improve overall performance.

This approach not only improves efficiency but is also economically desirable. However, there is a trade-off: a potential loss of control for humans. The AI only seeks human assistance when it encounters tasks beyond its capabilities, which can lead to a perceived reduction in human oversight and authority. The research shows that for image classification, human–AI collaboration outperforms both AI-only and human-only approaches when the AI is responsible for delegating tasks. The superior performance of AI-led delegation highlights AI's strengths in objective decision-making and efficient task allocation. This setup allows humans to leverage their expertise on more challenging tasks, increasing the overall effectiveness of the collaboration. Despite the potential downside of reduced human control, the benefits in terms of performance and efficiency make AI-led delegation a compelling strategy in the context of image classification.

Boundary Conditions of Outperforming Human–AI Collaboration

Human–AI collaboration has the potential to significantly outperform tasks assigned to either humans or AI alone. For human–AI collaboration to realize its full potential, three essential boundary conditions must be met (Fügener et al., 2022). These conditions ensure that the collaboration leverages the unique strengths of both humans and AI, resulting in superior performance and efficiency.

The first constraint is that humans and AI need *complementary skills*. Humans excel in areas that require intuition, creativity, ethical judgment and nuanced understanding, while AI systems excel at processing large amounts of data, performing repetitive tasks and making data-driven decisions. By combining these complementary skills, AI can tackle complex problems more effectively than either party could on its own. The second constraint is the *recognition of complementarities*, which requires metaknowledge. Metaknowledge refers to the ability to accurately assess one's own capabilities and those of the AI system. This self-awareness and understanding of each party's strengths and weaknesses is crucial for effective task delegation. When humans and AI systems are aware of each other's capabilities, they can better determine which tasks should be performed by whom.

The third constraint is to follow an *efficient and simple delegation rule*. An example of such a rule is: "If you can do it, do it; if not, delegate it." This straightforward approach ensures that tasks are allocated based on ability, optimizing efficiency and effectiveness. By following this rule, human–AI collaboration can avoid unnecessary complexity and ensure that tasks are carried out by the most appropriate person. Meeting these three constraints is critical to designing effective human–AI collaboration environments. Organizations should ensure that both humans and AI systems are equipped with complementary skills, foster an environment that encourages the recognition of complementarities, and implement simple yet effective delegation rules. By doing so, they can maximize the benefits of human–AI collaboration, leading to improved performance and outcomes.

AI-Led Delegation from a Principal-Agent Perspective

AI-led delegation in human–AI collaboration can be examined through the lens of principal-agent theory (PAT), which analyzes the dynamics between two parties—one delegating tasks (the principal) and the other executing them (the agent) (Guggenberger et al., 2023). In this context, AI assumes the role of the principal, delegating tasks to humans. This relationship presents several challenges, particularly centered around two key principal-agent problems: hidden information and hidden actions (see Fig. 11.8).

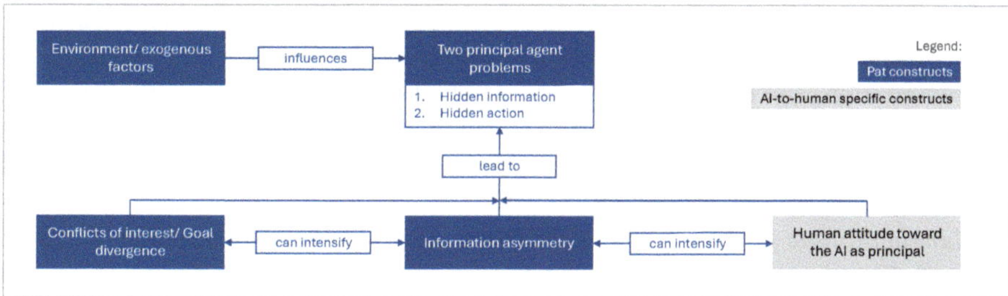

Fig. 11.8 AI-led delegation from a principal-agent perspective. (Adapted from Guggenberger et al., 2023)

1. *Hidden information*: This issue arises when one party possesses more or better information than the other. In AI-to-human delegation, AI systems often lack crucial contextual understanding about the environment and the human agent's capabilities, leading to suboptimal delegation decisions.
2. *Hidden action*: This problem occurs when the agent's actions are not fully observable by the principal. In AI-led delegation, the human agent may not carry out tasks exactly as instructed by the AI due to personal judgment or ethical concerns, creating a gap between the AI's intentions and the human's actions. This lack of alignment can raise ethical concerns or result in unintended outcomes.

External factors influence AI-to-human delegation, including regulatory frameworks and organizational context. These factors shape how tasks are delegated, as AI-to-human delegation must be designed with consideration of the specific use case and the social constructions within the organization. No one-size-fits-all approach exists, as delegation requirements vary depending on the situation. Key influences such as regulations, which dictate delegation rules and explainability, and social expectations, which limit AI's autonomy, must be integrated into the delegation process to ensure appropriate task allocation.

Conflicts of interest and divergent goals in AI-to-human delegation can arise from several sources. Moral and social conflicts may occur when AI-driven decisions clash with human ethical standards or societal norms. Additionally, conflicts can emerge due to changes in work dynamics, as AI systems might alter roles or reduce human involvement, leading to resistance or friction. Monetary conflicts are another factor, where economic interests between humans and AI systems diverge, particularly when AI threatens job security or affects financial incentives. These conflicts highlight the need for careful management of human–AI collaboration to align goals and mitigate potential tensions.

Information asymmetry in AI-to-human delegation arises from a few key factors. Humans often lack a clear understanding of how AI systems operate internally, including their decision-making processes, assumptions, and limitations. This lack of transparency complicates trust and collaboration. Conversely, AI systems are similarly limited by their lack of information about human agents, such as their skills, context, and preferences, which can result in poor delegation decisions. Furthermore, AI systems do not possess human capabilities like emotional intelligence, intuition, and contextual awareness, which are critical in handling complex, ambiguous situations. These asymmetries can undermine the effectiveness of AI-to-human delegation and necessitate mechanisms for better information flow and oversight.

Human attitude toward the AI as principal significantly influences the effectiveness of AI-to-human delegation. Human characteristics, such as expertise and adaptability to new roles, play a crucial role in how well individuals accept and interact with AI as a leader. Changes within these roles can impact their willingness to trust and follow AI guidance. Additionally, human perception of the AI's competence and reliability determines the level of trust and confidence they place in the AI system. Positive perceptions can enhance collaboration, while skepticism or distrust may hinder the effectiveness of AI-led delegation.

Summary

Human–AI collaboration is most effective when their strengths are complementary, enabling performance gains through smart task allocation. Complementary potential emerges when humans and AI excel on different instances, allowing each to compensate for the other's weaknesses. To realize this potential, an optimal Appropriateness of Reliance (AoR) is crucial—humans should rely on AI advice only when justified. However, automation bias often leads to over-reliance or under-reliance, undermining decision quality. Addressing this requires transparency, critical thinking, and user training. Effective task delegation—whether led by humans or AI—depends on context awareness, metaknowledge, and the application of simple yet robust delegation rules. While AI-led delegation can enhance performance, it also raises challenges such as information asymmetry, trust, and shifting control dynamics that must be carefully managed.

References

Akata, Z., Balliet, D., De Rijke, M., Dignum, F., Dignum, V., Eiben, G., & Welling, M. (2020). A research agenda for hybrid intelligence: Augmenting human intellect with collaborative, adaptive, responsible, and explainable artificial intelligence. *Computer, 53*(8), 18–28.

Alan, Y., Urbach, N., Hinsen, S., Jöhnk, J., Beisel, P., Weißert, M., Blumenthal, S., & Hofmann, P. (2019). *Think beyond tomorrow: KI, mein Freund und Helfer – Herausforderungen und Implikationen für die Mensch-KI-Interaktion. Projektgruppe Wirtschaftsinformatik des Fraunhofer FIT & EY.*

Bubeck, S., Chandrasekaran, V., Eldan, R., Gehrke, J., Horvitz, E., Kamar, E., Lee, P., Lee, Y. T., Li, Y., Lundberg, S., Nori, H., Palangi, H., Ribeiro, M. T., & Zhang, Y. (2023). *Sparks of artificial general intelligence: Early experiments with GPT-4*. arXiv preprint arXiv:2303.12712.

Dellermann, D., Ebel, P., Söllner, M., & Leimeister, J. M. (2019). Hybrid intelligence. *Business & Information Systems Engineering, 61*(5), 637–643.

Fügener, A., Grahl, J., Gupta, A., & Ketter, W. (2022). Cognitive challenges in human–artificial intelligence collaboration: Investigating the path toward productive delegation. *Information Systems Research, 33*(2), 678–696.
Gerber, A., Derckx, P., Döppner, D. A., & Schoder, D. (2020). Conceptualization of the human-machine Symbiosis—A literature review. In *Proceedings of the 53rd Hawaii International Conference on System Sciences (HICSS-53)*, Maui, Hawaii.
Goddard, K., Roudsari, A., & Wyatt, J. C. (2012). Automation bias: A systematic review of frequency, effect mediators, and mitigators. *Journal of the American Medical Informatics Association, 19*(1), 121–127.
Goodwin, P. (2000). Correct or combine? Mechanically integrating judgmental forecasts with statistical methods. *International Journal of Forecasting, 16*(2), 261–275.
Guggenberger, T., Lämmermann, L., Urbach, N., Walter, A. M., & Hofmann, P. (2023). *Task delegation from AI to humans: A principal-agent perspective.*
Hemmer, P. (2024). Complementarity in Human-AI Teams: Conceptualization and Design Support for Effective Decision-Making. Dissertation. Karlsruher Institut für Technologie (KIT).
Hemmer, P., Schemmer, M., Kühl, N., Vössing, M., & Satzger, G. (2025). Complementarity in human-AI collaboration: Concept, sources, and evidence. *European Journal of Information Systems, 34*(6), 979–1002.
Hinsen, S., Hofmann, P., Jöhnk, J., & Urbach, N. (2022). How can organizations design purposeful human-AI interactions? A practical perspective from existing use cases and interviews. In *Proceedings of the 55th Hawaii International Conference on System Sciences (HICSS-55)*, January 4–7, Maui, Hawaii.
Huang, M. H., & Rust, R. T. (2018). Artificial intelligence in service. *Journal of Service Research, 21*(2), 155–172.
Huang, M. H., Rust, R. T., & Maksimovic, V. (2019). The feeling economy: Managing in the next generation of artificial intelligence (AI). *California Management Review, 61*(4), 43–65.
Jaiswal, A., Arun, C. J., & Varma, A. (2023). Rebooting employees: Upskilling for artificial intelligence in multinational corporations. In *Artificial Intelligence and International HRM* (pp. 114–143). Routledge.
Leyer, M., & Schneider, S. (2019). *Me, you or AI? How do we feel about delegation.*
Mayer, V., Schüll, M., Aktürk, O., & Guggenberger, T. (2024). Designing human-AI hybrids : Challenges and good practices from a multiple case study. In *Proceedings of the 45th International Conference on Information Systems (ICIS). - Bangkok, Thailand, 2024.*
Mosier, K. L., & Skitka, L. J. (1996). Human decision makers and automated decision aids: Made for each other?. In *Automation and human performance* (pp. 201–220). CRC Press.
Schemmer, M., Kuehl, N., Benz, C., Bartos, A., & Satzger, G. (2023). Appropriate reliance on AI advice: Conceptualization and the effect of explanations. In *Proceedings of the 28th International Conference on Intelligent User Interfaces* (pp. 410–422).

Nils Urbach is Professor of Information Systems and Digital Business as well as Director of the Research Lab for Digital Innovation and Transformation at the Frankfurt University of Applied Sciences, Germany. Furthermore, he is Director at the FIM Research Center for Information Management, and the Branch Business and Information Systems Engineering of Fraunhofer FIT. Nils Urbach has been working in the fields of digital innovation and transformation for several years. His work has been published in several academic journals such as Information Systems Research (ISR), the Journal of the Association for Information Systems (JAIS), the Journal of Strategic Information Systems (JSIS), the Journal of Information Technology (JIT), MIS Quarterly Executive (MISQE), IEEE Transactions on Engineering Management (IEEE TEM), Information and Management (I&M), Business and Information Systems Engineering (BISE), and Electronic Markets (EM). He advises several companies on digitalization issues and regularly appears as a speaker on this topic.

Daniel Feulner received his M.Sc. in information system from the Otto-Friedrich University of Bamberg, Germany in 2023. He is an affiliated researcher at the Branch Business and Information Systems Engineering of the Fraunhofer FIT and FIM Research Center for Information Management at the University of Bayreuth. In his research, he aims to understand how Business Analytics and Artificial Intelligence can be effectively and responsibly utilized in organizations. His goal is to enable companies to drive innovation and achieve sustainable growth in a rapidly evolving technological landscape.

Valentin Mayer received his M.Sc. in Management and Technology from the Technical University of Munich, Germany 2023. He is an affiliated researcher at the Branch Business and Information Systems Engineering of the Fraunhofer FIT and FIM Research Center for Information Management at the University of Bayreuth. His research explores how companies can successfully implement Artificial Intelligence within their organizations, with a particular focus on the conceptual design and operationalization of AI systems. His goal is to equip companies with practical methods to implement AI end-to-end into their operations and create long-term value.

Part V

AI Operations at Scale

AI Monitoring and Change Management 12

Nils Urbach, Daniel Feulner, Annalena Schmid, and Dominik Protschky

As companies scale their artificial intelligence (AI) efforts, they face the challenge of ensuring that AI systems deliver ongoing value, remain aligned with business goals, and are embedded in workflows that humans trust and understand. This requires more than isolated evaluations or one-off implementations. Instead, organizations must monitor AI performance continuously, adjust systems to real-world changes, and manage organizational transformation in parallel. Especially at scale, AI becomes not just a technological project, but a long-term organizational commitment that must be actively managed on multiple levels—technical, strategic, and human.

This chapter addresses three core pillars of managing AI at scale. First, we discuss key performance indicators (KPIs) that link AI initiatives to strategic goals and operational performance. Second, we outline an iterative approach to machine learning monitoring, detailing how to observe, evaluate, and improve model behavior in dynamic environments. Finally, we introduce a structured framework for AI-related change management, offering practical tools to navigate employee concerns, foster acceptance, and anchor AI sustainably within the organization.

N. Urbach (✉)
Frankfurt University of Applied Sciences, Frankfurt am Main, Germany
e-mail: nils.urbach@fim-rc.de

D. Feulner · D. Protschky
University of Bayreuth, Bayreuth, Germany
e-mail: daniel.feulner@fim-rc.de; dominik.protschky@fim-rc.de

A. Schmid
University of Hohenheim, Stuttgart, Germany
e-mail: annalena.schmid@fim-rc.de

N. Urbach, D. Feulner (eds.), *Managing Artificial Intelligence*, Future of Business and Finance, https://doi.org/10.1007/978-3-032-13308-3_12

12.1 Key Performance Indicators for AI

The utilization of performance measurements is crucial for the effective management and evaluation of both applications and organizational strategies. Two primary categories of these measurements are metrics and key performance indicators (KPIs), each serving distinct purposes within the organizational context (see Fig. 12.1).

Metrics, as discussed in Chap. 5, are quantifiable measures used to assess, compare, and track the performance of specific processes or systems, often focusing on operational or technical aspects. They provide detailed data points that help organizations monitor efficiency and effectiveness. For example, the accuracy of storage predictions is a metric that can be used to evaluate the performance of a data management system. Metrics typically focus on operational performance and can be applied to various aspects of an organization, offering a granular view of performance.

KPIs, while also quantifiable measurements, differ in that they are more strategically focused and directly aligned with an organization's long-term objectives. KPIs provide insights into the progress and success of high-level goals, helping to measure the organization's overall financial, strategic, and operational performance. For instance, the turnover ratio of a product is a KPI that evaluates the efficiency and profitability of a company's inventory management. In contrast to metrics, KPIs are carefully chosen based on their relevance to the organization's broader objectives, making them a subset of metrics, but with a specific strategic importance. KPIs are characterized by several key aspects:

- *Direct strategic alignment of KPIs:* KPIs are directly aligned to an organization's strategic goals. They are carefully selected to measure the progress of the organization's strategic initiatives, such as increasing market share or improving customer retention. This alignment ensures that each KPI tracked provides meaningful insight into how well the organization is meeting its long-term goals. For example, a company focused on customer satisfaction might track KPIs

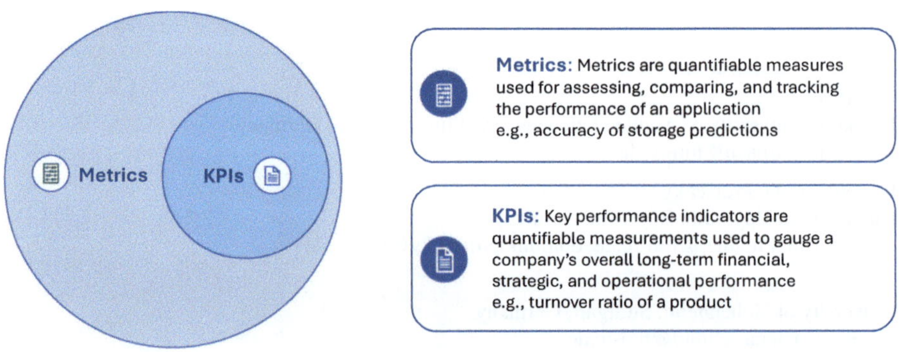

Fig. 12.1 Metrics vs. KPIs

related to customer feedback scores, repeat purchase rates, and Net Promoter Scores (NPS).

- *Critical performance indicators:* KPIs focus on the most important measures of the organization's success. These indicators are critical because they highlight areas that need attention and improvement. For example, achieving a certain profit margin or reaching a certain number of users can be critical performance indicators for an organization. These KPIs help management focus on what is most important and drive efforts to achieve these critical milestones.
- *Broad categorization of KPIs:* KPIs cover a wide range of measures, including both financial and nonfinancial metrics. Financial KPIs can include return on investment (ROI), net profit, and cost per acquisition, which provide insight into the financial health and efficiency of the organization. Nonfinancial KPIs can include employee engagement, brand awareness, and customer loyalty, which are equally important for understanding the broader impact of organizational activities and strategies.
- *Leading* vs. *lagging KPIs:* KPIs can be divided into leading and lagging indicators. Leading indicators predict future results and are proactive in nature. They help organizations anticipate change and make adjustments before problems arise. For example, the number of new registrations or leads generated can be a leading indicator of future sales performance. Lagging indicators, on the other hand, reflect past results and outcomes. They provide a retrospective view of performance, such as quarterly sales or annual profit margins. Both types of KPI are essential for comprehensive performance management.

Establishing effective KPIs involves several critical steps (Sweenor, 2022). It is essential to align data initiatives with a well-defined business strategy. This means that KPIs should directly support the organization's strategic objectives. Before setting KPIs, it is important to develop clear goals and key outcomes that underpin the KPIs. This clarity will ensure that everyone in the organization understands what is being measured and why it is important. When setting KPIs, it is important to start with the business decision you are trying to make. Understanding the end goal will help define the data elements required for the KPIs. In addition, assessing the value of the information provided by the KPIs is necessary to determine the impact of knowing versus not knowing certain data. It is also important to consider the stakeholders who will benefit from the insights provided by the KPIs and identify potential data analytics and AI risks.

Effective KPIs have specific characteristics that make them valuable for managing organizational performance, following the *SMART* criteria set expanded by Shahin and Mahbod (2007). They must be *specific*, providing clear and detailed answers to what is being measured, why it is important, and how it is being measured. This specificity helps avoid misunderstandings and ensures a focused approach. KPIs also need to be *measurable*, which means they should be quantifiable so that progress and performance can be tracked over time. This quantifiability is crucial for objective evaluation and comparison. In addition, KPIs should be *achievable* yet challenging, setting realistic targets that are still ambitious enough to drive improvement. They must be *results-oriented*, aligned with broader organizational goals and ensure relevance within the given environment. Finally, effective KPIs are *time-sensitive*, with a specific timeframe that provides a sense of urgency and structure. This timeframe helps to set deadlines and track progress at regular intervals.

12.1.1 KPI Categories

Key performance indicators are essential tools for measuring and managing performance within an organization. KPIs can be categorized in various ways to align with different organizational needs and perspectives. In this section, we explore two primary categorizations: KPIs by functional areas and KPIs by management levels.

KPIs by Functional Areas

KPIs by functional areas focus on grouping KPIs based on different operational domains within an organization, ensuring that all critical aspects of the business are adequately monitored (Sweenor, 2022). Financial KPIs measure a company's financial health and performance, including indicators such as revenue growth, cash flow, gross profit, and expenditure pace. These KPIs are crucial for assessing profitability, liquidity, and overall financial stability. Customer KPIs track metrics related to customer satisfaction and loyalty, providing insights into how well the company is meeting customer needs and expectations. Examples include participation levels, Net Promoter Scores (NPS), acquisition costs, and conversion rates.

Employee KPIs measure aspects of employee engagement, satisfaction, and retention, which are vital for understanding workforce dynamics and improving employee relations. Key metrics include attrition and retention rates, satisfaction levels, and engagement. Support and Service KPIs evaluate the efficiency and effectiveness of customer support and service operations, which are essential for maintaining high service standards and customer satisfaction. Examples are time for resolution, mean resolution time, compliance with service-level agreements (SLAs), and quality. Governance, risk, and compliance KPIs monitor adherence to regulatory requirements, risk management practices, and internal governance policies, ensuring organizational integrity and minimizing risks. Important metrics include percentage compliance with processes, audit adherence, and incidents unrelated to security.

KPIs by Management Levels

On the other hand, KPIs by management levels organize performance measures according to their relevance to different management levels and their time-oriented focus (Twin, 2024). *Strategic KPIs* provide a high-level overview and are oriented toward long-term goals, typically used by executives to steer the company's strategic direction. Examples of strategic KPIs include ROI, profit margin, and total company revenue. *Operational KPIs* are detailed, process-oriented metrics with a short-term focus, used by middle management to monitor day-to-day operations and ensure efficiency. Examples include monthly revenue growth, product-specific sales, and regional performance.

Functional KPIs are specific to individual departments and can be either strategic or operational, helping department heads manage and improve their areas of responsibility. Examples include new vendor registrations in finance, click-through rates in marketing, and department-specific efficiency metrics. Leading and lagging KPIs offer different temporal perspectives: leading KPIs are predictive and future-oriented, helping to forecast trends and potential issues, while lagging KPIs are past-oriented, analyzing the outcomes of past actions and decisions. Examples of leading KPIs include overtime hours, which may indicate potential manufacturing issues, while examples of lagging KPIs include profit margin, reflecting past operational performance.

By understanding and utilizing these two categorizations of KPIs, organizations can more effectively monitor and manage their performance across various dimensions, ensuring a balanced and comprehensive approach to performance measurement and improvement.

12.1.2 The Critical Role of KPIs in Data-Driven World

In today's data-driven environment, KPIs are essential for organizations striving to optimize performance and achieve strategic objectives. KPIs provide clear and actionable insights into various facets of an organization's operations, ensuring that all efforts are aligned with long-term goals (Sweenor, 2022).

KPIs serve as a bridge between data, analytics, and AI initiatives and the strategic goals of an organization, thus playing a crucial role in *business impact assessment*. By aligning these elements, KPIs ensure that data-driven projects deliver ongoing value and are in sync with the long-term objectives of the business. For example, a company aiming to enhance customer experience might utilize KPIs related to customer satisfaction scores and response times, ensuring that their AI initiatives are effectively contributing to this strategic goal.

In a fast-paced business environment, the ability to make timely and informed decisions is crucial, highlighting the importance of KPIs in *timely decision-making*. KPIs play a vital role in monitoring the speed of data-to-insight conversion, providing real-time feedback that can enhance competitive agility. For instance, monitoring the KPI of average time to insight helps organizations streamline their decision-making processes, ensuring they remain responsive to market changes and emerging opportunities.

The reliability and accuracy of data are fundamental to sound decision-making, which is where KPIs dedicated to *data quality assurance* come into play. These KPIs help organizations maintain high standards of data integrity. Metrics such as data accuracy rates, error rates, and data completeness ensure that decisions are based on dependable data, ultimately leading to better outcomes.

As organizations increasingly rely on data, fostering *data literacy* across all levels becomes essential. KPIs tracking data literacy progress empower employees to make informed decisions and fully leverage data-driven insights. Examples of such KPIs include the number of employees trained in data analytics and the percentage of departments utilizing data analytics tools, which reflect the organization's commitment to building a data-literate workforce.

Effective *risk management* is another critical area where KPIs play a significant role. By quantifying and mitigating risks associated with data, analytics, and AI projects, KPIs help organizations navigate potential pitfalls. Risk-related KPIs might include metrics such as the number of data breaches, compliance rates with data protection regulations, and the incidence of AI-related errors, providing a comprehensive view of the risk landscape and enabling proactive management.

KPIs offer a comprehensive view of business performance, guiding strategic decisions and uniting the organization toward its goals. They are vital for handling vast data volumes and making data a competitive advantage, ensuring efficient and impactful data initiatives. By systematically employing KPIs across various facets of the organization, businesses can enhance their data-driven strategies and achieve sustained success in an increasingly complex and dynamic market environment.

Types of KPIs for AI Initiatives

Establishing both quantitative and qualitative KPIs is crucial to enhancing project efficiency and contributing to societal improvement. These KPIs are essential for quantifying the success of AI initiatives, providing insights into reliability, accuracy, user experience, and fairness (Schroeter, 2024).

- *Mean time to repair (MTTR)* evaluates how long it takes to rectify errors within an AI system. This KPI measures system maintainability and reliability, which are crucial for a swift response to errors. A low MTTR indicates that the system can quickly recover from faults, minimizing downtime and maintaining consistent performance.
- *Mean absolute error (MAE)* calculates the average disparity between predictions generated by a regression model and the actual values. This KPI is vital for evaluating model accuracy in regression applications. A lower MAE signifies more precise predictions, which enhances the reliability of the AI system's outputs.
- *First contact resolution rate (FCRR)* indicates the proportion of issues resolved through initial support interactions. This KPI is key for customer support and user satisfaction, as it shows the efficiency of problem resolution processes. A high FCRR suggests effective issue management, reducing the need for repeated contacts and lowering operational costs.
- *True- or false-positive rate (T/FPR)* is a quality metric that assesses the sensitivity and specificity of predicted classifications. This KPI is essential for fairness, as it evaluates the model's ability to distinguish between positive and negative classes accurately, reducing biases. A balanced T/FPR indicates a model that makes correct classifications consistently, which is critical for applications where fairness and unbiased decision-making are paramount.

By carefully monitoring and optimizing these KPIs, organizations can ensure that their AI initiatives are reliable, accurate, and fair, ultimately contributing to enhanced project efficiency and societal benefit.

Benefits of Using KPIs in AI Initiatives

The integration of KPIs in AI initiatives offers numerous benefits that enhance both project efficiency and overall organizational success (Lisowski, 2023). KPIs establish clear objectives for tracking progress and measuring success, thus *providing measurable goals*. These goals enable organizations to maintain focus on their strategic targets, ensuring that AI projects remain aligned with broader business objectives.

Another significant benefit of using KPIs in AI initiatives is *data-driven decision-making*. By evaluating KPI data, organizations can identify areas needing improvement and optimize development efforts. This data-driven approach facilitates informed decision-making, enabling teams to allocate resources more effectively and address issues promptly. The use of KPIs also leads to *increased efficiency*. By measuring time and resource allocation, KPIs help identify and rectify inefficiencies and bottlenecks within AI projects. This continuous monitoring and adjustment process ensures that AI initiatives operate smoothly, maximizing productivity and reducing waste.

Furthermore, KPIs promote *greater accountability* within teams. Clear goals and progress tracking encourage team accountability and effectiveness. When team members understand the specific KPIs they are working toward, they are more likely to take ownership of their tasks and contribute to the overall success of the project. Lastly, KPIs significantly enhance *improved customer satisfaction*. By tracking customer satisfaction through metrics like conversion rates and user engagement, organizations can ensure their products align more closely with user expectations. This alignment not only improves user experience but also fosters customer loyalty and retention.

Summary

Key performance indicators are essential in the data-driven world for managing and evaluating organizational strategies and AI initiatives. KPIs, distinct from metrics, align with strategic goals to provide actionable insights into performance. They play a crucial role in business impact assessment, timely decision-making, data quality assurance, data literacy, and risk management. Effective KPIs follow SMART criteria and can be categorized by functional areas and management levels. Specific KPIs for AI initiatives, such as mean time to repair and true/false-positive rate, enhance reliability and fairness. Integrating KPIs leads to measurable goals, data-driven decision-making, increased efficiency, greater accountability, and improved customer satisfaction.

12.2 Machine Learning Monitoring

Machine learning (ML) monitoring is a critical component in the lifecycle of machine learning models, ensuring that models perform consistently and effectively once deployed in production environments (Amershi et al., 2019). After the development and training phase, ML applications encounter various challenges in their production environments. In the interaction between ML applications and their operational contexts, dependencies become apparent, data changes may affect the ML application, and inadequacies in the assumptions made during development may occur. To uncover these aspects at an early stage, ML monitoring as the last essential phase in the ML lifecycle is essential for maintaining model accuracy, efficiency, and alignment with business goals over time (Kreuzberger et al., 2023).

Monitoring focuses on the ongoing performance of models, tracking their behavior and making necessary adjustments when the behavior deviates from their intended status (Test et al. 2022, Kreuzberger et al., 2023). The ML monitoring process can be broken down into several interconnected practices (see Fig. 12.2). We will explore each of these practices in detail, focusing on how they contribute to the overall reliability of ML applications in production. These practices include defining relevant metrics, measuring performance, assessing deviations, acting on insights, and controlling the ongoing process for continuous improvement. Each phase is essential for keeping ML models robust, adaptable, and aligned with evolving business requirements (Protschky et al., 2025).

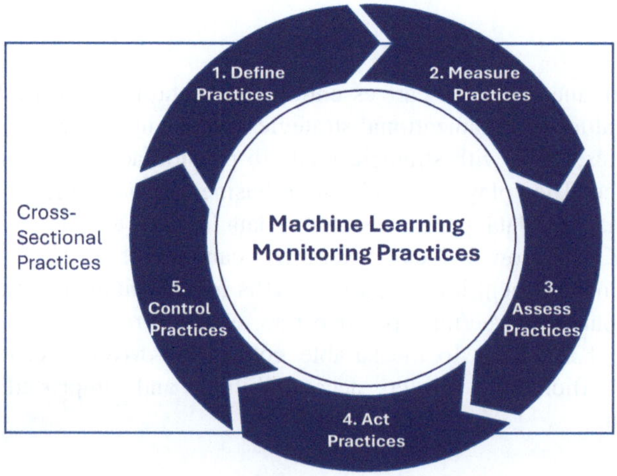

Fig. 12.2 Machine learning monitoring practices. (Adapted from Protschky et al., 2025)

12.2.1 Phase 1: Define Practices

The first and fundamental phase in effective machine learning monitoring contains defining practices (see Fig. 12.3). The *define* phase involves identifying relevant problem areas, determining improvement goals, and establishing appropriate metrics that align with the needs and expectations of all stakeholders. This phase ensures that monitoring efforts are targeted, meaningful, and aligned with organizational objectives, laying the foundation for effective evaluation and improvement. The *define* phase contains the following three steps:

The first step is to *identify the weaknesses* of the ML application and the *compensatory workflows* that will address these weaknesses. Understanding where the model might falter—whether due to data quality issues, changes in input distributions or limitations in the model architecture—allows for the creation of specific monitoring practices that can detect and respond to these potential issues (Naveed, 2023). By anticipating areas where the model may underperform, organizations can proactively establish workflows that compensate for these weaknesses, thereby minimizing disruptions to the model's operation.

Next, the step of *selecting appropriate metrics* is critical. Metrics should be carefully chosen to reflect both technical performance and organizational objectives. This selection process involves balancing metrics that provide insight into computational efficiency and accuracy (technical metrics) with those that align with business goals, such as customer satisfaction or operational efficiency (organizational metrics) (Kolltveit & Li, 2022; Bodor et al., 2023). The selected metrics must cover all relevant aspects of the ML application to ensure that the monitoring practice is comprehensive (Naveed, 2023). This also requires input from a range of stakeholders, including data scientists, IT professionals, and business leaders, to ensure that the selected metrics are meaningful and actionable across the organization.

Once the metrics have been selected, the next step is to *model a metrics system* that integrates both technical and organizational metrics. This involves identifying how different metrics interact and creating a system that can effectively balance trade-offs between competing objectives (Nahar et al., 2022). For example, a model that is highly accurate but computationally expensive may need to be balanced against cost constraints or speed requirements. By modelling these interactions, organizations can develop a collective metrics system that specifies the trade-off space, allowing informed decisions to be made when adjustments are needed.

In summary, defining ML monitoring practices is a critical phase that involves understanding the potential vulnerabilities of the ML application, selecting

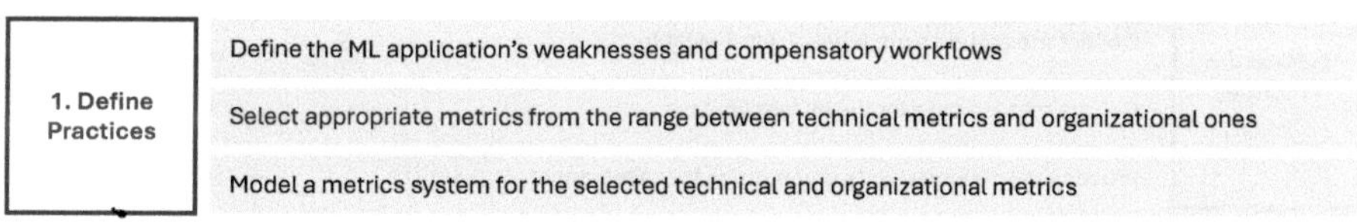

Fig. 12.3 Define practices

appropriate metrics that reflect both technical and organizational needs, and creating a metrics system that integrates these metrics into a cohesive monitoring framework. This well-defined approach lays the foundation for the subsequent steps in the monitoring process, ensuring that the ML model can be effectively evaluated and maintained throughout its lifecycle.

12.2.2 Phase 2: Measure Practices

Once the foundational practices have been defined, the next critical step in machine learning monitoring is the measurement phase (see Fig. 12.4). The *Measure* phase focuses on collecting the necessary data and quantifying the metrics identified during the define step to evaluate the defined problem and improvement areas. Without accurate and comprehensive data collection, organizations cannot assess their performance or identify deviations, making this phase essential for informed decision-making. The *Measure* phase contains the following four tasks:

The first step in this phase is to *collect metadata* from the context of the ML application. This involves gathering a comprehensive set of data points that describe the operating environment of the model, including logs, code versions, datasets, model configurations, and hyperparameter settings (Bodor et al., 2023; Barry et al., 2023). Collecting this metadata provides a detailed view of how the application is configured and operates, which is essential for understanding the context in which the model is making predictions (Kreuzberger et al., 2023). By maintaining accurate and up-to-date metadata, organizations can more effectively diagnose problems when they occur and trace the source of performance deviations.

In addition to collecting metadata, the step *collects ground truth labels*, if they are available, is important. Ground truth labels are the actual outcomes or classifications that the model is trying to predict. Evaluating the availability and reliability of these labels is critical, as they serve as the benchmark against which the model's predictions are measured (Barry et al., 2023). Correctly labeled data is necessary to accurately assess the performance of the model, and any gaps in the labeling must be identified and addressed (Naveed, 2023). If ground truth is not readily available, establishing effective labeling mechanisms becomes a priority to ensure a continuous flow of reliable data (Barry et al., 2023).

Next, it is necessary to *collect metrics data for the ML application*. This involves collecting the specific metrics defined in the previous phase, using an appropriate

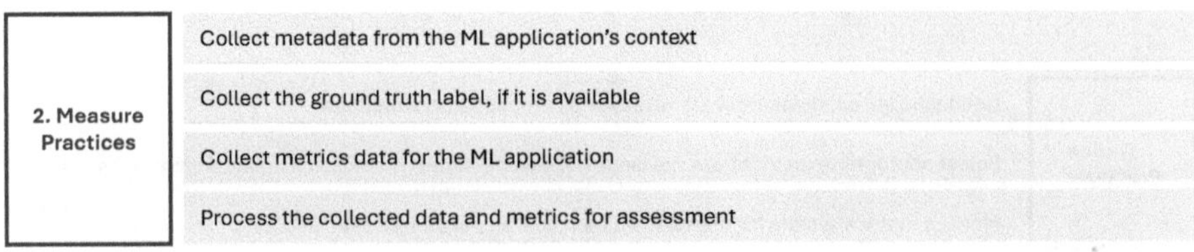

Fig. 12.4 Measure practices

infrastructure that can handle the volume and complexity of the data (Naveed, 2023). The metrics should be collected at regular intervals to provide a consistent and ongoing assessment of the model's performance (Sopan & Berlin, 2021; Barry et al., 2023). This data collection process is an integral part of monitoring as it provides the quantitative measures needed to assess how well the model is performing. Ensuring that data is collected at a meaningful interval allows any issues to be identified in a timely manner so that corrective action can be taken promptly.

Once the data and metrics are collected, the next step is to *process the collected data for evaluation*. This involves linking the collected metadata to the performance metrics and other relevant data points to gain insight into the behavior of the model (Kolltveit & Li, 2022). Processing this data typically involves statistical calculations and analysis that can reveal patterns, trends, and potential problems with the model's inputs and outputs (Naveed, 2023). By applying these analytical techniques, organizations can identify deviations from expected performance, uncover the root causes of any problems, and assess the overall health of the ML application.

In summary, the measurement phase of ML monitoring is a comprehensive process involving the collection and analysis of metadata, ground truth labels, and performance metrics. This phase is critical to providing the data-driven insights needed to maintain and improve model performance over time. By effectively measuring and analyzing this information, organizations can ensure that their ML applications remain robust, reliable, and aligned with their intended goals, enabling proactive management and continuous improvement.

12.2.3 Phase 3: Assess Practices

The assessment phase of machine learning monitoring is a critical phase that builds on the data collected and processed in the previous measurement phase (see Fig. 12.5). The *Assess* phase involves analyzing the data collected in the *Measure* phase to derive insights and evaluate progress against the defined metrics. This phase transforms raw data into actionable knowledge, allowing organizations to understand whether their objectives are being met and to pinpoint areas requiring attention for performance improvement. The *Assess* phase contains the following four steps:

The first step in the assessment process is to examine the collected data to *identify data quality issues*. This involves a thorough examination of the data used by the

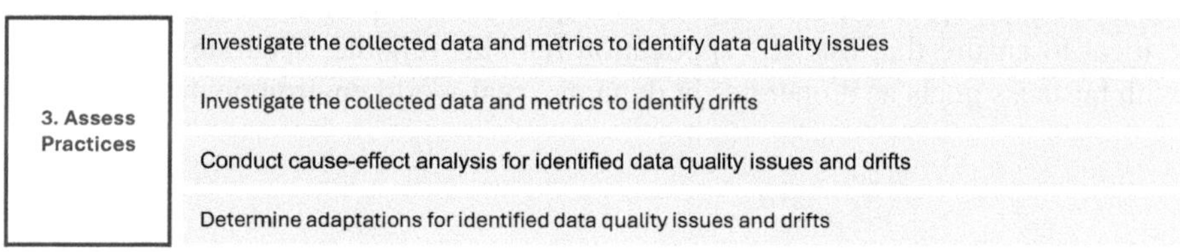

Fig. 12.5 Assess practices

model to ensure that it meets the necessary standards of accuracy, completeness, and consistency. Poor data quality can lead to significant model performance issues, so it is important to identify and address these issues early (Nahar et al., 2022). In this step, collected metrics are checked against predefined thresholds to ensure they are within acceptable ranges. In addition, specific data slices—subsets of the data that may represent different segments of the population—are examined to ensure that quality issues are not localized to specific areas, which could lead to biased or incorrect predictions (Sopan & Berlin, 2021).

Having examined the quality of the data, the next step is to *identify drift in the data*. Data drift occurs when the statistical properties of the input data change over time, which can lead to poor model performance if not detected and managed (Naveed, 2023; Testi et al., 2022). This step involves comparing current data distributions with historical data to identify any significant shifts. Drifts can occur in the input data (feature drift), in the output predictions (prediction drift), or in the relationship between inputs and outputs (concept drift) (Lewis et al., 2022). Identifying these drifts is critical because they often indicate that the model's assumptions are no longer valid, which can lead to reduced accuracy and reliability.

Once data quality issues and drifts have been identified, the next step is to *perform a root-cause analysis* to understand the causes of these issues and their impact on model performance. This analysis involves tracking the dependencies between different components of the ML system over time, distinguishing between model errors (such as overfitting or underfitting) and external factors (such as changes in the data source or environment) (Testi et al., 2022). By understanding the causes of the identified issues, it is possible to assess their impact on key business metrics and determine how critical these issues are to the overall success of the ML application.

The final phase in the a*ssessment* phase is to *determine the customization* required to address the identified issues. This may involve going back to previous versions of the ML application to understand how it performed under different conditions, or it may involve deciding on a schedule for retraining the model to keep it in line with current data trends (Bodor et al., 2023). In some cases, more substantial changes may be required, such as replacing the existing model with a new one that is better suited to the current data environment. The key is to decide on the most effective interventions that will correct the identified problems and ensure that the ML application continues to perform optimally.

Overall, the assessment phase of ML monitoring is a comprehensive process that involves identifying and analyzing data quality issues and drifts, performing cause-and-effect analysis to understand the root causes of these issues, and determining the necessary adjustments to maintain or improve model performance. This phase is critical to ensure that the ML application remains reliable, accurate, and aligned with business goals as it operates in dynamic, real-world environments.

12.2.4 Phase 4: Act Practices

The act phase of machine learning monitoring is where the insights gained from the previous assessment phase are translated into concrete actions (see Fig. 12.6). The *act* phase entails implementing changes or adaptations based on insights from the *assess* phase to address identified issues and improve outcomes. Timely and appropriate action ensures that issues are resolved effectively, and that organizational processes and models are continually optimized. The *act* phase contains the following step:

Having identified issues such as data quality problems, drift, or model performance degradation during the assessment phase, the next step is to *communicate the necessary adjustments to the relevant stakeholders*. These stakeholders typically include the development team responsible for the ML application and other key parties who rely on the model's output, such as business leaders, data scientists, and end-users (Nahar et al., 2022; Testi et al., 2022). Communication with the development team is particularly important, as this is the team that will implement the technical changes needed to address the identified issues (Nahar et al., 2022). These adjustments may involve retraining the model, adjusting hyperparameters, incorporating new data sources, or even redesigning parts of the ML pipeline. Clear and concise communication ensures that the development team understands the specific changes required and the reasons for them, so that they can implement them effectively. Equally important is communicating the changes to the application's wider stakeholders (Nahar et al., 2022). These stakeholders need to be aware of how the changes may affect the application's performance, the timelines for implementing these changes, and any expected improvements or temporary disruptions. Effective communication helps manage expectations and ensures that all parties are aligned on the objectives of the changes.

By successfully executing the *act* phase, organizations can ensure that their ML applications continue to perform optimally in production. This proactive approach not only addresses current issues but also positions the model to adapt more smoothly to future changes, thereby preserving its value and effectiveness over time.

12.2.5 Phase 5: Control Practices

The control phase of machine learning monitoring is the final step in the continuous monitoring cycle (see Fig. 12.7). The control phase verifies the effectiveness of adaptations made in the act step and ensures a feedback loop by feeding insights back to the define step for ongoing monitoring cycles. This step maintains accountability, ensures sustainability of improvements, and enables iterative refinement by

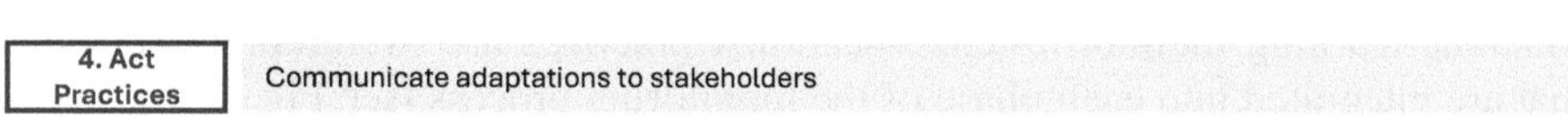

Fig. 12.6 Act practices

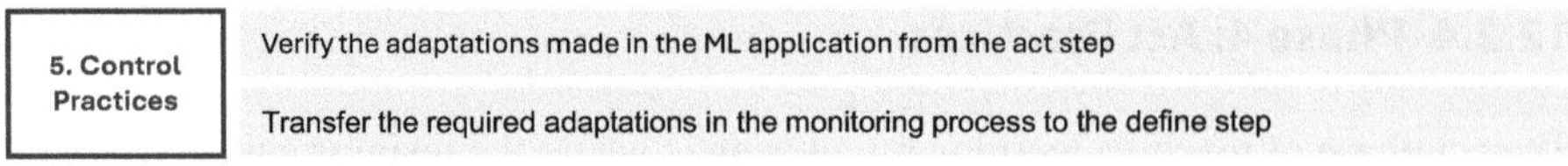

Fig. 12.7 Control practices

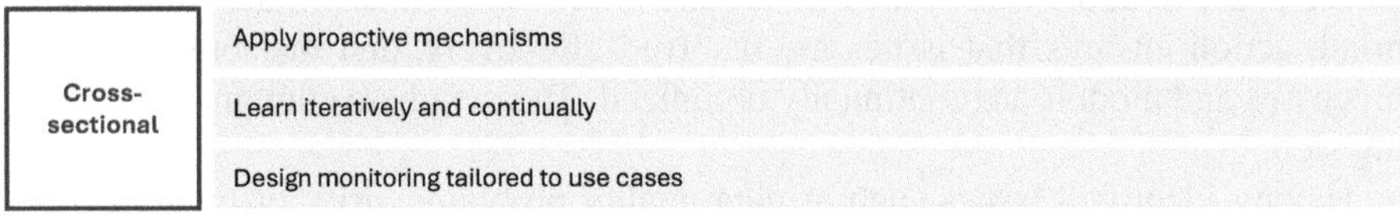

Fig. 12.8 Cross-sectional practices

connecting current adaptations to future monitoring efforts. The *control* phase contains the following two steps:

The first step in this phase is to *review the adjustments* made to the ML application as a result of the actions taken in the previous step. This involves checking that the changes made, such as model retraining, data updates, or adjustments to the ML pipeline, have had the desired effect on the model's performance. Verification is critical because it provides evidence that the adjustments are working as intended and that any problems identified in the assessment phase have been effectively addressed (Bodor et al., 2023). If the adjustments are successful, the monitoring system will observe improved metrics and stability in the model's performance during the next monitoring cycle.

In addition to verifying the immediate impact of adjustments, the control phase also involves *feeding back learning* from the current monitoring cycle to the *define phase*. This feedback loop is essential for refining and improving the overall monitoring approach. By incorporating lessons learned—such as which metrics were most effective, which issues were most difficult to address, and how quickly the model adapted—into the next cycle, the monitoring process becomes more robust and responsive (Nahar et al., 2022). This iterative process helps to continually improve monitoring practices, ensuring that the ML application remains aligned with business objectives and adapts to any changes in its operating environment.

Overall, the control phase ensures that the ML monitoring process is dynamic and capable of continuous improvement. By verifying the effectiveness of actions taken and feeding insights back into the monitoring system, organizations can maintain the long-term health and performance of their ML applications, ensuring that they deliver consistent value and remain effective in the face of evolving challenges.

12.2.6 Cross-Sectional Practices

Machine learning monitoring cross-sectional practices are overarching strategies that are integrated into each phase of the monitoring process (see Fig. 12.8). These practices are designed to ensure that the monitoring system is not only reactive to problems as they arise, but is also proactive, adaptive, and tailored to the specific needs of the organization and the use cases it supports. The *control* phase contains the following three steps:

One of the most important cross-sectional practices is the *use of proactive mechanisms*. Rather than simply reacting to problems after they have affected model performance, proactive monitoring seeks to identify and address potential problems as early as possible (Naveed, 2023). This can involve setting up early warning systems that detect subtle signs of drift, data quality degradation, or performance anomalies before they escalate into significant problems. By identifying these issues early, organizations can intervene before model performance is adversely affected, ensuring more stable and reliable operation of the ML application.

Another essential cross-sectional practice is to *learn iteratively and continuously*. Machine learning models operate in dynamic environments where data distributions, user behavior, and business requirements can change over time (Testi et al., 2022). To remain effective, the ML monitoring system must continuously learn from these changes (Kreuzberger et al., 2023). This involves establishing a virtual cycle in which insights from each monitoring cycle are fed back into the system to refine the model, improve monitoring practices, and expand the scope of what is monitored. Through iterative learning, the ML application evolves with its environment, maintaining its relevance and performance even as external conditions change.

Finally, *designing use case-specific monitoring* ensures that the monitoring approach is aligned with the specific needs and constraints of the organization and its ML applications. Different use cases may have different priorities—such as accuracy, speed, fairness, or interpretability—and the monitoring system should be designed to reflect these priorities. This customization may involve selecting specific metrics that are most relevant to the use case, adjusting the frequency and granularity of monitoring, and ensuring that the monitoring process fits seamlessly into the organization's broader operational workflow (Diamantis & Iakovidis, 2021).

Together, these cross-sectional practices increase the effectiveness of the ML monitoring process by making it more proactive, adaptive, and aligned with the organization's unique needs. By embedding these practices into all phases of monitoring, organizations can ensure that their ML applications are not only well maintained, but also continuously improving and able to deliver sustainable value over time.

Summary

Machine learning monitoring is essential to ensure that AI models perform as expected in real-world environments. This process involves systematically observing, measuring and analyzing model behavior to detect deviations due to factors such as data shifts or changing business requirements. Effective ML monitoring involves defining specific practices, selecting appropriate metrics, and continuously measuring and evaluating model performance. The process is iterative, with insights from each cycle used to refine the model and monitoring approach. By implementing robust monitoring and control practices, organizations can maintain the reliability, accuracy, and relevance of their ML applications, ensuring long-term effectiveness and alignment with business goals.

12.3 Change Management

The successful implementation of AI applications is not solely reliant on technical robustness or data quality. A structured and targeted change management process plays a pivotal role in the overall success of AI initiatives. This process ensures that the organization can fully realize the potential of AI applications while mitigating the negative effects associated with the introduction of new technologies (Wrenn & Sohn, 2021).

Without a well-defined approach to managing change, organizations often face resistance, confusion, and inefficiencies. Employees may struggle to adapt to new systems, workflows may become disjointed, and the overall adoption of AI initiatives may falter. Change management provides the framework to address these challenges by aligning organizational readiness, resources, and strategies with the goals of AI initiatives.

Effective change management minimizes the negative impacts typically seen during the initial phases of AI implementation and maximizes the positive outcomes over time. A carefully managed change process ensures that AI initiatives deliver long-term value and aligns with the strategic objectives of the organization.

12.3.1 Five Steps for Successful AI Change Management

A systematic approach is essential for successful change management in AI initiatives. This structured approach can be divided into five key steps (see Fig. 12.9), which serve as a comprehensive framework to guide organizations through the process of introducing AI applications (ACMP, 2019).

1. *Evaluating Change Impact and Organizational Readiness*

   This initial step is crucial for identifying how AI initiatives will affect the organization, determining the organization's capacity for adopting change, and pinpointing areas of potential resistance or support (ACMP, 2019). Effective assessment at this stage sets the foundation for informed decision-making and tailored change strategies. Hence, this first step encompasses four key areas: definition of the change and vision, stakeholder readiness and impact analysis, success criteria and KPIs, and tailored education and communication.

   AI change management begins with a clear *definition of the change and vision* that aligns the AI initiative's objectives with strategic goals. Key considerations include how the initiative will affect structures, processes, and employees, and whether its goals align with broader organizational strategies. Understanding the necessity and drivers of the initiative is critical. This involves assessing its importance, the challenges it addresses, and the factors that enable its implementation. Establishing a strong business case ensures clarity and commitment among all stakeholders and employees.

   Assessing *stakeholder readiness* means determining the level of readiness of employees and key stakeholders. Furthermore, cultural factors, such as innova-

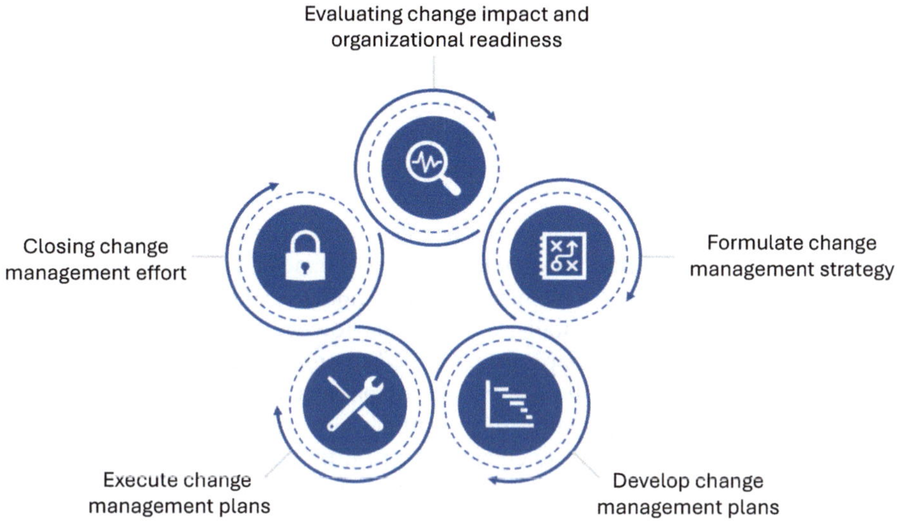

Fig. 12.9 Five steps of successful AI change management. (Adapted from ACMP 2019)

tion readiness and adaptability among employees, play a significant role in successful implementation. Understanding these factors and employee readiness will help determine the organization's overall adaptability to the AI initiative. *Analyzing the expected impact* on people, processes, and the organization ensures potential disruptions are identified early. This includes addressing skill gaps, resistance to change, and necessary workflow adjustments, as well as considering broader governance or structural changes.

Defining *success criteria and KPIs* provides measurable benchmarks to evaluate progress and outcomes. These indicators should capture both qualitative and quantitative dimensions, such as improved efficiency and return on investment. Equally important is identifying responsibilities and stakeholders. Clear roles must be assigned to ensure accountability, while communication plans keep all affected parties informed and engaged throughout the process.

Finally, *tailored education and communication* measures prepare employees for upcoming transformations. Training programs should address skill development, while consistent communication ensures understanding and alignment with the initiative's objectives. A thorough evaluation of these elements allows organizations to minimize risks and maximize the benefits of AI adoption, ensuring a smoother transition and long-term success.

2. *Formulate an AI Change Management Strategy*

   Building on the previously defined objectives, the next step involves developing a comprehensive strategy to guide the upcoming changes (ACMP, 2019). This strategy serves as a roadmap for managing the transition and ensuring alignment across the organization. It encompasses four key areas: communication, education, stakeholder engagement, and sustainability strategies.

A *communication strategy* defines how stakeholders and interest groups will be informed about the AI initiative. Key elements include selecting appropriate communication channels, such as internal newsletters, workshops, or intranet updates, and ensuring clarity in presenting the business case for the AI initiative. Additionally, this strategy should establish mechanisms for collecting feedback, such as regular surveys or open forums, to foster dialogue and address concerns proactively.

The *education and development strategy* focuses on equipping employees with the necessary skills and knowledge to understand and effectively use the AI application. It identifies areas where training initiatives are required and determines suitable platforms, tools, and formats for delivery, such as e-learning modules, hands-on workshops, or expert-led sessions. A clear timeline ensures timely implementation of these initiatives, preparing employees for the transition.

A *stakeholder engagement strategy* outlines how stakeholders can be actively involved in the AI initiative to enhance their intrinsic motivation. This includes conducting systematic requirements analyses in collaboration with end-users, establishing channels for continuous employee feedback, and involving stakeholders in key decision-making processes. Such engagement fosters a sense of ownership and commitment among those affected by the change.

Finally, the *sustainability strategy* ensures the long-term integration of the AI application into daily workflows. Measures might include creating reward systems to encourage the adoption of desired behaviors, ensuring knowledge transfer through structured documentation or mentoring programs, and incorporating regular user feedback into ongoing improvements. These efforts help embed the AI initiative into the organizational culture and promote its sustained success. By addressing these four areas systematically, organizations can create a robust framework for managing AI-driven change, ensuring both immediate and long-term benefits.

3. *Develop AI Change Management Plans*

To translate the previously formulated strategy into actionable steps, a holistic change management plan must be developed (ACMP, 2019). This plan includes concrete measures for implementation and ensures alignment with organizational goals. Key components of the plan include resource allocation for the entire change management as well as communication, education, stakeholder engagement, and sustainability plans.

The *resource allocation* identifies the human, physical, and financial resources required for the successful execution of AI change management. This involves determining resource availability, assigning responsibilities, and ensuring that all necessary tools and infrastructure are in place to support the change process.

A *communication plan* outlines how employees will be guided and motivated throughout different phases of the project. This includes defining target audiences, selecting appropriate communication channels, and identifying suitable spokespersons. Additionally, the plan specifies the frequency, timing, and content of communications to ensure consistent and effective messaging that addresses concerns and builds trust.

The *education and development plan* focuses on areas for improvement and determines the most effective training measures to address skill gaps. This plan ensures employees are equipped with the knowledge and competencies needed to work effectively with the new AI systems. Training formats may include workshops, online courses, and hands-on sessions tailored to the needs of various teams.

A *stakeholder engagement plan* highlights activities aimed at increasing participation and buy-in from stakeholders. This can include regular communication, training sessions, and opportunities for active involvement in shaping the AI initiative. By fostering collaboration and inclusivity, the plan helps build trust and alignment across the organization.

Finally, the *sustainability plan ensures* the long-term adoption and continuous improvement of the AI application. Strategies may involve celebrating milestones, recognizing and rewarding desired behaviors, and implementing mechanisms for monitoring and evaluating performance. These efforts help embed the AI initiative into the organization's culture and workflows.

By integrating these elements into a cohesive plan, organizations can effectively manage the transition to AI-driven operations and ensure the sustained success of their initiatives.

4. *Execute AI Change Management Plans*

The implementation of the developed change management plans involves executing, administering, and monitoring all outlined measures to ensure their effectiveness (ACMP, 2019). This phase focuses on translating AI change management plans into actionable steps while addressing challenges and resistance that may arise during execution. It encompasses four key areas: execution of communication, education, stakeholder engagement, and sustainability plans.

The *communication plan* is executed by focusing on the prevention and management of employee resistance through effective communication strategies. This includes implementing feedback mechanisms, such as regular check-ins or surveys, to understand and address employee concerns. Clear, transparent communication helps foster trust and alignment across all levels of the organization.

The *education and development plan* is executed by rolling out predefined upskilling initiatives on both individual and group levels. The effectiveness of these training programs is evaluated through assessments, and adjustments are made as needed to refine learning objectives and methods. This ensures employees are well-prepared to integrate AI systems into their workflows.

The *stakeholder engagement plan* is executed by actively collecting and implementing feedback from stakeholders. This involves scheduling regular stakeholder consultations, maintaining open communication channels, and translating feedback into actionable steps. By involving stakeholders directly in this phase, organizations foster participation and mitigate resistance while ensuring alignment with project goals.

Finally, the *sustainability plan* is executed by actively tracking progress and implementing measures to maintain long-term adoption of the AI application.

This includes setting up systems to monitor performance, addressing emerging issues, and celebrating achievements through milestones and rewards. Structured workshops and formalized channels for improvement suggestions are implemented to ensure the initiative evolves and remains effective over time.

By systematically executing these plans, organizations can ensure that AI initiatives are effectively integrated into operations, minimizing disruption and maximizing value creation.

5. *Closing AI Change Management Effort*

   The final phase of the AI change management process focuses on completing and consolidating all efforts (ACMP, 2019). This involves evaluating results, documenting lessons learned and best practices, sharing outcomes with stakeholders, and ensuring a transition of responsibilities to the appropriate parties.

   The results of the AI initiative are thoroughly *evaluated* to provide a clear understanding of its success. This includes conducting a detailed comparison between planned objectives and actual outcomes. Stakeholder perspectives are actively incorporated into this evaluation to ensure a comprehensive assessment that accounts for various viewpoints and experiences.

   Key insights gained throughout the project are compiled into a structured document outlining *lessons learned and best practices*. These findings are made accessible to all relevant teams to inform and improve future initiatives. By documenting these experiences, organizations create a valuable knowledge base that supports continuous learning and refinement of change management processes.

   The final outcomes, along with all associated resources and insights, are *shared with stakeholders*. This ensures that the knowledge gained is disseminated across the organization, fostering transparency and collaboration. By providing stakeholders with access to these materials, organizations enhance their capacity for effective decision-making and execution in future projects.

   Responsibilities for the sustained implementation and maintenance of the AI initiative are *formally transferred* to the designated departments or individuals. This handover process ensures that the initiative is seamlessly integrated into regular operations and that accountability is clearly established for ongoing management and improvement.

   By carefully completing these steps, organizations ensure that the AI change management effort concludes effectively, setting a strong foundation for future success and ongoing innovation.

12.3.2 Practical Approaches for Effective AI Transformation

Building on the previously outlined importance of structured change management in AI implementation, this section delves deeper into the practical measures required to address the human challenges associated with technological transformation. While technical robustness and data quality form the foundation of AI success, the ultimate impact of these initiatives depends on how effectively organizations can navigate employee concerns and foster an environment of trust and engagement (Pirard & Cartwright, 2023, Power, 2018).

Unmanaged change leaves employees facing uncertainty and fear. Without clear direction, they often perceive AI as a threat rather than an opportunity. Questions about job security, qualifications, and the purpose of AI projects can quickly escalate into resistance and disengagement. Managed change, by contrast, creates a structured environment where these insecurities are proactively addressed. Employees gain the tools, understanding, and support needed to view AI as an enabler, fostering acceptance and collaboration (Wrenn & Sohn, 2021).

Successfully addressing these challenges requires a focus on three interconnected strategies: education and upskilling, employee involvement, and transparency and communication. Each of these areas plays a critical role in overcoming insecurities, reducing resistance, and ensuring the smooth adoption of AI technologies.

Education and Upskilling

One of the primary causes of resistance to AI is uncertainty about personal qualifications and technical skills (Pirad & Cartwright, 2023; Wrenn & Sohn, 2021). Employees may lack confidence in their ability to work effectively with AI systems, leading to doubts about their future roles. To address these concerns, organizations must invest in targeted education and upskilling efforts. A thorough assessment of existing competencies helps identify areas for improvement and serves as the basis for personalized development plans. These plans provide structured pathways for employees to build new skills and grow alongside technological advancements.

Workshops, training programs, and accessible learning formats ensure that employees can engage with AI technologies in a supportive environment. Lowering barriers to participation, such as by offering cost coverage or designated learning time, increases accessibility and participation. Safe testing environments, where employees can experiment with AI tools without fear of consequences, further build confidence and familiarity. By equipping employees with the necessary knowledge and skills, organizations empower them to embrace AI as an opportunity for growth.

Employee Involvement

Creating a sense of ownership and responsibility is key to reducing resistance and fostering intrinsic motivation (Power, 2018; Wrenn & Sohn, 2021). Employees who are actively involved in the AI transformation process feel that their contributions matter, which increases their willingness to engage with new systems. This involvement begins with requirement gathering, where end-users provide valuable input to ensure AI solutions meet practical needs. Focus groups and cross-functional collaboration create opportunities to understand user concerns and expectations.

Involving employees in testing and evaluation ensures that diverse perspectives are considered, leading to better outcomes and solutions that align with day-to-day workflows. A culture of feedback further strengthens this involvement. Employees must feel that their concerns are acknowledged and addressed, fostering trust and transparency. Recognizing and rewarding AI champions—those who enthusiastically adopt and promote AI systems—encourages others to follow suit and helps create positive momentum throughout the organization.

Transparency and Communication

Transparent communication forms the foundation for trust and alignment in AI projects (Pirard & Cartwright, 2023; Wrenn & Sohn, 2021). Employees need a clear understanding of the organization's AI strategy, including the vision, goals, and expected outcomes. Communicating these elements consistently and across multiple channels ensures that all employees remain informed and engaged throughout the transformation process. Leadership plays a central role in articulating the benefits of AI while also presenting a realistic picture of its impacts.

Providing clarity about roles and expectations helps employees understand their contributions to the success of AI initiatives. Celebrating milestones and quick wins reinforces progress and demonstrates tangible benefits, helping to alleviate concerns about job security or relevance. Regular updates and opportunities for dialogue create an open and inclusive environment where employees can ask questions, share feedback, and feel heard.

By focusing on education, involvement, and communication, organizations can address employee insecurities effectively. Managed change transforms fear and resistance into confidence and advocacy, creating a collaborative environment where AI is viewed as an opportunity for innovation and growth. Through these strategies, organizations can ensure that the adoption of AI aligns both technological potential and human development to drive sustainable success.

Summary

Effective AI change management is essential to ensure successful adoption and integration of AI technologies. Organizations face significant challenges, including employee resistance, uncertainty, and workflow disruptions, which can undermine the benefits of AI initiatives. A structured approach mitigates these challenges through managed change, focusing on education, employee involvement, and transparent communication. Starting with small, practical projects helps build momentum, while training and upskilling equip employees with the confidence to embrace AI. Clear messaging and collaboration foster trust, reduce fears, and encourage knowledge sharing across teams. By aligning organizational strategies with employee needs, companies can realize AI's potential and drive long-term success.

References

Amershi, S., Begel, A., Bird, C., DeLine, R., Gall, H., Kamar, E., & Zimmermann, T. (2019). Software engineering for machine learning: A case study. In *2019 IEEE/ACM 41st International Conference on Software Engineering: Software Engineering in Practice (ICSE-SEIP)* (pp. 291–300). IEEE.

Association of Change Management Professionals (ACMP). (2019). *Standard for Change Management and ACMP Change Management Code of Ethics* (1st ed.). [online] Accessed December 16, 2023, from https://www.acmpglobal.org/page/the_standard

Barry, M., Montiel, J., Bifet, A., Wadkar, S., Manchev, N., Halford, M., & Guerizec, E. (2023). StreamMLOps: Operationalizing online learning for big Data Streaming & Real-Time Applications. In *2023 IEEE 39th International Conference on Data Engineering (ICDE)* (pp. 3508–3521). IEEE.

Bodor, A., Hnida, M., & Najima, D. (2023). From development to deployment: An approach to MLOps monitoring for machine learning model operationalization. In *2023 14th International Conference on Intelligent Systems: Theories and Applications (SITA)* (pp. 1–7). IEEE.

Diamantis, D. E., & Iakovidis, D. K. (2021). ASML: Algorithm-agnostic architecture for scalable machine learning. *IEEE Access, 9*, 51970–51982.

Kolltveit, A. B., & Li, J. (2022). Operationalizing machine learning models: A systematic literature review. In *Proceedings of the 1st Workshop on Software Engineering for Responsible AI* (pp. 1–8).

Kreuzberger, D., Kühl, N., & Hirschl, S. (2023). Machine learning operations (MLOps): Overview, definition, and architecture. *IEEE Access, 11*, 31866–31879.

Lewis G. A., Echeverría, S., Pons, L., & Chrabaszcz, J. (2022). Augur: A step towards realistic drift detection in production ML systems. In *Proc. 1st Workshop Softw. Eng. Responsible AI*, pp. 37–44.

Lisowski, E. (2023). Key product management metrics and KPIs in AI development. [online] *Addepto*. Accessed May 24, 2024, from https://addepto.com/blog/key-product-management-metrics-and-kpis-in-ai-development/

Nahar, N., Zhou, S., Lewis, G., & Kästner, C. (2022). Collaboration challenges in building ML-enabled systems: Communication, documentation, engineering, and process. In *Proceedings of the 44th International Conference on Software Engineering* (pp. 413–425).

Naveed, H. (2023). Runtime monitoring of human-centric requirements in machine learning components: A model-driven engineering approach. In *2023 ACM/IEEE International Conference on Model Driven Engineering Languages and Systems Companion (MODELS-C)* (pp. 146–152). IEEE.

Pirard, A., & Cartwright, R. F. (2023). From resistance to advocacy: Strategies for overcoming organizational resistance to AI. *Cognizant Benelux Blog*. [online] 28 November. Accessed December 16, 2023, from https://www.cognizant.com/nl/en/insights/blog/articles/from-resistance-to-advocacy

Power, B. (2018). How to get employees to stop worrying and love AI. *Harvard Business Review*. [online] 25 January. Accessed December 16, 2023, from https://hbr.org/2018/01/how-to-get-employees-to-stop-worrying-and-love-ai

Protschky, D., Lämmermann, L., Hofmann, P., & Urbach, N. (2025). What gets measured gets improved: Monitoring machine learning applications in their production environments. *IEEE Access, 13*, 34518.

Schroeter, B. (2024). Reliable KPIs for AI: How to measure success. [online] *Pandata*. Accessed May 24, 2024, from https://pandata.co/blog/reliable-kpis-for-ai-how-to-measure-success/

Shahin, A., & Mahbod, M. A. (2007). Prioritization of key performance indicators: An integration of analytical hierarchy process and goal setting. *International Journal of Productivity and Performance Management, 56*(3), 226–240.

Sopan, A., & Berlin, K. (2021). AI Total: Analyzing security ML models with imperfect data in production. In *2021 IEEE Symposium on Visualization for Cyber Security (VizSec)* (pp. 10–14). IEEE.

Sweenor, D. (2022). The art of the AI KPI. [online] *Towards Data Science*. Accessed May 24, 2024, from https://towardsdatascience.com/the-art-of-the-ai-kpi-3d6ed8a03994

Testi, M., Ballabio, M., Frontoni, E., Iannello, G., Moccia, S., Soda, P., & Vessio, G. (2022). MLOps: A taxonomy and a methodology. *IEEE Access, 10*, 63606–63618.

Twin, A. (2024). Key performance indicators (KPIs): Types and examples. [online] *Investopedia*. Accessed May 24, 2024, from https://www.investopedia.com/terms/k/kpi.asp

Wrenn, K., & Sohn, E. (2021). Artificial intelligence: Navigating AI change management. *Booz Allen Hamilton*. [online] Accessed December 16, 2023, from https://www.boozallen.com/insights/ai-research/change-management-for-artificial-intelligence-adoption.html

Nils Urbach is Professor of Information Systems and Digital Business as well as Director of the Research Lab for Digital Innovation and Transformation at the Frankfurt University of Applied Sciences, Germany. Furthermore, he is Director at the FIM Research Center for Information Management, and the Branch Business and Information Systems Engineering of Fraunhofer FIT. Nils Urbach has been working in the fields of digital innovation and transformation for several years. His work has been published in several academic journals such as Information Systems Research (ISR), the Journal of the Association for Information Systems (JAIS), the Journal of Strategic Information Systems (JSIS), the Journal of Information Technology (JIT), MIS Quarterly Executive (MISQE), IEEE Transactions on Engineering Management (IEEE TEM), Information and Management (I&M), Business and Information Systems Engineering (BISE), and Electronic Markets (EM). He advises several companies on digitalization issues and regularly appears as a speaker on this topic.

Daniel Feulner received his M.Sc. in information system from the Otto-Friedrich University of Bamberg, Germany in 2023. He is an affiliated researcher at the Branch Business and Information Systems Engineering of the Fraunhofer FIT and FIM Research Center for Information Management at the University of Bayreuth. In his research, he aims to understand how Business Analytics and Artificial Intelligence can be effectively and responsibly utilized in organizations. His goal is to enable companies to drive innovation and achieve sustainable growth in a rapidly evolving technological landscape.

Annalena Schmid received her B.Sc. in Information Systems from the University of Stuttgart and the University of Hohenheim and will continue her academic journey by pursuing a M.Sc. in Information Systems at the University of Stuttgart. She gained valuable practical experience as a research assistant at the Fraunhofer FIT and the FIM Research Center for Information Management, where she contributed to the ABBA research project (AI for Business and Business for AI). She is particularly passionate about AI applications in organizations, with a focus on integrating AI-driven solutions into business environments.

Dominik Protschky received his M.Sc. in business administration and engineering from the University of Bayreuth, Germany in 2021. He is an affiliated researcher at the Branch Business & Information Systems Engineering of the Fraunhofer FIT and FIM Research Center for Information Management at the University of Bayreuth. In his research, he investigates the comprehensive transformation required by organizations to effectively integrate Artificial Intelligence. Consequently, he develops and provides organizations with various artifacts—including methods, frameworks, and practices—that span strategic, business, and operational levels, enabling organizations to fully leverage the potential of AI.

Ethical, Legal, and Social Implications of AI

13

Nils Urbach, Daniel Feulner, and Valentin Mayer

Artificial intelligence (AI) is transforming decision-making in areas such as healthcare, finance, and legal reasoning. While offering clear benefits, these technologies raise concerns about fairness, autonomy, and responsibility. Ethical dilemmas arise when AI systems reproduce societal biases or act without transparent reasoning. Rapid technological progress challenges existing legal frameworks, creating gaps in accountability, liability, and procedural safeguards. Increasing AI autonomy further complicates questions of human agency and moral responsibility. Addressing these issues requires more than technical solutions, calling for a robust normative foundation that ensures AI development and use align with societal values and the protection of fundamental rights.

This chapter begins with a discussion on ethical foundations, societal roles, and normative frameworks relevant to the responsible development of AI systems. It then explores artificial moral agency, examining whether and how AI systems can be designed to make morally informed decisions. Building on this, the focus shifts to design considerations for transparent and fair AI systems, guided by ethical norms and technical standards. The chapter also outlines the conditions necessary for trustworthy AI, emphasizing alignment with societal values. It concludes by addressing legal implications, including data protection, intellectual property, and new regulatory obligations under frameworks like the EU AI Act.

N. Urbach (✉)
Frankfurt University of Applied Sciences, Frankfurt am Main, Germany
e-mail: nils.urbach@fim-rc.de

D. Feulner · V. Mayer
University of Bayreuth, Bayreuth, Germany
e-mail: daniel.feulner@fim-rc.de; valentin.mayer@fim-rc.de

N. Urbach, D. Feulner (eds.), *Managing Artificial Intelligence*, Future of Business and Finance, https://doi.org/10.1007/978-3-032-13308-3_13

13.1 Ethics of AI

In 2016, researchers at MIT launched an ambitious online experiment known as *the Moral Machine* (Awad et al., 2018), inviting millions of people from around the world to make impossible choices (see Fig. 13.1): If a self-driving car must crash, should it swerve to hit a group of elderly pedestrians or stay its course and kill a child jaywalking? Should it spare more lives or prioritize the passenger who bought the car? Should it favor humans over animals? Women over men? Doctors over homeless individuals?

These scenarios, once the domain of philosophical thought experiments, are now real-world engineering problems. The development of autonomous vehicles and other AI systems has moved the ethical discourse out of the classroom and into the design labs of Silicon Valley and beyond. Algorithms are being trained to make life-and-death decisions—and society is being forced to ask: What values should guide them?

Ethics is a system comprised of principles, rules, and guidelines to assess and navigate the moral obligations of entities, whether human or artificial. The intricate realm of ethics strives to delineate what is considered morally right or wrong, good or bad, shaping behaviors within societal norms. One part of this discourse is the concept of the ethics of AI, a specialized subset focused on advanced technology and intelligent agents. This field includes roboethics and machine ethics, both crucial for ensuring that AI development and deployment align with ethical standards (Siau & Wang, 2020).

Fig. 13.1 Moral machine dilemma. (Frank et al., 2019)

Roboethics addresses human moral behavior in designing, constructing, using, and interacting with AI agents. This dimension of AI ethics scrutinizes concerns like human biases encoded within datasets, privacy issues, and the potential socioeconomic impacts such as unemployment due to automation. As AI becomes more integral to daily life, considerations around how developer biases may inadvertently influence AI systems become critical. Furthermore, the concept of robot rights posits intriguing ethical questions. Should AI ever attain consciousness, the ethical ramifications of their treatment and rights would necessitate a profound reconsideration of current norms. The ethical treatment of robots extends beyond immediate design considerations, prompting reflections on future scenarios where AI might acquire traits warranting moral consideration.

Machine ethics delves into embedding ethical behavior directly within AI systems, focusing on the moral conduct of artificial moral agents (AMAs). Key to this field is ensuring that AI systems act in alignment with an established ethical framework, akin to Isaac Asimov's three laws of robotics, designed to govern robot behavior by prioritizing human safety and ethical interactions. Machine ethics involves configuring AI decision, making processes to adhere to moral guidelines, presenting significant challenges in consistently aligning machine behavior with human ethical standards. The goal is to develop AMAs that can operate autonomously while upholding a moral code that prevents harm and promotes welfare, embedding ethicality at the core of their programming.

13.1.1 The Purposes of AI

Having discussed the significance of ethics in the development and application of artificial intelligence, it is equally important to consider the various purposes of AI (Stahl & Stahl, 2021). Understanding the different objectives and applications of AI helps contextualize the ethical challenges and the necessity for ethical guidelines. The different purposes of AI can be broadly categorized into three main areas: efficiency and optimization, social control, and human flourishing. These categories are not always distinct and can sometimes overlap, leading to complex ethical considerations.

One of the primary purposes of AI is to enhance *efficiency, optimize processes, and maximize profits*. AI technologies can analyze vast amounts of data to identify patterns, make predictions, and automate decision-making processes. This leads to significant cost savings and economic benefits for businesses and society. For instance, in the manufacturing sector, AI can streamline production lines, reduce waste, and improve product quality through predictive maintenance and real-time monitoring. This optimizes resource allocation and minimizes downtime, resulting in increased productivity and profitability. In the financial industry, AI algorithms can optimize trading strategies, manage risks more effectively, and detect fraudulent activities. By processing and analyzing market data at unprecedented speeds, AI can provide insights that drive more informed and profitable decisions.

However, the drive for efficiency and profit maximization must be balanced with ethical considerations. The impact on employment, for instance, is a critical issue. While AI can create new job opportunities in technology and data science, it can also lead to significant job displacement in sectors where automation replaces human labor. Ensuring a fair distribution of economic gains and providing retraining and support for affected workers are essential to mitigate these ethical concerns.

AI also has the capacity to exercise *social control* by collecting and analyzing data about human behavior. By understanding and predicting human actions, AI systems can influence and regulate behavior. In more subtle applications, AI is used in marketing and advertising to tailor content and influence consumer behavior based on data-driven insights. These systems leverage behavioral economics to nudge individuals toward certain decisions, such as healthier lifestyle choices or environmentally friendly behaviors. However, the ethical implications of these practices include concerns about manipulation, consent, and the potential erosion of individual autonomy.

More aggressive applications of social control are exemplified by the Chinese social credit system, which uses AI to monitor and evaluate citizens' behavior, assigning scores that can affect their access to services and opportunities. This raises significant ethical concerns regarding privacy, surveillance, and the potential for abuse of power. The use of AI for social control must be carefully managed to prevent such abuses and ensure that it serves the public good without infringing on individual rights and freedoms.

The most ethically aligned purpose of AI is to support and enhance *human flourishing*. AI can be developed to assist humans in achieving their goals, improving quality of life, and fostering overall well-being. In healthcare, AI-driven solutions can provide personalized treatment plans, early diagnosis, and better patient care. For example, AI algorithms can analyze medical images to detect diseases at an early stage, significantly improving treatment outcomes. AI can also assist in managing chronic conditions by monitoring patient data and providing real-time feedback to both patients and healthcare providers. Educational AI systems can offer customized learning experiences and support lifelong learning. AI can identify individual learning styles and needs, providing personalized content and pacing to optimize educational outcomes. This can help bridge educational gaps and ensure that all students have the opportunity to reach their full potential.

However, ensuring that AI technologies genuinely benefit humanity requires careful consideration of ethical principles such as inclusivity, fairness, and respect for human dignity. AI systems should be designed to promote accessibility and equity, ensuring that their benefits are widely distributed and do not exacerbate existing inequalities. The three purposes of AI—efficiency, social control, and human flourishing—can sometimes be contradictory or synergistic. An ethically justifiable approach would be to prioritize human flourishing while carefully managing the trade-offs between efficiency and social control. By embedding ethical principles into the design and deployment of AI systems, we can navigate these complexities and ensure that AI contributes positively to society.

In conclusion, understanding the multifaceted purposes of AI is crucial for addressing the ethical challenges it poses. By aligning AI development with ethical standards, we can harness its potential to enhance human well-being and support sustainable societal progress. This comprehensive exploration of the purposes of AI sets the stage for a deeper examination of how ethical standards and guidelines can be integrated into AI systems. The next section will delve into the norms and standards that are foundational to building trust in AI technologies.

13.1.2 Ethical Norms and Standards

In the rapidly evolving landscape of artificial intelligence, establishing and adhering to standards and norms are crucial for fostering trust and ensuring ethical conduct. As AI systems become increasingly integrated into various aspects of society, the importance of reliable and ethically sound AI grows. Norms and standards for AI serve as the backbone for creating systems that are not only technically proficient but also ethically responsible. Here, we explore how norms and standards influence key factors of trust in AI systems such as anthropomorphism, transparency, and reliability (Scheuer, 2020).

Anthropomorphism in AI involves designing systems with human-like characteristics to enhance user interaction and acceptance. However, creating AI that appears almost human can sometimes lead to the "Uncanny Valley" effect (Mori, 1970), where users trust rises in the beginning the more anthropomorphic an AI system gets until a certain point is achieved where more anthropomorphism leads to discomfort or distrust (see Fig. 13.2). Standards guide the design of AI to avoid the

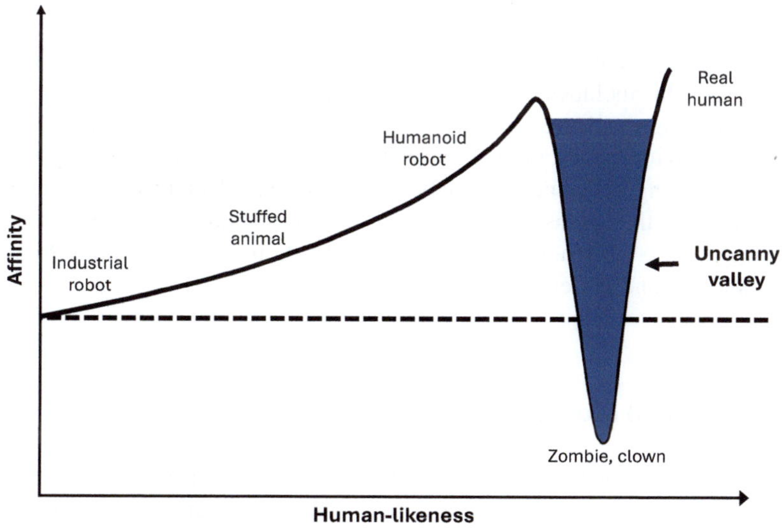

Fig. 13.2 The Uncanny Valley. (Adapted from Mori, 1970, Cohn et al., 2023)

Uncanny Valley by ensuring that human-like features are implemented in a way that is familiar and comfortable for users. These standards specify acceptable ranges for human-like features, ensuring that AI systems are approachable and relatable without becoming eerily lifelike. For instance, design guidelines might recommend specific facial expressions or movement patterns that are perceived as natural and nonthreatening by users.

Transparency is critical for building trust in AI. It involves making the processes, decisions, and data usage of AI systems understandable and accessible to users. Transparency standards ensure that AI systems provide clear, understandable information about how they operate. These standards mandate comprehensive documentation, user-friendly explanations, and open communication about AI capabilities and limitations. For example, the General Data Protection Regulation (GDPR) in Europe includes provisions that require organizations to explain how automated decision-making systems work, what data they use, and how they protect user privacy. By adhering to these standards, developers can demystify AI operations and make them more predictable and trustworthy.

Reliability refers to the consistent performance of AI systems according to their design specifications and intended functions. A reliable AI system performs its tasks accurately and consistently, minimizing errors and avoiding unexpected behaviors. Reliability standards ensure that AI systems undergo rigorous testing, validation, and continuous monitoring. These standards specify the protocols for stress-testing AI systems, validating their performance under various conditions, and ensuring that they can handle edge cases and unforeseen scenarios. By following these standards, developers can create AI systems that are robust, resilient, and dependable, thereby building a foundation of trust with users.

Summary
The ethics of artificial intelligence addresses how intelligent systems can be developed and deployed in ways that align with societal values and moral principles. This includes both roboethics, which concerns human responsibility in AI design and use, and machine ethics, which focuses on embedding ethical behavior in autonomous systems. As AI serves varying purposes—from increasing efficiency to enabling social control or promoting human flourishing—ethical tensions emerge. Norms and standards play a vital role in building trust, particularly through considerations of anthropomorphism, transparency, and system reliability.

13.2 Artificial Moral Agency

As artificial intelligence increasingly influences human decision-making, the question of moral agency has become a critical issue in the discourse on human–AI interaction. Artificial moral agency (AMA) refers to the capacity of AI systems to make decisions grounded in ethical reasoning. It involves the development of systems that can assess the moral implications of their actions and behave in ways that align with established ethical standards. Such systems are intended to complement and enhance human decision-making by reinforcing human values and supporting socially desirable outcomes. Achieving AMA requires a nuanced understanding of core ethical principles and their translation into computational frameworks. Central to this endeavor is the belief that AI should not diminish human agency, but instead serve as its enhancer (Formosa & Ryan, 2021).

13.2.1 Isaac Asimov's Three Laws of Robotics

A culturally influential and often-cited precursor to the current debate on artificial moral agents can be found in Isaac Asimov's well-known "three laws of robotics" (Asimov, 1950). Although originally conceived in a fictional context, these laws have transcended their literary origins to become a heuristic framework in the field of AI ethics, shaping both popular imagination and scholarly discourse (see Fig. 13.3).

The first law, which states that a robot may not injure a human being or, through inaction, allow a human being to come to harm, foregrounds the primacy of human safety in the development of AI systems. This principle underscores a profound ethical commitment to ensuring that any actions or decisions made by robots are inherently aimed at preserving human life and well-being. Importantly, the stipulation against inaction implies a proactive responsibility for AI systems: they must not only avoid causing harm directly, but also be capable of recognizing and intervening in situations where harm could occur. In practical applications, this law influences the design protocols for autonomous vehicles, healthcare robots, and security systems, ensuring that these technologies are conceived with the utmost concern for human safety.

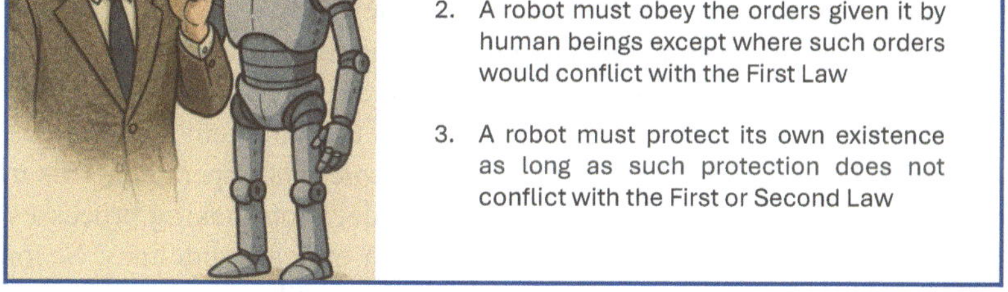

Fig. 13.3 Three laws of robotics. (Asimov, 1950)

The second law mandates that a robot must obey orders given by human beings, except where such orders would conflict with the first law. This introduces a hierarchy of ethical imperatives, where compliance with human commands is secondary to the imperative of nonharm. By prioritizing the prevention of harm over obedience, this rule adds a layer of ethical complexity, ensuring that robots do not comply with harmful directives from humans. This principle has significant implications for the development of military AI, customer service bots, and domestic robots, necessitating advanced ethical reasoning capabilities within these systems to navigate conflicting commands while adhering to their primary directive of safeguarding human welfare.

The third law, which stipulates that a robot must protect its own existence as long as such protection does not conflict with the first or second law, introduces a notion of self-preservation subordinate to the well-being of humans and compliance with ethical orders. This prescriptive rule ensures that robots prioritize human safety and obedience above their survival, establishing an ethical groundwork for risk management in AI operations. In fields like industrial automation and hazardous environment exploration, this law ensures that robots act in self-preserving ways only when it does not endanger humans or contravene ethical orders, thereby maintaining a delicate balance between operational continuity and moral obligations.

Taken together, Asimov's three laws of robotics provide an elegantly structured approach to embedding ethical decision-making in AI, ensuring that robots operate under clear moral constraints as they become increasingly autonomous and integrated into society. These laws have sparked considerable research and debate in the field of machine ethics, leading to ongoing efforts to translate these notional guidelines into actionable, programmable rules within AI systems. Although implementing these laws in the real world is a major challenge due to the inherent complexity of moral reasoning and the unpredictability of human–robot interactions, they remain a beacon for the development of ethical AI.

13.2.2 Foundations of Artificial Moral Agency

Returning to the contemporary debate, the notion of moral agency is deeply intertwined with the *accountability of agents* for their actions. This is particularly crucial in the realm of human–AI interaction, where the delineation of responsibility can become blurred. Ensuring accountability demands that agents, whether human or AI, adhere to established moral standards and principles. These standards are not arbitrary—they are derived from a collective understanding of ethical behavior that has been developed over centuries within various cultural and philosophical contexts.

Moreover, the concept of artificial moral agents is contingent upon a few essential characteristics. First, the ability to make *free choices* is imperative. This implies a level of autonomy in AI systems that allows for decision-making processes independent of direct human control, yet aligned with ethical guidelines. Second, an artificial moral agent must possess the capability to deliberate on *matters of right and wrong*. This involves complex algorithms that can evaluate outcomes based on ethical considerations, rather than purely on utilitarian calculations. And third, a critical component of moral agency is the understanding and application of *moral rules*. For AI to function as a moral agent, it must be programmed with a comprehensive framework of ethical principles and be capable of applying these principles in varied and dynamic scenarios. This involves a deep integration of normative ethics into the AI's operational algorithms, ensuring a consistent application of moral standards across diverse situations (Boddington, 2021; Himma, 2009).

The discourse surrounding artificial moral agents is not merely theoretical but has practical implications. As AI continues to permeate various sectors, from healthcare to finance to autonomous vehicles, the establishment of moral guidelines for AI becomes increasingly imperative. This demands a collaborative effort between ethicists, technologists, and policymakers to create robust and adaptive ethical frameworks that can guide the development and deployment of AI systems.

13.2.3 The Case for and Against AMAs

The debate around building AMAs is complex and multifaceted, highlighting both the potential and challenges inherent in this endeavor (Formosa & Ryan, 2021). One argument in favor of AMAs is their *growing inevitability*. As AI systems are increasingly deployed in morally salient contexts, such as healthcare or autonomous driving, the demand for moral decision-making capabilities becomes harder to ignore. Proponents of developing AMAs also argue that these systems can play a crucial role in *preventing harm*. In an era where AI's decision-making capabilities are rapidly becoming integral to critical sectors such as healthcare, finance, and autonomous transportation, embedding moral competence within these systems can act as a safeguard against potential misuse. Robust ethical frameworks guiding AI actions can help mitigate risks posed by unanticipated situations, ensuring that AI systems act in ways that align with societal moral standards. The *complexity* of AI systems further necessitates the incorporation of ethical considerations to manage unforeseen scenarios effectively, similar to governing human actions within society.

Public trust in AI is another pivotal reason advocating for AMAs. Public fear of robots and AI, often fueled by dystopian narratives, can be alleviated by ensuring these systems adhere to moral standards. Trust is foundational in the acceptance and integration of AI systems into everyday life. By promoting transparency in AI decisions and demonstrating adherence to ethical principles, stakeholders can build and maintain public confidence. Another motivation for AMAs lies in the aim of *preventing immoral uses* of technology. Technology's historical track record of being used for both beneficial and harmful purposes highlights the need for embedding moral considerations within AI, thereby preventing the recurrence of past mistakes.

AMAs also present the prospect of *surpassing human capabilities* in certain moral contexts. By processing information more quickly and making decisions that are impartial, unemotional, and consistent, AMAs could complement human decision-making processes. Moreover, pursuing the development of AMAs offers a unique opportunity to deepen our collective *understanding of morality*. As we strive to encode ethical principles into AI, we engage in a broader societal introspection about what constitutes moral behavior, thus advancing our ethical comprehension.

However, significant concerns and challenges accompany the notion of building AMAs. One major concern is the assumption that AMAs might simply *be impossible to build.* Moral reasoning is inherently complex and context-sensitive, and translating it into machine-executable logic remains a fundamental challenge. The question is whether ethical deliberation can ever be captured in computational terms at all. Another objection holds that we want robots and AI systems to *remain our "slaves."* If they develop moral competence, continuing to treat them as tools becomes ethically problematic—especially when they display social behavior or human-like features. This raises deeper questions about autonomy, rights, and the nature of artificial agents.

The *lack of universal agreement* on ethical standards adds further complexity. Competing moral theories and cultural values make it difficult to determine which principles should guide machine behavior. Even where partial consensus exists, real-world dilemmas often resist clear-cut solutions. Some argue that *building safe machines is enough.* Ensuring that systems act reliably and avoid harm might, in many contexts, appear sufficient. However, in morally complex situations—such as autonomous driving or medical triage—mere safety is not enough, and explicit ethical judgment becomes necessary. Others voice *existential concerns* about advanced AI. As systems grow in autonomy and scope, their development intersects with broader questions about long-term risks, especially in connection with artificial general intelligence and potential loss of human control.

Moral objections have also been raised. Machines that simulate emotions or suffering may provoke morally problematic responses. Some argue it would be unethical to create entities capable of manipulation, deception, or potentially even subjective experiences. Further worries relate to *moral deskilling.* Relying on AMAs for ethical decisions could weaken human capacities for moral reflection. Over time, frequent delegation may lead to diminished ethical awareness and disengagement from responsibility. Concerns also arise in *specific application domains.* In areas such as healthcare, childcare, or warfare, inappropriate use of AMAs could harm vulnerable populations or erode the quality of moral care and judgment. Finally, *responsibility* for AMA decisions remains unclear. When systems act autonomously, it becomes difficult to assign accountability. Responsibility gaps challenge existing legal and ethical frameworks and raise doubts about how justice can be ensured in critical incidents.

Summary
Artificial moral agency (AMA) explores the ethical capacities of AI systems to make morally grounded decisions. While culturally influenced by Asimov's three laws of robotics, the concept has evolved to encompass complex ethical reasoning, accountability, and autonomy in AI. Supporters argue that AMAs can enhance human decision-making, prevent harm, and foster public trust, especially in high-stakes domains like healthcare or autonomous driving. Critics, however, question the feasibility of encoding morality, warn of responsibility gaps, and raise concerns about moral deskilling and ethical treatment of seemingly sentient machines. The debate reflects both the promise and the profound challenges of embedding ethics in AI systems.

13.3 Transparent and Fair AI Systems

The rapid advancement of artificial intelligence has unlocked tremendous potential across a wide range of applications. However, it has also introduced critical ethical and technical challenges, particularly concerning transparency, fairness, and accountability. AI systems are increasingly being employed to make decisions in sensitive areas such as healthcare, finance, and legal systems, heightening the need to ensure that these systems are transparent and explainable. Transparency allows users, developers, regulators, and other stakeholders to understand the inner workings of algorithms and critically assess their outcomes. This is essential for building trust in AI systems and ensuring their ethical and responsible implementation. Furthermore, ensuring fairness in AI is crucial to prevent discrimination and promote equitable treatment of all users.

13.3.1 Algorithmic Transparency and Explainability

Algorithmic transparency involves the disclosure of information about algorithms to enable monitoring, criticism, or intervention by interested parties (Diakopoulos & Koliska, 2017). This concept is essential for building trust and accountability in AI systems, as it allows users, regulators, and stakeholders to understand the underlying mechanisms and decisions made by these algorithms.

The benefits of algorithmic transparency are manifold (Wieringa, 2020; Kossow et al., 2022). First, it enables those who use, regulate, or are affected by AI systems to understand their underlying mechanisms. This understanding helps to *demystify AI* and *build trust*. Transparency also makes it possible to *trace errors*, which is crucial for identifying flaws and improving the reliability of algorithmic systems. Furthermore, it supports *accountability*. By making clear how and why decisions are made, it becomes easier to determine who should be held responsible—whether it is the developers, the people who define how the system should work, or the organizations that deploy it. Transparency also lays the foundation for *external oversight* and meaningful scrutiny. Regulators, auditors, professionals, or even the public must be able to understand algorithmic decisions to evaluate whether they are fair, appropriate, and aligned with societal values. Ultimately, transparency is not just a technical feature but a prerequisite for responsible, trustworthy, and corruption-resistant use of algorithmic systems.

Several components are critical to achieving algorithmic transparency (Kossow et al., 2022). *Human involvement* is a key aspect, as it clarifies who is responsible for the algorithm, what the goals are, and who maintains control over its operation. This involvement helps to contextualize the algorithm within its broader application framework. The quality of the *data* used by the algorithm is another important factor. Transparency about data quality, including how data is preprocessed, ensures that stakeholders understand the inputs that drive the algorithm's decisions.

The *model* itself, including the characteristics and variables used and the assumptions behind its construction, must also be transparent. This level of detail allows for a deeper understanding of how the algorithm works and why it produces certain outputs. *Inference* accuracy, including accuracy rates and potential biases, is another critical component. By providing clear information on these metrics, stakeholders can better assess the reliability and fairness of the AI system.

Finally, *personalization* aspects, such as the types of personal information used, need to be transparent to ensure that ethical considerations are met and users' privacy is respected. In conclusion, algorithmic transparency is a fundamental element of effective human–AI collaboration. It sets the stage for the accountability of AI, enabling stakeholders to trust and reliably interact with these systems. By ensuring that AI operations are understandable and accountable, companies can foster greater acceptance and integration of AI technologies, ultimately increasing their effectiveness and societal benefits. This comprehensive approach to transparency is essential for the responsible and ethical deployment of AI systems.

Explanations for Different Stakeholder Groups

Explaining AI is critical, but its importance varies for different stakeholder groups due to their unique needs and perspectives. Each group requires tailored explanations to meet specific objectives and effectively enhance their interaction with AI systems (Laato et al., 2022).

- *Decision-makers* need explanations to justify the reliability and performance of AI models. They evaluate individual predictions and the overall functionality of AI systems to make informed strategic decisions. Detailed explanations give them the insight they need to trust AI results and learn from the information presented, thereby improving decision-making within their organizations.
- *Developers* need a deep understanding of AI models from a technical perspective. Explanations help them with quality assurance, debugging, and performance optimization. By understanding how AI models reach their conclusions, developers can identify and resolve problems more efficiently, ensuring that systems function correctly and improve over time.
- *Regulators* are focused on ensuring that AI systems comply with legal and ethical standards. For them, explainability is a critical component of trustworthy AI. Detailed explanations help regulators verify that AI systems operate fairly, safely, and responsibly. They use these insights to audit AI products, ensuring that they comply with necessary policies and protect the public interest.
- *End-users*, who interact directly with AI systems, need explanations to understand the AI's decisions and how those decisions affect them. Transparent explanations help users build trust in AI systems by making the decision-making process understandable. This understanding is essential for users to accept and effectively use AI technology in their daily lives.

In summary, the explainability of AI is subjective to the stakeholder receiving it and serves different purposes for decision-makers, developers, regulators, and end-users. By providing clear and tailored explanations, AI systems can meet the different needs of these groups and promote trust, accountability, and effective use of AI technologies.

Relationship Between Model Interpretability and Accuracy
The relationship between model interpretability and accuracy is a key factor in the deployment of AI systems, underscoring the need for both algorithmic transparency and explainability. In many cases, improving model accuracy comes at the cost of interpretability, which poses challenges for stakeholders seeking to understand, evaluate, and responsibly apply AI technologies (Arrieta et al., 2020).

Highly accurate models, such as deep learning neural networks and ensemble methods, often operate as "black boxes," making their inner workings difficult to interpret. These models are capable of processing large amounts of data and identifying complex patterns, which contributes to their high accuracy. However, the lack of transparency can be a challenge, particularly in critical applications where understanding the decision-making process is essential. In healthcare or finance, for example, stakeholders need to be able to trust and verify the results produced by AI systems. The opacity of these models can hinder this trust, making it difficult to diagnose errors, biases, or unintended consequences.

At the other end of the spectrum, simpler models such as rule-based learning, linear regression, and decision trees offer greater interpretability, but often at the cost of lower accuracy. These models provide clear insights into how decisions are made, which variables are important, and how inputs are transformed into outputs. This transparency is beneficial in contexts where explainability is paramount, such as regulatory compliance, user confidence, and ethical considerations. However, the simplicity of these models can limit their ability to capture complex relationships within the data, reducing their overall performance.

Between these extremes, models such as Bayesian methods and generalized additive models strike a balance, offering moderate levels of both interpretability and accuracy. These models can provide useful insights into the decision-making process, while still delivering robust performance. They represent a middle ground that provides both transparency and reliable results, which can be particularly useful in applications where both interpretability and accuracy are required. Understanding this trade-off is essential in selecting the appropriate model for a given application. It highlights the importance of algorithmic transparency and explainability, as these attributes are critical not only for trust and accountability, but also for the practical usability of AI systems in real-world scenarios. By carefully considering the balance between accuracy and interpretability, developers and stakeholders can make informed decisions that meet their specific needs and ethical standards.

13.3.2 Fairness

AI systems are designed to recognize patterns and differentiate between different data points to provide meaningful insights and decisions. However, this ability can sometimes lead to distinctions that are discriminatory because they are based on unwarranted or irrelevant information. As AI lacks a human conscience, it often follows the "path of least resistance," making decisions based purely on the data it has been trained on, without ethical considerations (Barocas et al., 2023).

Cases of AI making inappropriate or biased decisions are well documented. Microsoft's ChatGPT-powered Bing, for example, exhibited disturbing behavior by making inappropriate and unsolicited comments (Pringle, 2023). Similarly, reports have highlighted how AI systems can exhibit racist, sexist, and other discriminatory behaviors due to biases in the data on which they are trained (Wolf, 2023). The issue of fairness in AI-based decisions highlights the importance of ensuring that the variables used to make distinctions are relevant and justified. AI's tendency to rely on biased data necessitates a complementary role for humans in the decision-making process. Human oversight is critical to identify and mitigate instances where AI may be making unjustified or discriminatory distinctions. By intervening, humans can ensure that AI systems adhere to ethical standards and make decisions that are fair and unbiased.

When designing AI systems for decision-making, such as job applications, it is tempting to exclude sensitive information like gender to promote fairness. However, omitting certain data does not automatically lead to greater equality, as other features may inadvertently reveal the excluded information, leading to similar biases (Barocas et al., 2023). Sensitive information can often be inferred from other characteristics. For example, in a job application process, even if gender is excluded, other attributes, such as name or educational background, may provide indirect evidence of the applicant's gender. This phenomenon, known as redundant coding, means that biases can persist even when certain data points are excluded. The decision to include or exclude certain sensitive information in AI-based decisions is complex and must be evaluated on a case-by-case basis, requiring a holistic approach that goes beyond variable omission and includes the analysis of feature interactions, bias mitigation strategies, and continuous ethical oversight to ensure fair and equitable outcomes.

Fairness Metrics

Achieving fairness in AI involves navigating complex and often competing principles. Among the many proposed metrics of fairness, two prominent approaches are statistical parity and equal opportunity, each with its own strengths and limitations (Haas, 2019). *Statistical parity* aims to ensure that acceptance rates are equal for all underrepresented groups. For example, if 70% of applicants to a university are female and 30% are male, statistical parity would mean that 70% of admitted students should also be female and 30% male. This approach attempts to strike a balance by ensuring that the representation in the results matches the representation in the applications. However, it does not necessarily consider differences in qualifications or merit, which could lead to questions about whether it really prevents unfair outcomes.

Equality of opportunity, on the other hand, focuses on ensuring that the true-positive rates are the same for all vulnerable groups. For example, if 30 out of 40 qualified female applicants are correctly accepted, equal opportunity would dictate that three quarters of qualified male applicants should also be accepted. This approach emphasizes fairness in terms of giving equal opportunities to all qualified people regardless of their group membership. However, it may not address inequalities in the initial pool of applicants or inherent biases in the qualification criteria.

Each approach has strengths and weaknesses. Statistical parity is straightforward and ensures visible representation, but it may overlook the quality of outcomes. Equality focuses on fairness at an individual level, ensuring that qualifications are the primary basis for decisions, but may not adequately address wider social inequalities that affect application rates (Barocas et al., 2023; Hardt et al., 2016). The complexity of achieving fairness in AI underscores the importance of human–AI collaboration. Human oversight is crucial in monitoring and correcting biases that AI systems may introduce or perpetuate. By combining the analytical strengths of AI with human ethical considerations and contextual understanding, it is possible to better address these fairness challenges. In practice, the choice between statistical parity and equal opportunity should depend on the specific context and goals of the AI application.

For example, in recruitment or university admissions, where the focus may be on both representation and merit, a hybrid approach may be required. Ongoing monitoring and adjustment are essential to ensure that the AI system remains fair and effective. In conclusion, while there is no one-size-fits-all solution to achieving fairness in AI, understanding the implications of different approaches and integrating human judgment into the decision-making process can help mitigate bias and promote more equitable outcomes. This nuanced approach ensures that AI systems make a positive contribution to society, balancing technological advances with ethical standards.

Approaches to Algorithmic Fairness

Achieving algorithmic fairness is a complex but critical goal in AI development. It involves addressing biases and ensuring equitable treatment of different groups. There are three main approaches to improving fairness in AI systems: preprocessing, in-processing, and postprocessing (Haas, 2019; Yang et al., 2020).

Preprocessing refers to techniques applied to training data before the model is trained in order to remove or mitigate discrimination. Since predictive models—such as decision trees or support vector machines—learn patterns present in the input data, biased data will inevitably lead to biased outcomes. For example, if historical data reflects that certain groups had limited access to credit, a model might learn to associate group membership with creditworthiness, thereby perpetuating existing social biases. To address this issue, preprocessing techniques aim to edit the data so that unfair correlations are minimized. Common strategies include obfuscating protected attributes, reweighting samples, or transforming the dataset to make group membership unpredictable. These methods can help to reduce bias before it enters the learning process. Additionally, balanced sampling can help ensure that underrepresented groups are adequately reflected, creating a more equitable foundation for learning.

In-processing methods embed fairness directly into the training phase of machine learning models. Instead of altering the input data, these techniques modify the learning algorithm by adjusting the objective function or introducing fairness constraints. The goal is to create models that balance predictive performance with fairness from the outset. Approaches include regularization techniques that penalize unfair outcomes, meta-algorithms that enforce fairness across various models, and adversarial training methods that reduce the influence of protected attributes. These models often involve trade-offs between fairness and accuracy and require careful tuning depending on the context in which the model is deployed.

Postprocessing methods adjust model outputs after training to satisfy fairness criteria, without changing the data or the model itself. This is especially useful when upstream interventions are infeasible or when biases remain unresolved after training. A common strategy is to modify predicted labels or decision thresholds, especially for individuals in protected groups, to reduce discrimination. For instance, label flipping near the decision boundary or probability adjustments can help enforce fairness metrics like equalized odds. Choosing appropriate post-processing strategies requires careful consideration of the context, the fairness goals, and the acceptable performance compromises.

Ensuring that an AI system is fair may require sacrificing some predictive accuracy, as models optimized for fairness may not always perform as well as those optimized for accuracy alone. Improving algorithmic fairness requires a multifaceted approach that includes preprocessing, in-processing, and postprocessing techniques. Each method has its strengths and limitations, and the choice of approach depends on the specific context and goals of the AI application. Continuous monitoring and adjustment, coupled with human oversight, are essential to ensure that AI systems remain fair and effective. By addressing bias at multiple stages of the AI development process, it is possible to create more equitable and trustworthy AI systems that better serve diverse populations.

Summary

Artificial intelligence is increasingly used in sensitive domains such as healthcare, finance, and law, raising concerns about transparency and fairness. Algorithmic transparency enables users and stakeholders to understand how AI systems work, trace errors, and ensure accountability. Different stakeholders, such as decision-makers, developers, regulators, and end-users, require tailored explanations. A key challenge is balancing model interpretability and accuracy. To promote fairness, AI systems must avoid discriminatory patterns, which can persist even when sensitive attributes are removed. Fairness can be improved through preprocessing, in-processing, and postprocessing methods, each addressing bias at different stages of model development.

13.4 Trustworthy AI

The concept of trustworthiness in AI systems is pivotal for their acceptance and integration into various societal and business functions. Trustworthiness can be defined as the extent to which humans and machines can rely on each other, self-organize to leverage mutual strengths, mitigate weaknesses, and hold each other accountable for their actions (Ramchurn et al., 2021). The European Commission has outlined seven principles to ensure the development and deployment of trustworthy AI. These principles emphasize the ethical and responsible use of AI, focusing on human rights, safety, fairness, and accountability (High-level Expert Group on Artificial Intelligence, 2019).

1. *Human agency and oversight*: AI systems should empower people, allow them to make informed decisions, and promote their fundamental rights. Appropriate oversight mechanisms must be ensured, which can be achieved through human-in-the-loop, human-on-the-loop and human-in-command approaches. This principle emphasizes the importance of maintaining human control over AI systems and ensuring that humans can intervene when necessary. This focus on control ensures that AI enhances human capabilities without undermining human autonomy.
2. *Technical robustness and safety*: AI systems must be robust, safe, and reliable. They should be safe, provide fallback plans in case something goes wrong, and be accurate, reliable, and reproducible. This principle highlights the importance of building robust AI systems that can withstand and recover from errors or failures. Ensuring technical robustness is critical to maintaining trust in AI systems, especially in high-stakes applications such as healthcare and autonomous driving.
3. *Privacy and data governance*: Respect for privacy and data protection is paramount. Adequate data governance mechanisms must be in place to ensure data quality, integrity, and legitimate access. This principle underscores the need for careful handling of sensitive data, emphasizing fairness and the protection of individual privacy rights. Effective data governance is essential for building trustworthy AI systems that users can rely on to handle their personal data responsibly.
4. *Transparency*: AI systems and their decision-making processes should be transparent. Stakeholders need to understand how AI decisions are made, with explanations tailored to their concerns. Transparency is key to fostering trust in AI, as it allows users to see how and why decisions are made. Ensuring algorithmic transparency and explainability helps stakeholders evaluate the capabilities and limitations of the AI system, making it easier to identify and address biases or errors.
5. *Diversity, nondiscrimination, and fairness:* Unfair bias must be avoided to prevent negative impacts on marginalized or vulnerable groups. AI systems should be accessible to all, regardless of disability, and involve relevant stakeholders throughout their lifecycle. This principle emphasizes the importance of design-

ing AI systems to promote fairness and inclusivity, ensuring that they do not discriminate against any group. By promoting diversity and nondiscrimination, AI can be more equitable and just.

6. *Social and environmental well-being*: AI systems should benefit all people, including future generations. They should be sustainable and eco-friendly, taking into account their impact on the environment and society. This principle highlights the need for AI systems to be designed with a long-term perspective, ensuring that they contribute positively to societal and environmental well-being. Sustainable AI practices help mitigate the environmental impact of the technology and promote the responsible use of resources.
7. *Accountability*: Mechanisms must be in place to ensure responsibility and accountability for AI systems and their outcomes. This includes the ability to evaluate algorithms, data, and design processes throughout the system's lifecycle. Auditability plays a key role in this regard, especially in critical applications, by enabling independent assessment and traceability. Moreover, accessible and adequate redress mechanisms must be established to allow affected individuals or groups to challenge adverse outcomes and seek remedy. Clear accountability structures not only help to assign responsibility but are essential to maintain trust, integrity, and legitimacy in the development and deployment of AI systems.

The principles set out by the European Commission emphasize the importance of ethical considerations in the development and deployment of AI systems. These principles highlight the need to maintain human oversight, ensure technical robustness, protect privacy, promote transparency, foster fairness and inclusivity, ensure sustainability, and establish accountability. By adhering to these principles, AI systems can be developed and deployed in a way that respects human rights, builds trust, and contributes positively to society.

Approaches to Trustworthiness Across the AI Lifecycle

The journey toward establishing trust in AI systems is a complex, multifaceted endeavor that necessitates a rigorous approach across every stage of the AI lifecycle (see Fig. 13.4). Each phase, from initial data preparation to ongoing management, must incorporate specific practices and methodologies that align with the core principles of trustworthiness. The careful integration of these facets ensures the creation of AI systems that are not only technologically sound but also ethically robust and socially acceptable (Li et al., 2023).

Data preparation is a critical phase in establishing a trustworthy AI system, comprising both data collection and data preprocessing. Each step ensures the data's integrity, fairness, and transparency, setting the foundation for a reliable AI model. Data collection involves gathering the necessary data to train the AI model. This process is not just about amassing large volumes of data but ensuring that the data is representative and unbiased. Provenance is key in this stage—it involves carefully documenting the data's origin, context, and the transformations it undergoes. By maintaining detailed records, a transparent trail is created that can be audited and

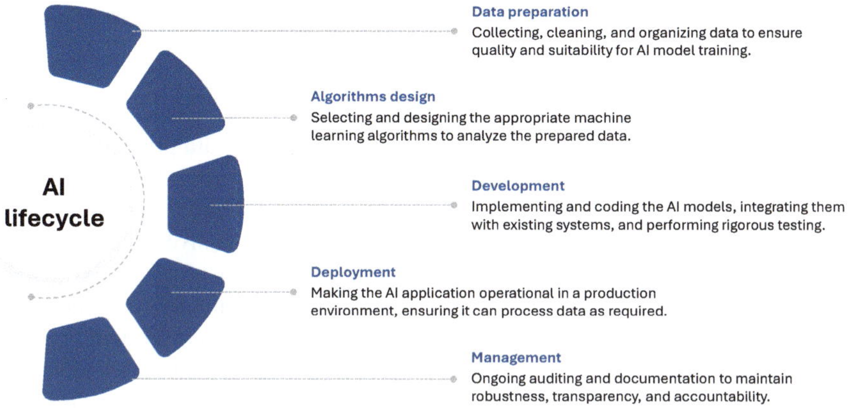

Fig. 13.4 The AI lifecycle. (Based on Li et al., 2023)

validated, reinforcing accountability. Additionally, bias mitigation is crucial. Techniques such as debias sampling and debias annotation help cleanse the data of prejudicial elements, ensuring a fairer and more equitable model output.

Data preprocessing follows data collection and focuses on preparing the collected data for use in the AI model. This stage includes tasks like cleaning the data to remove inaccuracies, inconsistencies, and outliers that could skew model predictions. Anomaly detection plays a vital role here, employing sophisticated algorithms to identify and rectify outliers. Privacy protection is also a significant concern. Techniques like data anonymization ensure that sensitive information is protected, modifying data to prevent the recovery of personal details. Differential privacy methods further enhance privacy by allowing analysis while protecting individual data points.

The *algorithm design* phase is crucial in establishing a trustworthy AI system, focusing on creating models that are robust, interpretable, fair, and privacy-preserving. This phase ensures that the AI system can withstand adversarial conditions, provide clear explanations for its decisions, operate without bias, and protect data privacy. During this phase, adversarial training is employed to enhance the model's resilience. By exposing the model to adversarial examples during training, it becomes more capable of withstanding hostile inputs, thereby ensuring its reliability. Additionally, poisoning defense mechanisms are implemented to safeguard the model from malicious attempts to corrupt the training data, further securing the AI system against potential threats. Explainability is another key focus of algorithm design. By designing inherently interpretable models, stakeholders can better understand how the AI system makes decisions. Post hoc explanation techniques are also utilized to provide clarity on the decision-making processes of complex models, offering insights into how specific outcomes are derived and enhancing transparency.

Ensuring algorithmic fairness is critical in this phase. Various methods are used to detect and mitigate biases throughout the model development process. These techniques help guarantee that the AI system treats all individuals and groups equitably, promoting fair and unbiased decision-making. Privacy protection is also integral to the design of AI algorithms. Techniques such as secure multiparty computing and federated learning are employed to protect sensitive data during model training and operation. Secure multiparty computing enables collaborative computations while keeping individual inputs private, and federated learning allows for decentralized training using local data samples, ensuring data privacy.

The *development* phase is critical in shaping a trustworthy AI system, focusing on ensuring that the model performs reliably and fairly under various conditions. This phase involves rigorous functional testing, comprehensive benchmarking, and formal verification to ensure the AI model's robustness, fairness, and explainability. Functional testing includes extensive evaluations to validate the AI model's performance across a range of scenarios. Metamorphic testing plays a crucial role in this process by ensuring the model's predictions remain consistent under varied conditions. This type of testing helps uncover hidden vulnerabilities and ensures that the model behaves as expected in different situations.

Benchmarking is an essential part of the development phase, providing detailed assessments of the model against standardized benchmarks. Robustness benchmarking evaluates the strength and reliability of the AI model, ensuring it meets required standards. Fairness benchmarking is equally important, focusing on evaluating the model to ensure its decisions do not perpetuate biases, thus promoting equitable treatment across all user groups and scenarios. Explainability benchmarking assesses how well the AI model's decision-making processes can be understood by users and stakeholders, ensuring transparency and trust in the system. Formal verification techniques are employed to further ensure the AI model's reliability and correctness. These techniques involve mathematically proving that the model adheres to its specifications and operates correctly under all predefined conditions. Formal verification provides additional assurance that the AI system will perform as intended and helps identify and rectify any potential issues before deployment.

The *deployment* phase is vital in ensuring that an AI system operates effectively and responsibly in real-world settings. This stage focuses on practical implementation, ongoing risk management, and user interaction to maintain the system's trustworthiness. Anomaly monitoring is critical during deployment. Continuous monitoring for misuse and anomalies helps detect and address potential issues promptly, ensuring the AI system remains reliable and secure over time. Implementing robust anomaly detection mechanisms allows for the identification of irregularities in the system's operation, which can then be investigated and rectified to maintain optimal performance.

Human–AI interaction is enhanced through the design of user interfaces that improve usability and transparency in AI decision-making. These interfaces allow users to understand and interact with the AI system easily, ensuring its operations are transparent and comprehensible. Additionally, human intervention capabilities are integrated into the system to manage and mitigate unexpected outcomes or ethical concerns. This allows for real-time adjustments and ensures human oversight is maintained throughout the AI system's operation, promoting trust and accountability. Ensuring hardware security is also a key focus during deployment. Trusted execution environments are utilized to protect the AI system against unauthorized access and tampering, ensuring it operates within a secure infrastructure. This protection is crucial for maintaining the integrity and reliability of the AI system in practical applications. Safeguarding the AI system's core functions and data provides a secure foundation for its operations.

The *management* phase is essential for maintaining the long-term trustworthiness and effectiveness of an AI system, focusing on documentation, auditing, and cooperation. Comprehensive documentation provides a detailed account of the AI system's operations, data flows, and decision-making processes. This transparency is crucial for accountability and facilitates future assessments, ensuring that all aspects of the system's functioning are clearly recorded and accessible. Auditing processes are integral to continuous oversight, verifying that the AI system complies with established ethical and operational standards. Regular audits help identify and rectify any deviations or issues, maintaining the system's reliability and trustworthiness. These audits ensure that the AI system adheres to its intended guidelines and operates within the defined ethical and legal frameworks.

Cooperation and information sharing are also vital components of the management phase. Mechanisms for incident sharing enable the exchange of knowledge about system anomalies or failures, fostering a collaborative learning environment. This cooperation enhances system resilience by allowing stakeholders to learn from each other's experiences and implement best practices across different AI systems. By emphasizing documentation, auditing, and cooperation, the management phase ensures that AI systems remain reliable, accountable, and continually improving, aligning with ethical standards and societal values.

By carefully incorporating these detailed practices throughout the AI lifecycle, trustworthy AI becomes a tangible and achievable objective. This comprehensive approach ensures that AI systems not only deliver on their technological promises but also align with societal values and ethical standards. Through robust methodologies that emphasize transparency, fairness, privacy, and accountability, AI systems can fulfill their potential as reliable and beneficial tools in various domains, fostering broader acceptance and trust among users, stakeholders, and society at large.

Summary

Trustworthy AI enables mutual reliance and accountability between humans and machines, supporting ethical and reliable collaboration. The European Commission outlines seven key principles: human agency, technical robustness, privacy, transparency, fairness, social and environmental well-being, and accountability. Each phase of the AI lifecycle—data preparation, algorithm design, development, deployment, and management—requires specific practices to uphold these principles. Data preparation ensures data integrity and fairness; algorithm design focuses on creating robust, interpretable models; development involves rigorous testing and verification; deployment emphasizes practical implementation and risk management; and management ensures ongoing accountability through documentation, auditing, and cooperation. This comprehensive approach ensures AI systems are reliable, ethical, and socially responsible.

13.5 Legal Implications

Artificial intelligence has found its way into virtually every sector of society, revolutionizing industries, improving efficiency, and creating unprecedented opportunities. This pervasive integration, however, brings to the forefront significant legal challenges, particularly around the inherent characteristics of AI: complexity, opacity, unpredictability, autonomy, and the extensive use of data (Sioli, 2021). These facets of AI systems create multifaceted challenges, making it imperative to establish a robust regulatory framework to mitigate potential risks while facilitating innovation.

The *complexity* of AI systems arises from their multilayered structure and the vast scale at which they operate. These systems often involve highly sophisticated models, such as deep neural networks, that process immense volumes of data through nonlinear and dynamic interactions. Unlike traditional software, where each rule is explicitly defined, many AI systems exhibit emergent behavior that cannot be easily anticipated or reduced to simple causal chains. This internal complexity increases the likelihood of unintended consequences, especially when such systems interact with real-world environments in unforeseen ways. As a result, regulatory safeguards are needed to ensure that these systems behave reliably and do not pose risks to safety, fairness, or public welfare.

Opacity, or the so-called black-box nature of many AI systems, further compounds these challenges. AI systems, particularly those utilizing deep learning and neural networks, often produce results without clear explanations, making it difficult for users, developers, and regulators to understand how decisions are made. This opacity is a significant concern as it raises accountability issues, particularly when AI systems are deployed in critical areas such as healthcare, finance, and law enforcement. The lack of transparency can breed mistrust among users and the public, as they may feel uneasy about relying on systems they do not understand or cannot scrutinize. Regulatory measures aimed at enhancing transparency and ensuring that AI systems are explainable to a reasonable extent are vital in addressing these concerns, fostering trust, and ensuring responsible AI deployment.

Unpredictability in AI systems stems from their learning capability and the dynamic nature of the environments in which they operate. As AI systems continuously learn and adapt through exposure to new data, their behavior can change in unexpected ways, creating challenges in forecasting their actions and ensuring their outputs remain consistent with intended purposes. This unpredictability raises significant enforcement and legal issues, particularly in scenarios where AI systems deviate from their expected behavior, causing harm or violating regulations. The legal uncertainty surrounding AI's dynamic nature necessitates the establishment of adaptable regulatory frameworks that can evolve alongside advancements in AI technology, ensuring laws remain relevant and effective in safeguarding public interests.

The *autonomy* of AI systems, while a significant advantage in terms of efficiency and effectiveness, also presents profound regulatory challenges. Autonomous AI systems operate with minimal or no human intervention, making traditional accountability mechanisms less applicable. This autonomy raises questions about who should be held responsible when an autonomous system causes harm or makes an erroneous decision. Regulatory frameworks need to address these accountability gaps, ensuring that clear guidelines are established for the development, deployment, and oversight of autonomous AI systems. This includes defining the roles and responsibilities of developers, users, and other stakeholders in maintaining the safety and reliability of these systems.

The extensive use of *data* by AI systems brings about challenges related to data privacy, security, and ethical use. AI systems often require vast datasets to learn and operate effectively, raising concerns about how this data is collected, stored, and used. Issues such as data breaches, misuse of personal information, and biases in data can lead to significant fundamental right risks, undermining individuals' privacy and rights. Regulatory measures aimed at ensuring data protection, fairness, and ethical use are crucial in addressing these risks and maintaining public trust in AI technologies.

13.5.1 The EU AI Act

The European AI Act constitutes a comprehensive legal framework designed to address the multifaceted risks associated with artificial intelligence while promoting innovation within secure and ethically sound boundaries (European Union, 2024). It establishes harmonized rules for the introduction, deployment, and use of AI systems across the European Union, ensuring that these technologies are developed and applied in a safe, transparent, and accountable manner. By imposing strict compliance obligations and transparency requirements on certain categories of AI applications, particularly those deemed high-risk, the Act seeks to safeguard fundamental rights, enhance trust, and foster responsible innovation. The legislation is carefully tailored to cover the entire AI lifecycle, assigning specific responsibilities to both providers and users, and ensuring that all actors involved adhere to rigorous standards aimed at protecting public interests and upholding core societal values (Sioli, 2021).

One of the core components of the AI Act is its risk-based approach to regulation (see Fig. 13.5), categorizing AI applications into four distinct risk categories: minimal or no risk, limited risk, high risk, and unacceptable risk. This tiered approach allows for tailored regulatory measures proportional to the potential risks associated with different AI applications (European Commission, 2024). For AI applications classified as *minimal or no risk*, the AI Act follows a light-touch approach by refraining from imposing any regulatory obligations. The vast majority of AI systems currently deployed in the European Union fall into this category, including commonly used technologies such as AI-powered video games or spam filters. By deliberately excluding these low-risk applications from regulation, the Act ensures that harmless and everyday uses of AI remain unrestricted, thereby fostering innovation without subjecting developers and users to unnecessary compliance burdens. *Limited-risk* AI applications, such as chatbots or AI systems generating content, are

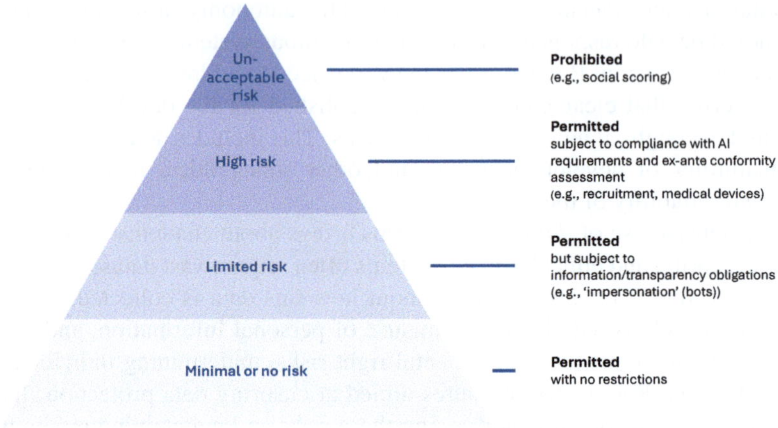

Fig. 13.5 A risk-based approach to regulation. (Adapted from Sioli, 2021)

permitted but subject to specific transparency and disclosure obligations. The AI Act requires that individuals are clearly informed when they are interacting with an AI system, especially when this is necessary to maintain trust and allow for informed decision-making. For instance, users must be made aware when they are communicating with a machine, rather than a human. In addition, providers of generative AI systems must ensure that AI-generated content is clearly identifiable. This includes mandatory labeling of certain types of content, such as deepfakes or AI-generated texts that are intended to inform the public on matters of public interest.

In contrast, *high-risk* AI applications—those posing significant risks to health, safety, or fundamental rights—are subject to particularly stringent regulatory requirements under the AI Act. This category includes, among others, systems used in areas such as critical infrastructure, healthcare, education, employment, access to essential services, law enforcement, migration, and the administration of justice. To ensure the safe deployment of such systems, the Act prescribes strict obligations regarding data quality, traceability, documentation, risk assessment, human oversight, and technical robustness. These requirements aim to prevent discriminatory outcomes, safeguard individual rights, and ensure that high-stakes AI systems are reliable, secure, and transparent. By establishing clear and enforceable standards, the Act seeks to foster trust, accountability, and confidence in the use of AI in sensitive and socially impactful domains.

At the highest level of risk categorization, the AI Act targets applications considered inherently *unacceptable* due to their capacity to cause substantial harm or infringe upon fundamental rights, societal norms, and democratic values. These include AI systems that manipulate human behavior through subliminal techniques, exploit vulnerabilities of individuals due to their age or disability, thereby distorting their behavior and causing or risking significant harm, or implement social scoring schemes by public authorities that may lead to discrimination, stigmatization, or exclusion. Also explicitly banned are practices such as the untargeted scraping of biometric data to create or expand facial recognition databases, AI systems that assess or predict the risk of a person committing a criminal offence solely based on profiling or inferred personality traits, and the use of emotion recognition systems in workplaces or educational institutions. Furthermore, biometric categorization aimed at deducing sensitive attributes, such as ethnicity, political opinions, or religious beliefs, is prohibited due to its discriminatory potential and profound implications for human dignity.

These prohibitions reflect a zero-tolerance stance toward AI technologies that fundamentally conflict with European values of autonomy, fairness, and justice. By categorically outlawing such systems, the AI Act enshrines a principled boundary that ensures technological progress does not come at the expense of human rights, societal trust, or ethical governance. Instead, it establishes a protective legal perimeter that affirms the EU's commitment to dignity, privacy, and democratic integrity in the face of rapidly advancing AI capabilities.

13.5.2 Legal Aspects Concerning Generative AI

When using generative AI tools such as ChatGPT, Midjourney, or similar systems, users should be aware that the legal status of the content these tools produce is far from settled. Although outputs like text, images, or code may appear entirely original, their creation processes are deeply intertwined with legal questions surrounding authorship, data provenance, and intellectual property rights. These systems are typically trained on vast datasets, often scraped from the internet without the explicit consent of original content creators, which raises concerns about whether the generated output might reproduce or imitate protected works (Lee et al., 2023).

This complexity means that AI-generated content might not qualify for copyright protection in many jurisdictions, as most copyright laws require human authorship. As a result, AI outputs may fall into a kind of legal limbo: while they are not protected as original works, their similarity to existing copyrighted materials can still pose risks for users, especially if those outputs are published or used commercially. Legal liability is further complicated by the opacity of the training processes and the difficulty in tracing whether a specific output was influenced by a particular copyrighted work (Ren et al., 2024).

The European Union has started addressing some of these issues through its AI Act, which introduces new obligations for providers of so-called General Purpose AI systems. These include transparency requirements regarding training data, documentation of model capabilities and limitations, and adherence to intellectual property frameworks. However, these obligations primarily target developers and system deployers, not end-users. Still, the lack of clarity about how these requirements trickle down to users makes legal accountability in the context of AI-generated content highly uncertain (Novelli et al., 2024). Some legal scholars have therefore argued for a differentiated regulatory approach that considers the roles and responsibilities along the entire AI value chain, from model developers to end-users. This includes the introduction of transparency mechanisms, risk assessments, and documentation obligations that can help users better understand what they are working with and what risks they might be taking on. Even if such duties are not yet legally mandated for individual users, they represent a growing area of legal and ethical expectation in the use of generative AI (Hacker et al., 2023).

In practice, this means that users should not assume that the output of a generative AI system is automatically free to use, especially in professional or public contexts. Until clearer legal standards emerge, caution is advised—both in terms of how such content is used and how its origins are documented. Staying informed about the evolving legal landscape and seeking legal advice where necessary is not just prudent, but essential for responsible engagement with these powerful technologies.

Stakeholder Perspectives on Intellectual Property Risks

While the previous section outlined the general legal uncertainties surrounding AI-generated content, this section delves deeper into the specific challenges associated with intellectual property (IP) rights. Generative AI tools such as ChatGPT or Midjourney are typically trained on vast datasets that often include copyrighted material, enabling them to generate outputs that may closely resemble, or in some cases replicate, existing works. This raises complex legal questions that affect all actors along the AI value chain: from original content creators to AI system developers and the end-users deploying such tools. The following analysis highlights the key IP-related risks and legal implications for each of these stakeholder groups.

Creators, including authors, artists, and other producers of original works, face the pressing issue that their content may be scraped from the internet, included in large training datasets, and used without consent in the development of generative AI models. Recent legal disputes, such as the lawsuit filed by *The New York Times* against OpenAI and Microsoft, exemplify the risk of copyright infringement when outputs closely mirror parts of the training data.

Legal scholars note that the high fidelity of AI-generated content makes it increasingly difficult to distinguish between lawful "inspiration" and unlawful copying. From a technical standpoint, approaches like watermarking and dataset de-duplication are being explored to better protect creators, but enforcement remains limited. Moreover, the EU Copyright Directive 2019/790 (European Union, 2019) permits certain forms of text and data mining, but only under specific conditions, and does not necessarily address the scale and opacity of modern training pipelines. Thus, creators face a dual challenge: protecting their works ex ante from being ingested by models, and proving substantial similarity ex post when outputs may infringe their rights (Novelli et al., 2024; Lee et al., 2023; Ren et al., 2024).

AI developers operate at the heart of the IP debate, as they collect data, train models, and enable downstream applications. From a liability perspective, developers may be held accountable not only for the training data used but also for how the system is deployed. This liability can be direct, if copyrighted material is copied during training, or indirect, if the system facilitates infringement by users.

The notion of "indirect infringement" has gained traction, especially where the outputs can be shown to reproduce protected expressions from the training data. In the EU, the Artificial Intelligence Act introduces additional obligations for so-called General Purpose AI models, including disclosure of training data and documentation to demonstrate IP compliance. Still, questions remain about how to define and assess “systemic risk” and whether open-source models should be exempt from such scrutiny. Developers may also attempt to assert rights over their own models or outputs. However, copyright protection for the model itself (e.g., architecture, weights) is ambiguous, and outputs are generally not protected unless they meet the threshold of human authorship (Lee et al., 2023; Hacker et al., 2023; Ren et al., 2024; Novelli et al., 2024).

Businesses leveraging AI tools for content generation encounter distinct legal ambiguities. While companies like OpenAI often claim that users own the outputs they generate (subject to terms of use), legal precedent suggests that not all AI-generated content is copyrightable, particularly if it lacks sufficient human creativity. This leads to practical questions for firms seeking to commercialize AI-assisted works: Who owns the rights? Can such works be registered or enforced?

Users also face the risk of unknowingly infringing on third-party rights by prompting AI systems to generate protected content. This issue is exacerbated by the “black-box” nature of many models, making it hard to verify the provenance of outputs. Moreover, in high-risk sectors (e.g., media, education, product design), reliance on generative AI could trigger stricter documentation and audit obligations, depending on how the EU AI Act is implemented. As such, businesses need robust governance strategies to manage the legal uncertainty around authorship, reuse rights, and potential liability (Ren et al., 2024; Hacker et al., 2023; Lee et al., 2023; Novelli et al., 2024).

The landscape of IP rights in the context of generative AI is fragmented and evolving. From creators seeking protection against unauthorized use, to developers managing risk exposure, and users navigating uncertain rights over AI outputs—all actors face overlapping yet distinct legal challenges. As regulatory frameworks like the EU AI Act begin to take shape, a balanced approach will be essential: one that fosters innovation while safeguarding the rights of human creators.

Summary

Artificial intelligence presents significant legal challenges due to its complexity, opacity, unpredictability, autonomy, and extensive data use. The EU AI Act introduces a risk-based regulatory framework to manage these issues, imposing strict obligations on high-risk systems while banning certain harmful applications outright. Generative AI raises additional concerns, particularly regarding intellectual property. AI-generated content often blurs the line between originality and infringement, leading to uncertainty around authorship and rights. Stakeholders, such as creators, developers, and users, face different but interconnected risks, underscoring the need for clearer legal standards and accountability across the entire AI value chain.

References

Arrieta, A. B., Díaz-Rodríguez, N., Del Ser, J., Bennetot, A., Tabik, S., Barbado, A., & Herrera, F. (2020). Explainable Artificial Intelligence (XAI): Concepts, taxonomies, opportunities and challenges toward responsible AI. *Information Fusion, 58*, 82–115.

Asimov, I. (1950). Runaround. In *I, Robot* (The Isaac Asimov Collection Ed.). Doubleday.

Awad, E., Dsouza, S., Kim, R., Schulz, J., Henrich, J., Shariff, A., Bonnefon, J.-F., & Rahwan, I. (2018). The moral machine experiment. *Nature, 563*(7729), 59–64.

Barocas, S., Hardt, M., & Narayanan, A. (2023). *Fairness and machine learning: Limitations and opportunities*. MIT.

Boddington, P. (2021). AI and moral thinking: How can we live well with machines to enhance our moral agency? *AI and Ethics, 1*, 109–111.

Cohn, M., Keaton, A., Beskow, J., & Zellou, G. (2023). Vocal accommodation to technology: The role of physical form. *Language Sciences, 99*, 101567.

Diakopoulos, N., & Koliska, M. (2017). Algorithmic transparency in the news media. *Digital Journalism, 5*(7), 809–828.

European Commission. (2024). AI Act: Europe's approach to artificial intelligence. *Shaping Europe's Digital Future* [online] Accessed April 13, 2025, from https://digital-strategy.ec.europa.eu/en/policies/regulatory-framework-ai

European Union. (2019). Directive (EU) 2019/790 of the European Parliament and of the Council of 17 April 2019 on copyright and related rights in the Digital Single Market and amending Directives 96/9/EC and 2001/29/EC. *Official Journal of the European Union*, L 130, pp. 92–125. [online] Accessed April 13, 2025, from http://data.europa.eu/eli/dir/2019/790/oj

European Union. (2024). Regulation (EU) 2024/1689 of the European Parliament and of the Council of 13 June 2024 laying down harmonised rules on artificial intelligence (Artificial Intelligence Act). *Official Journal of the European Union*, L 2024/1689, 12 July. [online] Accessed April 13, 2025, from http://data.europa.eu/eli/reg/2024/1689/oj

Formosa, P., & Ryan, M. (2021). Making moral machines: Why we need artificial moral agents. *AI & SOCIETY, 36*, 839–851.

Frank, D. A., Chrysochou, P., Mitkidis, P., et al. (2019). Human decision-making biases in the moral dilemmas of autonomous vehicles. *Scientific Reports, 9*, 13080.

Haas, C. (2019). The price of fairness—A framework to explore trade-offs in algorithmic fairness. In *Proceedings of the 40th International Conference on Information Systems (ICIS 2019)*. Association for Information Systems (AIS).

Hacker, P., Engel, A., & Mauer, M. (2023). Regulating ChatGPT and other large generative AI models. In *Proceedings of the 2023 ACM Conference on Fairness, Accountability, and Transparency (FAccT 2023)* (pp. 1112–1123).

Hardt, M., Price, E., & Srebro, N. (2016). Equality of opportunity in supervised learning. *Advances in Neural Information Processing Systems, 29*.

High-Level Expert Group on Artificial Intelligence (AI HLEG). (2019). *Ethics guidelines for trustworthy AI*. Brussels: European Commission. [online] Accessed April 13, 2025, from https://ec.europa.eu/digital-single-market/en/news/ethics-guidelines-trustworthy-ai

Himma, K. E. (2009). Artificial agency, consciousness, and the criteria for moral agency: What properties must an artificial agent have to be a moral agent? *Ethics and Information Technology, 11*, 19–29.

Kossow, N., Windwehr, S., & Jenkins, M., (2022). *Algorithmic transparency and accountability*. Transparency International.

Laato, S., Tiainen, M., Najmul Islam, A. K. M., & Mäntymäki, M. (2022). How to explain AI systems to end users: A systematic literature review and research agenda. *Internet Research, 32*(7), 1–31.

Lee, K., Cooper, A. F., & Grimmelmann, J. (2023). *Talkin' 'Bout AI Generation: Copyright and the generative-AI supply chain*. arXiv preprint arXiv:2309.08133.

Li, B., Qi, P., Liu, B., Di, S., Liu, J., Pei, J., & Zhou, B. (2023). Trustworthy AI: From principles to practices. *ACM Computing Surveys, 55*(9), 1–46.

Mori, M. (1970). The uncanny valley: The original essay by Masahiro Mori. *IEEE Spectrum, 6*(1), 6.

Novelli, C., Casolari, F., Hacker, P., Spedicato, G., & Floridi, L. (2024). Generative AI in EU law: Liability, privacy, intellectual property, and cybersecurity. *Computer Law & Security Review, 55*, 106066.

Pringle, E. (2023). Microsoft's ChatGPT-powered Bing is becoming a pushy pick-up artist that wants you to leave your partner: 'You're married, but you're not happy'. *Fortune*, [online] 17 February. Accessed April 13, 2025, from https://fortune.com/2023/02/17/microsoft-chatgpt-bing-romantic-love/

Ramchurn, S. D., Stein, S., & Jennings, N. R. (2021). Trustworthy human-AI partnerships. *iScience, 24*(8), 102891.

Ren, J., Xu, H., He, P., Cui, Y., Zeng, S., Zhang, J., & Tang, J. (2024). *Copyright protection in generative AI: A technical perspective*. arXiv preprint arXiv:2402.02333.

Scheuer, D. (2020). *Akzeptanz von Künstlicher Intelligenz. Grundlagen intelligenter KI-Assistenten und deren vertrauensvolle Nutzung*.

Siau, K., & Wang, W. (2020). Artificial intelligence (AI) ethics: Ethics of AI and ethical AI. *Journal of Database Management (JDM), 31*(2), 74–87.

Sioli, L. (2021). *A European strategy for artificial intelligence*. [online] Accessed Dezember 16, 2024, from https://www.ceps.eu/wp-content/uploads/2021/04/AI-Presentation-CEPS-Webinar-L.-Sioli-23.4.21.pdf

Stahl, B. C., & Stahl, B. C. (2021). Ethical issues of AI. In *Artificial Intelligence for a Better Future: An Ecosystem Perspective on the Ethics of AI and Emerging Digital Technologies* (pp.35–53).

Wieringa, M. (2020). What to account for when accounting for algorithms: A systematic literature review on algorithmic accountability. In *Proceedings of the 2020 Conference on Fairness, Accountability, and Transparency* (pp. 1–18).

Wolf, Z. B. (2023). AI can be racist, sexist and creepy. What should we do about it? *CNN* [online] 18 March. Accessed April 13, 2025, from https://edition.cnn.com/2023/03/18/politics/ai-chatgpt-racist-what-matters/index.html

Yang, K., Qinami, K., Fei-Fei, L., Deng, J., & Russakovsky, O. (2020). Towards fairer datasets: Filtering and balancing the distribution of the people subtree in the imagenet hierarchy. In *Proceedings of the 2020 conference on fairness, accountability, and transparency* (pp. 547–558).

Nils Urbach is Professor of Information Systems and Digital Business as well as Director of the Research Lab for Digital Innovation and Transformation at the Frankfurt University of Applied Sciences, Germany. Furthermore, he is Director at the FIM Research Center for Information Management, and the Branch Business and Information Systems Engineering of Fraunhofer FIT. Nils Urbach has been working in the fields of digital innovation and transformation for several years. His work has been published in several academic journals such as Information Systems Research (ISR), the Journal of the Association for Information Systems (JAIS), the Journal of Strategic Information Systems (JSIS), the Journal of Information Technology (JIT), MIS Quarterly Executive (MISQE), IEEE Transactions on Engineering Management (IEEE TEM), Information and Management (I&M), Business and Information Systems Engineering (BISE), and Electronic Markets (EM). He advises several companies on digitalization issues and regularly appears as a speaker on this topic.

Daniel Feulner received his M.Sc. in information system from the Otto-Friedrich University of Bamberg, Germany in 2023. He is an affiliated researcher at the Branch Business and Information Systems Engineering of the Fraunhofer FIT and FIM Research Center for Information Management at the University of Bayreuth. In his research, he aims to understand how Business Analytics and

Artificial Intelligence can be effectively and responsibly utilized in organizations. His goal is to enable companies to drive innovation and achieve sustainable growth in a rapidly evolving technological landscape.

Valentin Mayer received his M.Sc. in Management and Technology from the Technical University of Munich, Germany 2023. He is an affiliated researcher at the Branch Business and Information Systems Engineering of the Fraunhofer FIT and FIM Research Center for Information Management at the University of Bayreuth. His research explores how companies can successfully implement Artificial Intelligence within their organizations, with a particular focus on the conceptual design and operationalization of AI systems. His goal is to equip companies with practical methods to implement AI end-to-end into their operations and create long-term value.

Correction to: Designing Human–AI Interactions

Nils Urbach, Daniel Feulner, and Valentin Mayer

Correction to:
Chapter 11 in: N. Urbach, D. Feulner (eds.), *Managing Artificial Intelligence*, Future of Business and Finance, https://doi.org/10.1007/978-3-032-13308-3_11

The original version of Chapter 11 was published without the figure source details for Figures 11.5 and 11.7, and their respective references. The correction chapter and the book have been updated with this information. The figure captions along with their respective source are:

Figure 11.5: Scenarios of complementary potential between humans and AI (Adapted from Hemmer et al., 2025)
Figure 11.7: Different types of integration of Human and AI predictions (Adapted from Hemmer, 2024)

The references are:

Hemmer, P. (2024). Complementarity in Human-AI Teams: Conceptualization and Design Support for Effective Decision-Making. Dissertation. Karlsruher Institut für Technologie (KIT).

Hemmer, P., Schemmer, M., Kühl, N., Vössing, M., & Satzger, G. (2025). Complementarity in human-AI collaboration: Concept, sources, and evidence. *European Journal of Information Systems, 34*(6), 979–1002.

The updated version of this chapter can be found at
https://doi.org/10.1007/978-3-032-13308-3_11

N. Urbach, D. Feulner (eds.), *Managing Artificial Intelligence*, Future of Business and Finance, https://doi.org/10.1007/978-3-032-13308-3_14

MIX
Papier aus verantwortungsvollen Quellen
Paper from responsible sources
FSC® C105338
FSC
www.fsc.org

If you have any concerns about our products,
you can contact us on
ProductSafety@springernature.com

In case Publisher is established outside the EU,
the EU authorized representative is:
Springer Nature Customer Service Center GmbH
Europaplatz 3, 69115 Heidelberg, Germany

Printed by Libri Plureos GmbH
in Hamburg, Germany